". . . An admirable, handsome and handy addition to the library of popular, easy-to-use and . . . inspiring Bible dictionary-encyclopedias."

—*Christian Science Monitor*

"A grade-A book . . . as a reference book in the field of religion, it is great."

—*Chattanooga Times*

"As a reference work it would be invaluable; for religious students; fascinating; for the ordinary reader (it) depicts beautifully an important aspect of day-by-day life."

—*The San Diego Union*

About the Author

Ronald Brownrigg is rector of a progressive Anglican parish in the south of England. He is the author of several books on Israel and Jerusalem, including Holy Places *(with Christopher Hollis).*

Educated at Shrewsbury and Emmanuel College, Cambridge, he served for four years as an infantry and general staff officer and was in charge of an Educational Training Center at Mount Zion, Jerusalem.

Who's Who in the New Testament

Ronald Brownrigg

PILLAR BOOKS   NEW YORK

The Scripture quotations in this publication are from the *Revised Standard Version Bible,* copyright 1946 and 1952 by the Division of Christian Education, National Council of the Churches of Christ in the U.S.A., and used by permission.

Advisory editors for this volume:

The Reverend Canon E. Every,
St George's Cathedral, Jerusalem

The Very Reverend Wolfgang E. Pax, OFM,
Convent of the Flagellation,
Via Dolorosa, Jerusalem

WHO'S WHO IN THE NEW TESTAMENT

A PILLAR BOOK
Published by arrangement with Holt, Rinehart and Winston

Pillar Books edition published February 1977

ISBN: 0-89129-203-9

Library of Congress Catalog Card Number: 75-153654

Copyright © 1971 by Ronald Brownrigg

Printed in the United States of America

PILLAR BOOKS
Pyramid Publications
(Harcourt Brace Jovanovich, Inc.)
757 Third Avenue
New York, New York 10017
U.S.A.

Contents

CONTENTS

Author's acknowledgments

I should like warmly to express my gratitude to the following for their academic advice and encouragement in the production of this book: The Reverend Anthony Harvey, Warden of St Augustine's College, Canterbury; The Reverend Canon Edward Every, St George's Cathedral, Jerusalem; The Very Reverend Wolfgang E. Pax, OFM, Convent of the Flagellation, Via Dolorosa, Jerusalem.

For their endless typing and proof-reading my friends Elna Charleson and Kathleen Clarke, of Blechingley, and Philip and Susan Richardson for their 'prophet's chamber'.

Most particularly I should like to mention John Curtis of Weidenfeld and Nicolson for his skill, perception and never failing good will, throughout this project.

Introduction

The scope of this work is comprehensive and includes all the people mentioned by name in the New Testament as well as some who remain unnamed like the centurions at Capernaum and Cavalry, together with certain political and religious groups. The articles are necessarily limited and selective in content, but are primarily planned for the general reader, students and others needing concise, accurate and readable information. They are not intended for scholarly research, but are meant to answer questions raised by ordinary reading.

Considerable space has been given to those personalities thought to be essential to the New Testament story. Thus, such characters have been briefly introduced, their biography outlined without commentary and their significance assessed. In the process, some attention has been paid to sources of information and authorship, and, where relevant, to environment and archaeological evidence. Very little knowledge of places and persons has been assumed, and the reader is often reminded of names and dates, the topography and chronology of events.

The names have been compiled from the Revised Standard Version, but include some variants from the King James Version. The R.S.V. New Testament, the work of American scholars first published in 1946, was an authorised revision of the American Standard Version of 1901, itself a revision of the King James version published in 1611.

The derivation of each character's name, its origin from Hebrew, Greek or Latin, is given — where it is

9

known and appears to be of interest. Relevant scripture references are listed at the end of each article and in some cases scripture passages are quoted at length. A table of abbreviations is to be found on page 22.

Repetition has been reduced to a minimum, so have cross-references, in the hope that each entry may stand on its own. No Old Testament names have been included, unless there is a New Testament character of the same name. The selection of groups and types of people, for example scribes and centurions, may appear to be arbitrary, but has tended towards those playing a major role in the life of the central character, Jesus. There is an article on the Essenes, who are not mentioned in the New Testament, since many of their ideas are reflected in the Gospels.

The background of the land

The Holy Land was the bridge between the riverside civilizations of the ancient world, spanning the routes between Egypt, Babylon, Persia, Greece and finally Rome. A buffer state, exposed to, yet detached from, these great civilizations, its history is one of constant political disaster and prophetic reconciliation.

The geography of the country is remarkably simple, consisting of consecutive parallels running north and south. From east to west, the pattern is coastal plain, foothills, spine, mountainous desert, descending to the Rift Valley far below sea-level through which runs the River Jordan. This north-south pattern is broken only by the fertile plain of Esdraelon, a narrow bottleneck, avoided by armies of the ancient world. Instead of circumventing the cape of Carmel and risking ambush, the military and trade routes struck through the Carmel range from the coastal plain of Sharon to Esdraelon by narrow passes of considerable tactical importance.

The nature of the country tended to break up the population into small and closely-packed communities among the tangle of hills. The River Jordan, whose name means 'Descender', rises in the foothills of Mount Hermon and enters the Sea of Galilee at 680 feet below sea-level, before sinking deeper and deeper into the Rift Valley to empty itself into the Dead Sea at 1,300 feet below sea-level. Standing back from the coastal highways, the hill-country of Judea and Samaria, of limestone rock strata, is hard to cultivate and breeds a hardy, God-fearing people, whose livelihood depends largely upon the climate.

As the Land influenced the people, so it did also their writings. The awe and majesty of the scenery, in its ruthless immensity, provoke a sense of the nearness of God.

The Land was thus a well-prepared seed-plot for the sowing of the Word and Message of God. Bethlehem was the traditional city of David, from whose line the coming Messiah was expected. Nazareth, a cosmopolitan township overlooking the trade-routes through Esdraelon, provided a rugged schooling for an intinerant, open-air ministry. Capernaum and the lakeside of Galilee, with a crowded and hot-blooded population in the climate of the Rift Valley, were conducive to the spread of the Gospel, to be carried on the wind of the Spirit throughout the Roman world.

The time of Jesus's birth

'When the time had fully come,' said the Apostle Paul, 'God sent forth his Son, born of a woman, born under the Law . . .' The long process of progressive prepara-

11

tion, through the revelation of God and the reason of Man, culminated in a remarkable sequence of events. During the exile in Babylon, Hebrew prophecy flowered into a rich monotheism and universalism; religion was momentarily emanciapated from nationalism; personal religion developed within the synagogue, apart from the Temple. With the return, the spiritual life and worship of the people prospered. The Canon of the Law and the Prophets was compiled and the Scribal interpretation developed.

The world at large was enriched by the universal ideals of Alexander and the philosophy of Aristotle. With the Ptolemaic domination of Greater Syria, Jewish communities fled to Egypt and throughout the eastern Mediterranean, taking their scriptures with them, establishing their synagogues and attracting their Gentile proselytes and God-fearers.

Under the Hellenistic persecution of the Seleucids, Judaism was further refined in the furnace of affliction. The Jews consoled and comforted themselves with apocalyptic hopes of the coming of a Messiah (Deliverer). Jewish philosophers, such as Philo in Alexandria, began to interpret the nature and purpose of their God in terms understandable to the pagan world – as the mind and reason that made sense of all created life.

With the advent of the Augustan age and stable government from Rome, law and order was established on land and sea; robbery and piracy were reduced to a minimum. Travel facilities and communications had never been better. Colloquial Greek was the lingua franca of the whole Mediterranean world. A sense of imperial unity and a wise colonial policy enabled a limited freedom in both local government and in matters of religion. East and West were united and Alexander's dream was realized. Into such a world and at such a time, Jesus was born. Nor is it a coincidence that the four years of good government prior to Nero's persecution marked the climax of the ministry of Paul the Apostle.

How the Gospels came to be written

On the day of Pentecost, the first Whitsunday – sometimes called the birthday – of the Christian Church, Peter proclaimed the gospel of Jesus. 'Men of Israel, hear these words: Jesus of Nazareth, a man attested to you by God with mighty works and wonders and signs which God did through him in your midst, as you yourselves know – this Jesus, delivered up according to the definite plan and foreknowledge of God, you crucified and killed by the hands of lawless men. But God raised him up, having loosed the pangs of death, because it was not possible for him to be held by it . . . Let all the house of Israel therefore know assuredly that God has made him both Lord and Christ.' (Acts 2:22-24, 36)

The first followers of Jesus preached 'Christ risen from the dead' and expected his early return to establish his kingdom. At first the apostles stayed in Jerusalem, which remained the headquarters of the Christian Church despite the siege and destruction in the years 69-70, until the end of the 1st century. An advance headquarters was established at Antioch, from which missionary enterprises were conducted throughout the whole Mediterranean world.

As the years passed, the surviving apostles were now scattered far and wide, sometimes under bitter persecution from outside the Christian community, sometimes faced with disunity and false teaching within the local Church congregations. All the original eye-witnesses to

13

the life, death and resurrection of Jesus were growing older and some written record and authoritative account of the facts behind the Christian faith became essential to the sound progress and development of the Church. However much the scattered Christian communities treasured and exchanged their letters from Paul and other missionary apostles, these congregations needed an accurate record of the life and teaching of Jesus on which to base their own teaching and practical living.

Following a great fire in the city of Rome in the year 64, the Christians were blamed by the government and suffered a reign of terror under the Emperor Nero. Among the victims of this persecution were the two Apostles Peter and Paul, who had both been preaching and teaching about Jesus for some thirty years. Almost immediately after their death there began to be circulated 'The Gospel of Jesus Christ', which we now call the 'Gospel according to Mark'. An early Christian bishop linked this Gospel directly with the Apostle Peter. Papias in around the year 130 quoted the Elder as saying: 'Mark was the interpreter of Peter and wrote down accurately, but not in order, all that Peter remembered.' Fifty years later, Irenaeus said that after the death of Peter and Paul Mark wrote his Gospel to record the story while there were still eye-witnesses to the events in the life of Jesus. The result was a vigorous, vivid and dramatic series of episodes in the life of Jesus, whom the reader is encouraged to recognize as the 'Son of God', as well as the Jewish Messiah.

Mark's account, however, recorded little of the teaching of Jesus, of which there was already a separate account in circulation. Probably in answer to a demand for an enlarged edition of 'The Gospel of Jesus Christ', to include both narrative and teaching, two further Gospels were published within the next twenty-five years.

Although their authors were very different people — Matthew, a Jew brought up on the Old Testament scriptures, and Luke, probably a Gentile of Greek culture and education — they both made extensive use of Mark's narrative and a contemporary collection of the teaching and sayings of Jesus. This last is sometimes called 'Q', being the first letter of the German Quelle, 'source'. The first three Gospels are grouped together as 'Synoptic', for they largely follow the substance, language and order of Mark and can thus be 'viewed together'. Nearly all of Mark's work is to be found in the other two: 90% in Matthew, 50% in Luke, and only 6% in neither. Again, in language Matthew and Luke are often identical with Mark and never agree to differ from him, though each sometimes revises him for the sake of reverence, brevity or accuracy. Both Matthew and Luke seem to have had also their own written sources of information, such as Matthew's Sermon on the Mount and the long parables peculiar to Luke's Gospel. Both seem to have drawn information from their own personal contacts or traditions; thus Luke's accounts of the birth of Jesus reflect the feelings of Mary, whereas those of Matthew describe the experience of Joseph.

The Fourth Gospel did not emerge until the end of the 1st century. It is quite different in style, order and even sometimes in substance. Looking back over almost a century, it aims at an interpretation rather than a record of events. Recently, however, scholars have recognized an independent historical tradition and a knowledge of Judea in this gospel. John's readers in the sophisticated Greek city of Ephesus were far removed in time and space from the days and home of Jesus. This Gospel was written primarily to explain the place of Jesus, the Jewish Messiah, in God's wider and universal plan of salvation, to provoke belief in and response to his son Jesus as the Way, the Truth and the Life for all mankind.

Despite their differences in detail and presentation, the Gospels constitute a serious record of historical events, vouched for by honest and well-informed witnesses. They support each other in giving a clear portrait of Jesus within a framework of events entirely consistent with the history of his day.

The spreading of the Gospel

The Gospel according to Luke was followed by a second volume, addressed to the same person, in the same literary style, with the same motives and approach as the Gospel. 'Acts of Apostles', as it is correctly translated, is no exhaustive or consecutive history of the early Church, but rather a selection of adventures of certain apostles vividly and accurately recorded. Yet, apart from the Letters, the Book of Revelation and some occasional comments from heathen writers, Acts is the main source of information about the apostolic age. As an adventure book, it is full of people, of plots and intrigues; its hero is Jesus; its chief character is first Peter and then Paul, both working in the power of the Spirit of God. The zeal and enthusiasm of the early leaders of the missionary Church come alive in the condensed yet vivid narrative of the personal travelling companion of the Apostle Paul. It is Paul's many friends and acquaintances who provide the greater part of the entries in this book.

It was some six years after the crucifixion of Jesus that Paul experienced his sudden and unique encounter with the risen Jesus and his commission as the apostle to the Gentiles. In the momentous thirty years that followed, Paul carried the good news throughout the Mediterranean world, establishing in many cities and towns small Christian communities which survived, in spite of persecution and apparent isolation. It is the problems and controversies, the progress and practice of these early Christian congregations that are revealed in Paul's remarkable correspondence which occupies so great a part of the New Testament.

Whether theological treatises or direct communications dealing with particular persons in specific and concrete situations, the epistles of Paul bear the stamp of apostolic authority. They are real letters to real people, often personally known to the writer, and they reveal his own very real personality and genius for friendship. Composed and dictated in longhand, laboriously written between constant interruptions to his train of thought, compressed no doubt by a shortage of time and papyrus, it is not surprising that the arguments are sometimes hard to follow.

Besides all this, the vast distances travelled, his constant 'thorn in the flesh', the continual physical and mental strain, not least the severe bodily violence he suffered, are inevitably reflected in his correspondence. Paul's theology is deeply rooted in the crucible of his own conversion, his continuing experience of suffering, and in the life of the Christian community.

Interpretation of Jesus's message

At first glance the New Testament may appear almost equally divided into the historical account of Jesus and the interpretation of his message, between past events and present faith. On closer inspection, however, the Gospels are seen to include a great deal of interpretation and of faith. Each account, written well after the events of the crucifixion, the resurrection and the coming of the Spirit, inevitably interprets the good news for the benefit of its particular readers. Thus the Palestinian Jews, Mark and Matthew, provoke their readers to a recognition of the central character as the Messiah, who is also the Son of God. Luke, possibly a doctor-slave and Gentile, emphasizes the universality of the rule of the Messiah, whose love and forgiveness embrace all races and all levels of society. The Fourth Gospel, written at the close of the apostolic age, when the primitive hopes and momentum of the good news were somewhat spent, when Christianity could no longer be confined within Judaistic language and thought, is even more full of interpretation and of faith than the others. In John's presentation, as in that of Paul, it is not so much who Jesus was that matters, but rather what he had become to those who have experienced his spiritual presence within the believing community. Past events are overshadowed by present experience and future hopes.

Under the guise of historical narrative, John records a series of seven signs each demonstrating the difference that Jesus makes in the lives of his followers, as their Lord, their healer, their strength, their food, their guide, their light and their life. The frequent brief episodes and comments within the Synoptic Gospels are replaced by a few selected scenes with explanatory conversions or speeches; the many short parables give way to carefully worked out allegories and illustrations. Those of the 'Good Shepherd' and the 'True Vine' are explored at considerable length and depth. John's Gospel seems to record not just the impressions of eye-witnesses among the crowd, but rather the insight and the hindsight into these far-off events of the more mature faith of the apostles.

The writer expressed himself in terms and language understood by both the Jews and Greeks of his day, to claim that the very 'Word', 'Thought' or 'Mind' of God had become 'enfleshed' in the person of Jesus. As the Apostle Paul had already stated: 'In him the whole fulness of deity dwells bodily', so John proclaimed: 'The Word became flesh and dwelt among us, full of grace and truth; we have beheld his glory, glory as of the only Son from the Father.' Thus God communicated himself to mankind, revealing his glory in a supreme act of self-giving love, in Jesus. Both Paul and John perceived that it was God's plan, in this very act of revealing his love, to bring into being a new humanity – a new community – bound by a new commandment to love one another and empowered to do so by their union with himself.

The formation of the New Testament

The compilation of each Gospel from the oral tradition and written material from a variety of sources had been a lengthy and complicated process; so was the formation of the canon (literally 'measure') of the New Testament. This process took place in three stages: the writing (in a space of approximately sixty years) and preservation, the collection of such writings as were of apostolic authority by the catholic Church, and finally their recognition or rejection.

The primitive Christian Church was more concerned with preaching the good news than with recording it in writing. The kernel of the good news was therefore the story of the passion of Jesus 'crucified and risen from the dead', told as history and preached as gospel. To this were added accounts of his ministry, collections of his sayings, and practical guidance in Christian living.

Some compendium of instruction was necessitated by

the growth in the number of converts, particularly Gentiles. Thus Paul and Barnabas would have set out on their missionary travels armed with the Old Testament, an account of the passion of Jesus, an outline of his ministry, and perhaps a collection of his sayings and parables.

The first book of the New Testament to be written may have been the letter (or sermon) of James. All Paul's letters had been written, however, before the first Gospel (of Mark) was in circulation, but they were not all collected into one group until considerably later. In the last half of the 1st century sections of Paul's correspondence found their way to libraries at the main centres of the Christian Church in Jerusalem, Antioch, Ephesus and Rome. All four Gospels were used in Rome by the early Christian apologist and martyr, Justin, in about the year 150: Irenaeus, bishop of Lyons, in 180 accepted the four Gospels without question.

The selection and recognition by the catholic Church of a canon of authorized and apostolic writings were precipitated by the independent selections of certain individuals and heretical sects wishing to promote their own personal interpretations of the Christian faith. During the 2nd century, most churches had come to acknowledge a canon which included the present 4 Gospels, Acts, 13 Letters of Paul, 1 Peter and 1 John, but they still disputed the inclusion of Hebrews, James, 2 Peter, 2 and 3 John, Jude and Revelation. The final stage of sifting, accepting and rejecting lasted well into the 4th century. Eusebius, bishop of Caesarea and 'Father of Church History', classified the Christian writings into three groups: recognized, disputed and spurious. It was not until 367 that the 27 books now contained in the New Testament were finally listed by Athanasius, bishop of Alexandria, as exclusively canonical. Formal sanction was accorded this list by the synod of Carthage in the year 397.

The original manuscripts have long disappeared, but there are nearly 5,000 ancient Greek manuscripts of all or parts of the New Testament. Of these the oldest, written on papyrus or parchment, number more than 300 and date from the 2nd to the 8th centuries.

List of abbreviations

The following abbreviations have been used for the books of the New Testament:

Matt.	Matthew	Thess.	Thessalonians
Rom.	Romans	Tim.	Timothy
Cor.	Corinthians	Philem.	Philemon
Gal.	Galatians	Heb.	Hebrews
Phil.	Philippians	Jas.	James
Eph.	Ephesians	Pet.	Peter
Col.	Colossians	Rev.	Revelation

The following abbreviations have been used for the derivations of the names:

Aram.	Aramaic	Heb.	Hebrew
Gk.	Greek	Lat.	Latin

A

ABADDON (Heb. 'ruin', 'perdition', 'destruction') In the Old Testament books of Job and Proverbs, Abaddon has the general sense of death and destruction or even of Sheol, the place of the dead. The word occurs only once in the New Testament, in the vision of John the Divine on Patmos. John sees the fifth angel blow his trumpet and the bottomless pit open up to emit billowing clouds of black smoke. Within the smoke are seething swarms of locusts, like squadrons of warhorses. Against such a pest the world of men is defenceless. 'They have as king over them the angel of the bottomless pit; is anme in Hebrew is Abaddon, and in Greek he is called Apollyon.' (Rev. 9:11)

Abaddon may be interpreted within the context of this vision as the master-mind of evil, directing the hosts of temptation to their targets in the world of mankind, who without divine grace fall an easy prey. [Rev. 9:11]

ACHAICUS (Gk. 'native of Achaia') A Corinthian Christian of the household of Stephanas, he was named after Achaia, the province of which Corinth was the capital.

Writing from Ephesus in about the year 55, during his Third Journey, to the Church in Corinth which he had founded some four years before, Paul affectionately and courteously closes his letter: 'I rejoice at the coming of Stephanas and Fortunatus and Achaicus, because they have made up for your absence; for they refreshed my spirit as well as yours. Give recognition to such men.' (1 Cor. 16:17)

Apparently the household of Stephanas included

23

slaves and employees, such as Fortunatus and Achaicus. This was the first household to have been converted by Paul – and the only household to have been baptized by Paul – in Corinth, on his Second Journey in around the year 51. These three men had travelled to Ephesus on business, possibly carrying a letter to Paul from Corinth, and were probably present with Paul as he completed the dictation of his answering letter. In this, he commends to the loyalty of the Corinthians all such people who have dedicated themselves to serve the Christian community. [1 Cor. 16:17]

AENEAS (Gk. 'praise') A paralytic, bedridden for eight years, who was healed by the Apostle Peter at Lydda. 'Peter said to him, "Aeneas, Jesus Christ heals you; rise and make your bed." ' Luke, the recorder of this incident in Acts, adds, 'And immediately he rose. And all the residents of Lydda and Sharon saw him, and they turned to the Lord.' [Acts 9:33-35]

AGABUS (Gk. from the Heb. 'to love') One of the prophets, acknowledged within the primitive Christian Church to rank next to the apostles, Agabus is twice recorded as exercising a prophetic ministry in the presence of Paul.

On the first occasion, Agabus and others had come down from Jerusalem to Antioch. Agabus foretold a severe famine, which actually occurred in the reign of the Emperor Claudius. In fact there were acute shortages of food in different parts of the Roman Empire over the period of years 41–54. Josephus, the Jewish historian, relates that there was a famine in Jerusalem during the procuratorship of Tiberias Alexander and that the poor were relieved by the generosity of Queen Helena of Adiabene between the years 46 and 48.

On another occasion Agabus came down from Judea to Caesarea, to meet Paul in the house of Philip the deacon. This would have been in about the year 58, when Paul had returned by sea from Corinth to make his last visit to Jerusalem. Agabus acted in the same symbolic manner as the Old Testament prophets, binding his own hands and feet as a token that Paul would suffer a similar fate in Jerusalem – which indeed he did. [Acts 11:28; 21:10]

AGRIPPA *see* HEROD **5.** *and* **6.**

ALEXANDER (Gk. 'defender of men')

1. Son of Simon of Cyrene

2. Relative of Annas, the high priest

3. Jewish spokesman at Ephesus

4. Convert turned apostate

5. Coppersmith from Asia

1. One of the sons of Simon of Cyrene, 'the father of Alexander and Rufus', who was compelled by the Roman execution and Rufus', who was compelled by the Roman execution squad to carry the cross-piece for Jesus on his way to Calvary. Only Mark mentions the sons by name, perhaps because they had become Christians and were known to his readers. Mark's Gospel is said to have been written in Rome during the year 64-5. Paul, in the final chapter of his letter to the Christians in Rome, includes a greeting to 'Rufus, eminent in the Lord, also his mother and mine'. Whether this greeting and others were in fact addressed to Rome or to Ephesus, there cannot be any certain identification of this family with that of Simon of Cyrene. The respect of Paul for the mother of Alexander and Rufus, coupled with Mark's mention of them by name, would seem, however, to strengthen the tradition that Simon of Cyrene and his family were converted to Christianity. [Mark 15:21]

2. A relative of Annas, the high priest, in Jerusalem. This Alexander is only mentioned once among the members of high-priestly families, within the Sanhedrin. The Supreme Council was, on this occasion, convened in emergency to deal with the situation caused by the powerful preaching of the apostles in Jerusalem. Peter and others were arrested and detained overnight, possibly in the guardroom at the high priest's palace where Jesus himself had been imprisoned overnight. The modern church of 'St Peter in Gallicantu' probably covers the site of this house of Caiaphas and, on a series of levels cut into the rock of the cliff face, enshrines the courtroom of the Council, the guardroom complete with the whipping-block and staples for prisoners' chains, and a bottle-necked condemned cell.

This Alexander is reported to have met with the rulers, elders and scribes together with Caiaphas, John, and other Sadducees. Their decision was to warn the apostles and forbid them to preach in the name of Jesus, but for fear of the people they dared not punish them. [Acts 4:6]

3. A spokesman of the Jewish community in Ephesus. At the height of the confusion in the silversmiths' riot at Ephesus incited by Demetrius (*see* DEMETRIUS), the Jews tried to put forward Alexander as their spokesman, but he was howled down by the mob. Alexander's intention was to defend the two travelling-companions of the Apostle Paul, Gaius and Aristarchus, who had been dragged into the great theatre by members of the offended trade-guilds. When the excited crowd saw that the speaker was a Jew, rather than one of themselves, they began to chant in chorus 'Great is Diana of the Ephesians'. Alexander had seemingly attached himself to Paul but had then joined his fellow-countrymen in opposing Paul. (*see* ALEXANDER **4.** *and* **5.**) Luke adds that the majority of the crowd had no idea what it was all about and that after two hours of tumult the town clerk managed to obtain a hearing, conciliated his audience, and dispersed the disorderly meeting. [Acts 19:33]

4. A convert of Paul's turned apostate. This Alexander may well have been the man involved in the silversmiths' riot (*see* ALEXANDER **3.**). He was a heretical teacher within the Christian community, probably at Ephesus or Troas, on the coast of Asia Minor, whom Paul found it necessary to excommunicate, as his teaching represented a real threat to the faith and loyalty of the local congregation. As Paul puts it in his first letter to Timothy, 'By rejecting conscience, certain persons have made shipwreck of their faith, among them Hymenaeus and Alexander, whom I have delivered to Satan that they may learn not to blaspheme.' (1 Tim. 1:19-20) In his last letter to Timothy, Paul is even more insistent in his warnings against false teachers. Timothy needs to be a 'sound workman', 'handling the word rightly', avoiding 'what is ignoble', and exercising a strict supervision of his congregation. [1 Tim. 1:20]

5. A coppersmith, probably from Troas or Ephesus, bitterly opposed to Paul. This Alexander may possibly have been the same as the heretical teacher, and even the same man who was involved in the silversmiths' riot at Ephesus. (*see* ALEXANDER **3.** *and* **4.**) If so, then the progressive opposition and hostility of this man to the work and person of the Apostle Paul may have culminated in the final arrest of Paul and the ending of his missionary activity. Certainly the final paragraph of Paul's last letter to Timothy implies that he had been arrested at Troas, for Timothy was asked to bring his cloak and scrolls left behind there. The letter could also imply that his arrest was due to the treachery of a certain Alexander. 'Alexander the coppersmith did me great harm; the Lord will requite him for his deeds. Beware of him yourself, for he strongly opposed our message. At my first defence no one took my part; all deserted me. May it not be charged against them!' [2 Tim. 4:14-16]

There would seem to be a case for identifying the last three Alexanders. The first Alexander was concerned in the silversmiths' riot in the year 57, though not specified as himself a craftsman. The last Alexander was described by Paul as a 'smith', using the general Greek word for a worker in copper or brass. The first Alexander was probably a renegade Christian convert of Paul's, yet put forward by the Jews as prepared to give evidence which was more likely to support their case than that of his former teacher. The second Alexander with his plausible but misleading teachings of the Christian faith was active, probably, during Timothy's ministry at Ephesus. Paul certainly felt the need to warn Timothy against this man and wrote to this effect from his first captivity in Rome, during the years 61–2. Three years or so later, after Paul's acquittal by the imperial tribunal and following the resumption of his missionary activities, his re-arrest and final deportation back to Rome, Paul again wrote to Timothy of a third Alexander. This man's bitter hostility and malicious gossip seem to have got Paul into trouble with the civic authorities; moreover he represented a potential menace to the future progress of the Christian Church. The character of this Alexander appears to have been all too consistent with that of the other two references. It would seem that in fact Paul was speaking from hard and bitter experience of a man whom he had known for a decade, and that all three Alexanders were one and the same man.

ALEXANDRIANS Traditionally before the dispersion of the Jews there were said to have been 480 synagogues in Jerusalem. These were the meeting-places for prayer and discussion – particularly about the Law – of many different peoples of Jewish faith. Alexandrian Jews had emigrated to Jerusalem to escape persecution. At the time of Stephen's martyrdom, it was the natives of Alexandria and Cyrene in Africa, and of the Roman provinces of Asia and Cilicia (the home of Saul the Persecutor who was to become Paul the Apostle), who took the initiative in Stephen's arrest. It was the members of these synagogues who took most offence at Stephen's teaching, but could not successfully dispute with his wisdom and enthusiasm.

In consequence, they instigated the crowd to accuse him of blasphemy against Moses and God, for the Jew the ultimate wickedness. The mob dragged Stephen off to the Council and accused him of speaking both against the Temple, as the official centre of worship, and against the Law. Members of the synagogue of the Alexandrians were among the foremost in securing his condemnation and stoning. [Acts 6:9]

ALPHAEUS 1. Alphaeus, father of Levi the tax-collector (better known as the Apostle Matthew). *see* MATTHEW, *and* ALPHAEUS **2.** [Mark 2:14]

2. Alphaeus, father of James the Younger. In the three Synoptic Gospels and in the Acts, the name of this Alphaeus is linked with that of James the Younger, but is not otherwise mentioned. If he was the same person as Alphaeus, father of Levi the tax-collector, Matthew and James the Younger would have been brothers.

The name 'Alphaeus' is derived from the same Aramaic word as the name 'Clopas' (John 19:25); it is possible that these two may have been one and the same person. In this case, 'Mary the wife of Clopas', who watched by the cross of Jesus, would have been the mother of James the Younger, if not also of Matthew.

The 2nd-century historian Hegesippus supposed that

29

Clopas was the brother of Joseph the carpenter. If this were correct, together with the identification of Alphaeus with Clopas, then Alphaeus would have been uncle to Jesus. [Matt. 10:3; Mark 3:18; Luke 6:15; Acts 1:13]

AMPLIAS *see* AMPLIATUS

AMPLIATUS One of the Christians greeted warmly by Paul as 'my beloved in the Lord', at the close of his letter to the Christian congregation in Rome. The Aurelii family at Rome used this common surname and the Christian members of that family are buried in the 1st-century cemetery of Domitilla, on the Via Ardeatina. Here, one tomb in an early style bears the single word 'Ampliati' in lettering of the 1st or 2nd century. The identification is uncertain, but possible, as the position and character of this tomb indicate a person held in considerable respect. [Rom. 16:8]

ANANIAS (Gk. from the Heb. 'Jehovah has been gracious')

1. False Christian at Jerusalem

2. Christian disciple at Damascus

3. High priest in Jerusalem

1. False Christian at Jerusalem. The hypocrite who sold property, but appropriated some of the purchase-money with the connivance of his wife Sapphira, and only brought part of its value to give to the apostles for the Church. The Apostle Peter rebuked him sharply. 'Ananias, why has Satan filled your heart to lie to the Holy Spirit and to keep back part of the proceeds of the land? While it remained unsold, did it not remain your own? And after it was sold, was it not at your disposal? How is it that you have contrived this deed in your heart? You have not lied to men but to God.' (Acts 5:3, 4) This terrible indictment caused his immediate death. Three hours later, his wife Sapphira arrived and, after similar cross-examination and for the same lie, was instantly punished by death. [Acts 5:1-5]

2. The Christian disciple in Damascus who welcomed the baptized Saul. In a vision 'the Lord said to him, "Rise and go to the street called Straight, and inquire in the house of Judas for a man of Tarsus named Saul; for behold, he is praying, and he has seen a man named Ananias come in and lay his hands on him so that he might regain his sight." But Ananias answered, "Lord, I have heard from many about this man, how much evil he has done to thy saints at Jerusalem; and here he has authority from the chief priests to bind all who call upon thy name." But the Lord said to him, "Go, for he is a chosen instrument of mine to carry my name before the Gentiles and kings and the sons of Israel; for I will show him how much he must suffer for the sake of my name." ' (Acts 9:11-16) Then Ananias went to the house in Straight Street 'and, laying his hands on him, he said, "Brother Saul, the Lord Jesus who appeared to you on the road by which you came, has sent me that you may regain your sight and be filled with the Holy Spirit." And immediately something like scales fell from his eyes and he regained his sight. Then he rose and was baptized, and took food and was strengthened.' (Acts 9:17-19) That was in about the year 36.

Later, at his trial in Jerusalem in about the year 58, Paul described before the Council his conversion and baptism at Damascus. He emphasized the character of Ananias, 'a devout man according to the Law, well spoken of by all the Jews who lived there'. Ananias had said, 'The God of our Fathers appointed you to know his will, to see the Just One and to hear a voice from his mouth; for you will be a witness for him to all men of what you have seen and heard. And now why do you wait? Rise and be baptized, and wash away your sins,

31

calling on his name.' (Acts 22:12-16) Paul wished to show that those Jews who strictly kept the Law approved of him at the time of his conversion, and he spoke with affection of Ananias. [Acts 9:10-17; 22:12-16]

3. The high priest in Jerusalem and chairman of the Council at Paul's trial. At the order of the Roman tribune, the Council met to draw up the charges against Paul. When Paul began to defend himself, the high priest, Ananias, commanded those who stood by to strike him on the mouth. This drew from Paul a blistering rebuke, ' "God shall strike you, you whitewashed wall! Are you sitting to judge me according to the law, and yet contrary to the law you order me to be struck?" Those who stood by said, "Would you revile God's high priest?" And Paul said, "I did not know, brethren, that he was the high priest; for it is written, 'You shall not speak evil of a ruler of your people'." ' (Acts 23:3-5)

Five days later, the Roman governor, Felix, summoned Ananias and the elders to Caesarea. They brought a barrister called Tertullus to act as prosecutor in presenting the charges against Paul. But all Felix could do was to confine Paul for the next two years, until he was succeeded by the new governor, Festus.

Ananias was murdered by his fellow-countrymen in Jerusalem, during the siege of the city by Titus in the years 69-70, in revenge for Ananias's pro-Roman tendencies. [Acts 22:12; 23:2; 24:1]

ANDREW (Gk. 'manly') One of the first disciples of Jesus and the brother of Simon Peter, Andrew appears in all the lists of the apostles. All three Synoptic Gospels – Matthew, Mark, and Luke – and the first chapter of the Acts describe the call of Simon Peter and Andrew, though Luke does not mention Andrew in his account of the event by name, but adds the story of the miraculous draught of fish and Peter's penitence. 'And passing along by the Sea of Galilee, he saw Simon and Andrew the brother of Simon casting a net in the sea; for they were fishermen. And Jesus said to them, "Follow me and I will make you become fishers of men." And immediately they left their nets and followed him.' (Mark 1:16-18)

After the exorcism of an unclean spirit in the synagogue at Capernaum, all three Gospels again record that Jesus entered the home of Peter. Mark adds, 'And immediately he left the synagogue, and entered the house of Simon and Andrew', implying that the house was directly outside the synagogue and that it was the home of both the brothers as well as of Peter's mother-in-law. An octagonal Byzantine shrine of 'Peter's house' has long been shown opposite the entrance of the site of the synagogue at Capernaum. Recently, however, the Byzantine pavement has been lifted to permit the excavation of 1st-century houses beneath, thus confirming the occupation of the site in the life-time of Jesus.

Andrew was present on the Mount of Olives with the inner cycle of Jesus's disciples, Peter, James, and John, when Jesus foretold the destruction of the Temple. The four disciples questioned him privately, 'Tell us, when will this be, and what will be the sign when these things are all to be accomplished?' (Mark 13:4) Mark uses their question to introduce the long discourse that follows in his Gospel and which is repeated in both Matthew and Luke.

There is no further reference to Andrew in the first three Gospels, apart from the list of apostles, where he is linked with Philip, as he is also in the list of apostles in the Upper Room before Pentecost.

33

Andrew and John the Baptist

The Fourth Gospel is far more specific about Andrew and his particular function within the group of disciples. It seems that Andrew and another disciple, possibly Philip, were disciples of John the Baptist during his evangelistic mission by the River Jordan. It was thanks to the words of John the Baptist that his disciples first took notice of Jesus: 'John was standing with two of his disciples; and he looked at Jesus as he walked, and said, "Behold, the Lamb of God!" The two disciples heard him say this, and they followed Jesus. Jesus turned, and saw them following, and said to them, "What do you seek?" And they said to him, "Rabbi" (which means Teacher), "where are you staying?" He said to them, "Come and see." They came and saw where he was staying; and they stayed with him that day.' (John 1:35-9)

Early next morning Andrew met his brother Simon Peter and declared, 'We have found the Messiah', and introduced Simon Peter to Jesus. Jesus looked hard at Peter and said, ' "So you are Simon the son of John? You shall be called Cephas" (which means Peter).' The writer goes on to speak of Philip, Simon Peter, and Andrew as being natives of the fishing town Bethsaida.

The next reference to Andrew in the Fourth Gospel is in the story of the feeding of the five thousand. His friend Philip, possibly the caterer of the party, has just commented on the fact that two hundred denarii would hardly buy enough bread to give such a crowd a mere mouthful apiece. At this point in the dilemma, Andrew produces a little boy with his picnic meal of five barley loaves and two small fishes, saying, 'But what are they among so many?' Nevertheless, he introduces the boy to Jesus, who takes what the boy has to offer, says grace, and divides it for distribution by the disciples. And all are fed.

The last appearance of Andrew is before the Passover festival in Jerusalem, after the triumphal entry on the first Palm Sunday. Some Greeks came up to Philip with the request, 'Sir, we wish to see Jesus.' Philip promptly told his friend Andrew, and together they told Jesus. Andrew once again seems to have been the willing witness and missionary, introducing first his own brother, Peter, then the boy with the loaves and the fishes, and finally a Gentile delegation to Jesus.

St. Andrew's Cross

A 3rd-century apocryphal *Acts of St. Andrew* describes his ministry, persecution, imprisonment, and execution at Patrae, on the north-west coast of Achaia, in the year 60. He was said to have hung alive on the cross for two days, preaching to and encouraging his watchers. The 4th-century bishop of Caesarea and 'Father of Church History', Eusebius, relates that Andrew's ministry was among the backward and ruthless barbarians of Scythia – now the southern steppes of Russia and the Ukraine.

The Muratorian Fragment, the earliest list of New Testament writings, dating from the end of the 2nd century, connects Andrew vaguely with the writing of the Fourth Gospel.

Since about 750, Andrew has been the patron saint of Scotland, and his festival has always been kept in the Anglican Church as a time of prayer for missionaries and the mission of the Church. It was not until the 14th century that the tradition of his crucifixion on the 'X'-shaped cross appeared, presumably because the 'X' was the Greek 'Ch', the first letter of 'Christos', meaning 'Messiah'. [Matt. 10:2; Mark 1:14-18, 29; 3:18;

13:3; Luke 6:14; John 1:40-44; 6:8-12; 12:20-22; Acts 1:13]

ANDRONICUS (Gk. 'man of victory') One of the Christians greeted by Paul at the end of his letter to the Christian Church in Rome, Andronicus is linked with Junias. Paul refers to them as his 'kinsmen', probably meaning that at least they were fellow-Jews, if not blood-relatives. Paul also calls them his 'fellow-prisoners', though during which of his imprisonments is uncertain. Paul goes on: 'They are men of note among the apostles, and they were in Christ before me.' This immediately places their conversion within five years of the crucifixion of Jesus and connects them with the Church in Jerusalem, rather than at Antioch. In fact they may well have been associated with the Stephen group of Hellenized Jews who dispersed to found branches of the Church in Antioch, Cyprus, and elsewhere in the eastern Mediterranean. It is just possible that Junias should be read as 'Junia', in the feminine, which would then suggest the wife of Andronicus and a woman apostle. [Rom. 16:7]

ANGEL (Gk. 'messenger') For centuries before Jesus, people felt protected, guided and advised by the angels of God – and not just Jewish people, but those of many races and cultures, whether from primitive superstition, oriental imagination, or from divine inspiration. The New Testament never questions the existence of angels, but simply states the fact. Jesus often spoke of them in the terms of his day and age. He told us that they rejoice over the penitent, they bear up souls to paradise, that the guardian angels of little children always see the Father's face, that the angels neither marry nor are given in marriage.

The angels, moreover, were closely linked with the crises of his own life. They announced the birth of his cousin John the Baptist to the old priest Zechariah and his own birth to Mary at Nazareth. Angels sang at his birth, in the fields of Bethlehem. Angels ministered to him during his temptation in the wilderness. Angels strengthened him during his agony in the Garden of Gethsemane. Angels rolled away the stone from the tomb and announced his resurrection. Angels encouraged his apostles after his ascension. Angels supported his followers. An angel led Peter out of prison. An angel stood by Paul throughout his shipwreck off the island of Malta. In the Revelation of John the Divine, the worship of the angels in heaven is the prototype of the worship of the Church. From St Augustine of Hippo to St Francis of Assisi and to Joan of Arc, the more simple and humble-minded Christians have felt that they enjoyed the guidance, comfort and protection of angels.

Catholic Christianity today teaches their existence, their pure spirituality and their creation before that of mankind – while the Protestants tend to disregard rather than define their place in the order of creation. The Eastern Churches are on the whole far more aware of the presence of the angels, for whom Monday is a weekly Orthodox day of commemoration. The Book of Common Prayer collect for Michaelmas well sums up Christian belief thus: 'God who hast ordained and constituted the services of Angels and men in a wonderful order; mercifully grant that, as thy holy angels always do thee service in heaven, so, by thy appointment, they may succour and defend us on earth.' *see* GABRIEL *and* MICHAEL [Matt. 1.20; 2:13, 19; 4:6, 11; 13:39; 16:27; 18:10; 25:41; 28:2, 5; Mark 1:13; 8:38; 13:27; 16:5; Luke 1:11, 18, 19, 26, 34; 2:9, 10, 13, 15; 22:43; 24:23; John 1:51; Acts 1:10; 5:19; 6:15; 8:26; 10:30; 27:23, 24; Rom. 8:38; 1 Cor. 6:3; 13:1; 2 Cor. 12:7; Gal. 4:14; Eph. 3:10; Col. 1:16; 2:15; 2 Thess. 1:7;

Heb. 1:4-14; 2:1-16; 13:2; 1 Pet. 1:12; 3:22; 2 Pet. 2:4; Jude 6; Rev. 2:1, 12, 18; 3:1, 7, 14; 5:2, 11; 22:6]

ANNA (Gk. from the Heb. 'grace') An elderly prophetess – in the tradition of Moses's sister Miriam (Exod. 15:20), Deborah (Judg. 4:4), and Huldah (2 Kgs. 22:14), who served in the Temple at Jerusalem, as did the aged priest Simeon, when the child Jesus was presented in the Temple by Joseph and Mary. Luke says that after only seven years of marriage she had been widowed, since when she had hardly left the Temple area, spending her time by day and night in fasting and prayer. 'And coming up at that very hour she gave thanks to God, and spoke of him to all who were looking for the redemption of Jerusalem.' (Luke 2:38) It would seem that Anna thanked God for living to see the baby Jesus, whom she openly pronounced to be the fulfilment of God's Messianic promises [Luke 2:36-38]

ANNAS (Gk. from the Heb. 'gracious', 'merciful') This Jewish high priest was appointed at the age of 36, in the year 6, and nine years later was deposed by the Roman procurator of Judea, Valerius Gratus. Annas was succeeded by his son-in-law Caiaphas, a member of the priestly aristocracy, the wealthy class resident traditionally in the upper city of Jerusalem. The house of Annas to which Jesus was first taken after his arrest (according to the Fourth Gospel) had a spacious courtyard, a portress on the gate, and other servants. The traditional site of this building is now that of an Armenian church of the 15th century on the Western Hill outside the wall.

The hierarchy tended to fill all the chief positions from their own families as a matter of course. The ruling house of Annas held perhaps all the chief-priestly positions within its control, besides operating a flourishing trade in sacrificial victims within the court of the

Gentiles, in the Temple. No less than eight members of this family held the supreme office of high priest: Annas himself, five sons, Caiaphas his son-in-law, and his grandson Matthias, from the year 65. Such a family virtually established the political as well as religious leadership of the nation.

Luke dates the beginning of the ministry of John the Baptist as 'within the high priesthood of Annas and Caiaphas'. John describes the arrest and escort of Jesus to Annas. It was here, according to the Fourth Gospel, that young John Bar-Zebedee (*see* ZEBEDEE) obtained entrance for Peter into the courtyard, where he thrice denied Jesus. There, 'the high priest then questioned Jesus about his disciples and his teaching. Jesus answered him, "I have spoken openly to the world: I have always taught in synagogues and in the Temple, where all Jews come together; I have said nothing secretly. Why do you ask me? Ask those who have heard me, what I said to them; they know what I said." When he had said this, one of the officers standing by struck Jesus with his hand, saying, "Is that how you answer the high priest?" Jesus answered him, "If I have spoken wrongly, bear witness to the wrong; but if I have spoken rightly, why do you strike me?" Annas then sent him bound to Caiaphas the high priest.' (John 18:19-24) As retired high priest, Annas would retain considerable prestige and influence.

Luke again mentions Annas, first on account of his age and influence, in a list of 'rulers' in Jerusalem for a meeting of the Sanhedrin. This supreme court was convened to try the Apostles Peter and John for their healing of the lame man at the Beautiful Gate of the Temple. The court warned and acquitted the apostles without punishment. No further mention is made of Annas in the New Testament, though it was openly rumoured in his day that, as a wealthy man, he had lent money to the Romans and was so able to blackmail them into doing as he wished. Certainly he and his family were deep in a highly successful political intrigue and were able to claim the privileges and immunity of priesthood.

Jesus had few contacts with the aristocratic Sadducees, as he moved rather among the common people, but no doubt the Sadducees watched the development of his movement with increasing dislike and restlessness. [Luke 3:2; John 18:13-24; Acts 4:5-6]

ANTICHRIST (Gk. 'against' or 'instead of Christ') One who assumes the place and office of the Messiah, but is directly opposed to him, the man of sin epitomizing all that is impious and abominable.

Christian belief about the 'Last Things' or the 'End' inherited much from Judaism. Jewish apocalyptic thought posed a programme of events to come: the world was under the limited and temporary sway of evil powers, but at the 'End', God would establish his rule or kingdom and destroy the control or kingdom of the 'adversary'. It was an ancient belief, however, that this final victory would be preceded by the final desperate stand of the powers of evil. For this, one supreme adversary – either a man of diabolical power and wickedness, or a supernatural being from another world – would appear as a sort of Antichrist. In Mark's Gospel, the prediction of the end of the world put into the mouth of Jesus (Chapter 13) refers to 'desolating sacrilege' which will defile the Temple. Paul foretells 'the coming of the lawless one' (2 Thess. 2:9) who will set himself up in the Temple and claim to be God. The coming of the Antichrist was to herald the 'End' and at the second coming of the Messiah the Antichrist would be finally defeated.

John the Divine in his Book of Revelation sees the Antichrist as the 'Beast', the power of Rome, which desecrated and destroyed the Temple in the year 70. The author of the letters of John, most probably another John, tends to rationalize the ancient mythology of the 'Last Things' by thinking of Antichrist as not one but many opponents and false teachers. 'Children, it is the last hour; and as you have heard that antichrist is coming, so now many antichrists have come; therefore we know that it is the last hour. They went out from us, but they were not of us; for if they had been of us, they would have continued with us; but they went out, that it might be plain that they all are not of us. . . . Who is the liar but he who denies that Jesus is the Christ? This is the antichrist, he who denies the Father and the Son.' (1 John 2:18, 19, 22) 'For many deceivers have gone into the world, men who will not acknowledge the coming of Jesus Christ in the flesh; such a one is the deceiver and the antichrist.' (2 John 7) [1 John 2:18, 19, 22; 2 John 7]

ANTIPAS 1. An early martyr at Pergamum, the northernmost of the seven Christian parishes on the mainland of Asia Minor, encircling Ephesus.

Paul could have passed through Pergamum during his Third Journey, when travelling from Ephesus north to Troas on his way to Macedonia. These Christian congregations were possibly founded by teachers trained by Paul during his three-year stay in Ephesus in the years 54-7. Later, John the Divine inherited this ministry and, when deported to the island of Patmos as a Christian agitator, wrote to his beloved 'Seven Churches', referring to Antipas as 'Antipas my witness, my faithful one, who was killed among you, where Satan dwells'. [Rev. 2:13]

2. Antipas, Herod *see* HEROD ANTIPAS

APELLES (Gk. abbreviation for 'Apollonius') One of the Christian converts greeted by Paul, as 'approved in Christ', at the close of his letter to the Christian congregation in Rome. A variant reading in an important manuscript, the *Codex Sinaiticus,* identifies Apelles with Apollos – but without further confirmation. The name 'Apelles' is frequently found in Jewish inscriptions and in the works of Philo, Josephus, and Horace. [Rom. 16:10]

APOLLOS A learned Alexandrian Jew, who arrived with others at Ephesus in the year 53, during Paul's absence at Antioch between his Second and Third Journeys.

Apollos and his twelve companions were teachers of the 'baptism of John' but had never received baptism in the name of Jesus. Apollos himself was an erudite and eloquent scholar of the Old Testament scriptures and an enthusiastic teacher with an accurate knowledge of the story of Jesus; but he had little knowledge of the purpose and progress of the Christian movement. Aquila and Priscilla, left at Ephesus by Paul, heard him speaking in the synagogue and immediately recognized the potential power of his message – once he had grasped the significance of what he was already trying to teach. They took him aside and completed his Christian education, explaining the 'Way of God' more perfectly. As he was bound for Corinth, they also commended him to the newly-founded Christian community there, where his forceful preaching and illustrations from the scriptures of the Messiahship of Jesus were of immediate use.

After Apollos's arrival in Corinth, Paul reached Ephesus to find the little group of disciples of John the Baptist, who after instruction received baptism in the name of Jesus. Paul laid his hands upon them and they received the gift of the Spirit.

Meanwhile Apollos made a deep impression, probably by the allegorical style (in the Alexandrian tradition; and expertise of his preaching. The Corinthian community had little sense of unity and quickly came to regard Apollos as a rival, rather than a successor to Paul, as the pastor of their immature little Christian congregation. To many of them Apollos's gift of exposition and oratory compared favourably with the blunt technique and insignificant physical appearance of Paul. Consequently, some of the Corinthian congregation remained loyal to Paul; others were attracted and overwhelmed by the preaching of Apollos; yet others rallied to the name of Peter.

Paul dealt with their party-spirit frankly, in his Corinthian correspondence, upbraiding them for their lack of spirituality as 'men of flesh' and 'babes in Christ'. 'For when one says, "I belong to Paul," and another, "I belong to Apollos," are you not merely men? What then is Apollos? What is Paul? Servants through whom you believed, as the Lord assigned to each. I planted, Apollos watered, but God gave the growth. . . . He who plants and he who waters are equal, and each shall receive his wages according to his labour. For we are fellow workers for God; you are God's field, God's building.' (1 Cor. 3:4-9) 'So let no one boast of men. For all things are yours, whether Paul or Apollos or Cephas or the world or life or death or the present or the future, all are yours; and you are Christ's; and Christ is God's.' (1 Cor. 3:21-23)

After working with Paul in Ephesus during his long teaching mission, Apollos returned to take charge of the Corinthian congregation and, according to Jerome, the

43

4th-century biblical scholar, became the first bishop of Corinth.

A final reference in the letter addressed to Titus asks him to send Apollos to meet Paul at Nicopolis, on the Adriatic coast of Greece, though the Pauline authorship of this request is very uncertain. [Acts 18:24; 19:1; 1 Cor. 1:12; 3:4-6; Titus 3:13]

APOLLYON (Gk. 'destroyer') *see* ABADDON

APPHIA (Gk. from the Phrygian 'beloved') The mistress and hostess of the well-to-do household in which the Christian congregation gathered at Colossae. Together with Philemon, who was apparently her husband, and Archippus, probably their son, Apphia was an addressee of Paul's personal plea that they should forgive and welcome back the runaway slave, Onesimus. (*see* PHILEMON) According to tradition, Apphia and her family were martyred at Colossae during the persecutions in the time of the Emperor Nero. [Philem. 2]

AQUILA (Lat., Gk. 'eagle') Aquila and his wife Priscilla, always called 'Prisca' by Paul, were very close friends of the Apostle Paul. Aquila, originally a Jew from Pontus in Asia Minor, had migrated to Rome. In the year 49 he had been exiled, with his wife, by the edict of Claudius expelling all Jews from the imperial city. They met Paul, probably in the following year, at Corinth, where they had a business as tentmakers, in which trade Paul also earned a living. Paul went to live with them, probably working under Aquila, either in canvas or leather.

It is not certain whether Aquila and Priscilla were Christians before their expulsion from Rome, or whether they were converted at Corinth. They soon, however, became partners with Paul in Christian evangelism, as well as in the tent trade. In about the year 52, they sailed with Paul from Cenchrae, the Aegean port of Corinth, for Syria; but they seem to have stopped at Ephesus, where they awaited Paul on his return from Antioch. They may well have been opening a branch of their business in Ephesus, for Paul was able to spend the next two years there in a concentrated teaching mission. It was during this time that an Alexandrian Jew called Apollos, who had been baptized after the manner of John the Baptist, but had not experienced the gift of the Holy Spirit, arrived in Ephesus. An eloquent and learned man, Apollos argued powerfully in the Jewish synagogue for the Messiahship of Jesus. When Aquila and Priscilla heard him, they took him aside and instructed him more accurately in the Christian faith. Later, Paul gave him charge of the Christian congregation at Corinth.

Whether Aquila and Priscilla were involved in the silversmiths' riots at Ephesus, or in some other dangers there, is unknown. Paul, however, includes in his greetings to the Christian congregation at Rome 'Prisca and Aquila, my fellow workers in Christ Jesus, who risked their necks for my life, to whom not only I but also all the churches of the Gentiles give thanks'.

Following the death of the Emperor Claudius, the edict of banishment was no longer in force and Aquila and Priscilla probably returned to Rome. On the other hand, they probably retained their business in Ephesus and travelled freely between the two cities. This would explain Paul's greeting to them, at the end of his last letter to Timothy, when he had left Timothy as his representative in Ephesus and was himself writing from prison in Rome.

It is interesting that of the six times that Aquila and his wife are mentioned in the New Testament, four times Priscilla's name is put first — twice by Luke and twice by Paul. This might be taken to imply that she was a more prominent member of the Church than her husband Aquila. [Acts 18:2, 18, 26; Rom. 16:3; 1 Cor. 16:19; 2 Tim. 4:19]

ARABIANS (Heb. 'steppe') At the feast of Pentecost – for the Jew, the giving of the Law; for the Christian, the giving of the Spirit – Arabians, Elamites, Medes, Parthians are included in the list of nationalities enumerated as present in Jerusalem. The gift of the Spirit enabled the apostles of the early Christian Church to make themselves understood in all languages. The Greek implies that each heard his own dialect. This miracle was thought to be symbolical of the coming universality of the gospel of Jesus.

On their return home to many Jewish communities throughout the eastern Mediterranean, those who had heard the preaching of the apostles might well have taken with them the news of a Messiah. [Acts 2:11]

ARCHELAUS (Gk. 'ruling the people') *see* HEROD AR-CHELAUS

ARCHIPPUS (Gk. 'master of the horse') Described by Paul as a 'fellow soldier', he was probably in charge of Church affairs at Colossae, in the absence of Epaphras, the pastor and evangelist. Paul indeed sent him a message, 'And say to Archippus, "See that you fulfil the ministry which you have received in the Lord." '

The letter to Philemon is addressed also to Apphia and to Archippus, 'and the church in your house'. It has been suggested that Apphia was the wife of Philemon and that Archippus was their son – besides being the responsible leader in the Colossian Church at that time. This might mean that Paul's plea to the father and family of Archippus, to forgive and welcome back the runaway slave Onesimus, was in fact addressed to the most influential Christian family at Colossae, in whose house

46

the local congregation met for worship. *see* PHILEMON
[Col. 4:17; Philem. 2]

AREOPAGITE (Gk. 'member of the court of Areopagus', i.e. of Mars Hill) *see* DIONYSIUS

ARETAS (Gk. 'pleasing' or 'virtuous') The Nabatean king, the fourth of that name (9 BC-AD 40), whose daughter was married to and divorced from Herod Antipas; he ruled Damascus at the time of the conversion of Paul, and his governor there tried to arrest the future apostle.

The capital of his kingdom was Petra, some 170 miles south of Amman. This city of rock is famous for its complex of fantastic hills and chasms, and for the multiplicity of its monuments carved in the rose-red sandstone of an exquisite, natural, and strategic setting.

The Nabateans began as a wandering Bedouin tribe living on the plunder of caravans from Arabia. From Petra they sallied forth on the 'King's Highway', first to pillage and then to protect. In fact, they were the forerunners of the protective racketeers, extorting high taxes for providing escorts to passing caravans. Thus their city of Petra became a prosperous trading metropolis, perhaps identifiable with Sela, Nebaioth and the strong city of Edom. The Nabatean kingdom, famous also for its agriculture and its architecture, with familiar egg and arrow motifs, reached the height of its history under its kings, particularly Aretas IV.

The power of the Nabateans extended over the caravan routes south and east of Judea from the 7th century BC to the 2nd century AD. Their influence may be inferred from references in the New Testament. Antipas, son of Herod the Great and tetrarch of Galilee, had married the daughter of Aretas, but divorced her in favour of Herodias, his brother Philip's wife. It was opposition to this liaison that cost John the Baptist his life

47

(Matt. 14:3). Aretas promptly revenged his daughter by invading Antipas's territory and Antipas was able to escape only with the help of Roman forces.

Paul relates that 'At Damascus, the governor under King Aretas guarded the city of Damascus in order to seize me, but I was let down in a basket through a window in the wall, and escaped his hands.' (2 Cor. 11:32-33) The Roman Emperor Caligula had apparently limited the power of the Jewish high priests and, not trusting Antipas, had given the control of the Hellenistic city of Damascus to Aretas, who had put the city in the charge of a governor. Why the governor co-operated with the Jewish enemies of Paul is not known. There is today an unconvincing site of Paul's descent in the basket, but the atmosphere of the story is more vividly illustrated by the ancient brick walling, with its Turkish overhanging lattice windows, nearby. [2 Cor. 11:32]

ARISTARCHUS (Gk. 'the best ruler') A faithful fellow-traveller and constant companion of the Apostle Paul, Aristarchus is first mentioned together with Gaius. They were both Macedonians; Aristarchus came from Thessalonica and was probably a convert from Judaism.

At the very height of the silversmiths' riot at Ephesus, towards the close of Paul's teaching ministry in about the year 57, Aristarchus and Gaius were seized by the mob and dragged into the great theatre. The silversmiths felt their trade in shrines and images of Artemis (Diana of the Ephesians) threatened by the teachings of Paul, and stirred up the crowd to demonstrate against Paul and his companions. In the resultant confusion, Aristarchus and Gaius seem to have borne the brunt of the grievance and Paul was warned not to come to their rescue. The town clerk finally called an end to the disorder and we may assume that Aristarchus and Gaius escaped, if a little the worse for wear.

The following year, they are both mentioned among the representatives of Christian congregations accompanying Paul, and the money-offering for the relief of the poor, from Troas to Jerusalem. Only Aristarchus, however, is recorded as sailing with Paul and Luke from Caesarea, on Paul's long and eventful voyage to Rome.

It is probable that, during Paul's long imprisonment in Rome, his friends took turns in keeping him company and sharing captivity along with him. This would account for Paul's mention in his later letters of different 'fellow prisoners'. Certainly when Paul wrote his letter to the Christian Church at Colossae, Aristarchus was his companion in prison. By the time Paul writes his personal letter to Philemon, it is Epaphras whom he mentions as his fellow-prisoner, whereas Aristarchus is listed, together with Mark, Demas, and Luke, as a fellow-worker.

Thus all five references to Aristarchus, covering a period of seven critical years in the life of Paul, seem to refer with little doubt to one and the same faithful and staunch companion of the apostle. [Acts 19:29; 20:4; 27:2; Col. 4:10; Philem. 24]

ARISTOBULUS (Gk. 'the best counsellor') His family was greeted by Paul at the close of his letter to the Christian congregation in Rome. The name 'Aristobulus' was also that of a grandson of Herod the Great, resident in Rome earlier in the 1st century. It is possible that Paul's friend had been a slave in the household of Herod Aristobulus. [Rom. 16:10]

ARTEMAS (Gk. 'gift of Artemis') A companion of Paul during his stay at Nicopolis, on the Adriatic coast of Greece, perhaps after his release from his first captivity in Rome, and during the years 64-5. Paul intended to send Artemas or Tychicus to Titus in Crete, and wanted Titus to return and spend some of the winter with him at Nicopolis. According to tradition, Artemas became bishop of Lystra in the Roman province of Galatia, in the south of Asia Minor. [Titus 3:12]

ARTEMIS The great goddess of the Ephesians, whose name and cult were the oriental equivalent of the Roman huntress-goddess, Diana. Artemis was represented as the many-breasted goddess of fertility. In the times of the Apostle Paul and of John the Divine of Patmos, the vast temple of Artemis in Ephesus was one of the seven wonders of the world and a centre of pilgrimage as famous as Jerusalem. To the progress of the early Christian Church in Asia, the cult of Artemis presented the most profound and incipient opposition. Today, the vast sanctuary complex of the Temple of Artemis below the acropolis is buried under layers of sand, rubble and silt. The Roman historian Pliny relates that the temple was destroyed seven times. It was completely sacked by the Goths in the year 263. Some of its columns were used in the building of the church of S. Sophia, at Constantinople. *see* EPHESIANS [Acts 19:28, 34]

ASYNCRITUS (Gk. 'incomparable') The first of a list of five men, mentioned in a special greeting from Paul at the close of his letter to the Christian congregation in Rome. Perhaps Asyncritus, his fellows, and 'the brethren who are with them' formed a household or small group within the larger Christian community. [Rom. 16:14]

ATHENIANS Within the New Testament, the men of Athens present a rather disdainful audience on Mars Hill to the Apostle Paul on his Second Journey, in about the year 51.

Paul was making his way south from Thessalonica to Corinth, but left his companions up in Macedonia, while he probably sailed down the coast of Achaia to land at Piraeus, the port of Athens, and passed over the isthmus to Corinth.

Three hundred years previously, Athens had been the intellectual centre of the world. The Athenians, therefore, were hardly likely to be impressed by the insignificant figure and rough-and-ready oratory of the Jew from Tarsus who impertinently proclaimed: 'Men of Athens, I perceive that in every way you are very religious. For as I passed along, and observed the objects of your worship, I found also an altar with this inscription, "to an unknown God". What therefore you worship as unknown, this I proclaim to you.' (Acts 17:22-23)

The altar probably 'belonged' to a goddess of the mystery cults; Paul, stirred by the progressive philosophy of the Athenians, preached in the synagogues and the market-place. At the request of Epicurean and Stoic philosophers, Paul gave an exposition of his teaching before the Council of the Areopagus on Mars Hill. It was a masterpiece of tact, insight, and condensation but in practical terms it was a complete failure. The Greek conception of the human body was of a tomb imprisoning the spirit of the man. They rejected out of hand any mention of the resurrection of the body. They did not believe resurrection would lead to redemption and liberation. Paul made few converts and, filled with disappointment, made his way in fear and trembling to Corinth. [Acts 17:21-23]

AUGUSTUS (Gk. 'majesty') Gaius Octavius was born at Rome in 63 BC, the great-nephew of Julius Caesar. At the age of 20, on the assassination of Caesar, he learned that he had been adopted as Caesar's heir. He conquered his rival, Anthony, at the battle of Actium in 31 BC and held supreme power in the Roman world for the

51

next 45 years. The Senate awarded him the title of 'Augustus', which has continued to grace the age of progress and peace marked by his reign. On his death in AD 14, he was succeeded by his stepson, Tiberius.

Luke dates the census which required Joseph and Mary's presence at Bethlehem as being in the reign of Augustus. An imperial enrolment, such as Luke describes, was not in accordance with Roman practice, though provincial enrolments, for taxation purposes and carried out by the governor, were well known. It is just possible that such a census was instigated by Herod the Great, but no Roman census was held until after Judea came under direct Roman rule in AD 6. Unless, however, Luke was mistaken, this was not perhaps the census that resulted in the birth of Jesus taking place in Bethlehem some twelve years previously, within the lifetime of Herod the Great who died in 4 BC.

It was in honour of Augustus that Herod built both Caesarea, on the Mediterranean coast, and Samaria in the hill country. The Greek name for Samaria, *Sebastos,* means 'Augustus'. [Luke 2:1]

B

BARABBAS (Gk. from the Heb. 'son of a father' or 'teacher') The Jewish prisoner whose release was demanded, according to a customary Passover amnesty, by the crowd in preference to the release of Jesus offered by Pilate, the Roman procurator, in the year 30.

All four Gospels mention Barabbas and the Apostle Peter refers to him as a 'murderer' in a speech to the people of Jerusalem, shortly after Pentecost. Matthew and Mark record that the chief priests incited the mob to call for Barabbas rather than Jesus. 'Now at the feast he used to release for them one prisoner whom they asked. And among the rebels in prison, who had committed murder in the insurrection, there was a man called Barabbas. And the crowd came up and began to ask Pilate to do as he was wont to do for them. And he answered them, "Do you want me to release for you the King of the Jews?" For he perceived that it was out of envy that the chief priests had delivered him up. But the chief priests stirred up the crowd to have him release for them Barabbas instead.' (Mark 15:6-11)

Luke describes Barabbas as 'a man who had been thrown into prison for an insurrection started in the city, and for murder'. (Luke 23:19) In John's more detailed and exact account, probably taken from the official records of the trial of Jesus, Pilate does not even mention Barabbas. After considerable cross-examination of the prisoner Jesus, Pilate, aware that the case was being fraudulently presented and that he was expected to act as a destructive tool of the Sanhedrin, looked for a means of escape. He suggested the offer of the customary Passover amnesty; but he had forgotten Barabbas. Again he went to the Jews and told them, ' "I find no crime in him. But you have a custom that I should release one man for you at the Passover; will you have me release for you the King of the Jews?" They cried out again, "Not this man, but Barabbas!" Now Barabbas was a robber.' (John 18:38-40) John emphasizes the tragedy of their choice by his choice of word for Barabbas; the word 'robber' is better translated 'bandit'.

A number of early manuscripts of Matthew's Gospel give Barabbas a forename. Possibly very early in the life of the original manuscript a copyist transcribed the

Greek words 'to you' (release *to you* Barabbas') as the abbreviation for the common name Jesus, or Joshua.

So, in such manuscripts, the words of Pilate to the people appear as: 'Whom do you want me to release, Jesus Barabbas or Jesus who is called the Messiah?' The dramatic force of the choice thus offered to the people is heightened by the identical names of the prisoners. It was noted in the 3rd century by the biblical scholar Origen.

The Barabbas incident has become permanently incorporated in Christian tradition with the story of the trial of Jesus. It is, however, all too possible to perceive here the polemical purpose to blame not only the Jewish priests but the Jewish people for the death of Jesus. And yet the choice of Barabbas rather than of Jesus would have been absolutely consistent with the contemporary political situation.

Barabbas was almost certainly a Zealot (*see* ZEALOTS) and a member of the *Sicarii,* the guerrillas or commandos, literally 'dagger-men', dedicated to the expulsion of the hated Roman occupation forces. Jesus, on the other hand, in teaching and practice was an exponent of nonresistance, appearing even at his own arrest and trial to yield feebly to the occupying power. Faced with such a choice, the crowd without hesitation, even with enthusiasm, chose the violent nationalist rather than the patient idealist, so useless to the nationalist cause. To coin Jesus's own dictum, they took the sword and perished by the sword, in Roman hands. It may be that the rabble outside the Antonia Fortress (*see* PILATE) included a group of the partisans of Barabbas and this may account for their clamorous insistence for his release. In any case Pilate's device to free Jesus was self-defeating, for the crowd demanded the release of their real rebel. In a sense, the choice was and is symbolical. The world still chooses violence and banditry. [Matt. 27; Mark 15; Luke 23; John 18]

BAR-JESUS (Gk. from the Heb. 'son of Jesus', 'son of Joshua') A Jewish sorcerer in the retinue of the Roman proconsul, Sergius Paulus, at Paphos, on the island of Cyprus.

When Paul, Barnabas, and Mark visited Cyprus in the year 46, on the first of Paul's journeys, they fell in with a false prophet and sorcerer, who belonged to the suite of the Roman proconsul. It is quite in keeping with what is known of Roman colonial life that a learned Jew should have been attached to his household, that is, one who combined his philosophy with the exercise of magic or divination. When Sergius Paulus invited Paul and Barnabas to present 'the word of God' to him, Elymas Bar-Jesus attempted to baulk the teaching of the Christian gospel to his Roman master. Paul pronounced a curse upon him, as it were 'beating him at his own game' and inducing a temporary blindness, which both silenced the opposition and so impressed the governor that he accepted and believed the gospel proclaimed by Paul. [Acts 13:6]

BAR-JONAH (Gk. from the Heb. 'son of Jonah', 'son of John') *see* PETER

BARNABAS (Gk. from the Heb. 'son of exhortation', 'son of consolation') This Cypriot Jew, of the tribe of Levi, is described by Luke in Acts as 'a good man, full of the Holy Spirit and of faith', as a result of whose devotion and encouragement 'a large company was added to the Lord'. Barnabas was instrumental in introducing the newly-converted Paul to the leaders of the Christian Church both in Jerusalem and in Antioch. Together with Paul he conducted a mission to the churches of Galatia, and later with Mark firmly established the Christian Church in the island of Cyprus.

When the early Christian community in Judea was setting up a system of stewardship of money and property, Barnabas sold his only piece of land and presented the proceeds to the apostles for distribution to needy members of the congregation. He showed the same generosity in his personal relationships. When Paul arrived in Jerusalem after his conversion, and probably after a period of retirement in the desert to the east of Damascus, the disciples in Jerusalem gave him a cool reception, for they could not believe that Paul, until lately the 'grand inquisitor' and arch-persecutor of the Church, was really a disciple of Jesus. Barnabas, who may indeed have known Paul in Tarsus, trusted and sponsored Paul, taking charge of him and introducing him personally to the leaders of the Church in Jerusalem.

Because of the persecution of Hellenized Christians in Judea after the stoning of Stephen, the Gentile Christian community had scattered throughout the Levant as far as Phoenicia and Syria. Whether because of the Hellenized Christians from Cyprus and Jerusalem, or through Paul himself, or by means of both, the Church was firmly established at Antioch, capital of Syria, which was to become the headquarters of Paul's future journeys. The leaders in Jerusalem sent Barnabas to superintend the Church at Antioch, and Barnabas in turn chose Paul as his assistant, collecting him from Tarsus. For a whole year they conducted a teaching mission together. It was at that time that the possibly derisive title of 'Christians' was first given to the members of the Church at Antioch.

In all this success, Barnabas did not forget his old friends in Jerusalem. There the stewardship experiment was breaking down under the strain of poor crops and other difficulties in maintaining regular support. The Antiochene Christians had started a Judean relief fund.

Barnabas and Paul were chosen for the happy task of delivering their contributions to Jerusalem, whence they returned to Antioch, bringing with them John Mark. There the spontaneous success of the young Christian Church promoted new enterprise and it was natural that the same pair, Barnabas and Paul, should be sent off on what has now come to be called the First Journey, in the year 45 or 46.

On a journey that was to cover 1,400 miles, they set off down the Orontes valley to sail from the port of Seleucia for Salamis, the eastern harbour of Cyprus. There were many Jews working in the copper-mines of Cyprus and a number of Hellenized Christians had come to Cyprus after the persecution in Jerusalem in the year 36. Now, ten years later, Barnabas and Paul landed on the island and proceeded to Paphos, seat of the Roman proconsul Sergius Paulus, who may have been a God-fearing attendant at the local synagogue. One of the proconsul's household was a Jewish magician called Elymas Bar-Jesus, who tried to prevent the preaching of the Christian gospel to his master. Paul very quickly and mercilessly exposed him, and the proconsul accepted Paul's teaching about Jesus.

Crossing over to the mainland of Pisidia, on the south coast of Asia Minor, they landed at Attalia and set off inland, climbing the western spurs of the rugged Taurus range, infested with robbers and other hazards. A few miles inland, John Mark (see MARK) left them and returned to Jerusalem. The rest arrived at Antioch, the capital of Pisidia – not of Syria – a hundred miles north from the coast, an important centre with a large Jewish community. In their synagogue, Paul delivered an address (fully recorded in Acts 13) to both Jews and Gentiles. By the following morning, opposition had crystallized and Paul and Barnabas were expelled from the city – but not before Paul had convinced many pagans, who were later to form the core of the Christian community in Pisidian Antioch.

Paul and Barnabas now turned eastwards and after nearly a hundred miles of rough travelling came to Iconium – a city of Lycaonia now called Konya. Here again their visit followed the same pattern and a Church was formed before – under threat of being stoned – Paul and Barnabas went on to Lystra, 25 miles towards the coast. Here there was no synagogue, so Paul spoke in the open air and healed a cripple. When the crowd realized what had happened, they declared Paul and Barnabas to be gods and attempted to offer them sacrifices.

Barnabas, however kindly, must have had a commanding presence, because in this amusing if (for a Jew) highly embarrassing incident at Lystra, the crowd decided that Barnabas must be Jupiter, lord of the gods, while to the talkative and eloquent Paul they assigned the subordinate role of Mercury.

After a most successful journey, the two reported to headquarters in Jerusalem and had to face a barrage of questions about the freedom with which they had admitted pagans into the Church by baptism, without causing them first to be circumcised. In the end it was decided that the free admission of Gentiles to the Church would be allowed, if they would conform with certain particular social customs of the Jews.

On the next journey, because Barnabas proposed to take Mark with them, the party split up and Paul chose to go with other companions. Barnabas went to Cyprus with Mark.

In any case, the dispute did not end the friendship between Paul and Barnabas. Even on his last journey, when he was writing to the Corinthians, Paul shows that they had kept in touch. He mentions Barnabas as an example, with himself, of apostles who still maintain themselves by working at their old trade and refuse to live on the charity of the Church. It may be said that without the sympathy and encouragement of Barnabas, the vital contributions of Paul and Mark to the Christian faith and the New Testament might never have been made. [Acts 4:36; 11:22, 25, 30; 12:25; 13:1-50; 14:12-20; 15:2-37; 1 Cor. 9:6; Gal. 2:1, 9, 13; Col. 4:10]

BARSABBAS (Gk. from the Heb. 'son of Sabbas' or 'born on the Sabbath') **1. Justus Barsabbas** (sometimes called Joseph) The unsuccessful candidate proposed together with Matthias to fill the gap left by the death of the traitor Judas, and so to complete the number of the twelve apostles of Jesus. *see* MATTHIAS [Acts 1:23]
2. Judas Barsabbas One of two eminent and respected members of the first General Assembly or Christian Council in Jerusalem, held in the year 49 or 50, who were commissioned to convey their decision or decree to the Church in Antioch.

The Council, under the chairmanship of James the brother of Jesus, had received a deputation from the Judean Church stating that circumcision was necessary for salvation.

The Council repudiated the Judaizers and refused to impose the Law on the Gentiles, only forbidding specific offensive practices. Their decision was conveyed to the Church at Antioch by the official delegates Judas and Silas, accompanying Paul and Barnabas on their return. 'So when they were sent off, they went down to Antioch; and having gathered the congregation together, they delivered the letter. And when they read it, they rejoiced at the exhortation. And Judas and Silas, who were themselves prophets, exhorted the brethren with many words and strengthened them.' (Acts 15:30-32)

Judas Barsabbas is carefully distinguished from Justus with the same patronymic, the near-apostle of twenty years before. (*see above*) [Acts 15:22, 27, 30-32]

3. Joseph Barsabbas *see* BARSABBAS **1.** and MATTHIAS

BARTHOLOMEW (Gk. from the Aramaic 'son of Tomai' or 'Talmai') This name is mentioned in the Gospels of Matthew, Mark, and Luke, within the lists of the twelve apostles, where each time Bartholomew is linked with Philip. Otherwise he is listed in Acts among the apostles present at the election of a substitute apostle for the traitor Judas. As the name of Bartholomew is simply a patronymic indicating that he was the son of Tolmai, he must also have had a personal name. This is often identified as 'Nathanael', by which name the writer of the Fourth Gospel calls the apostle-companion of Philip in both his first and last chapters. Here, Nathanael is introduced to Jesus by Philip and is said to come from Cana of Galilee. The identification of Nathanael with Bartholomew has been widely accepted by biblical scholars from the 9th century to the present day.

Eusebius, the early 4th-century historian and bishop of Caesarea, records that an Alexandrian traveller in India discovered a *Gospel of Matthew,* written in Hebrew and left behind by 'Bartholomew, one of the apostles'. According to tradition, Bartholomew was flayed alive in Armenia. He is often represented in art with his skin over his arm and the knife in his hand. *see also* NATHANAEL [Matt. 10:3; Mark 3:18; Luke 6:14; Acts 1:13]

BARTIMAEUS (Gk. from the Heb. 'son of Timaeus') The blind beggar at Jericho, healed by Jesus on his final journey to Jerusalem. All the first three Gospels relate the story of the blind man by the roadside at Jericho, though Matthew duplicates the central character into two blind men; only Mark mentions his name and parentage, and Luke, unlike the other two, says that Jesus was on the way to Jericho.

The story is significant, and full of dramatic irony, for, apart from Peter at Caesarea Philippi, and also certain 'evil spirits' in possession of people whom Jesus healed, this blind man is the first person mentioned in Mark's Gospel to recognize the identity of Jesus as Messiah. He is sitting by the road, probably begging, when he hears the hubbub of the approaching crowd. Hearing that 'Jesus of Nazareth is passing by', the blind man calls out not 'Jesus of Nazareth', but 'Jesus, Son of David, have mercy on me!', thus using the title reserved for the expected Messiah/Deliverer. At this point, all three Gospels portray the bystanders telling him to be quiet, but depict the blind man calling all the more insistently 'Son of David, have mercy'. Now, Jesus comes to a standstill and calls for the blind man, who stands up, drops his cloak and comes, guided through the crowd, to Jesus. Jesus asks him what he wants him to do for him, and Bartimaeus asks, 'Master, let me receive my sight'. The irony lies in the fact that the blind man is the only member of the public who has the insight to recognize the Messiahship of Jesus, and yet he asks to receive his sight. Jesus's answer immediately pinpoints his faith as the real source of his sight, 'Go your way; your faith has made you well.' Whereupon Bartimaeus, now seeing, follows Jesus with the crowd.

Bartimaeus is one of very few persons miraculously healed and restored who are mentioned by name in the first three Gospels. [Mark 10:46-52]

BE-ELZEBUL (*or* BEELZEBUB) (Heb. 'Baal' or 'Lord of the flies') Be-elzebul (in the original Greek) was the

61

ancient pagan god worshipped by the Philistines at Ekron. The word 'baal' was a Canaanite term for 'lord' and the whole word meant 'Lord of heaven'. The Hebrews came to think of him as the prince of the demons and changed his name to Beelzebub, 'Lord of the flies', equating him with the devil. Thus the scribes from Jerusalem said of Jesus: 'He is possessed by Be-elzebul, and by the prince of the demons he casts out the demons.' Jesus at once replied: 'How can Satan cast out Satan? If a kingdom is divided against itself, that kingdom cannot stand. And if a house is divided against itself, that house will not be able to stand. And if Satan has risen up against himself and is divided, he cannot stand, but is coming to an end.' (Mark 3:22-26) *see* SATAN [Matt. 10:25; 12:24-27; Mark 3:22; Luke 11:15]

BELIAL (Gk. from the Heb. 'vain fellow', 'fool', 'good-for-nothing') An Old Testament term of scorn. 'Sons of Belial' were 'useless' and sometimes 'wicked' fellows. In the intertestamental period, the term became synonymous with Satan. In the writings of the Apostle Paul, the term implied 'antichrist'. *see* SATAN [2 Cor. 6:15]

BELOVED DISCIPLE *see* JOHN **3.**

BERNICE (Gk. 'victorious') This daughter of Herod Agrippa I and great-granddaughter of Herod the Great was present with her brother Herod Agrippa II to hear Paul's defence at Caesarea. The procurator, Festus, wished to draw up the charges against Paul before despatching him to Rome, and invited the opinion of Agrippa. The impression of Agrippa and Bernice given by Luke in the Acts of the Apostles is a pleasing one of Roman aristocrats of Jewish birth, courteously attentive, genuinely interested, and well-informed of the political and religious implications of Paul's defence.

Paul's respect for Agrippa is sincere. He says: 'I think myself fortunate that it is before you, King Agrippa, I am to make my defence today against all the accusations of the Jews, because you are especially familiar with all customs and controversies of the Jews.' And Agrippa's comment at the end of Paul's eloquent speech may well have been equally sincere. 'And Agrippa said to Paul, "In a short time you think to make me a Christian!" ' (Acts 26) Bernice seems to have been included in the discussion which followed and may well have influenced Festus's report to Rome, which appears to some to have resulted in Paul's acquittal after two years under house-arrest.

The constant companionship of this brother and sister, Herod Agrippa II and Bernice, caused considerable scandal, as recorded in the satires of Juvenal. Both, however, in the family tradition, were skilled and courageous diplomats. Bernice risked her life for the Jews during the massacre by the infamous procurator Gessius Florus. Agrippa did his best to avert the Jewish War. Bernice is also said to have married King Ptolemy of Sicily, and to have been the mistress of the Emperor Titus. [Acts 25:13, 23; 26:30]

BLASTUS (Gk. 'sprout') The royal chamberlain to Herod Agrippa I, who arranged an audience for the people of Tyre and Sidon, at Caesarea, to settle their differences with the king.

The story told by Luke in Acts is interesting because it is partly corroborated by Josephus in his *Antiquities*. Both sources record an important gathering at Caesarea, at which the audience with true oriental flattery acclaimed Agrippa as a god. Both describe his royal robes, his oration, and his miserable death. The complete independence of Luke's account is indicated by the fact that he alone mentions Blastus, the king's chamberlain. Luke alone records the solution of the feud by the submission of the two cities to the chamberlain. For his master was the ruler of Galilee, upon which the food-supply of the Phoenician coastal cities depended.

Josephus's account adds some interesting details: 'The king went to Caesarea . . . and gave a spectacle in honour of Caesar, at which all the chief personages were present. On the second day of the show, Herod put on a marvellously woven robe of silver, which shone wondrously when the rays of the sun caught it. Thereupon his flatterers cried out, "Be propitious; if we reverenced thee hitherto as a man, from henceforth we acknowledge thee to be more than mortal." The king did not rebuke them, but as he looked up he saw an owl sitting on a rope, and realized that the bird which had once been a messenger of good fortune to him was now an omen of evil. He was seized with violent internal pains, and told his friends that he, whom they saluted as a god, was about to depart from life. He lingered in agony for five days, and died, to the great grief of his countrymen at Caesarea.'

Although Blastus and the feud with the coastal cities do not figure in Josephus's account, yet the 'persuasion' of Blastus, possibly by bribery, the consequent overtures for peace and the resultant reconciliation are typical within the context of the royal magnanimity of such a festal occasion. [Acts 12:20]

BOANERGES (Gk. from the Heb. 'sons of thunder') The name given by Jesus to the two sons of Zebedee, James and John, recorded only by Mark.

The lists of the disciples of Jesus reveal the nickname given to John and his brother James as 'Boanerges'. This means 'sons of thunder' and presumably refers to their angry temperaments, or glowering faces. 'Son of' implies 'having the quality of' thunder. Whether the nickname implies honour or rebuke, it is certain that John and sometimes his brother too were reproved by Jesus. John once said to Jesus at Capernaum, 'Master, we saw a man who is not one of us casting out devils in your name; and because he was not one of us we tried to stop him.' But Jesus said, 'You must not stop him: no one who works a miracle in my name is likely to speak evil of me. Anyone who is not against us is for us.' When James and John asked Jesus to reserve the seats of honour on either side of him at his Messianic banquet in heaven, Jesus replied, 'You do not know what you are asking.' And he went on to ask if they could share his destiny. They confidently affirmed that they could, whereupon Jesus answered, 'The cup that I must drink you shall drink . . . but as for the seats at my right hand or my left, these are not mine to grant. . . .' James was in fact the first of Jesus's apostles to suffer martyrdom, as early as AD 44, under Herod Agrippa. John and James received a further rebuke from Jesus when his messengers were not welcome in a Samaritan village, and the 'sons of thunder' suggested, perhaps typically, 'Lord, do you want us to call down fire from heaven to burn them up?' Jesus and his disciples shared the rigours of his intinerant ministry, often forced to go without shelter: 'The Son of Man has nowhere to lay his head'.

Despite their temperament and Jesus's frank rebukes, the two brothers, James and John, together with Peter, formed an inner circle within the group of disciples and it is these three whom Jesus took with him on at least three important occasions. They accompanied him into the house for the raising of Jairus's daughter; they were permitted to witness the glory of Jesus's transfiguration on the mountain; they were chosen to support him and to witness his agony in the Garden of Gethsemane. [Mark 3:17]

C

CAESAR The title of the Roman emperors until the 3rd century AD, denoting to the people of the provinces the concept of the imperial throne rather than its particular occupant.

The name originally was that of a Roman family, prominent from the 3rd century BC, whose most well-known member was Julius Caesar, the conqueror of Gaul (102-44 BC). Julius Caesar adopted Octavius as his heir, thereby conferring on him and his successors the title of 'Caesar', to which the Senate added for Octavius, in 31 BC, the title 'Augustus'.

Always acknowledging the doubt in dating the writings, the emperors during the events of the New Testament were:

Augustus (27 BC-AD 14) – Jesus was born and grew up.

Tiberius (AD 14-37) – Jesus taught in Galilee and Judea; Jesus was crucified, rose, and ascended; the Christian Church received the Spirit at Pentecost; Paul was converted.

Caligula (Gaius) (AD 37-41) – Paul was received by the Christian leaders in Jerusalem; the Church was established at Antioch in Syria.

Claudius (AD 41-54) – The First Journey of Paul and Barnabas to Cyprus and Galatia; the first Council of Jerusalem; the Second Journey of Paul and Silas to Europe; Paul's Letters to Thessalonica, Galatia, and Corinth.

Nero (AD 54-68) – The Third Journey of Paul; the Teaching Mission at Ephesus; Paul's return to arrest in Jerusalem; Paul's trials and imprisonment under Felix and Festus; Paul's appeal to Caesar and journey to Rome; Paul's captivity, and possible release; (the writing of Mark's Gospel?); the writing of 1 Peter, James, and Jude; the remainder of Paul's Letters, except Timothy and Titus; the arrest and martyrdom of Peter and Paul.

Galba (AD 68-9), *Otho* (AD 69), *Vitellius* (AD 69), *Vespasian* (AD 69-79) – The fall of Jerusalem; the establishment of the Christian congregation at Pella; the writing of the Gospel of Matthew.

Titus (AD 79-81) – The writing of the Gospel of Luke; (the writing of the Letters to Timothy and Titus?).

Domitian (AD 81-96) – The writing of the Fourth Gospel; the exile of John to Patmos; the three Letters of John; (the second Letter of 'Peter'?); the Revelation of John. *see also* ROMANS [Matt. 22:17; Mark 12:14; Luke 2:1; 20:22-25; John 19:12; Acts 17:7; 25:8-21; Phil. 4:22]

CAIAPHAS Joseph, surnamed Caiaphas, was the Jewish high priest (AD 18-37) by whose calculation and cunning Jesus was arrested, convicted, and crucified by the Roman authorities in Jerusalem.

He married the daughter of Annas the high priest (AD 6-15). It was customary for a priest to marry the daughter of a priest, especially among the priestly aristocracy and the priests of Jerusalem, whose prestige and education gave them a superior standing. The high priests tended to appoint their sons and sons-in-law into the more lucrative posts in the Temple, consequently it was not surprising that Caiaphas succeeded

67

his father-in-law, who virtually founded a dynasty of high priests.

The ruling house of Annas held perhaps all the chief-priestly positions within its control, besides operating a flourishing trade in sacrificial victims in the court of the Gentiles, within the Temple. No less than eight members of this family held the supreme office of high priest: Annas himself, five sons, Caiaphas his son-in-law, and his grandson Matthias, from the year 65. Such a family virtually established the political as well as the religious leadership of the nation. Both Caiaphas and his father-in-law, Annas, were appointed from Rome but removed from office by the Roman procurator, in the case of the unpopular Caiaphas by Vitellius. The patriarchal figure of Annas long continued as the 'power behind the throne'. Luke dates the beginning of the ministry of John the Baptist as 'within the high priesthood of Annas and Caiaphas'.

Jesus, a threat to the Council

The Fourth Gospel describes the arrest and escort of Jesus to the house of Annas from where, after an unsuccessful examination, he was sent to Caiaphas, the officiating high priest who convened the Sanhedrin for the trial and sent Jesus to Pilate. Mark, on the other hand, does not specify the high priest by name, but Matthew does. In any case, it was Caiaphas who presided at the Sanhedrin's trial of Jesus.

The Sadducees had long watched Jesus and the development of his movement with increasing dislike and restlessness, as they had done that of John the Baptist. Again and again the messengers of Caiaphas had tried to trap Jesus into self-conviction, until they had begun to ask themselves, 'What are we to do? For this man performs many signs. It we let him go on thus, every

68

one will believe in him, and the Romans will come and destroy both our holy place and our nation.' (John 11:47-48) But Caiaphas had answered them: ' "You know nothing at all; you do not understand that it is expedient for you that one man should die for the people, and that the whole nation should not perish." He did not say this of his own accord, but being high priest that year he prophesied that Jesus should die for the nation, and not for the nation only, but to gather into one the children of God who are scattered abroad. So from that day on they took counsel how to put him to death.' (John 11:49-53).

No doubt the outcome of their consultations was a very clever and crafty solution, possibly the product of the fertile cunning of Caiaphas himself. This was to hand Jesus over to the Roman authorities: in any case they could not execute him. They could, however, label him guilty of treason and a danger to the imperial security and let the Romans cope with him. They could then convince their people that it was better for one man to die for the whole nation. Thus in one act they would destroy Jesus, put the blame on the Romans, and pretend their own loyalty to the Roman authority in the process.

Very shortly followed the incident involving the expulsion of the dealers from the Temple and the overthrowing of the kiosks of the money-changers, nicknamed 'the booths of Annas'. This was a clear threat to the vested interest and authority of Caiaphas himself, for the Temple was a thriving trading-colony and an excellent source of income from the sale of sacrificial animals and offerings, augmented by an exorbitant rate of exchange on the Temple coinage needed to purchase them. Josephus, in his *Antiquities* says, 'Such was the shamelessness and effrontery which possessed the high priests, that they were actually so brazen as to send their servants to the threshing-floors to receive the tithes due to the priests, so it happened at that time that those of the priests who in olden days were maintained by the tithes now starved to death.'

Only a fear of the common people restrained the Temple authorities from arresting Jesus then. On the first Palm Sunday, the day of Jesus's final entry into Jerusalem, the city was in an uproar and many expected him to declare himself the 'Son of David' at the Passover festival. Caiaphas must have realized that it was 'now or never', and that he must act before the beginning of the feast.

Caiaphas at the trial of Jesus

Caiaphas may well have feared the miraculous power of Jesus as well as being nervous of the reaction of the crowds of Galilean pilgrims, with whom Jesus was a popular hero. Hence the marks of haste in the arrest and trial of Jesus: the arrest in the dark, the nocturnal trial, the witnesses badly prepared. It was illegal to try a capital charge at night; it was illegal for the president (Caiaphas) to invite the prisoner to convict himself; it was illegal for him not to be acquitted once the witnesses had disagreed. Of the charges: Jesus's threat to destroy the Temple was manifestly unproven; Jesus's claim to be the Messiah was the direct outcome of the coercion of the high priest Caiaphas, who, seeing the charges fail, intervened to cross-examine the prisoner himself.

Invoking the most solemn oath binding on any Jew, Caiaphas 'stood up in the midst, and asked Jesus, "Have you no answer to make? What is it that these men testify against you?" But he was silent and made no answer. Again the high priest asked him, "Are you

70

the Christ, the Son of the Blessed?" And Jesus said, "I am; and you will see the Son of Man sitting at the right hand of Power, and coming with the clouds of heaven." And the high priest tore his mantle, and said, "Why do we still need witnesses? You have heard his blasphemy. What is your decision?" And they all condemned him as deserving death.' (Mark 14:60-64)

The conviction for blasphemy in the Sanhedrin was disregarded in favour of the more appealing charge of treason, when the case was referred to Pilate. The very speed and expedition of the arrangements for the trial in the early hours of the morning before Pilate reflects the pressure and power of the influential high priest, Caiaphas. This was most probably not the first time that Caiaphas had presented a threat to the procuratorial reputation of Pilate, who was ultimately exiled for his tactless and inept brutality. He was a child in the hands of Caiaphas, and the argument: 'If you release this man, you are not Caesar's friend; everyone who makes himself a king sets himself against Caesar' was the final twist of the screw necessary to secure conviction. (*see* PILATE)

Caiaphas in Acts

Caiaphas figures several times in the story of the early Church. Twice he presided over examinations of Peter, John, and the other apostles, in connection with their preaching and healing activities in the Temple. Finally, on the advice of the Pharisee Gamaliel, Caiaphas had them beaten, warned, and discharged. He also presided at the trial of Stephen and took the initiative in the persecution of Hellenist Christians that followed the stoning of Stephen. Indirectly, Caiaphas contributed thereby to the diaspora of these potential Christian missionaries throughout the Mediterranean. Caiaphas was also the

71

high priest who commissioned Saul (later to become the Apostle Paul) with letters of authority to persecute Christians as far as Damascus, then under his ecclesiastical authority.

The house of Caiaphas

A possible site of the house of Caiaphas in the upper city, on the Western Hill of Jerusalem, provides many vivid illustrations of all the paraphernalia of the high priest's palace: the store-house, treasury, palace, court of justice, guardroom, and cells.

Various churches have been built on this site to commemorate the trial and imprisonment of Jesus by Caiaphas, as well as St Peter's denial and repentance. The Pilgrim of Bordeaux in 533, commenting on the ruins of the high priest's palace, wrote: 'In the same Valley of Siloam, you go up to Mount Zion and (in the same valley) you see the spot where the House of Caiaphas stood.' Between 457 and 459, a fine basilica dedicated to St Peter was built on the ruins by the Empress Eudocia. In 530, Theodosius went from the Cenacle to the House of Caiaphas, 'which is now St Peter's Church'.

The present church includes at least three different storeys or levels, being built on a steep, if not almost sheer, hillside. Perhaps the one man-made feature common to both the city of the 1st century and that of the Byzantine age, and still to be seen, is that magnificent rock-hewn staircase ascending the hillside from the Pool of Siloam. It was on to this equivalent of the city highway that the palace of the high priest faced.

The main west doorway of the present church leads into the top level, and from a balcony outside the east end the visitor can look down on the vast storage-chambers below the palace. Staircases lead down into corn-stores; oil-stores are lined with plaster and have round bottle-necks. There is a complete grinding-mill here, with an underground rock-hewn stable for the donkey that operated it. Complete sets of weights and measures, used only by the priests, have been discovered in this 'treasury', also a huge stone door-lintel inscribed: 'This is Korban or offering'. Such facilities on such a scale indicate the storage of Temple dues.

Within the church, over the high altar, is an illustration of the trial which was conducted in the rock-hewn courtroom on the next level below the church. The prisoner is standing on a raised platform or dock, in the centre and with his back to the wall, chained by the wrists to escorts sitting on either side of him. It is easy to picture this scene on the lower level, facing westwards into the hillside in which are cut staircases and galleries. On one of these Peter must have sat with the soldiers, warmed himself by the fire, and denied knowing his master. On either side of the wall, behind the raised rock platform, the corners of the courtroom are cut square to a height of almost ten feet.

In the very centre of the courtroom is the mouth of the bottle-necked prison, into which the condemned prisoner could be lowered after trial.

Descending to a third level there is a complete guardroom, all round the walls of which are still the staples for the prisoners' chains. On one side is a small window opening on to the bottle-necked condemned cell. Below this window, and left projecting from the floor when the guardroom was excavated out of the rock, is a block in which the guard stood to peer down into the gloom of the cell below him. On the opposite side of the guardroom is the whipping-block. Here, tied up by the wrists with leather thongs through staples at the top, a belt round his waist secured to a staple at each side, the prisoner would be stretched up taut and helpless. At his feet

73

were two bowls carved in the rock, one for salt to disinfect his scars, one for vinegar to revive him. Here, the apostles of the early Church received the legal number of 'forty lashes less one' (thirteen on each shoulder from the back and thirteen on the chest from the front), were commanded not to preach Jesus as Christ, then sent home. Yet they returned daily to the Temple to teach and to preach this very thing, despite the threats and warnings of Caiaphas. [Matt. 26:3; Luke 3:2; John 11:49; 18:13, 14, 24, 28; Acts 4:6]

CANAANITE (Gk. from the Aramaic 'native of Cana') *see* SIMON

CANDACE (Gk. from the Ethiopian) The general title of the queens of Meroe in Ethiopia, then meaning Nubia in the area of the upper Nile. The story of the Ethiopian eunuch, treasurer to the Candace, probably himself a pilgrim visiting Jerusalem, his conversion and baptism by Philip the Evangelist on the road to Gaza, is included by Luke in Acts immediately before the conversion of Paul. *see also* ETHIOPIANS [Acts 8:27]

CARPUS (Gk. from the Heb. 'harvest') The Christian in whose house at Troas Paul left his cloak and scrolls, following his arrest, perhaps through the treachery of Alexander the coppersmith, possibly between the years 64 and 67. Paul wrote from Rome to Timothy in Ephesus, asking him to collect his things from Carpus 'and above all the parchments', before his execution.

Tradition claims that Carpus became bishop of Beroea. [2 Tim. 4:13]

CENTURION (Lat. 'hundred')
1. Centurion at Capernaum
2. Centurion at Calvary
3. Cornelius, centurion at Caesarea
4. First centurion at the Antonia Fortress
5. Second centurion at the Antonia Fortress

6. Julius, centurion of the Augustan cohort

The centurion was a non-commissioned officer in charge of a hundred soldiers in the Roman army. He was always promoted from the ranks and was the equivalent of a company sergeant-major. There were sixty centurions to each legion of 6,000 men. Just as sergeant-majors are a byword for comic swagger and policemen for their alleged flat feet, so, according to Juvenal, centurions were caricatured for their fat calves and hob-nailed boots. Julius Caesar mentions several centurions who earned his praise for their loyalty and initiative. Polybius, the Greek historian of Rome, in his well-known description of the army, says of the 'centurions' that they are not expected to be so much 'venturesome seekers of danger, as men who can command, steady in action, and reliable; they ought not to be over-anxious to rush into the fight, but when hard-pressed, they must be ready to hold their ground and die at their posts'.

No less than six centurions are mentioned in the New Testament, and they all stand out very creditably in the narrative. Of these, two are linked with the life of Jesus: the centurion at Capernaum in Matthew and Luke, and the centurion in charge of the crucifixion squad appearing in all three Synoptic Gospels, Matthew, Mark, and Luke. One other centurion, Cornelius, was converted by Peter, and three others are linked with Paul.

1. Centurion at Capernaum He sent a message to Jesus begging his help. Luke says that the centurion had a servant – presumably the equivalent of a batman – who was desperately ill. Matthew adds that he was paralysed and in great pain. In Luke's account, the centurion himself never appears, but the Jewish elders commend him and his request to Jesus. The centurion's friends then bring the message that he is not worthy to receive Jesus into his house – 'Lord, do not trouble yourself . . . But say the word, and let my servant be healed,' runs the message. Jesus then says to the crowd following him, 'I tell you, not even in Israel have I found such faith.' And when the messengers get back to the house they find the servant in perfect health.

It is strange that at a solemn moment of the Catholic Mass of the Latin Rite the priest, before receiving Communion, says the words of that Roman centurion. Three times he repeats, 'Lord, I am not worthy that thou shouldst come under my roof, but speak the word only . . .' Some scholars think that the story in John's Gospel (4:46) of the cure of the nobleman's son records the same incident, retold in the manner and for the purpose of the later writer. Certainly he shows that the act of healing took place over a distance of 20 miles, from Cana to Capernaum.

This centurion was probably one of the Gentiles who attended worship at the Jewish synagogue, a 'God-fearer', as Paul called them. Luke describes how the elders reported that 'he loves our nation, and he built us our synagogue'. Today, at Capernaum, is to be seen a 3rd-century reconstruction into which are incorporated both Roman and Jewish designs. This synagogue has been partially restored; it was well built of white limestone, contrasting vividly with the black lava of the surrounding houses. The prayer hall was rectangular, nearly 80 feet long and 53 feet wide. To the east of the prayer hall was an open courtyard, entered by two doors, on the south side. Both hall and courtyard were colonnaded, the columns in the hall supporting the gallery, those in the courtyard forming a cloister facing a doorway into the hall. Through this doorway the Gentile 'God-fearers' might listen to the synagogue service. The whole building was elaborately decorated with carved stone ornaments. Its walls may have been covered with frescoes, like those of the nearly contemporary Dura synagogue, built in AD 244. As Professor Albright has pointed out, the catacombs in Rome and the necropolis at Beth She'arim demonstrate the dependence of early Christian art on Jewish frescoes of the Roman period. What is really striking at Capernaum is the variety of the motifs, particularly the mixture of Jewish and Roman symbols. Among the former are the *menorah* (the seven-branched candlestick), the *shofar* (the ram's horn), the *magen David* (the shield of David), the Ark of the Covenant, the manna pot, and that old symbol of the land, the palm-tree.

Among the Roman symbols, two have particular significance for the Christian. The first is the regimental crest of the Tenth Legion, two eagles back to back and beak to beak. The second is the Roman army's equivalent of the Victoria Cross: it was awarded to a soldier who saved the life of an officer in battle. It is a victor's laurel-wreath tied in a circle with a reef-knot and enclosing a round sea-shell. The eagles in the regimental crest are holding the same laurel-wreath in their beaks. What is the explanation of this combination of symbols?

Although this is a late 2nd-century or early 3rd-century building, Professor Albright is certain that it stands on the site of an earlier synagogue. This latter may possibly have been that in which Jesus worshipped, taught, and healed. It may well be that carvings of this synagogue were moved on to the later building. Coupled with the story in Luke's Gospel, this could explain how the regimental crest of a Roman legion came to adorn the very keystone of a Jewish synagogue. [Luke 7:1-10]

2. Centurion at Calvary As commander of the Roman execution squad, he gives us the only independent eyewitness account of the conduct of Jesus up to the moment of his death. What this rough and honest soldier exclaimed came from the depth of his own military and human experience.

As a Roman soldier he was trained in the hard school of courage, endurance, and fortitude in uncomplaining suffering. He had had the opportunity to watch the prisoner – if he was in charge of him – from his trial before Pilate; he would have watched the scourging, the mocking, the barrack-room horseplay with the crown of thorns. He would have whipped back the mob thronging the Via Dolorosa of cobbled streets, out through the Judgment Gate to the rocky mound of execution. He would have watched the falls beneath the weight of the cross, the stripping, the nailing, and the hideous moment when the cross was reared and the tortured body dropped to hang upon the nails. Then he would have shared the hours of waiting for the end – the agonized conversations, first with the two thieves and then with the mother and the 'son'. He was there in the darkness; he heard the cry of desolation – and he heard the final cry of triumph, 'It is finished'.

And out of this experience – however little he may have grasped what was going on, or the significance of what he himself was doing as executioner – he gave his personal verdict of utter admiration. He allowed himself bravely and honestly to be heard, in complete insubordination, contradicting and criticizing his superior authority – the Roman governor: 'Certainly this man was innocent!'; 'Truly this was the Son of God!' [Matt. 27:54; Mark 15:39; Luke 23:47]

3. Cornelius, centurion at Caesarea see CORNELIUS

4. First centurion at the Antonia Fortress When Paul came to Jerusalem after this Third Journey, James, the first bishop of Jerusalem, warned him that his loyalty to the Jewish Law was being questioned. James recommended that Paul associate himself publicly in the Temple with four other men under a vow of purification, which he did. But Paul was soon recognized by some Asiatic Jews, who accused him of 'teaching men everywhere against the people and the law and this place'. The mob dragged Paul out of the Temple to kill him. The Tribune and commander of the Antonia Fortress 'turned out the guard' to Paul's rescue, put him under protective custody, and attempted to retire with him up the stairway into the fortress. Despite the violence of the mob, Paul obtained permission to speak to them and in a mercurial speech related his own Jewish background as a Pharisee at the feet of Gamaliel, his own ardent persecution of the Christian communities, his own remarkable conversion on the road to Damascus, and finally his own vocation to the Gentiles.

At this point the mob went berserk, and the commander ordered Paul to be taken into the fortress for examination under the lash. When he was already strapped up, Paul turned to the centurion on duty and asked, 'Is it lawful for you to scourge a man who is a Roman citizen, and uncondemned?' At once the centurion informed the commander – 'What are you about to do?' – that Paul was a Roman citizen. The commander questioned his citizenship and arranged for a confrontation between Paul and the Jewish Sanhedrin for the next day. [Acts 22:25]

5. Second centurion at the Antonia Fortress The meeting with the Sanhedrin (*see above*) broke up in confusion, Paul being supported by the Pharisees but condemned by the Sadducees. Again, the commander took Paul into protective custody. Some of the Jews, however, held a meeting and made a solemn vow to hunger-strike until such time as they should have killed Paul.

They planned to ambush him on the way to the Sanhedrin, but Paul's nephew got wind of the plan and warned him. Paul called one of the centurions and asked him to conduct his nephew to the commander, who at once acted on the information. Summoning two centurions, he arranged for the despatch of Paul, under infantry and cavalry escort, to Caesarea, with a letter of explanation to the governor, Felix. [Acts 23:17, 23]

6. Julius, centurion of the Augustan cohort see JULIUS

CEPHAS (Gk from the Aramaic 'rock' or 'stone') see PETER

CHLOE (Gk. 'verdant') The Corinthian woman, the members of whose household, possibly her slaves, informed Paul at Ephesus of the party strife within the Christian Church at Corinth. [1 Cor. 1:11]

CHRIST (Gk. 'anointed', 'Messiah')

The Messianic hope

The title 'Messiah', in the Hebrew *Mashiah* and in the Greek *Christos,* from which we derive the term 'Christ', is found in the Old Testament as an adjective meaning anointed or consecrated to an office. Kings, priests and prophets were thus anointed. The king was the 'Anointed of the Lord'. The prophet Nathan told King David that his house would remain on the throne; from this prophecy expectations arose about future kings descended from David. But an anointed king does not come into all the pictures to be found in the Old Testament of a better world coming in the future. In many prophetic utterances God is said to be the only true king of Israel. However, for some time before the period in which the New Testament books were written, the ideal future king of Israel was called the Messiah.

Jewish expectations underwent considerable change

in periods of persecution of the Jewish people. In the reign of Antiochus Epiphanes (175-163 BC), according to many scholars, the Book of Daniel was written and in this the 'People of the saints of the Most High', the future possessors of the kingdom which God will establish, are represented symbolically by a human figure: 'One like a son of man came with the clouds of heaven'. The Book of Enoch, generally thought to have been written about the same period, envisaged a superhuman being, the 'Elect One', waiting in heaven to descend upon the world in judgment. The writer of eighteen psalms attributed to Solomon, generally believed to have been written about 70-40 BC, perpetuated the idea of a Davidic king who would rule from Jerusalem. The last two of these psalms refer to the 'righteous and pure Davidic king who will build up Jerusalem', who will punish sinners, subdue the nations hostile to Israel and rule in righteousness.

In the time of Jesus expectation was divided between a warrior king who would, as a political ruler, introduce the reign of God on earth, and a supernatural deliverer, a figure from the world beyond the sky, the 'Son of Man' of the Book of Daniel or the 'Elect One' of the Book of Enoch. The followers of Jesus believed that he had fulfilled Messianic expectation in his ministry and by his death and resurrection. In this redemption and deliverance, according to their perception of the matter, he had fulfilled their expectation. The writers of the Gospels of Matthew and Luke had evidently expected the Messiah to be of the family of David and they traced the ancestry of Jesus, through Joseph, back to David, although such a genealogy may seen to us inconsistent with the story of the virgin birth of Jesus which they also included in their Gospels.

Jesus as Messiah

All four Gospels state that Jesus knew himself to be the Messiah. The Gospels differ from one another in their presentation of the style or kind of Messiahship which he envisaged and of the extent to which he actually claimed Messiahship. Jesus is never represented as saying that he was the Messiah, using that actual word. Nor is he represented as denying that he was the Messiah. In the Gospels of Mark, Matthew and Luke, generally known as the Synoptic Gospels, it appears that Jesus tried to keep secret his identity as Messiah, ordering those who recognized him to remain silent about it. Especially in the Gospel of Mark the dramatic irony of this secret is to be found in the fact that it was only the evil spirits possessing the mentally handicapped who did recognize him, until the last few months of his life. Then Peter and other disciples said to him, 'You are the Christ', only to be ordered to keep silent and say nothing about it. At his examination in front of the high priest, when asked under oath the question, 'Are you the Christ, the Son of the Blessed?', Jesus answered, 'I am', according to Mark's Gospel. The Gospels of Matthew and Luke state that he said, 'You have said so' or, 'you say that I am'. This has been said to introduce an element of ambiguity into the frank admission recorded in the Gospel of Mark. But whatever ambiguity there is in the phrase used in the Gospels of Matthew and Luke may belong to the original Aramaic words of Jesus.

The purpose of Jesus in keeping the 'Messianic Secret' seems to lie in the radical difference between his conception of the Messianic function and the current conceptions and expectations. Public recognition would inevitably have resulted in general misunderstanding of his purpose. Thus when he chose to enter Jerusalem on a donkey, as a man of peace, he was acclaimed as a conquering hero.

The Gospel of John, often called the Fourth Gospel, is unlike the other three Gospels and was written later. It describes an open acknowledgement by the disciples of Jesus that he was the Messiah, even at the beginning of his ministry. Before Jesus invited his disciples to be with him, Andrew said to Peter, 'We have found the Messiah' and Nathanael addressed Jesus as 'Son of God and King of Israel'. Martha said to Jesus that she knew that he was the Messiah. When the woman of Samaria mentioned the Messiah to Jesus he said to her, 'I who speak to you am he'. It is thought by many scholars that when this Gospel was written the words 'Christ' and 'Jesus' had in the writer's circle almost become two names of one person. But the Gospel of John concludes that 'These things are written that you may believe that Jesus is the Christ, the Son of God'.

Jesus as the Son of Man

Jesus applied to himself the title of 'Son of Man', to be found in his speeches eighty times within the Gospels, always with reference to Jesus himself. Outside the Gospels it is used little in the New Testament; but Stephen, among the first Christian martyrs, uses it at his trial as a title of Jesus. (Acts 7:56) Jesus certainly seems to have applied the title to himself in a prophetic and authoritative or official context. Before telling a paralytic to take up his pallet and walk, since his paralysis was healed, Jesus declares that 'The Son of Man has authority on earth to forgive sins.' (Mark 2:10) On another occasion, defending his disciples who had plucked ears of grain on the Sabbath Day, he said, 'The Son of Man is lord even of the Sabbath.' (Mark 2:28) He uses the title in the context of his quotations from the Suffering

Servant passages in the Book of Isaiah. Thus he says, 'The Son of Man . . . came not to be served but to serve and to give his life as a ransom for many.' (Mark 10:45) In the Fourth Gospel the title is used in a prediction of his death on the cross, 'as Moses lifted up the serpent in the wilderness, so must the Son of Man be lifted up'. (John 3:14) Finally, according to the Synoptic Gospels of Mark, Matthew and Luke, Jesus when confronting the high priest at his trial quoted from the prophecy in the Book of Daniel, 'You will see the Son of Man sitting at the right hand of Power and coming with the clouds of heaven.'

Jesus as the Suffering Servant

According to all the Gospels, Jesus associated his Messiahship and his identity as the Son of Man with his future sufferings and his death. From his baptism and temptation onwards, Jesus saw in the passage which we find in the Book of Isaiah about the 'Suffering Servant of the Lord' the mode of his Messiahship.

In the Gospel of Mark, Jesus predicts his passion in detail. 'Behold, we are going up to Jerusalem; and the Son of Man will be delivered to the chief priests and the scribes, and they will condemn him to death, and deliver him to the Gentiles: and they will mock him, and spit upon him, and scourge him, and kill him: and after three days he will rise.' The Gospel of Luke describes Jesus directly quoting from the Book of Isaiah on the way to the place where he was arrested. 'For I tell you that this scripture must be fulfilled in me, "And he was reckoned with transgressors": for what is written about me has its fulfilment.' At the Last Supper, Jesus had said, 'I am among you as one that serves.'

Perhaps the many indirect allusions to the Suffering

Servant passages are more significant than the direct quotations. For example, Jesus said to his disciples: 'For the Son of Man came not to be served but to serve, and to give his life a ransom for many.' (Mark 10:45) The costly suffering of the obedient servant of the Lord in the Suffering Servant passages is well described by the word 'ransom'. There are several places in these passages where the word 'many' is used and the suffering of the servant is said to be beneficial to many nations and many individual people. (Isa. 52:14, 15; 53:11, 12)

The actions of Jesus described in the Gospels and the teaching about human conduct attributed to him in the Gospels seem to be related to these prophetic passages. He is silent at his trial before Pilate: 'Like a lamb that is led to the slaughter, and like a sheep that before its shearers is dumb, so he opened not his mouth.' (Isa. 53:7) He was treated as a criminal, yet was buried in the tomb of a rich man, Joseph of Arimathea. 'And they made his grave with the wicked and with a rich man in his death.' (Isa. 53:9) The teaching of Jesus about non-resistance reflects the action of the Suffering Servant in offering 'cheeks to those who pulled out the beard'. (Isa. 50:6) So the follower of Jesus is to turn the left cheek to those who strike him on the right cheek. (Matt. 5:39)

All the imagery used in the New Testament to portray the Messianic function of Jesus is derived from the Old Testament. But in the Old Testament, outside the Suffering Servant passages, the conception of the Messiah and the conception of vicarious suffering are not combined or united. It may be said, in general terms, that the Messiah belongs to the future, while suffering, whether it is vicarious or not, belongs to the present age. Jesus identified the Suffering Servant with the

Messiah, in the context of his own life and time, combining the two conceptions.

Jesus the Son of God

In Hebrew, phrases as 'son of' and 'father of' may indicate the character of a person, rather than parenthood. Jesus called the devil the 'Father of Lies'. (John 8:44) 'Sons of Belial' is a common biblical term for evil men. So also the phrase 'son of Righteousness' can describe an honest man and a godly man can be called 'son of God'. Jesus pronounced the peacemakers blessed, 'for they shall be called sons of God'. (Matt. 5:9) Hosea the prophet referred to Israel as God's son and Nathan the prophet addressed the anointed king of Israel as God's son. (Hos. 11:1; 2 Sam. 7:14)

In the days of Jesus the term the 'Son of God' was used for the Messiah. It is so used in the first words of the Gospel of Mark: 'The beginning of the Gospel of Jesus Christ, the Son of God.' In that Gospel, when Peter recognizes Jesus as the Messiah, he says: 'You are the Christ.' In the Gospel of Matthew, at the same point, the words are: 'You are the Christ, the Son of the Living God.' Jesus is reported in the Gospels of Matthew and Luke as saying: 'No one knows the Son except the Father and no one knows the Father except the Son'. It is the belief of Jesus that he was the Son of God which has given to his followers their most vivid idea of the Fatherhood of God. It is reported in all the Synoptic Gospels that, when Jesus was baptized by John the Baptist and on the occasion when he was transfigured in the presence of three of his disciples, he heard a voice from heaven. The words of that voice were: 'You are [or 'This is'] my beloved Son, in whom I am well pleased.' The words seem to come from two passages in the Old Testament, one of which refers to the King-

Messiah (Ps. 2:7) while the other concerns the Suffering Servant (Isa. 42:1). It was this union of 'Sonship' with 'Suffering Service' that made the conception of the Messianic function in the mind of Jesus, as he is pictured in all the Gospels, radically different from all other conceptions of the Messiah. The inauguration of the kingdom of God was the function of the Messiah according to Jesus, as well as in the popular conceptions; but the kingdom of God was seen according to a different pattern. The contrast is shown in the story of the temptation of Jesus in the wilderness, at the beginning of his public ministry according to the Synoptic Gospels, when he rejected popular conceptions of the Messiah as an economic benefactor or a political ruler overcoming the enemies of his people by miracles.

In the parable of the vineyard, his assessment of his situation and his purpose are revealed. It describes a man planting a vineyard, fencing it, ditching it and building a tower to protect it, before letting it to tenants and going abroad. In due time he sends a series of servants to collect the produce due to him from the vineyard. Each time the tenants maltreat or kill his servants. He still has someone left to send, his beloved son. Last of all he sends his son and they kill him and throw his body out of the vineyard. In this story given in the Synoptic Gospels (Mark 12:1-8; Matt. 21:33-39; Luke 20:9-15) Jesus accuses his opponents among the priests and scribes of disregarding the messages of the prophets of the past and makes a prediction of a violent death for himself, similar to the deaths of many prophets. Jesus believed that his task, as the Son of God, was to reveal the loving purpose of his Father to his people. 'I, when I am lifted up from the earth, will draw all men to myself.' (John 12:32) It was his consciousness of his sonship to God and his vivid experience of God's fatherly purpose that shaped his Messianic destiny to save by suffering. He went to his death in the certainty that it was the will of God, completely aware of what was coming to him, completely accepting it and utterly determined that nothing should prevent the will of God being done. Throughout the Passion, he is the master of the situation, in the Upper Room, in Gethsemane, before the high priest, before Pilate and finally on the cross. The writer of the Gospel of John, the Fourth Gospel, declares that it is the belief of the followers of Jesus that the death of Jesus was according to the purpose of God for the world, 'that whoever believes in him may have eternal life. For God so loved the world that he gave his only Son, that whoever believes in him should not perish, but have eternal life.'

Jesus Christ as God Incarnate

The disciples of Jesus and their successors in the Christian Church came to believe that Jesus had created a new relationship between man and God, through his life and teaching, his death and his resurrection. His achievement could not be fitted into the traditional picture of the Messiah. They believed that he had not just brought a new message about God; in him God had come to save and to draw mankind to himself, by love and by the example of his self-sacrifice. He had come into human history from a 'beyond', from the heart of God himself, to redeem mankind that men might live with him as fellow sons of God. As Athanasius wrote in the 4th century: 'He became human, that we might become divine.'

The Christian doctrine of the incarnation, that God became Man in the Person of Jesus, is not to be identified with the belief that Jesus had no human father, which is the Christian doctrine of the virgin birth. The

Muslim believes in the virgin birth, without believing in the Incarnation. In modern times many Christians consider the doctrines of the incarnation to be true, while doubting the historical character of the story of the virgin birth. The speeches attributed to Peter in the Acts of the Apostles, the Letters of Paul and the Gospel of John do not use the virgin birth as an argument for the Messiahship of Jesus. Paul writes that 'God sent forth his Son, born of woman, born under the law'. (Gal. 4:4) But this need not be a reference to the virgin birth; it implies that the Son of God whom Paul proclaims to the Gentiles is a man and a Jew. The doctrine of the virgin birth was taken by the Church from the Gospels of Matthew and Luke, where it dominates the accounts of the infancy of Jesus. Some Christian scholars regard these accounts of the infancy as the expression in the form of a story of the idea that Jesus as the Son of God came into history and not out of history, having in him a new life and a new hope, which the world itself could not produce. [The Suffering Servant passages in the Book of Isaiah are Isa. 42:1-4; 49:1-6; 50:4-9; 52:13; 53:12] *see* JESUS, JOHN, LUKE, MARK, MATTHEW, COLOSSIANS, HEBREWS

CHUZA The domestic administrator or steward at the court of Herod Antipas, whose wife Joanna was one of the women – together with Mary of Magdala, Susanna, and others – who accompanied Jesus and the Twelve on his teaching tour of Galilee. These women provided for the disciples 'out of their means'. No doubt Chuza was a man of some income and substance and may well have told Antipas about the miraculous ministry of Jesus. For Luke records that 'Herod the tetrarch heard of all that was done, and he was perplexed, because it was said by some that John had been raised from the dead, by some that Elijah had appeared, and by others that one of the old prophets had risen. Herod said, "John I beheaded; but who is this about whom I hear such things?" And he sought to see him.' (Luke 9:7-9) [Luke 8:3]

CLAUDIA One of the four who sent their personal greetings at the close of Paul's final letter to Timothy in Ephesus, perhaps the last he ever wrote. From the grouping of the names, Claudia may possibly have been the wife of Pudens and the mother of Linus. Paul is writing from prison, presumably in Rome, after his conviction, and expecting execution. This family, not elsewhere mentioned in the New Testament, may have ministered to the final needs of Paul, along with the 'beloved physician' Luke, Paul's fellow-prisoner to the end. [2 Tim. 4:21]

CLAUDIUS The Roman emperor, AD 41-54, mentioned twice by name in Acts. First, Luke established the date of the fulfilment of a prophecy of famine, foretold by the prophet from Jerusalem, called Agabus, which famine 'took place in the days of Claudius'. (see AGABUS)

Secondly, Luke comments on the arrival in Corinth from Rome of two Jews, Aquila and his wife Priscilla, 'because Claudius had commanded all the Jews to leave Rome'. This edict of the explusion of Jews from Rome took effect in the year 49. (see AQUILA)

It was during the reign of Claudius that the first two missionary journeys set forth from Antioch, by then the headquarters of the Gentile Christian mission, and that the first Christian Council was held in Jerusalem. [Acts 11:28; 18:2]

CLAUDIUS LYSIAS The Roman tribune commanding the troops of the Antonia Fortress, at the time of the assault on Paul by the Jews in the Temple area, on his final visit to Jerusalem. The tribune is faced with constant responsibilities and decisions in the face of the tremendous emotional forces at play in a highly combustible situation. Throughout, he conducts himself and disposes his forces with skill and efficiency. His report, however, to his superior, the governor Felix at Caesarea, abbreviates and manipulates the record of events in such a manner as to give a logic to his actions that was not originally there. Only in the opening address of this report is the tribune's name revealed as Claudius Lysias, after two whole chapters of fast-moving events in which the tribune plays the leading role.

On his arrival in Jerusalem, Paul, in deference to the wishes of the Jewish leaders of the Christian Church, had agreed to undergo a week's ritual purification in the Temple, with four other men under a vow, to show that he personally kept the Law. When the week's ritual was almost completed, some Asian Jews had recognized Paul and, stirring up the crowd, had accused him of bringing Greeks into the Temple. They would have lynched Paul, if the guard had not turned out to protect him and hustle him up the steps of the Antonia Fortress. Paul, speaking in Greek and declaring his Roman citizenship, requested a final opportunity to address the mob, which he did in Aramaic.

The tribune himself seems to have taken command and in considerable force to have charged the mob, thinking that the dishevelled figure of Paul was that of a dangerous Egyptian brigand, who had only recently brought an army of assassins (literally 'dagger-men') against the city. His astonishment to hear a request in educated Greek from a 'Jew of Tarsus, a citizen of no mean city' must have been considerable, and so he gave permission for Paul to speak. Luke's description of the riot and the scenes that followed is a masterpiece and certainly the work of an eye-witness of the events.

At this point, Paul 'motioned with his hands to the people; and when there was a great hush, he spoke to them in the Hebrew language [dialect] saying: "Brethren and fathers, hear the defence which I now make before you . . ." '

When he described his own conversion, all listened in silence, but when he declared his commission to the Gentiles he was shouted down. The tribune accordingly took him into the fortress for scourging in preparation for his interrogation. Not until Paul was actually strapped up for this literally crippling torture did he say to the centurion standing by: ' "Is it lawful for you to scourge a man who is a Roman citizen, and uncondemned?" When the centurion heard that, he went to the tribune and said to him, "What are you about to do? For this man is a Roman citizen." So the tribune came and said to him, "Tell me, are you a Roman citizen?" And he said, "Yes." The tribune answered, "I bought this citizenship for a large sum." Paul said, "But I was born a citizen." So those who were about to examine him withdrew from him instantly; and the tribune also was afraid, for he realized that Paul was a Roman citizen and that he had bound him.' (Acts 22:25-29)

The tribune had put himself in a difficult situation, for Paul and influential relatives in Jerusalem, and had just brought an enormous sum of money to the city for the relief of the poor, which had been collected in several different Roman provinces. The next day, therefore, the tribune ordered a meeting of the high priest and the whole Council and placed Paul before them.

With the Council, Paul skilfully divided the Pharisees from the Sadducees, by claiming to be a Pharisee and basing his claim to orthodoxy on the resurrection of the dead, a doctrine unacceptable to the Sadducees. Paul was withdrawn from the debate that followed and returned to the fortress. Some forty zealous opponents of Paul vowed to fast until they had killed Paul. Information, however, of their plot reached the Roman tribune and he sent Paul with both an infantry and cavalry escort, at nine o'clock that night, down to Antipatris, a Roman staging-post on the way to the coast. On the following day the cavalry took Paul on to Caesarea and presented him to the Roman governor, Felix, with a covering letter from the tribune.

The tribune's letter has every appearance of being genuine, being as brief and objective as it is misleading of the real motives of the man, but if fulfilled its purpose admirably. 'Claudius Lysias to his Excellency the governor Felix, greeting. This man was seized by the Jews, and was about to be killed by them, when I came upon them with the soldiers and rescued him, having learned that he was a Roman citizen. And desiring to know the charge on which they accused him, I brought him down to their council. I found that he was accused about questions of their law, but charged with nothing deserving death or imprisonment. And when it was disclosed to me that there would be a plot against the man, I sent him to you at once, ordering his accusers also to state before you what they have against him.' (Acts 23:26-30)

Had Claudius Lysias been an imcompetent and corrupt official, he might well have connived at Paul's death at any one of a number of moments in this sequence of events. Yet he took every precaution to ensure Paul's protection until the governor should decide his innocence or guilt. Thus Claudius Lysias became one of several who together enabled Paul to reach Rome. [Acts 21, 22, 23. By name Acts 23:26]

CLEMENT A fellow-worker with Paul and others at Philippi 'whose names are in the book of life', commended by Paul in the final and happy chapter of his letter to the Christian congregation in Philippi. Clement is such a common Roman name that the 3rd-century theologian Origen's identification of this Philippian Clement with Clement, bishop of Rome at the turn of the 1st century, is barely possible. [Phil. 4:3]

CLEOPAS One of two disciples walking over the hills from Jerusalem to a village called Emmaus on the first Easter Day. While they were discussing the events of the last few days, Jesus joined them, walking and talking with them, but they did not recognize him. 'And he said to them, "What is this conversion which you are holding with each other as you walk?" And they stood still looking sad.' (Luke 24:17) Then Cleopas answered, ' "Are you the only visitor to Jerusalem who does not know the things that have happened there in these days?" And he said to them, "What things?" They said to him, "Concerning Jesus of Nazareth, who was a prophet mighty in deed and word before God and all the people, and how our chief priests and rulers delivered him up to be condemned to death, and crucified him. But we had hoped that he was the one to redeem Israel. Yes, and besides all this, it is now the third day since this happened. Moreover, some women of our company amazed us. They were at the tomb early in the morning and did not find his body; and they came back saying that they had even seen a vision of angels, who said that he was alive. Some of those who were with us went to the tomb, and found it just as the women had said; but him they did not see." ' (Luke 24:18-24) Jesus, still unrecognized, turned to them and said, ' "O foolish men, and slow of heart to believe all that the prophets has spoken! Was it not necessary that the Christ should suffer these things and enter into his glory?" And beginning with Moses and all the prophets, he interpreted to them in all the scriptures the things concerning himself.' (Luke 24:25-27)

As they drew near to their destination, Jesus made as if to continue further on his journey, but they persuaded him, 'Stay with us, for it is toward evening and the day is now far spent.' (Luke 24:29) And so he turned in to eat with them. As the guest, he was invited to give thanks before the meal. 'When he was at table with them, he took the bread and blessed, and broke it, and gave it to them. And their eyes were opened and they recognized him; and he vanished out of their sight. They said to each other, "Did not our hearts burn within us while he talked to us on the road, while he opened to us the scriptures?" And they rose that same hour and returned to Jerusalem.' (Luke 24:30-33)

Perhaps the companion of Cleopas was his wife, though surely Luke, of all people, would have said so. In any case, they were probably Judean rather than Galilean disciples.

There are no less than four sites for Emmaus, though all with differing merits and at varying distances from Jerusalem. The Roman *stadia* was approximately equivalent to the modern furlong, but the number of *stadia* differs in some of the major manuscripts. An unlikely site is that of Kaloniyeh (so named after a colony of Roman veterans), only half the recorded distance from Jerusalem. Another site is at Qubeibe, 60 *stadia* (or 7 miles) away, as quoted in most of the major biblical manuscripts; this was a small town on the Roman road (still to be seen) from Jerusalem to Caesarea This site is supported only by the Crusaders and the Franciscans. Yet another site, favoured by the Crusaders, with a magnificent church built over the Roman masonry and water-supply for the detachment of the Tenth Legion from Fretensis in Sicily, is to be found at Abu Ghosh.

Again, this site is the correct distance away from Jerusalem and on another and perhaps earlier Roman road to the coast.

Paradoxically, the earliest traditional and archaeological evidence, probably 4th-century Byzantine as well as Crusader, supports a location at Amwas (Arabic for Emmaus), one hundred and sixty *stadia* from Jerusalem, as quoted in *Codex Sinaiticus,* which was known to both Bishop Eusebius of Caesarea and to Jerome, who translated the Vulgate. Over the hills from Jerusalem, however, Amwas is only 15 miles. Therefore, this site is within reach of the possibility of the double journey from and back to Jerusalem in an afternoon.

Wherever the Emmaus appearance of the risen Jesus took place, Luke's narrative of this story of Cleopas and his companion is of great value as typical of the post-resurrection experience of Jesus's disciples. Excavations at Amwas and Qubeibe prove that the whole region supported some sort of agricultural community. Cleopas, therefore, was not likely to have been a dreamer, but a sober business man. As Luke himself says: 'To them he presented himself alive after his passion by many proofs, appearing to them during forty days, and speaking of the kingdom of God.' (Acts 1:3) [Luke 24:18]

CLOPAS The husband of Mary, whom John describes as watching by the cross of Jesus. 'Standing by the cross of Jesus were his mother, and his mother's sister, Mary the wife of Clopas, and Mary Magdalene.' (John 19:25) The 2nd-century historian, Hegesippus, supposed that Clopas was the brother of Joseph the carpenter, and brother-in-law to Mary the mother of Jesus. Were this correct, Clopas would have been uncle to Jesus. [John 19:25]

COLOSSIANS Colossae was one of three cities within the fertile valley of the River Lycus, about 100 miles inland and to the eastward of Ephesus. All three cities were probably evangelized by Epaphras, a convert of Paul, trained during Paul's long and systematic period of teaching at Ephesus, in the course of his Third Journey.

Paul's letter to the Christian community at Colossae was primarily concerned with countering a peculiar type of false teaching, which devalued the importance of Jesus in God's plan for the world. This was probably a local heresy, the result of a wish to incorporate into Christian theology the best of both pagan and Jewish philosophies. Paul roundly declared Jesus Christ the supreme power for salvation, the ultimate reality, and the all-sufficient redeemer and intermediary between God and man.

A letter from captivity

The so-called 'pastoral epistles' to Timothy and Titus belong to a period of Paul's imprisonment after his first trial and acquittal in Rome. The letters to Philippi, Colossae, Philemon, and the circular letter now entitled 'to the Ephesians' may have been written during any of three previous imprisonments, at Ephesus, Caesarea, and Rome. The last two each lasted at least two years, while the first, to which Paul refers on three occasions (1 Cor. 15:32; 2 Cor. 1:8-10; Rom. 16:3, 4), seems to have been very brief, however critical and severe.

There is some doubt as to during which imprisonment Paul wrote his letter to the Colossians. Together with a personal letter to Philemon, himself a Colossian, the two letters were written at the same time and despatched to Colossae by the same messenger, Tychicus. Both letters include greetings from Epaphras, Luke the physician, Demas, Aristarchus, and Mark, nephew of Barnabas. Both refer to Paul's prison chains. Together with his letter to Philemon, Paul returns the fugitive slave, Onesimus. It might seem more profitable that Paul despatched Onesimus the comparatively short distance of 100 miles from Ephesus to Colossae, rather than from Caesarea or from Rome. Again, both letters are sent by Paul and Timothy, Paul's companion during his time at Ephesus. Moreover, those who send greetings also belong to the band of Paul's associates on his Third Journey and stay in Ephesus in the years 56 and 57. But there is no evidence that Paul's imprisonment in Ephesus was long enough for him to receive reports and send considered answers. During his first long imprisonment in Rome in the years 61-63, he was only under house arrest and his friends had free access to him. The vast cosmopolitan city of Rome was a notorious hideout for runaway slaves such as Onesimus.

Heresy at Colossae

Wherever Paul was imprisoned at the time, he was visited by Epaphras with a report from Colossae, favourable except for one ominous detail. Certain strange teachings were gaining ground, and Epaphras himself was not sufficiently confident to deal with them. Paul therefore wrote to correct this false doctrine and at the same time gave some practical advice on domestic relations. It seems that the teachers at Colossae had tried to combine within Christianity what they considered to be the best in both Judaism and Hellenism. On the one hand they stressed the demands of the Mosaic Law, the keeping of festivals, of the Sabbath, and of the hygiene laws. On the other, they devalued the material and physical, regarding the human body with contempt, not considering the physical birth and death of the Man Jesus as able to secure the reconciliation of the world with God. They questioned the uniqueness of Jesus Christ in God's scheme of salvation, which they felt could only be achieved by supernatural means. We do not know exactly what form this heresy took. We only have Paul's reply, which seems an attempt to combat pagan theosophy and to reaffirm the total sufficiency of Jesus Christ within God's purpose and scheme of salvation.

Stressing the role of Jesus

The theme of the letter to the Colossians is to be found more fully expressed within the circular letter now known to us as the Letter to the Ephesians. (*see* EPHESIANS) The importance of this letter to the Colossians is that it includes the first known Christian statement of the cosmic significance of Jesus. This is all the more remarkable, appearing as it does more than thirty years before the *Logos* declaration of Jesus as the source of universal life, in the prologue of the Fourth Gospel. (*see* JOHN 4.)

'He is the image of the invisible God, the first-born of all creation; for in him all things were created, in heaven and on earth, visible and invisible, whether thrones or dominions or principalities or authorities – all things were created through him and for him. He is before all things, and in him all things hold together. He is the head of the body, the church; he is the beginning, the first-born from the dead, that in everything he might be pre-eminent. For in him all the fullness of God was pleased to dwell, and through him to reconcile to himself all things, whether on earth or in heaven, making peace by the blood of his cross.' (Col. 1:15-20)

Such a magnificent formal statement is followed rapidly by personal witness of his own sufferings, by which Paul claims to make up all that still has to be endured by Jesus for the sake of his body, the Church.

Then Paul warns his readers to hold to the true faith in Jesus, rather than to any false teaching: 'As therefore you received Christ Jesus the Lord, so live in him, rooted and built up in him and established in the faith, just as you were taught, abounding in thanksgiving. See to it that no one makes a prey of you by philosophy and empty deceit, according to human tradition, according to the elemental spirits of the universe, and not according to Christ. For in him the whole fullness of deity dwells bodily, and you have come to fullness of life in him, who is the head of all rule and authority.' (Col. 2:6-10)

Paul warns his readers against forms of asceticism: 'Therefore let no one pass judgment on you in questions of food and drink or with regard to a festival or a new moon or a sabbath. These are only a shadow of what is to come; but the substance belongs to Christ. . . . If with Christ you died to the elemental spirits of the universe, why do you live as if you still belonged to the world? Why do you submit to regulations?' (Col. 2:16, 17, 20)

Paul's closing exhortation concerns general rules of Christian behaviour and the morals of home and household relationships. Finally, he adds to the dictated letter a message in his own bold hand: 'Remember my fetters. Grace be with you.' [Col. 1-4]

CORINTHIANS It was at Corinth, during his Second Journey, that Paul conducted a mission (from perhaps the winter of the years 49 and 50 to the summer of the year 51), described by Luke in Acts 18:1-18. Later, during his Third Journey, he conducted a considerable correspondence with the Christian community at Corinth, writing from Ephesus between the years 54 and 57, during which time he also paid a brief visit to Corinth. Although Paul built up a flourishing Christian congregation at Corinth, which he left in the care of Apollos, a learned Alexandrian Jewish convert, the

Corinthian Church played a relatively small part in the later history of the Christian Church in the eastern Mediterranean.

Corinth was an important and wealthy city astride the Isthmus of Corinth and controlling the ports on either side, Lechaeum on the west, Cenchreae on the east. Corinth was the capital of the Roman province of Achaia, the southern part of Greece, and the seat of the Roman proconsul. It was a city of great commerce, wealth, and squalor, renowned for its culture and notorious for its immorality. Lying on the great trade-route between Rome and the East, with a very mixed commercial and cosmopolitan community, Corinth was of strategic importance in the spreading of Christianity throughout the eastern Mediterranean. Travellers could avoid the dangerous voyage round the Peloponnese by crossing the Isthmus of Corinth from harbour to harbour. The international character of the city fostered the development of a variety of cults from as far away as Egypt and Phoenicia. The chief shrine, however, was the temple of the Greek goddess of Love – Aphrodite – although the cult was debased by foreign influences. The priestess-prostitutes of Aphrodite at Corinth are said to have numbered a thousand.

Paul came to Corinth after his highly unsuccessful visit to Athens. Filled with disappointment, in fear and trembling he made his way over the isthmus to the city in the winter of 49-50. There he remained for eighteen months, living and working as a tentmaker with Aquila and his wife Priscilla, Jews expelled from Rome by the edict of Claudius in the year 49. On the arrival of Timothy and Silas, they taught both Jews and Greeks in the synagogue and then in a private house. As a result, a large Church was formed at Corinth, mostly from the poor and slave classes. During this time Paul, receiving

101

Timothy's report from Thessalonica, sent his first letter to that Church about the second coming of Jesus. Following further reports he sent his second letter, warning the Thessalonians not to use the teaching of justification by faith as an excuse for lawlessness, but to persevere in faith and well-doing. In both these letters, Paul's intensity and affection are conveyed and reveal the power of his personality.

With the arrival of a new proconsul of Achaia, called Gallio, in the year 51, certain members of the Jewish community at Corinth accused Paul of teaching religion 'contrary to the Law'. Gallio refused to adjudicate, but the time had come for Paul and his party to move on. Sailing from Cenchreae, the eastern harbour of Corinth, he reached Ephesus, on the west coast of Asia Minor. After a brief preliminary visit to the synagogue and promising to return on his next journey, Paul sailed for Caesarea, where he greeted the Christian Church on his way north by road to Antioch. This Second Journey of 2,800 miles must have taken three years, the greater part of which was spent at Corinth.

Broadside against immorality

The following is one of many theories of the circumstances of Paul's correspondence with Corinth.

During his time in Ephesus, Paul had heard news from Corinth that made it necessary for him to write to warn that Christian community against associating with immoral persons. He then probably wrote what is now to be found in 2 Cor. 6:14-7:1. Shortly afterwards, he received an official letter from the Corinthian Church asking advice on specific matters, such as the celebration of the Eucharist and the doctrine of the resurrection. Paul had also heard that a party spirit prevailed in

102

that community and that a particularly grave case of immorality had arisen within the Church. Paul dealt with these questions in a letter now known to us as 1 Corinthians, which he sent by sea, while Timothy took the land route to deal with the situation in person. Neither the letter nor Timothy's visit achieved the desired effect, and Paul himself sailed for Corinth. Even he was not able to secure a reform within the Corinthian Christian community and, after being grossly insulted, he sailed back to Ephesus. From there, he wrote a 'severe letter', his third, part of which is probably to be found in 2 Cor. 10-13, which was carried by Titus, an older and more experienced man than Timothy. This letter demanded a proper respect both for Christian morality and for Paul, as founder of the Church in Corinth.

When Paul finally closed his ministry at Ephesus, he travelled north overland to Troas, whence he sailed once again for Macedonia to visit Philippi, Thessalonica, and Beroea. Somewhere *en route* he met Titus, who at last brought him the good news that the Corinthian Church was ready to conform, and that they had already by a majority vote censured the person who had insulted Paul. Paul immediately wrote his fourth letter, to be found in 2 Cor. 1-9. In this last letter, he forgave his antagonist, closed the controversy, and arranged for a collection to be taken for the poor at Jerusalem. Paul seems to have travelled overland to Corinth, where he spent the winter months, in which time he wrote his letter to the Christian Church in Rome, to prepare them for his coming and to secure their support for a journey to Spain.

Paul's plan to sail directly from Corinth for Jerusalem, taking his poor-relief collection, was thwarted by some threat of ambush. Consequently he returned overland to Macedonia.

'Temples of the living God'

Only a fragment of Paul's first letter is to be found in 2 Cor. 6:14-7:1, but the theme is crystal clear: an appeal for purity and the consecration of life to God. 'We are the temple of the living God.' As the membership of the Christian Church had been drawn from a motley of pagans with a variety of standards of conduct, many such problems were to arise in the newly-formed Christian community. Here, in this fragment of the initial letter, we get only a glimpse at the sort of problems to be dealt with at length in the later letters.

The second letter – our 1 Corinthians – must have been sent soon after the first. A member of Chloe's household (1 Cor. 1:11) brought Paul depressing news of the faction rife in Corinth, and a letter (1 Cor. 7:1) arrived, asking for Paul's ruling on a variety of points concerning the ordering of worship and relationships with the pagan society within the city. Our first letter to the Corinthians is Paul's reply: an effort to deal with these disciples and their problems.

The early Corinthian Church had little sense of unity, little sense of sin, or of the need for salvation. Paul's successor as pastor of the embryo Christian Church at Corinth had been the Alexandrian Apollos, and his gifts of exposition and oratory had compared favourably with Paul's technique. Some of the congregation remained faithful to Paul, others were attached to the preaching of Apollos, yet others rallied to the name of Peter. To all these Paul now preached Christ's leadership alone. 'Is Christ divided? Was Paul crucified for you? Or were you baptized in the name of Paul?' (1 Cor. 1:13), and again, 'For Jews demand signs and Greeks seek wisdom, but we preach Christ crucified, a stumbling block to Jews and folly to Gentiles, but to those who are called, both Jews and Greeks, Christ the power of God and the wisdom of God.' (1 Cor. 1:22-24)

Paul goes on to comment on a case of incest within the Christian congregation, which had cheerfully tolerated a liaison between a man and his stepmother. The man must be excommunicated. Such sin should be hunted out of the Christian household, as the Jews hunted out leaven before their Passover. 'Cleanse out the old leaven that you may be a new lump, as you really are unleavened. For Christ, our paschal lamb, has been sacrificed. Let us, therefore, celebrate the festival, not with the old leaven, the leaven of malice and evil, but with the unleavened bread of sincerity and truth.' (1 Cor. 5:7, 8) And this must be a personal choice: 'For what have I to do with judging outsiders? Is it not those inside the church whom you are to judge? God judges those outside. "Drive out the wicked person from among you." ' (1 Cor. 5:12, 13)

Paul then complains of Christians going to law against each other in the pagan courts, which is further evidence of their lack of unity. 'I say this to your shame. Can it be that there is no man among you wise enough to decide between members of the brotherhood, but brother goes to law against brother, and that before unbelievers?' (1 Cor. 6:5-7) He warns his flock against immorality of all kinds. To 'become one' means surely to establish a close personal relationship. To do so with a harlot who has served in the pagan temple is forbidden to a Christian, who is linked with his Lord and is of one spirit with Christ Jesus. 'Do you not know that your body is a temple of the Holy Spirit within you, which you have from God? You are not your own; you were bought with a price. So glorify God in your body.' (1 Cor. 6:19, 20)

Then Paul deals one by one with the questions which

he has been asked. As a bachelor, Paul points out the advantages of celibacy that Christian loyalties may be first and foremost to God. Those who need to marry should do so and there can be no question of divorce, says Paul, citing Jesus's own teaching. Paul's discouragement of marriage was most likely due to the current expectation of the End.

A thorny question was that of food offered to idols. Much of the meat sold in the markets had been offered as sacrifice in the pagan temples, and Paul gave three simple rulings. Christians could buy meat in the open market without scruple, but if the host at a dinner-party declared that the meat was sacrificial meat, then a Christian guest must refuse for the sake of his pagan friend, that nothing must be allowed to become an obstacle to his conversion. Any attendance at pagan feasts by Christians was expressly forbidden.

Because of the different backgrounds among the Christian community there was a variety of conduct, even at the agape or 'common meal' eaten together before the Eucharist. The Gentile Christians did not have the same sacremental respect for all meals which the Jewish Christians had. Consequently their conduct at the meal was sometimes a scandalous preparation for the Eucharist that followed. Paul reminded them sharply of the sacramental nature of the Last Supper, declaring that 'Whoever, therefore, eats the bread or drinks the cup of the Lord in an unworthy manner will be guilty of profaning the body and blood of the Lord' (1 Cor. 11:27), and sums up, 'So then, my brethren, when you come together to eat, wait for one another – if any one is hungry, let him eat at home – lest you come together to be condemned. About the other things I will give directions when I come.' (1 Cor. 11:33-34)

One of the questions raised in the letter to Paul must

have concerned the 'speaking with tongues' during religious fervour. Paul listed the various spiritual gifts within the Church, such as preaching, teaching, believing, healing, miracles, prophecy, and lastly the 'gift of tongues'. He showed that the spiritual community, or Body of Christ, like the human body, has different members with different functions. The test of their reality was whether they contributed to the corporate life of the Church as a whole. And Paul went on to extol the greatest gift – love – using the Greek word agape, denoting the highest form of self-giving love, like that of Jesus himself.

'Love is patient and kind; love is not jealous or boastful; it is not arrogant or rude. Love does not insist on its own way; it is not irritable or resentful; it does not rejoice at wrong, but rejoices in the right. Love bears all things, believes all things, hopes all things, endures all things. Love never ends; as for prophecies, they will pass away; as for tongues, they will cease; as for knowledge, it will pass away. . . . So faith, hope, love abide, these three; but the greatest of these is love.' (1 Cor. 13:4-8, 13)

The final question Paul answers concerns the resurrection. The Greek conception of the human body was of a tomb imprisoning the spirit of man, and so they rejected out of hand any mention of the resurrection of the body, which the Jews and the Christians accepted. Paul gives a long testimony of the Easter faith of the early Christian Church. He reminds his readers what he had taught them about the resurrection and gives what must be the earliest record of the resurrection appearances of Jesus, through which mankind was redeemed to share in the resurrection. The resurrection of the body would involve both a difference and a continuity between the earthly personality and the risen 'body'. As the seed is sown in one form but grows up to be a plant, so the individual soul will retain the individual's personality in some recognizable spiritual form. God gives his creations bodies suitable for their environment; the physical body of flesh and blood in this life will be replaced by an immortal body in the life to come.

'When the perishable puts on the imperishable, and the mortal puts on immortality, then shall come to pass the saying that is written: "Death is swallowed up in victory. O death, where is thy victory? O death, where is thy sting?" The sting of death is sin, and the power of sin is the law. But the thanks be to God, who gives us the victory through our Lord Jesus Christ.' (1 Cor. 15:54-57)

Paul closes this letter with final commendations and greetings, after outlining his plan for a collection of money to be taken for the Church in Jerusalem. He saw this as a way of uniting both the Jewish and the Gentile elements in the Churches he had founded in Asia and Europe. He planned to take a representative group of Gentile and Jewish Christians to deliver the offering to the Mother Church in Jerusalem. The letter ends with a prayer in the form of a versicle and a response that may have been part of the liturgy, perhaps between the *agape* and the Eucharist: 'The grace of the Lord Jesus be with you. My love be with you all in Christ Jesus.'

Paul's 'severe' letter

Neither Paul's letter to Corinth nor the personal visit of Timothy managed to clear up the situation in the Corinthian Church, and Paul, disturbed by the news, decided to visit Corinth himself. But even he was unable to achieve a reform within the Christian community, and, after being publicly insulted, he sailed back to Ephesus. There he wrote a third letter and sent it back by the hand of Titus, an older and more experienced man than Timothy.

The four chapters we have of this letter were perhaps only the beginning of it. If we had the rest, we might have known why it was so effective in bringing the Corinthian congregation to heel. It appears to begin with an appeal, 'by the meekness and gentleness of Christ', at the 10th chapter of 2 Corinthians; but the military metaphors in which it proceeds show that it is little less than a declaration of war. 'For though we live in the world we are not carrying on a wordly war, for the weapons of our warfare are not worldly but have divine power to destroy strongholds. We destroy arguments and every proud obstacle to the knowledge of God, and take every thought captive to obey Christ, being ready to punish every disobedience, when your obedience is complete.' (2 Cor. 10:3-6)

Paul proceeds to vindicate himself against charges of being arrogant and self-seeking, however pitiable a public speaker he may be. It seems that one of the apostles, passing through Corinth, accepted hospitality as by right of his apostleship. In consequence, some Corinthians seem to have denied that Paul, who worked for his living, was in fact a genuine apostle at all. 'I think that I am not in the least inferior to these superlative apostles. Even if I am unskilled in speaking, I am not in knowledge; in every way we have made this plain to you in all things. Did I commit a sin in abasing myself so that you might be exalted, because I preached God's gospel without cost to you? I robbed other churches by accepting support from them in order to serve you.' (2 Cor. 11:5-8)

In a deliberately sarcastic passage, Paul challenges the Corinthians, if they did take him for a fool, to listen to some of his folly. Then, after a caustic apology for boasting, he gives them an autobiographical account of his life and sufferings for Jesus. 'But whatever any one dares to boast of – I am speaking as a fool – I also dare to boast of that. Are they Hebrews? So am I. Are they Israelites? So am I. Are they descendants of Abraham? So am I. Are they servants of Christ? I am a better one – I am talking like a madman – with far greater labours, far more imprisonments, with countless beatings, and often near death. Five times I have received at the hands of the Jews the forty lashes less one. Three times I have been beaten with rods; once I was stoned. Three times I have been shipwrecked; a night and a day I have been adrift at sea; on frequent journeys, in danger from rivers, danger from robbers, danger from my own people, danger from Gentiles, danger in the city, danger in the wilderness, danger at sea, danger from false brethren; in toil and hardship, through many a sleepless night, in hunger and thirst, often without food, in cold and exposure. And, apart from other things, there is the daily pressure upon me of my anxiety for all the churches. Who is weak, and I am not weak? Who is made to fall, and I am not indignant? If I must boast, I will boast of the things that show my weakness. The God and Father of the Lord Jesus, he who is blessed for ever, knows that I do not lie.' (2 Cor. 11:21-31)

But Paul had learned that his weaknesses and sufferings for Jesus's sake were a source of strength, and his severe language changes to an appeal as he declares, 'I will all the more gladly boast of my weaknesses, that the power of Christ may rest upon me. For the sake of Christ, then, I am content with weaknesses, insults, hardships, persecutions, and calamities; for when I am weak, then I am strong.' (2 Cor. 12:9, 10) '. . . since you desire proof that Christ is speaking in me. He is not weak in dealing with you, but is powerful in you. For he was crucified in weakness, but lives by the power of God. For we are weak in him, but in dealing with you we shall live with him by the power of God. Examine yourselves, to see whether you are holding to your faith. Test yourself. Do you not realize that Jesus Christ is in you? – unless indeed you fail to meet the test!' (2 Cor. 13:3-5)

Paul concludes with the promise of a third visit to Corinth, on which he duly set out from Ephesus, via Troas and Macedonia. There, on his way, Titus met him with the good news that the Corinthian Church was ready to reform and that they had already, by a majority vote, censured the person who had insulted Paul. He therefore immediately wrote his fourth letter, from Macedonia – our 2 Corinthians 1-9 (omitting 6:14-7:1).

A paean of praise

Paul sent his own apostolic greeting, to which he added the greetings of Timothy. He thanked God for the sufferings and the comfort that both he and the Corinthian congregation shared in Christ Jesus. He refers to some dire and distressing danger he had undergone when in Asia, asking for their continued prayers. (This was probably some persecution Paul had endured in Ephesus, but which is not recorded in the Acts.) The second chapter of this fourth letter gives a vivid picture of Paul's concern for the Church at Corinth. He had dispatched his 'severe' letter in great anxiety. 'For I wrote you out of much affliction and anguish of heart and with many tears, not to cause you pain but to let you know the abundant love that I have for you.' (2 Cor. 2:4)

Paul simply could not bear to wait in Ephesus for their reply to his 'severe' letter, so he went up to Troas to meet Titus. There was no sign of him there, so Paul crossed by sea to Macedonia, where at last Titus met him with an answering letter and a reassuring report. Paul accordingly broke into a paean of praise, his anxiety dispersed by the good news. The rest of his journey he compares to a triumphal and sacrificial journey in which incense is burned with the fragrance of the knowledge of Christ. Paul here feels that in a sense he himself is the victim being burned and offered up for the life of his beloved Corinthians. 'But thanks be to God, who in Christ always leads us in triumph, and through us spreads the fragrance of the knowledge of him everywhere. For we are the aroma of Christ to God among those who are being saved and among those who are perishing, to one a fragrance from death to death, to the other a fragrance from life to life. Who is sufficient for these things?' (2 Cor. 2:14-16)

For a moment Paul is almost embarrassed by his self-recommendation, and then tells his Corinthians that they themselves are his best reference. 'Are we beginning to commend ourselves again? Or do we need, as some do, letters of recommendation to you, or from you? You yourselves are our letter of recommendation, written on your hearts, to be known and read by all men; and you show that you are a letter from Christ delivered by us, written not with ink but with the Spirit of the living God, not on tablets of stone but on tablets of human hearts.' (2 Cor. 3:1-3)

Paul proceeds to defend the apostles and to describe his own trials and hopes. He is essentially a realist, whose every word is tested in the fire of experience. 'For what we preach is not ourselves, but Jesus Christ as Lord, with ourselves as your servants for Jesus's sake. . . . But we have this treasure in earthen vessels, to show that the transcendent power belongs to God and not to us. We are afflicted in every way, but not

112

crushed; perplexed, but not driven to despair; persecuted, but not forsaken; struck down, but not destroyed; always carrying in the body the death of Jesus, so that the life of Jesus may also be manifested in our bodies. For while we live we are always being given up to death for Jesus's sake, so that the life of Jesus may be manifested in our mortal flesh.' (2 Cor. 4:5, 7-11)

Paul, the tentmaker, compares the body to the canvas tent that is to be replaced by 'a building from God, a house not made with hands, eternal in the heavens'. (2 Cor. 5:1) He appeals to the Corinthians in Christ's name to be reconciled to God while they have time. Finally, he outlines his plan for taking up a collection from the missionary congregations for the Mother Church in Jerusalem. He says that this is not obligatory for them, but that he is testing the genuineness of their love against the keenness of others. 'For you know the grace of our Lord Jesus Christ, that though he was rich, yet for your sake he became poor, so that by his poverty you might become rich . . . So give proof, before the churches, of your love and of our boasting about you to these men.' (2 Cor. 8:9, 24) [Acts 18; First and Second Letters to the Corinthians]

CORNELIUS (Gk. 'of a horn') Cornelius was a centurion of the Italian cohort, the equivalent of a regiment, stationed in Caesarea a year or two after the crucifixion of Jesus. He is described as 'a devout man who feared God with all his household, gave alms liberally to the people, and prayed constantly to God'. (Acts 10:2) He was probably a pious Roman who, disillusioned by polytheism and disappointed by pagan philosophy, had gravitated spiritually towards Judaism.

At three o'clock one afternoon, Cornelius distinctly saw in a vision an angel who told him that his prayers and alms had been accepted by God and that he was to send to Joppa (Jaffa) to fetch Simon, called Peter, staying with Simon the Tanner, whose house was by the sea. Cornelius dispatched a soldier and two slaves to Joppa. Just before they arrived the next day, Peter at noon fell into a trance, in which he too had a vision. A great sheet was let down from the sky, full of strange animals and birds; a voice called to him, saying, 'Rise, Peter; kill and eat,' to which Peter answered, 'No, Lord; for I have never eaten anything that is common or unclean.' The voice replied, 'What God has cleansed, you must not call common.' This sequence was repeated three times before the sheet was taken up into the sky again. While Peter was puzzling out the meaning of his vision, the messengers of Cornelius arrived on the doorstep, calling out to know whether Simon, called Peter, was staying there. It was then that the Spirit told him, 'Behold, three men are looking for you. Rise and go down, and accompany them without hesitation; for I have sent them.' So Peter went to greet them and asked them why they had come; the next day he set off with them and with six brothers from Joppa to go to Caesarea.

It is interesting to note that the centurion at Caesarea, like the centurion at Capernaum, sends others with a message for help.

On Peter's arrival, Cornelius, his family and friends were assembled and waiting. Cornelius prostrated himself at Peter's feet, then each explained their visions and Peter added, 'Truly I perceive that God shows no partiality, but in every nation any one who fears him and does what is right is acceptable to him.' (Acts 10:34-35). Peter then announced the good news of Jesus, his life, death, and resurrection, and proclaimed the eternal purpose of God in sending Jesus to be the Saviour. While he was speaking, the Spirit came to all who were listening, to the astonishment of Peter and his Jewish companions from Joppa, because these Gentiles had not yet been baptized. Whereupon Cornelius and his whole household were baptized 'in the name of Jesus Christ'.

This is a unique chapter in the story of the early Church, just because it brought to a head the controversy between Peter and the 'circumcision party' at Jerusalem. It was not until the first Council of Jerusalem, under the chairmanship of James the brother of Jesus, that the issue was finally settled with only minimal demands being made of Gentile Christians. (Acts 15) This was largely the result of reports from Paul and Barnabas, together with Peter's own account of the conversion of Cornelius, the Roman centurion. [Acts 10:1-31]

CRESCENS (Gk. 'increasing') A companion of Paul in his final imprisonment, who left him to visit Christian churches in Galatia. Tradition claims that he became bishop of Chalcedon, in northern Asia Minor, the scene of the fourth Ecumenical Council of the Christian Church in the year 451. [2 Tim. 4:10]

CRETANS The long island of Crete in the eastern Mediterranean forms a natural bridge with the island of Cythera on the north-west and those of Salmone and Rhodes on the north-east; a bridge between Europe, Asia Minor and Phoenicia. There was a large community of Jews in Crete, some of whom came to attend the festival of Pentecost in Jerusalem, heard and understood the message of the apostles of Jesus. The Apostle Paul, on his way from Caesarea, sailed 'under the lee of Crete off Salmone. Coasting along it with difficulty . . . to a place called Fair Havens, near which was the city of Lasea.' Against Paul's advice, the captain and owner of the ship preferred to sail further round the island to the more commodious harbour of Phoenix for the winter. Although they kept inshore along the coast, they were blown offshore by a north-east gale and being forced off course, never actually landed in a Cretan harbour. (Acts 27:7-15)

There is no record in Acts or allusion in his letters to any visit of Paul to Crete, though, writing to Titus, he says, 'This is why I left you in Crete, that you might amend what was defective, and appoint elders in every town as I directed you.' (Titus 1:5) Paul well knew the proven tact and experience of Titus, from his successful dealings with the demanding task of organizing the Church in Corinth. If the letter to Titus was in fact written by Paul, then it is just possible that Paul visited Crete after his release from captivity in Rome. There are many other directions in which Paul might have preferred to conduct a final Christian mission. He had no high opinion of Cretans, as his advice to Titus shows (if indeed the letter is his). 'One of themselves, a prophet of their own, said, "Cretans are always liars, evil beasts, lazy gluttons." This testimony is true. Therefore rebuke them sharply, that they may be sound in the faith, instead of giving heed to Jewish myths or to commands of men who reject the truth. . . . They profess to know God, but they deny him by their deeds; they are detestable, disobedient, unfit for any good deed.' (Titus 1:12-14, 16) [Acts 2:11; Titus 1:12]

CRISPUS (Gk. 'curled') The ruler of the Jewish synagogue in the pagan city of Corinth, who became a Christian and was probably baptized by Paul the Apostle during his eighteen-month stay in about the years 51 and 52. Tradition records that he became bishop of Aegina. [Acts 18:8; 1 Cor. 1:14]

CYRENIANS (Gk. 'wall') Traditionally there were 480 synagogues in Jerusalem. These were the meeting-

116

places for prayer and discussion — particularly about the Law — of many different peoples of Jewish faith. At the time of Stephen's martyrdom, it was the natives of Alexandria and Cyrene in Africa and of the Roman provinces of Asia and Cilicia (the home of Saul the Persecutor, who was to become Paul the Apostle), who took the initiative in Stephen's arrest. It was the members of these synagogues who took most offence at Stephen's teaching, but could not successfully dispute with his wisdom and enthusiasm.

In consequence, they instigated the crowd to accuse him of talking blasphemy against Moses and God, for the Jews the ultimate wickedness. The mob dragged Stephen off to the Council, and accused him of speaking both against the Temple and against the Law. Members of the synagogue of the Cyrenians were foremost among those who secured Stephen's condemnation and stoning. [Acts 6:9]

CYRENIUS see QUIRINIUS

D

DAMARIS An Athenian woman, mentioned by name with only one other Athenian, called Dionysius the Areopagite, as believing and joining with Paul on the occasion of his visit to Athens. The great bishop of Constantinople in the 4th century, John Chrysostom, in his *Priesthood* declared that Damaris was the wife of Dionysius. see DIONYSIUS [Acts 17:34]

DEMAS (Gk. 'popular') Linked with Luke as a loyal prison-companion of Paul in Rome, on at least one occasion, Demas has yet left a doubtful reputation behind him because of a disparaging reference in the last letter to Timothy.

He was certainly with Paul at the time of his writing the captivity letters – his letters to the Christian congregation at Colossae and to Philemon, a member of that congregation. In both these letters, Paul sends the greetings of Demas, along with those of Luke, 'the beloved physician'. In the final letter of Paul, if indeed it was written by Paul at all, to Timothy, Demas is mentioned with some bitterness. He is there said to have stayed with Paul for some time and then to have forsaken him, having returned to his worldly business.

In his *Pilgrim's Progress,* John Bunyan depicts Demas as the type of half-hearted Christian who goes part of the way and then turns back. If the pastoral letters to Timothy are not authentically Pauline, then some early tradition must have branded Demas with disloyalty. [Col. 4:14; Philem. 24; 2 Tim. 4:10]

DEMETRIUS (Gk. 'belonging to Demeter') **1.** The silversmith at Ephesus who, suffering a slump in his sales of silver shrines and trinkets of the goddess Artemis, blamed Paul's teaching and stirred up his fellow-tradesmen to make a riotous demonstration.

For the significance of Artemis in Ephesus, *see* ARTEMIS.

Demetrius must have catered for a very considerable pilgrim and tourist trade entirely centred on the vast temple and cult of the goddess Artemis, for Ephesus was the Benares of the eastern Mediterranean. It was probably the month of the festival, the *Artemision,* the people would be keeping holiday and the city would be crowded with visitors and customers for the purchase of the shrines and images of the sanctuary. The Ephesians and even the provincials of Asia, however, had been so affected by the mission of Paul and his companions that there was little sale for these objects of devotion.

Demetrius, therefore, appealed to the pockets of the silversmiths and the piety of the people. Paul's teaching was bad for both trade and religion. The great goddess Artemis herself was threatened: 'Men, you know that from this business we have our wealth. And you see and hear that not only at Ephesus but almost throughout all Asia this Paul has persuaded and turned away a considerable company of people, saying that gods made with hands are not gods. And there is danger not only that this trade of ours may come into disrepute but also that the temple of the great goddess Artemis may count for nothing, and that she may even be deposed from her magnificence, she whom all Asia and the world worship.' (Acts 19:25-27)

In the riot that followed, Paul was conspicuous by his absence. It was two of his travelling companions who were dragged into the theatre, until the town clerk called for order and dismissed the assembly, appealing to Demetrius to bring the matter to court rather than cause such a commotion. [Acts 19:24, 38]

2. The bearer of the third letter of John the Elder to Gaius, reproving one Diotrephes for flouting the authority of the elder, calling for his reader's support and quoting Demetrius as a witness in the writer's cause. [3 John 12]

DEVIL (Gk. 'slanderer') *see* SATAN, BE-ELZEBUL, BELIAL

DIANA *see* ARTEMIS

DIDYMUS (Gk. 'twin') Each of the three times that Thomas is mentioned in the Fourth Gospel he is called 'the Twin'. The word Didymus, to be found in the King James Version, is not a surname but a Greek translation of the Hebrew for Thomas, which itself means 'Twin'.

Didymus was probably the nickname by which Thomas was known to Greek Christians in Asia Minor. It is possible that this disciple's real name was not known, but that he was in fact just called 'the Twin', in whatever language. see THOMAS [John 11:16; 20:24; 26; 21:2]

DIONYSIUS A member of the Council of the Areopagus (the High Court of Athens that used to meet on Mars Hill), called Dionysius, is mentioned by name with only one other Athenian, a woman called Damaris, as believing and joining with Paul on the occasion of his visit to Athens.

The Areopagus (Mars Hill) would have been admirably suited to public meetings, being a low but large outcrop of rock just below the main stairway entrance to the Acropolis, in full view of the Parthenon and the statue of Athena. Here the ancient religion of the Greeks was confronted by the Christian Faith, presented by an insignificant little Jew.

At the request of Epicurean and Stoic philosophers, Paul gave an exposition of his teaching before the Council of the Areopagus. It was a masterpiece of tact, insight, and condensation but in practical terms it was a complete failure. The Greek conception of the human body was of a tomb imprisoning the spirit of the man, therefore they rejected out of hand any mention of the resurrection of the body. Paul made few converts on this occasion, of which Dionysius was, however, traditionally one and destined to become the first bishop of Athens and to be martyred under the Emperor Domitian. [Acts 17:34]

DIOTREPHES (Gk. 'nurtured by Zeus') A domineering elder, if not leader of the Christian congregation to which Gaius, the addressee of 3 John, belonged. Diotrephes appears from this letter to have flouted the writer's authority as an elder and to have been highly critical of him. The writer is more concerned, however, with Diotrephes's refusal to receive messengers from him and with his hostility to all of those who offer hospitality to his messengers. He writes to thank Gaius for giving them a welcome and providing for their needs, in spite of the threats of Diotrephes. [3 John 9]

DORCAS (Gk. 'gazelle') *see* TABITHA

DRUSILLA The Jewish wife of the Roman procurator Felix, himself born a Greek and made a freedman by the Roman Emperor Claudius, of whom Felix and his brother Pallas were favourites. Drusilla, the youngest of the three daughters of Herod Agrippa I, at the age of fourteen had been married to Azizus, king of Emesa (Homs) in Syria. Azizus accepted circumcision in order to obtain her. With the help of a Syrian sorcerer, Drusilla was persuaded to desert her husband and marry Felix, for whom she bore a single son, later killed in an eruption of Mount Vesuvisus.

During a period of violent Jewish resistance to the occupying Roman forces in Palestine, the Emperor Claudius appointed Felix as procurator in the year 52, because of his tolerant disposition to Jewry and of his Jewish wife, Drusilla. This, however, only served to strengthen the position of the Zealot party and their fanatical loyalty to the Law of the Temple, and to correspondingly weaken the independence of the young Christian Church. In about the year 58, following the return to and arrest of the Apostle Paul in Jerusalem, Paul appeared before Felix at Caesarea in the presence of his wife Drusilla. A Syriac text of this passage implies that Drusilla herself was interested in Paul, and induced Felix to have Paul brought to him. It seems that Paul had virtually convinced Felix of his innocence and certainly he was well treated, if kept under arrest for the rest of Felix's procuratorship. Drusilla accompanied Felix when he was recalled to Rome to answer for his misgovernment. [Acts 24:24]

E

ELAMITES (Gk. 'inhabitants of Elamais') *see* ARABIANS

ELDERS Whether within the Jewish or Christian communities, the elder had a double function – both to rule and to teach.

The elders of ancient Israel were called by Moses to direct the affairs of the community, to make decisions and announcements of importance. The elders announced the institution of the Passover, and they accompanied Moses up Mount Sinai to meet with God. On the settlement in Canaan, elders functioned in each town and were consulted by the central government. On the return from exile in Babylon, the elders continued to function locally but formed a third grade of laymen within the Sanhedrin or central council of justice.

From the Gospels, it is clear that they were still the leaders of religious life in three clear respects. In local affairs, they were of considerable influence. It was the elders of Capernaum who came to Jesus to ask him to help the Roman centurion, 'for he loves our nation, and he built us our synagogue'. (Luke 7:5) In matters of biblical interpretation, too, the elders inherited a tradition handed down from the earliest times. This 'tradition of the elders' took the form of an endless extemporization and extension of the Old Testament Law to enable its application in all circumstances. It began as an oral tradition added to the written Law, but in the hands of the scribes it was preserved in writing, constantly extended and transmitted to include the whole range of conduct in every possible situation. Consequently, it had become near impossible of fulfilment and was often criticized by Jesus as a burden too heavy to bear. 'So, for the sake of your tradition, you have made void the word of God,' he said, referring to the fact that any man could allocate his earnings to the Temple, according to the tradition of the elders, and in so doing avoid supporting his parents as demanded by the Law of Moses. (Matt. 15:1-9)

It was the elders who questioned Jesus's authority in turning the dealers out of the Temple. (Mark 11:27) The elders gave judgment at the trial of Jesus. The elders in consultation with the high priest and scribes drew up the charges for the trial before Pilate, as the lay members of the Sanhedrin.

Within the early Christian Church, the presbyters or elders were among the first officers to be appointed. In the pastoral epistles, the functions of the Christian elders are clearly seen. 'Let the elders who rule well be considered worthy of double honour, especially those who labour in preaching and teaching; for the scripture says, "You shall not muzzle an ox when it is treading out the grain," and, "The labourer deserves his wages." Never admit any charge against an elder except on the evidence of two or three witnesses.' (1 Tim. 5:17-19)

Titus is called upon to appoint elders in every town on the island of Crete. At least ten years, however, before these letters were written Paul had himself already appointed elders at Ephesus, to whom on his last journey to Jerusalem he gave these final instructions: 'Take heed to yourselves and to all the flock, in which the Holy Spirit has made you guardians, to feed the church

123

of the Lord which he obtained with his own blood. I know that after my departure fierce wolves will come in among you, not sparing the flock; and from among your own selves will arise men speaking perverse things, to draw away the disciples after them. Therefore be alert, remembering that for three years I did not cease night or day to admonish every one with tears. And now I commend you to God and to the word of his grace, which is able to build you up and to give you the inheritance among all those who are sanctified.' (Acts 20:28-32) [Matt. 15:2; 16:21; 21:23; 26:57; 27:1, 20; Mark 7:3; 8:31; 15:1; Acts 4:5, 8, 23; 6:12; 11:30; 14:23; 15:4, 6, 22, 23; 16:4; 20:17; 1 Tim. 5:1, 17, 19; Titus 1:5; Jas. 5:14; 1 Pet. 5:1; 2 John 1; 3 John 1; Rev. 4:4, 10; 5:5, 6, 8, 11, 14; 7:11, 13; 11:16; 19:4]

ELIZABETH (Gk. from the Heb. 'God is my oath') Elizabeth, the mother of John the Baptist, was visited by her cousin Mary, mother of Jesus, when they were both expecting their first babies. The story of the parents and birth of John the Baptist is recorded only by Luke.

Elizabeth was the wife of a village priest called Zechariah. They were both of priestly descent, she from Aaron, he from Abijah. Both were devout and scrupulous in their observance of the Law; but they were childless, for Elizabeth was barren and they were getting on in years. The twenty-four families of the 'sons of Aaron' were responsible in rotation for service in the Temple at Jerusalem. Within each family the individual priest was chosen by lot to tend the brazier on the altar of incense in front of the Most Holy Place. When Elizabeth's husband Zechariah was carrying out this privileged task, he received a vision in which the Archangel Gabriel made him a promise: 'Do not be afraid, Zechariah, for your prayer is heard, and your wife Elizabeth will bear you a son, and you shall call his name John.' (Luke 1:13) It was Elizabeth who at the child's circumcision was to insist on his being named 'John' rather than 'Zechariah' after his father.

After his service in the Temple, Zechariah returned home. Elizabeth conceived and remained in retirement for five months, saying 'Thus the Lord has done to me in the days when he looked on me, to take away my reproach among men.' (Luke 1:25) Meanwhile, Elizabeth's cousin Mary of Nazareth had had a vision and the promise of a son, Jesus. The Archangel Gabriel had told Mary the news of Elizabeth. 'And behold, your kinswoman Elizabeth in her old age has also conceived a son; and this is the sixth month with her who was called barren. For with God nothing will be impossible.' (Luke 1:36-37)

Mary promptly set out to visit her cousin Elizabeth at her home in the 'hill country, to a city of Judah'. Elizabeth met her with the words, 'Blessed are you among women, and blessed is the fruit of your womb! And why is this granted me, that the mother of my Lord should come to me? For behold, when the voice of your greeting came to my ears, the babe in my womb leaped for joy.' (Luke 1:42-44)

At this point Luke introduces the paean of praise that has come to be included in the liturgies of all the Christian Churches as the 'Magnificat'. In nearly all manuscripts it is put into the mouth of Mary, but in a few it is attributed to Elizabeth.

The feast of the Visitation, kept within the Eastern and Western Churches, is a commemoration of the significant role of these two women in God's plan of redemption, as perceived by Luke, who stresses the agency of the Holy Spirit in the life of Elizabeth as well as in the life of Mary. The visitation would have been

125

the most natural event. Mary would have welcomed an opportunity to escape from prying eyes and malicious tongues in Nazareth, and the three months' rest with her cousin would have been a most welcome retreat. Elizabeth, the older woman, herself going through the same experience, would have been a great comfort and support to the young peasant girl Mary, plunged so unexpectedly though so willingly into pregnancy.

Apart from the normal course of personal relations, each woman had an added incentive to seek the society of the other. Each knew that there was something altogether exceptional about the promise of her child. Elizabeth's age, quite apart from her husband's vision, had alerted her to the marvel that was happening to her. Mary's virginity, together with the message of the angel, had left her in no doubt that she was being used as a willing agent in the hand of God.

They understood quickly the respective roles they had to play, and what would be the relative positions of their children. With the advantage of hindsight we are inclined to read rather more than is warranted into the words addressed by the angel Gabriel to Elizabeth's husband in the Temple. But there may have been enough to suggest to Zechariah that work of a preparatory nature would be the destiny of his son-to-be. Perhaps some communication had already passed between Mary and Elizabeth, so that the older woman knew of the wonderful circumstances attending Mary's pregnancy. In any case, Elizabeth had no hesitation in joyfully accepting the minor role for her child, and so establishing, even before the birth, the position of John as the forerunner and of Jesus as the Messiah.

When the time came, the two boys were born within six months of each other, in towns within sight of each other. Joseph and Mary had come to Bethlehem for the census; the home of the priest Zechariah and Elizabeth was below Mount Orah in Ein Karem, the 'Gracious Spring'. Before the time of the Russian pilgrim Daniel in 1107 the birthplace of John was located, within the village, in a cave that is now shown in the Franciscan Church of St. John. On the other side of the valley is the Franciscan Church of the Visitation, within the crypt of which is shown the spring that according to a medieval tradition appeared at the meeting-place of Mary with Elizabeth. This is the spring which gives a name to the town today. In the wall of the crypt is a hollowed rock in which, according to another medieval tradition, the child John was concealed at the time of the Massacre of the Innocents by Herod's order. An apse of the Crusader Church of the Visitation can be seen in the upper church today, which is covered in murals.

The Russian Convent of Elizabeth, surrounded by little whitewashed cottages, rises among the trees on the slopes of Mount Orah above the Church of the Visitation at Ein Karem. On the feast of the Visitation, the Russian nuns from the Garden of Gethsemane used until 1947 to bring icons representing Mary to meet their sisters of Ein Karem with icons representing Elizabeth. At the village well, called Mary's Spring, they would touch icons together in a kiss of greeting, before carrying them in procession up the flower-strewn steps to the Convent of Elizabeth. [Luke 1]

ELYMAS (Gk. from the Aramaic 'powerful') *see* BAR-JESUS

EPAENETUS (Gk. 'praised') One of the Christians greeted warmly by Paul, at the close of his letter to the Christian Church in Rome. Paul refers to him as 'My beloved Epaenetus, who was the first convert in Asia for Christ'. Some manuscripts read 'in Achaia' rather than in Asia, referring to the mainland of Greece, rather than that of Turkey. This would seem to conflict with Paul's nomination of Stephanas and his household (1 Cor. 16:15) as the first Christians in Achaia. As one of the leading Christians at Ephesus, Epaenetus may well have visited the congregation in Rome. [Rom. 16:5]

EPAPHRAS A Christian probably taught by Paul during his long and systematic period of teaching at Ephesus, in the course of his Third Journey over the years 54-7. Epaphras took a leading part in the evangelization of the cities within the fertile valley of the River Lycus, 100 miles east and inland from Ephesus, particularly Colossae, Laodicea, and Hierapolis.

Some years later, Epaphras reported to Paul, in prison in Rome, on the good progress of the Church at Colossae. Paul wrote back to Colossae a letter in which he corrected some false teaching and gave some practical advice. He mentions Epaphras twice, first paying tribute to him as the evangelist and faithful steward of the gospel message, secondly praising his prayerful and pastoral concern for his fellow Colossians. 'We always thank God, the Father of our Lord Jesus Christ, when we pray for you, because we have heard of your faith in Christ Jesus and of the love which you have for all the saints, because of the hope laid up for you in heaven. Of this you have heard before in the word of the truth, the gospel which has come to you, as indeed in the whole world it is bearing fruit and growing – so among yourselves, from the day you heard and understood the grace of God in truth, as you learned it from Epaphras our beloved fellow servant. He is a faithful minister of Christ on our behalf and has made known to us your love in the Spirit.' (Col. 1:3-8)

A short time before the writing of this letter, a great earthquake had taken place in the Lycus valley; it is just possible that Epaphras's journey to Rome may have been with the specific purpose of requesting some Christian aid for the victims of this disaster. The historian Tacitus records that financial help from Rome was offered on a large scale. Paul thus mentions Epaphras at the close of his letter to Colossae: 'Epaphras, who is one of yourselves, a servant of Christ Jesus, greets you, always remembering you earnestly in his prayers, that you may stand mature and fully assured in all the will of God. For I bear him witness that he has worked hard for you and for those in Laodicea and Hierapolis.' (Col. 4:12, 13)

It is probable that, during Paul's long imprisonment in Rome, his friends took turns in keeping him company and sharing his captivity with him. This would account for Paul's mention in his later letters of different 'fellow-prisoners'. Certainly when Paul wrote his letter to the Christian Church at Colossae, Aristarchus was his companion in prison. By the time Paul writes his personal letter to Philemon, it is Epaphras whom he mentions as his fellow-prisoner.

Epaphras is shown to have been a very useful and faithful friend both to Paul personally and to the development of the Christian Church in Asia. [Col. 1:7; 4:12; Philem. 23]

EPAPHRODITUS (Gk. 'lovely') The messenger of the Christian congregation at Philippi entrusted with a gift of money for Paul during his first imprisonment in Rome, who was also the bearer of Paul's letter back to Philippi.

Epaphroditus stayed some time with Paul, perhaps taking a turn with others in sharing his captivity. During that time of caring for Paul, he himself became severely ill. On his recovery, Paul decided to send him back to the congregation at Philippi with the letter that we know as the Letter to the Philippians. (*see* PHILIPPIANS) In that letter, among other things, Paul thanks them for their very acceptable gift, referring to their record of generosity over some ten years of acquaintance. 'Yet it was kind of you to share my trouble. And you Philippians yourselves know that in the beginning of the gospel, when I left Macedonia, no church entered into partnership with me in giving and receiving except you only; for even in Thessalonica you sent me help once and again. Not that I seek the gift; but I seek the fruit which increases to your credit. I have received full payment, and more; I am filled, having received from Epaphroditus the gifts you sent, a fragrant offering, a sacrifice acceptable and pleasing to God. And my God will supply every need of yours according to his riches in glory in Christ Jesus.' (Phil. 4:14-19)

Paul's letter includes a personal discharge and warm commendation of Epaphroditus, revealing the depth of Paul's pastoral relationships, even during the rigours of his imprisonment. 'I have thought it necessary to send to you Epaphroditus my brother and fellow worker and fellow soldier, and your messenger and minister to my need, for he has been longing for you all, and has been distressed because you heard that he was ill. Indeed he was ill, near to death. But God had mercy on him, and not only on him but on me also, lest I should have sorrow upon sorrow. I am the more eager to send him, therefore, that you may rejoice at seeing him again, and that I may be less anxious. So receive him in the Lord with joy; and honour such men, for he nearly died for the work of Christ, risking his life to complete your service to me.' (Phil. 2:25-30) [Phil. 2:25; 4:18]

EPHESIANS Ephesus was the headquarters of Paul's great Third Journey. It was later the centre of the mission and pastoral activities of John the Divine. From

Ephesus, Paul conducted his correspondence with the Christian community at Corinth and possibly also wrote his letter to the congregation at Philippi. To the Church at Ephesus, along with other congregations in Asia, Paul wrote a circular letter or encyclical when under house-arrest during his first visit to Rome. This so-called Letter to the Ephesians is a magnificent exposition of the 'mystery' of God's purpose in history and of the new life within the Christian Church. It has been called 'the very crown of all his epistles'.

Paul in Ephesus

Paul spent three years – perhaps 54-7 – at the very heart of Greco-Roman civilization, at Ephesus, the great city of paganism in Asia. Its temple of Diana was the centre of pagan worship for all the Mediterranean lands. The proud title of this great commercial and religious centre was 'Neocorus' – temple-keeper or sacristan – of Artemis. Ancient writers considered that this Benares (place of pagan pilgrimage) of the ancient world outshone even the gardens of Babylon and the Colossus of Rhodes. Its temple was the centre of a dark, licentious, and mysterious oriental culture, very different from the healthy-minded open-air huntress-goddess known in Greece as Artemis and in Rome as Diana. Wherever the deity of a race was female, women took a prominent part in the life of the place and people. Asia Minor had been the land of the fabled moon-worshipping Amazons. Consequently the Temple of Artemis enjoyed the services of an army or virgin-prophetesses, eunuch-priests, choristers, vergers, and even acrobats in a spate of infamous and immoral excess. Ephesus in the early Christian era – was a city of magic and necromancy, the home of a superstition so ancient and deeply rooted that it outlived the gods of Olympus.

To the little Christian communities founded along the coast-line, in the 50s, the Temple of Artemis at Ephesus was an infernal counterpart to the Temple at Jerusalem. A vast stone staircase led up past the many-breasted statue of the Ephesian Artemis to the glistening colonnade and façade. The Temple was the size of St Paul's Cathedral in London but the same shape and style as the Parthenon in Athens, white marble colonnades without, dark and numinous within, containing no statue but a single colossal meteorite.

Before the 4th century BC, the Temple of Artemis had formed the centre of the city. When the harbour became silted up, the city was moved a mile and a half towards the sea, and a sacred pilgrim's way linked the city to the sanctuary. In the 6th century AD, the city was moved back to the acropolis where it was more easily defensible than on the low marshland by the river. Little stands on the acropolis today but the magnificent Byzantine Basilica of St John. The Greco-Roman city remains, however, forming a magnificent complex of temples, libraries, baths, gymnasia, and theatres, linked by a splendid marble street which still today runs from the Magnesia Gate to the Roman *Agora or* market-place.

Here, Paul spent the first three months of his ministry teaching in the synagogue. When the final break with the Jewish community occurred, he moved to the lecture-room of Tyrannus. There he worked daily in teaching and discussion among Jews and Greeks, over a period of two whole years, in the siesta hours of noon to four in the afternoon. Remarkable progress followed this systematic instruction, accompanied also by a ministry of healing. Both Jews and Greeks came to respect the name of Jesus, rather than the magical arts of Diana. Paul despatched teachers to Colossae and Macedonia; at this time also the Seven Churches of Asia, mentioned by John in the Book of Revelation, were founded. (*see* JOHN **9.**) Paul, when he closed his ministry in Ephesus, travelled overland to Troas, crossed into Macedonia and, visiting his Greek congregations, made his way down to Corinth for the winter months of the year 57-8. In the spring, wishing to reach Jerusalem by Pentecost, Paul summoned the elders of the Church at Ephesus to meet him on the coast at Miletus, where he bade them a fond farewell.

It is not certain that Paul managed to return to Asia and Ephesus, following his release from his first captivity in Rome. His letters to Philemon and Timothy, however, imply that he did so, before being finally arrested at Troas some 150 miles north of Ephesus.

Paul's letter: a masterpiece

Until very recently there has been no doubt that this was an authentic letter of Paul and indeed his masterpiece. Its thought and language are echoed in Peter's first letter written in the 1st century, and the letter was often quoted by the Fathers of the Church in the 2nd century. The letter reveals a careful reconsideration of some of the themes explored in his earlier letters, together with a splendid and original statement of God's purpose for man as seen in the establishing of the universal Church of Jesus Christ. Doubts as to the letter's genuine Pauline authorship spring from its difference in style and approach from the earlier letters. Such peculiarities, however, whether intentional or even unconscious, may be due to the fact that the whole letter is in the form and language of a prayerful meditation. Consequently ideas follow one upon the other, born of the inspiration of the moment and with little regard for punctuation. It has been said that in his letter to the Romans Paul flies off at a tangent, but that in his letter to the Ephesians he ties himself in knots! It is within the context of a meditation that he borrows ideas from his own letter to the Colossians, but tends to modify and develop his conclusions. No editorial comment or recent criticism can conceal the distinctly Pauline stamp on the thinking and expression of this letter.

The destination of this letter is perhaps less certain than its authorship. At least three of the most ancient manuscripts omit the address 'at Ephesus' within the opening verse. In the year 140, the heretical writer Marcion substitutes the address 'to the Laodiceans'. We know from Paul's letter to the Colossians (4:16) that he did in fact write a letter to the Laodiceans and that he suggested that the congregations at Colossae and Laodicea should exchange letters after they had read their own. Both letters were sent by the hand of Tychicus and his route would inevitably take him to many other Asian congregations during the course of his journey. It may well be, therefore, that what we know as the letter to the Ephesians was a circular letter of which perhaps half a dozen copies were carried by Tychicus. The bearer may have been instructed to fill in the blank address before delivering each copy of the letter, but probably failed to do so on at least one copy. This theory is widely accepted; it explains the somewhat abstract and impersonal nature of the letter, almost devoid of greetings for any one person among the multitude of Paul's friends at Ephesus.

God's purpose: unity through the Church

The letter is clearly the result of a private meditation of the writer, but is expressed with practical ends in view. He is concerned with the sectarianism within the Christian congregations – made up as they were of Jews and Gentiles of different nationalities and backgrounds. The letter is in two clearly marked sections, expressing two aspects of a single theme. The first three chapters describe God's purpose to unite all things through his Church. If the Church is to be the unifying factor within God's world, it must itself be united. The duties of the individual Christian churchman are analysed in the final chapters of the letter, in the light of the unifying purpose for which the Church exists. The whole letter is woven together into a single prayer for world-wide reconciliation in Jesus. Out of a divided humanity God has made a united community in the Christian Church. Jesus is the 'principle' of reunion; his Church is to be the 'instrument' of reconciliation.

'For he has made known to us in all wisdom and insight the mystery of his will, according to his purpose which he set forth in Christ as a plan for the fullness of time, to unite all things in him, things in heaven and things on earth.' (Eph. 1:9-10)

Paul is deeply aware of the age-old warfare between good and evil. It is against this background that he sees the hidden purpose of God from the beginning to 'unite all things in him, things in heaven and things on earth'. When men grasped the 'mystery' of this inner purpose of God, then they held the clue to all his doings. 'Having the eyes of your hearts enlightened, that you may know what is the hope to which he has called you, what are the riches of his glorious inheritance in the saints, and what is the immeasurable greatness of his power in us who believe, according to the working of his great might which he accomplished in Christ when he raised him from the dead and made him sit at his right hand in the heavenly places.' (Eph. 1:18-20)

Meanwhile, the Church of Jesus is the continuation of his life and work in God's world. The life of the risen Lord is expressed through his Church. As he assumed a

135

human body for his earthly life, so now he works his purpose through his eternal Body, the Church. He has solved the problem of the mutual alienation of Jew and Gentile by the creation of this single and united Body. 'For he is our peace, who has made us both one, and has broken down the dividing wall of hostility, by abolishing in his flesh the law of commandments and ordinances, that he might create in himself one new man in place of the two, so making peace, and might reconcile us both to God in one body through the cross, thereby bringing the hostility to an end.' (Eph. 2:14-16)

The first section of this letter closes with a magnificent prayer for all the congregations of the Church who may receive it. It is hard to realize that the entire Christian Church at this time consisted of a few thousand people meeting in small groups in the back streets of such cities as Antioch, Ephesus, and Rome. To Paul, however, the Church was God's instrument to carry out his infinite purpose of reconciliation, planned from the beginning of time, guided and energized by his indwelling Spirit. 'For this reason I bow my knees before the Father, from whom every family in heaven and on earth is named, that according to the riches of his glory he may grant you to be strengthened with might through his Spirit in the inner man, and that Christ may dwell in your hearts through faith; that you, being rooted and grounded in love, may have power to comprehend with all the saints what is the breadth and length and height and depth, and to know the love of Christ which surpasses knowledge, that you may be filled with all the fullness of God.' (Eph. 3:14-19)

The Christian's duty

In Paul's eyes, the essential unity of the Church has been planned and provided for in Jesus, but it can only

136

come into being by every individual member co-operating in the purpose of Jesus. All their actions must be directed towards love, peace, and understanding. Each in his own family circle and community must be centre of reconciliation, as Jesus is for the whole world. Each is to hold close to the person and teaching of Jesus, that they may draw their strength and unity from him.

'I therefore, a prisoner for the Lord, beg you to lead a life worthy of the calling to which you have been called, with all lowliness and meekness, with patience, forbearing one another in love, eager to maintain the unity of the Spirit in the bond of peace. There is one body and one Spirit, just as you were called to the one hope that belongs to your call, one Lord, one faith, one baptism, one God and Father of us all, who is above all and through all and in all.' (Eph. 4:1-6)

Each individual member of the Church has been given different spiritual gifts and abilities, 'for the equipment of the saints, for the work of the ministry, for building up the body of Christ, until we all attain to the unity of the faith and of the knowledge of the son of God, to mature manhood, to the measure of the stature of the fullness of Christ.' (Eph. 4:12, 13) Meanwhile, however, there is a need for organization in the Church, for sound teaching and frank speaking. 'Rather, speaking the truth in love, we are to grow up in every way into him who is the head, into Christ, from whom the whole body, joined and knit together by every joint with which it is supplied, when each part is working properly, makes bodily growth and upbuilds itself in love.' (Eph. 4:15, 16)

Finally, Paul comes to the practical details of the new life in Christ. He deals with personal relationships: truth, honesty, decency, and forgiveness. He deals with the morals of the Christian home and family, husbands

137

and wives, parents and children, masters and slaves. He closes with an exhortation to all his readers to stand their ground against evil in the strength of the 'armour of God', and begs their support for himself in prison, 'an ambassador in chains'.

So ends what is perhaps the most remarkable of all Paul's letters. For Paul, Jesus is the central principle of existence, because the whole visible creation exists not for its own sake, but simply to unfold the divine purpose shown in Jesus. Those who, like Paul, know Jesus, share the hidden plan of God for his universe. By their response to the law and life of Jesus, in their homes and in their communities, men co-operate with God in his eternal purpose. [Eph. 1-6]

EPICUREANS The Greek philosophers who, together with the Stoics, questioned the teachings of Paul in Athens, and brought him to speak publicly on the Areopagus, during his Second Journey in the years 50-2.

The Epicureans followed the teachings of a Greek thinker called Epicurus, 342-270 BC, who claimed that reality lay in the world of nature rather than in the reason of man. In a world of matter and space, the pursuit of happiness was the primary and attractive purpose of man. For Epicurus and his early followers, who lived in small communities of friends, happiness lay in intellectual and spiritual exercises, but for lesser mortals in more basic satisfactions. Consequently the high intellectual standards of the founder of this philosophy degenerated into lower and more common forms of pleasure-seeking.

It was hardly surprising, therefore, that Paul's teaching about God as the Maker and 'Lord of heaven and earth', who now calls 'all men everywhere to repent', who has 'fixed a day on which he will judge the world in righteousness' by someone already appointed 'by

138

raising him from the dead', did not much appeal to the Epicureans. [Acts 17:18]

ERASTUS (Gk. 'beloved') This name occurs three times in the New Testament, each person of that name being linked with the work of the Apostle Paul. All three references may be to one and the same person, who may well have been a Corinthian.

1. A helper of Paul during his long ministry in Ephesus, on his Third Journey. Erastus and Timothy were sent by Paul into Macedonia, while Paul himself stayed on in Ephesus. Following the riot of the silversmiths, Paul took leave of his friends in Ephesus and then followed Timothy and Erastus to Macedonia. [Acts 19:22]

2. A representative of Paul remaining at Corinth, after Paul's arrest and second journey to Rome. In his final letter to summon Timothy from Ephesus to Rome, Paul outlines the whereabouts of his representatives and leaders of the Christian Church in the eastern Mediterranean. Among these, perhaps, were some who had accompanied him on this final journey towards Rome. He had left Trophimus ill at Miletus; Erastus had remained at Corinth; only Luke was still with him in Rome. [2 Tim. 4:20]

3. The city treasurer of Corinth, who joined with Paul in sending greetings, at the close of Paul's letter to the Church in Rome. His name is grouped with those of Gaius and Quartus. [Rom. 16:23]

ESSENES (Gk. from the Syriac 'holy ones') The Essenes were a Jewish sect which grew up in the two centuries before the Christian era. One branch of this sect settled at Qumran. Recently they have found new fame as the probable writers of the Dead Sea Scrolls and the pioneers of a monastic community in the wilderness of Judea.

Community in the wilderness

A schismatic movement of priests broke away from the worship of the Temple and from the theocratic rule of the Maccabean high priesthood. They did so because they considered that the Maccabees were not entitled to be high priests, not being of the correct tribe of Levi. The Hasmoneans had simply claimed the high priesthood as the spoils of conquest in war. If, therefore, the priesthood was invalid, so were its sacrifices in the Temple at Jerusalem.

During the Greek domination, there had been many cultic innovations and the calendar had had to be remodelled to the more exact lunar cycle. The conservative Essenes considered this calendar invalid together with its appointed sacrifices. In their eyes, consequently, there was feasting on fast days and fasting on feast days, with which God was displeased. The Essenes were highly apocalyptic and, following the Book of Daniel, expected an early end of the world. Remembering the Mosaic experience in the wilderness as a necessary means of purification, they retired to form a monastic community at Qumran, in the wilderness of Judea, overlooking the Dead Sea. There they prepared for the final battle between good and evil. We can not be certain, however, that the Qumranis were truly representative of the Essenes.

So, led by a Teacher of Righteousness, as a community of guaranteed purity – of the individual, of the priesthood and of the calendar – they set up a framework of monasticism as early as 150 BC. Surprisingly enough, however, this sect is not mentioned by name in the New Testament. The name 'Essenes' probably comes from the Syriac 'holy ones', 'pious ones'.

Until 1947, comparatively little was known about

this sect and the principal sources of information were from outside the community at Qumran, which may have been the headquarters of the Essenes. From the Jewish philosopher Philo, born in 20 BC, the Roman writer Pliny, and the Jewish historian Josephus, both writing about AD 110, the Essenes were known to be a priestly order of about 4,000 in number, isolating themselves in communities and observing a strict disicipline of conduct, ritual purity, and communal living, being bound together by the sharing of a sacred meal.

The Dead Sea Scrolls

In the summer of 1947, a young Arab shepherd chanced upon a cave, near the Wadi Qumran, containing several parchment scrolls carefully wrapped in linen cloths and stowed in tall, wide-necked jars. These scrolls were examined and proved to be part of the library of an Essene community. It was not long before archaeologists discovered and excavated a monastic settlement on the nearby plateau overlooking the Dead Sea. The discovery of ten other scroll caves followed, the last of which was found in 1956. These proved to contain 500 different documents from a great library, of which some biblical fragments go back to the 3rd century BC. Until then, the earliest Hebrew manuscripts of the Old Testament were of the 9th century AD. These 'Dead Sea Scrolls', as they have come to be called, throw much light on the transmission of the Bible text over a period of nearly a thousand years. The scrolls concerning the monastic life and discipline of the Essene community reveal many of the ideas, customs, and hopes that appear later in the New Testament. Perhaps the most important significance of these scrolls is that they portray, more vividly than before, the Jewish background of the early Christian Church and of the New Testament.

There are parallels between some of the ideas expressed in the scrolls and some in the four Gospels, particularly in the Fourth Gospel. Among these are 'eternal life', 'light', and the 'spirit of truth'. There is, too, the same conflict of opposites, such as 'truth and error', 'spirit and flesh', 'light and darkness'. Perhaps the John who wrote this Gospel was influenced by the Essenes, their practices and their terminology, as was possibly John the Baptist. The Essenes seem to have been possessed enthusiastically, if not obsessed, by their vivid expectation of the coming of the Messiah and the end of the world. They believed that the world was to end by a final conflict between the forces of good and evil, after which God would establish his kingdom of righteousness.

Community and fortress

The ruins of the Essene monastery at Qumran stand on a projecting spur of a marl plateau above the floor of the Rift Valley. The spur is surrounded by precipitous ravines and joined by a narrow neck to cliffs which form a steep scarp overlooking the Dead Sea. From the valley a path leads up on to the spur, passing through a cemetery of over a thousand tombs in orderly rows. Each body lies, head to the south and hands crossed, at a depth of at least six feet on a slab within a single tomb. The path leads up to the main gate and directly ahead in the cliff-face is the gorge or waterfall of the Wadi Qumran. From this, the remains of a broad water-canal can be seen entering the north-west of an enclosed compound. This conduit feeds seven large cisterns scattered throughout the settlement. These cisterns are mostly rectangular with steps leading down into them; they were probably indispensable as baptisteries for the ritual ablutions of the community. On the west side is the reconstructed watch-tower which affords both an excellent bird's-eye view of the monastery layout and also commands views of several miles north to the head of the Dead Sea and south along the narrow valley between the cliffs and the water's edge. Perhaps it was its situation and strategic position that caused the capture of the monastery and its adaptation as a fortress by the Romans in AD 68.

South of the tower rose a long double-storeyed building, the top floor of which was the scriptorium. A long table ran the length of the wall complete with inkwells and a bench; here probably the scrolls were written or copied. The largest room in the monastery, more than sixty-five feet long, was within the south wall of the settlement and served as an assembly hall and dining-room or refectory. Opposite the entrance was a raised dais, from which a speaker could address the meeting. Next to the dining-hall was the pantry, discovered complete with about a thousand dishes and platters stacked according to size, but shattered by the collapse of the roof. Whether, however, this was caused by earthquake or during the Roman assault remains a matter of conjecture. These large structures were surrounded by a number of smaller rooms, with the functions necessary to an isolated community: there are still clearly to be distinguished a laundry, a pottery, a kitchen, a bakery, a mill, and food stores. The most impressive and essential item of all remains the water system, penetrating the length and breadth of the walled enclosure by a series of canals and conduits linking tanks and basins from the waterfall of the wadi to the farthest cistern. Two or three miles to the south of the settlement is still a fresh and plentiful spring, where once the Essenes had considerable plantations and fields which enabled them, even in the desert, to be self-sufficient through their own careful and skilful agricultural efforts.

All members lived outside the monastery proper in settlements, under canvas or in caves, coming in to eat, work, and worship. They shared a variety of skills within the community. There were farmers, potters, writers, and healers using roots and herbs, who claimed to be able to cast out evil spirits. The Jewish historian Josephus says that there were astrologers and interpreters of dreams. The women lived in the camp outside the walls, but the leaders of the community were probably celibate. Some members married, but put their wives outside the community when they became pregnant. Twice every day, the community gathered in the assembly hall to sing hymns and give thanks to God. They sat down in a strict order of priority: the priest reading the scriptures, the overseer expounding them, members of the Council of Twelve in front, the 'many' sitting in rows behind them with the unbaptized novices at the back. On the Sabbath they ate a ritual meal of bread and wine. On important festivals, they held a love-feast, which was for them a foretaste of the none too distant last days, when the Messiah and Prince of Israel would arrive to conquer the world and invite the faithful to share his triumph.

Every other Jewish sect is mentioned in the New Testament, but nothing is said either of the Essenes or their remote headquarters at Qumran, either within the New Testament or the Mishnah. Their omission appears to remain an unsolved mystery. Despite their disciplines of secrecy, Jesus must have known something about them, their teaching, and their Messianic expectation. Indeed, at his own baptism only a few miles from Qumran, he became acutely aware of his own Messianic vocation, which was so different from the apocalyptic and nationalistic conception of Messiahship in his day among the Essenes and other religious groups.

The significance of the Essenes is that their writings have not only bridged a gap in the literary history of the Jewish people, but that they have provided a background canvas against which the transition from the Old to the New Testament era will become progressively and more clearly understood. [There is no mention of the Essenes by name in the New Testament.]

ETHIOPIAN The only Ethiopian mentioned in the New Testament was the eunuch, treasurer to the Candace of Ethiopia, converted and baptized by Philip the Evangelist on the road to Gaza. The man was possibly a court official from the train of the queen at Meroe, in Nubia, and probably himself also a Jew, though, being a eunuch, he was outside the covenant and forbidden by the Law to enter the congregation. (Lev. 21:20; Deut. 23:1)

The story told by Luke in Acts is of an incident completely isolated from the rest of the narrative. Philip is described as intercepting the chariot on the road from Jerusalem to Gaza. The site is still pointed out to pilgrims on the road to Hebron. The Ethiopian Jewish eunuch was returning from a pilgrimage to Jerusalem and was reading aloud as he journeyed, from the prophet Isaiah. Philip ran up, heard what he was reading, and asked him if he really understood. He answered, ' "How can I, unless someone guides me?" And he invited Philip to come up and sit with him. Now the passage of the scripture which he was reading [from the 'Suffering Servant' songs of the Second Isaiah] was this:

"As a sheep led to the slaughter
  or a lamb before its shearer is dumb,

145

so he opens not his mouth.

In his humiliation justice was denied him.

Who can describe his generation?

For his life is taken up from the earth."

And the eunuch said to Philip, "About whom, pray, does the prophet say this, about himself, or about some one else?" Then Philip opened his mouth, and beginning with this scripture he told him the good news of Jesus. And as they went along the road they came to some water, and the eunuch said, "See, here is water! What is to prevent my being baptized?" And he commanded the chariot to stop, and they both went down into the water, Philip and the eunuch, and he baptized him.' (Acts 8:32-8)

This well-known 53rd chapter of Isaiah is rarely, if at all, applied to the Messiah in Hebrew literature, although it is constantly quoted of the Christ in the New Testament. (Matt. 8:17; Luke 22:37; John 12:38; Acts 3:18; 1 Pet. 2:22, 24; Heb. 9:28; Rev. 13:8; 14:-5)

It is not possible to link the conversion of the Ethiopian eunuch with the foundation of the Christian Church in what is now Ethiopia, but when, in the 4th century, Frumentius and Edesius, missionaries from Tyre, set about the conversion of Ethiopia, they found there already an early form of the Christian faith. [Acts 8:27]

EUBULUS (Gk. 'of good counsel') A Christian in Rome, known to Timothy, whose greetings Paul sent to Timothy in Ephesus, when he, Paul, was imprisoned in Rome and awaiting execution. [2 Tim. 4:21]

EUNICE (Gk. 'conquering well') The mother of Timothy, a lieutenant of Paul destined to become bishop of Ephesus, Eunice was a Christian Jewess married to a Greek (Acts 16:1) and living with her family at Lystra.

Paul may well have persuaded Timothy, his mother Eunice, and his grandmother Lois, to become Christians on the very first visit to Lystra with Barnabas in the year 46. (Acts 14:8-20) Certainly Timothy knew of Paul's stoning by the Jews on that occasion. (2 Tim. 3:11) When Paul passed through Lystra again, on his Second Journey some four years later, he collected Timothy from his home and family. Because he wanted to use Timothy for evangelism among the Jews, who knew that his father was Greek, Paul personally took Timothy and circumcised him, to convince them of his adherence to the Jewish Law.

Paul, in his correspondence with Timothy, acknowledges generously the careful training of Timothy in the Jewish faith and scriptures, within his own home and family. 'I am reminded of your sincere faith, a faith that dwelt first in your grandmother Lois and your mother Eunice and now, I am sure, dwells in you.' (2 Tim 1:5) And again, 'Continue in what you have learned and have firmly believed, knowing from whom you learned it and how from childhood you have been acquainted with the sacred writings which are able to instruct you for salvation through faith in Christ Jesus.' (2 Tim. 3:14-15)

Presumably Eunice remained at Lystra, for Paul did not send her greetings in his letters to Timothy at Ephesus. [2 Tim. 1:5]

EUODIA (Gk. 'prosperous journey' or 'fragrance') One of two women members of the Christian congregation at Philippi who had been disagreeing. Probably news of their quarrel was brought to Paul in prison by Epaphroditus. In the letter which Epaphroditus now took back to Philippi, Paul wrote this appeal, 'I entreat Euodia and I entreat Syntyche to agree in the Lord. And I ask you also, true yokefellow, help these women, for they have laboured side by side with me in the gospel together with Clement and the rest of my fellow workers, whose names are in the book of life.' (Phil. 4:2, 3) The 'true yokefellow' referred to might well be an elder in their congregation, or may be read as the proper name 'Syzygus'. [Phil. 4:2]

EUTYCHUS (Gk. 'fortunate') a boy member of the Christian congregation at Troas who, listening to a long sermon from the Apostle Paul, was overcome by sleep and fell from a second- or third-storey window. Paul ran downstairs and hugged him, though he was taken for dead, and declared, 'Do not be alarmed, for his life is in him.' Paul then returned to the upper room, where he 'broke the bread' and talked until daybreak before leaving. The boy revived, much to the comfort of the congregation.

The description of this assembly throws some light on the form of early Christian Eucharist. The points of particular interest include the fact that it was the first day of the week, that is, late Saturday or Sunday night, the use of many lamps either for light or ritual, the assembly in an upper dining-room or cenacle, the division between a liturgy of the Word and a liturgy of the Eucharist. The preaching of the Word in the sermon was separated from the breaking of the bread and the meal that followed, by the rescue and restoration of the boy Eutychus. [Acts 20:9]

F

FELIX (Gk. from the Lat. 'happy') Procurator of Judea 53-60, during the critical period of revolts of the Zealots and *Sicarii,* Felix conducted the first trial of

Paul the Apostle at Caesarea, and left him in custody two years later for his successor, Porcius Festus.

Antonius Claudius and his brother Pallas were Greek subjects, made freedmen by the Emperor Claudius, 41-54. They became favourites first of Claudius and then of Nero, 54-68. Antonius, who had received the name of Felix, enters the New Testament story of the early Christian Church on his appointment as procurator of Judea in the year 53. The impression of him given by Luke's narrative in Acts, particularly in his dealings with Paul, is one of dilatory inefficiency. There is no need to doubt Luke's eyewitness account and careful report of these events. Other historians of the time are far less generous and more caustic in their assessment of his character.

The Jewish historian, Josephus, describes Felix's heavy hand in suppressing the constant disorder within his territory. Felix appears to have been compromised in the murder of the high priest, Jonathan, and to have sent other priests for trial to Rome, despite his appointment by Claudius on the grounds of his sympathy with Jewry and his marriage to a Jewish princess. (see DRUSILLA) Josephus wrote two accounts of Felix, one in the *War* about 80, one ten years later in the *Antiquities* which enumerates the 'crimes' of Felix. The Roman historian, Tacitus, accused Felix of fomenting strife between the Jews and Samaritans for his own personal profit and said that Felix 'revelled in cruelty and lust, and exercised the powers of a king with the outlook of a slave'. Suetonius regarded Felix as a military adventurer, who married three queens in the course of his adventurous career.

Luke's narrative in Acts, of the trial of Paul by Felix, gives perhaps the earliest and most independent eyewitness impression of Felix. Both the prosecution and the defence felt that he would respond to flattery and began accordingly. However impressive the prosecutor Tertullus may have been, the defence of Paul, trained in the famous law school of Tarsus, was more than a match for him. Felix, 'having a rather accurate knowledge of the Way', as Luke puts it, adjourned the trial until the arrival of the Roman tribune from Jerusalem. *see* CLAUDIUS LYSIAS) Paul must have convinced Felix of his innocence, for the procurator behaved kindly, allowing him some liberty and permitting Paul's friends to care for his needs.

A few days later, Felix sent for Paul and, together with his Jewish wife Drusilla, listened to Paul speaking about the 'faith in Christ Jesus'. As Paul argued about 'justice and self-control and future judgment', Felix became alarmed and dismissed him, thinking perhaps that Paul would bribe him to secure release. After two years in protective custody, Paul was left by Felix under close arrest. Felix had in fact been recalled to Rome to stand his own trial for misgovernment, and, seeking favour with the Jews, left Paul in prison.

Felix suffered banishment, and lost his only son by Drusilla in the great eruption of Mount Vesuvius in the year 79. [Acts 23, 24]

FESTUS (Gk. 'joyful') The Roman procurator who succeeded Felix in Judea, of whom little is known before this particular appointment by the Emperor Nero. Porcius Festus, according to the Jewish historian Josephus, did what he could to restore peace by the vigour of his methods, but died only two years after his appointment.

On his arrival at Caesarea, Festus soon started for Jerusalem to consult with the leading Jews, for his predecessor (*see* FELIX) had left the Apostle Paul unconvicted after two years in custody, but now under close arrest. The chief priests demanded Paul's transfer to Jerusalem for trial, but arranged for him to be ambushed *en route*. Festus in turn requested them to accompany him down to Caesarea and there to accuse Paul.

Ten days later, at Caesarea, Festus presided at a tribunal at which many serious charges were brought against Paul, who denied them all with the words, 'Neither against the law of the Jews, nor against the temple, nor against Caesar have I offended at all.' (Acts 25:8) Festus, apparently to placate the Jews, then invited Paul to accompany him to Jerusalem for trial, not by the Jews but by himself as procurator. At this point Paul felt he had no alternative but to make his appeal to Caesar, the ancient right of all Roman citizens since the year 449 BC. 'I am standing before Caesar's tribunal, where I ought to be tried; to the Jews I have done no wrong, as you know very well. If then I am a wrongdoer, and have committed anything for which I deserve to die, I do not seek to escape death; but if there is nothing in their charges against me, no one can give me up to them. I appeal to Caesar.' (Acts 25:10, 11) After consulting his advisers, Festus answered, 'You have appealed to Caesar, to Caesar you shall go.'

Some days afterwards, King Agrippa and his sister Bernice arrived at Caesarea with pomp to welcome the new procurator. Festus took the opportunity to present Paul's case to the king, in order to enable him, as procurator, to draw up a report of the charges against Paul. Paul rose to the occasion with a magnificent defence calculated to appeal to the Jewish sympathies of Agrippa and Bernice, and summing up the Christian gospel as a proclamation of the fulfillment of Messianic prophecy. 'For this reason the Jews seized me in the temple and tried to kill me. To this day I have had the help that comes from God, and so I stand here testifying both to small and great, saying nothing but what the prophets and Moses said would come to pass: that the Christ must suffer, and that, by being the first to rise from the dead, he would proclaim light both to the people and to the Gentiles.' (Acts 26:21-23)

At this point, Festus loudly declared, ' "Paul, you are mad; your great learning is turning you mad." But Paul said, "I am not mad, most excellent Festus, but I am speaking the sober truth." ' (Acts 26:24-25) After further exchanges between Agrippa and Paul, the king and the governor withdrew and agreed together, ' "This man is doing nothing to deserve death or imprisonment." And Agrippa said to Festus, "This man could have been set free if he had not appealed to Caesar." ' (Acts 26:31-32) Despite Agrippa's considered verdict of 'not guilty', Festus could not legally disregard Paul's own appeal to Caesar and made the necessary arrangements for his escort and journey as a prisoner to Rome.

There is no comparison between the inefficient procrastination of Felix and the efficient despatch of Festus, who died unexpectedly at his post two years later. [Acts 25, 26]

FORTUNATUS (Gk. 'blessed', 'fortunate') Fortunatus was a Christian member of the household of Stephanas in Corinth.

Writing from Ephesus in the year 55, during his Third Journey to the Church in Corinth which he had founded some four years before, Paul closes his letter: 'I rejoice at the coming of Stephanas and Fortunatus and Achaicus, because they have made up for your absence; for they have refreshed my spirit as well as yours. Give recognition to such men.'

Apparently the household of Stephanas included slaves and employees, such as Fortunatus and Achaicus.

This was the first household to have been converted by Paul – and the only household to have been baptized by Paul – in Corinth, on his Second Journey in the year 51. These three men had travelled to Ephesus on business, possibly carrying a letter to Paul from Corinth, and were probably present with Paul as he completed the dictation of his answering letter. [1 Cor. 16:17]

FREEDMEN (*also* LIBERTINES) (Gk. 'free') 'Libertine' is a Latin word for freedman, referring to a Roman Jew who had obtained his liberty. Following Pompey's capture of Jerusalem in the year 63 BC, many captives had been deported to Rome, where by now they or their children had obtained their liberty to return home. It seems that there was in Jerusalem a synagogue of such men, though some scholars, such as Moffat, would transpose 'Libertine' into 'Libyan' within this context, in order to form a list of three groups of Jews from Africa: Libyans, Cyrenians, and Alexandrians.

Traditionally there were 480 synagogues in Jerusalem. These were the meeting-places for prayer and discussion – particularly about the Law – of many different peoples of Jewish faith. At the time of Stephen's martyrdom, it was the natives of Alexandria and Cyrene in Africa and of the Roman privinces of Asia and Cilicia (the home of Saul the Persecutor who was to become Paul the Apostle) who took the initiative in Stephen's arrest. It was the members of these synagogues who took most offence at Stephen's teaching, but could not successfully dispute with his wisdom and enthusiasm.

In consequence, they instigated the crowd to accuse him of talking blasphemy against Moses and God, for the Jew the ultimate wickedness. The mob dragged Stephen off to the Council and accused him of speaking both against the Temple as the official centre of worship, and against the Law. Members of the synagogue of the Freedmen were first mentioned among those who secured Stephen's condemnation and stoning. [Acts 6:9]

G

GABRIEL (Heb. 'man of God') One of the seven archangels, the messenger of divine comfort, Gabriel is accorded a place in Jewish theology second only to Michael. Appropriately, his feast-day is the day before that of the Annunciation of the Blessed Virgin Mary. Only in the Book of Enoch is he given the status of archangel (Chapters 9, 20 and 40). Twice in the Book of Daniel he appears to interpret visions. Twice in Luke's Gospel he appears to announce miraculous births: first to Zechariah, the priest in the Temple, the birth of John the Baptist, forerunner and cousin of Jesus; second to Mary, the mother of Jesus.

On the occasion of Zechariah's turn in the Temple in Jerusalem, when he was chosen for the great privilege of entering the sanctuary to burn incense there, the congregation remaining outside at prayer, Zechariah received a vision.

He saw an angel standing by the altar of incense, and he was overcome with fright. He heard the angel speaking to him: ' "Do not be afraid, Zechariah, for your prayer is heard, and your wife Elizabeth will bear you a son, and you shall call his name John. And you will have joy and gladness, and many will rejoice at his birth; for he will be great before the Lord, and he shall drink no wine nor strong drink, and he will be filled with the Holy Spirit, even from his mother's womb.

And he will turn many of the sons of Israel to the Lord their God, and he will go before him in the spirit and power of Elijah, to turn the hearts of the fathers to the children, and the disobedient to the wisdom of the just, to make ready for the Lord a people prepared." And Zechariah said to the angel, "How shall I know this? For I am an old man, and my wife is advanced in years." And the angel answered him, "I am Gabriel, who stand in the presence of God; and I was sent to speak to you, and to bring you this good news. And behold, you will be silent and unable to speak until the day that these things come to pass, because you did not believe my words, which will be fulfilled in their time." ' (Luke 1:13-20)

The visit of Gabriel to the peasant girl Mary at Nazareth is told also with consummate artistry by Luke. 'In the sixth month the angel Gabriel was sent from God to a city of Galilee named Nazareth, to a virgin betrothed to a man whose name was Joseph, of the house of David; and the virgin's name was Mary.' (Luke 1:26-27) In a single sentence, the sender, the messenger, and the receiver are introduced: God Almighty, the angel Gabriel and the girl betrothed to the village carpenter. 'And he came to her and said, "Hail, O favoured one, the Lord is with you!" But she was greatly troubled at the saying, and considered in her mind what sort of greeting this might be. And the angel said to her, "Do not be afraid, Mary, for you have found favour with God." ' (Luke 1:28-30) The divine choice of Mary implies her utter devotion and dedication; even the angel delivers his message with reverence and humility: 'Hail Mary, full of grace'; she is disturbed and ashamed at the extravagant greeting.

Then the burden of the message (is it a command or an invitation?): 'And behold, you will conceive in your womb and bear a son, and you shall call his name Jesus. He will be great, and will be called the Son of the Most High; and the Lord will give to him the throne of his father David, and he will reign over the house of Jacob for ever; and of his kingdom there will be no end.' (Luke 1:31-33) Mary's reply is no refusal, but only an enquiry as to how she is to accept. 'And Mary said to the angel, "How can this be, since I have no husband?" ' (Luke 1:34) It is only then that the messenger can unfold the divine plan of the sender. 'And the angel said to her, "The Holy Spirit will come upon you, and the power of the Most High will overshadow you; therefore the child to be born will be called holy, the Son of God." ' (Luke 1:35) Momentarily, the divine plan for the redemption of mankind waited upon the acceptance of this little Jewish girl, before she sealed her acceptance with that stupendously humble *fiat*: 'And Mary said, "Behold, I am the handmaid of the Lord; let it be to me according to your word." And the angel departed from her.' (Luke 1:38) [Luke 1:19,26]

GADARENES (Gk. 'inhabitants of Gadara') One of the three names for the people in whose country Jesus cured a savage and untamable demoniac, who lived in the tombs and mountains overlooking the Lake of Galilee. The unclean spirits were exorcised from the man, whose very name was Legion (they were so many), and at their own request were allowed to go into a herd of pigs, who immediately ran over the cliff into the lake and were drowned. The proximity to the pagan cities of the Decapolis would account for the presence of the pigs.

The story is virtually the same in all three Synoptic Gospels, though the original narrative in Mark is understandably more graphic in detail, but the names, or cities, of the people concerned vary. Thus in Mark it is the country of the Gerasenes, from the city of Gerasa (the modern Jerash) 50 miles south-east of the Lake of Galilee, beyond Ajlun. This, however, is obviously a mistaken identification by Mark, the Palestinian, who seems to have been muddled between the various cities of the Decapolis, for Gerasa is too far from the lakeside to be appropriate. Then, in Matthew, it is the country of the Gadarenes, from the city of Gadara (possibly identified with Um Keis, whose ruins are on a steep hill) 5 miles south-east of the lake and south of the Yarmuk River. Like Gerasa, Gadara was a city of the Decapolis with its own hot springs, baths, and public buildings, though on a far smaller scale than those still to be seen at Jerash. 'The country of the Gadarenes' is a more likely identification with the story.

Luke's Gospel poses yet a third possibility in some manuscripts, some of which have 'the country of the Gergesenes' instead of either Gerasenes or Gadarenes. Gergesa has been identified with the ruins of Khersa, well to the north of Hippos and the modern Ein Gev, at the only point on the east coast where the steep slopes reach right down to the shore. It is possible that Gergesa, a smaller town, may have been under the jurisdiction of the city of Gadara, the 'best fortified city in Perea', and that the area of Gergesa was rightly called 'the country of the Gadarenes'. Certainly the cliffs of Khersa illustrate the dramatic events of the story very well indeed. [Matt. 8:28; Mark 5:1; Luke 8:26]

GAIUS (Gk. 'the name of a Christian') **1.** One of the converts baptized personally by Paul at Corinth. [1 Cor. 1:14]

2. A prominent member of the Christian community at Corinth, who joined his greetings to those of Paul, at the close of Paul's letter to the Church in Rome. Paul was staying in his house while the letter was being written, and his house seems to have been the meeting-place for Christians at Corinth, or perhaps a lodging-house for Christians travelling over the Isthmus of Corinth. [Rom. 16:23]

3. A Macedonian travelling-companion of Paul, arrested in Ephesus during the silversmiths' riot. Gaius and Aristarchus were dragged into the great theatre, still to be seen at Ephesus, which was the scene of a vast demonstration in the name of Artemis (Diana) of the Ephesians, whose famous temple was the cathedral shrine of paganism in the eastern Mediterranean. Paul was dissuaded from venturing into the theatre at the height of the commotion. The assembly was dismissed by the town clerk and, presumably, Gaius and Aristarchus were released, if a little the worse for wear. [Acts 19:29]

4. A Galatian from Derbe, who accompanied Paul from Corinth to Jerusalem, as one of the many representatives of the newly-founded churches, chosen to deliver the money collected for the poor of Jerusalem. The name of Aristarchus is also listed, which implies that possibly both the men arrested at Ephesus travelled with Paul to Corinth and later returned to Jerusalem with him. [Acts 20:4]

5. The addressee of the last letter of John the Elder. This man lived on after the turn of the 1st century, that is, well after the life of Paul. He was a respected and influential member of some congregation in Asia Minor, within range of Ephesus, the probable home of John the Elder who encouraged his continued support and leadership. [3 John 1]

GALATIANS Paul's letter to the Galatians has been described as the *Magna Carta* of Christian freedom. His plea for freedom from legalistic codes presents timeless

Christian principles. Paul's attack on the influence of extraneous religious practices on the belief in God, as revealed through Jesus, is nowhere so clearly stated as in this letter. He singled out the danger of the rigid observance of external rules as a fundamental stumbling-block of his day; and it is still a relevant issue in the Christian Church today.

There were two Galatias in New Testament times: the old kingdom of Galatia along the south coast of the Black Sea, and the Roman province of Galatia, an enlargement of the kingdom and bordering the Mediterranean to include those towns visited by Paul and Barnabas on the First Journey. Paul's letter was intended either for the Christian Churches of the Roman province at Iconium, Lystra, and Derbe, or for other Christian communities further north which Paul visited briefly during his Second Journey on the way to Ephesus. It is possible that his letter to the Galatians was written either from Syrian Antioch on his return from the Second Journey, or from Ephesus during his Third Journey, between the years 53 and 57.

His letter to the Galatians is second only in writing among Paul's letters to the Thessalonian correspondence. It reveals many valuable details of Paul's earlier life and activity, with which the parallel accounts in Acts are not always easily reconciled. It may be that Luke's history of the early Church in Acts was written as a brief for the legal defence of Paul in Rome, but even its powerful and polished presentation does not carry the same authority as the more personal and spontaneous witness of Paul's own letters. Luke's description of Paul's visit to the Galatian Churches with their particular problems is wholly compatible, however, with the contents of the letter of Paul which was intended to tackle those problems.

The challenge to orthodoxy

Paul had heard that agents of a party among the Jewish
Christians had 'furtively crept in to spy on the liberty
we enjoy in Christ Jesus and wanted to reduce us all to
slavery'. The emissaries of that party were insisting that
Paul's Gentile converts in Galatia should be circumcised
and keep the Mosaic Law, as a necessary condition for
entering the Christian Church. To Paul this demand
seemed a complete contradiction of the free grace of
God and a denial of the sufficiency of redemption
through Jesus. 'We ourselves, who are Jews by birth
and not Gentile sinners, yet who know that a man is not
justified by works of the law but through faith in Jesus
Christ, even we have believed in Christ Jesus, in order
to be justified by faith in Christ, and not by works of
the law, because by works of the law shall no one be
justified. . . . For I through the law died to the law,
that I might live to God. I have been crucified with
Christ; it is no longer I who live, but Christ who lives in
me; and the life I now live in the flesh I live by faith in
the Son of God, who loved me and gave himself for me.
I do not nullify the grace of God; for if justification
were through the law, then Christ died to no purpose.'
(Gal. 2:15, 16; 19-21)

Paul saw in the demands of these Jewish Christians
the danger that Christianity would become a party
among believers in Judaism rather than a universal
faith. Paul was willing that Jewish Christians should
continue to keep their ancient national customs, but
they should not try to impose them on Christians of
other cultures and nations. Such observances were not
necessary for salvation.

The Council of Jerusalem (described in Acts 15)
had already ruled on this issue with an absolute mini-

mum of regulation. 'And when they perceived the grace that was given to me, James and Cephas and John, who were reputed to be pillars, gave to me and Barnabas the right hand of fellowship, that we should go to the Gentiles and they to the circumcised; only they would have us remember the poor, which very thing I was eager to do.' (Gal. 2:9, 10) Paul, seeing clearly that some of the Jewish Christians wanted to turn the Christian Church into a select circle within Judaism rather than the universal society intended by Jesus, held the whole Christian Church to the decision of the Council. In order to convince the Jewish Christians from their own scriptures, Paul justified his action by a careful exposition of Old Testament history.

First, he boldly cites the blessing and faith of Abraham, father of the Jewish race: 'Thus Abraham "believed God, and it was reckoned to him as righteousness". So you see that it is men of faith who are the sons of Abraham. And the scripture, foreseeing that God would justify the Gentiles by faith, preached the gospel beforehand to Abraham, saying, "In you shall all the nations be blessed." So then, those who are men of faith are blessed with Abraham who had faith.' (Gal. 3:6-9) Paul then quotes the Book of Deuteronomy to show that the law brings a curse upon all who fail to keep it in full, but states that Jesus has redeemed man by taking that curse upon himself, through the shameful death of crucifixion. The Book of Leviticus says, 'Cursed be everyone who hangs on a tree.' This was done, says Paul, 'that in Christ Jesus the blessing of Abraham might come upon the Gentiles, that we might receive the promise of the Spirit through faith'. (Gal. 3:14)

In other words, the promise of Abraham is fulfilled in the death and resurrection of Jesus. And since the Law was given 430 years later than the promise, it is secondary to the promise which has been fulfilled in Jesus. In fact, says Paul, the Law served the purpose of a tutor or guardian for mankind, until mankind 'came of age' with the coming of Jesus.

'Now before faith came, we were confined under the law, kept under restraint until faith should be revealed. So that the law was our custodian until Christ came, that we might be justified by faith. But now that faith has come, we are no longer under a custodian; for in Christ Jesus you are all sons of God, through faith. For as many of you as were baptized into Christ have put on Christ. There is neither Jew nor Greek, there is neither slave nor free, there is neither male nor female; for you are all one in Christ Jesus. And if you are Christ's, then you are Abraham's offspring, heirs according to promise.' (Gal. 3:23-29)

Finally, Paul takes the analogy of 'coming of age' one step further. If faith in Jesus is the condition of adoption into the family of Abraham and of the inheriting of the promise to Abraham, so the Spirit of Jesus in people's hearts make them both the sons and heirs of God himself. 'But when the time had fully come, God sent forth his son, born of woman, born under the law, to redeem those who were under the law, so that we might receive adoption as sons. And because you are sons, God has sent the Spirit of his Son into our hearts, crying, "Abba! Father!" So through God you are no longer a slave but a son, and if a son then an heir.' (Gal. 4:7) [Gal. 1-6]

GALILEANS (Gk. from the Heb. 'circuit') The mixed population of the Roman-ruled district between the Mediterranean and the Lake of Galilee, ruled successively by Herod Antipas (4 BC-AD 39) from Sepphoris and then Tiberias, by Agrippa I (39-44) and, after a short time within the Roman province of Syria, by Agrippa II (48-53).

The name Galilee, from the Hebrew *galil* meaning 'circuit', is applied to any well-defined region. Galilee of the Gentiles, *Galil ha-Goim,* the 'Region of the Gentiles', was the name given to the northern province of Israel, because it was surrounded on three sides by foreigners. Following the return from Babylon, the district remained largely Gentile, but by the 1st century BC was thoroughly Judaized. The words 'of the Gentiles' were dropped from the title of the district, which then became proudly known as 'The Region'.

The most striking feature of Galilee, in the time of Jesus, was the system of roads crossing the district in all directions, from the Levant to Damascus and the East, from Jerusalem to Antioch, from the Nile to the Euphrates. The fertility and the good communications of the district resulted in the growth of a considerable population, engaged in local industry and commerce, concentrated largely upon the lakeside. Unlike Judea, whose desert borders exerted an austere influence on that province, Galilee was surrounded by pagan and colonial townships, which poured upon Galilee the full influence of Greek life and leisure.

All these features – the wealth of water, the extreme fertility, the great highways, the considerable population, the Greek influences – were crowded into the Rift Valley, in tropical heat, round a blue and lovely lake. These were the conditions in which Jesus taught and worked – and under which Christianity began to grow. It takes very little imagination today, as one looks down on the rather sleepy and deserted lakeside, to picture the nine cities round the lake, each of not less than 15,000 inhabitants. Of these cities, Tiberias and Magdala were on the western shore, Gadara and Hippos on the

163

eastern hills, Bethsaida, Capernaum, and Chorazin to the north, but the remaining two are unlocated.

The catalogue of towns around the lake conjures up for us an almost unbroken line of buildings. Little remains of the city walls, houses, synagogues, wharves, and factories; of the castle, temples, and theatres of Tiberias, the bath-houses at Hammath, the hippodrome of Tarichae, the amphitheatre and the Greek villas at Gadara. All this was once imposed on the simple open-air life of fields, roads, and boats that we see in the Gospels.

Jesus drew his disciples from the hardy fisherfolk of Galilee. He called them out of a highly temperamental and turbulent population, concentrated within the deep trench and intense heat of the Rift Valley, which further served to inflame the spirit of nationalism and revolt among the Galileans. Jesus, however, went to a trade which had no private wrongs and which was content to work from day to day, whose members had the time and opportunity to escape from the crowds to the fishing-grounds out on the lake in peace. So it is not the jargon of the fanatics or brigands, or of the Zealots hiding in the highlands of Galilee, but the speech of the fishermen and their simple craft that have become the language and symbolism of Christianity. Even the Gospels reflect a Judean disrespect for the rugged rustics and strangers of Galilee, referring to Peter's Galilean patois, which betrayed him at the trial of Jesus. Pilate's mingling of Galilean blood with their sacrifices was a foretaste of the frightful suppression of the Zealot revolt in 66, when the lake ran red with the blood of Galileans.

At Bethphage on the Mount of Olives there was a Galilean settlement, indicated by the discovery of a 1st-century ossuary with the name of 'Galileans', in 1923.

The inhabitants of Bethany were also mostly Galileans, therefore Jesus when visiting Mary, Martha and Lazarus stayed with his compatriots. This fact may also explain the ease with which the disciples were able to procure the donkey for the triumphal entry of Jesus into Jerusalem, on Palm Sunday. The men at the crossroads were probably fellow-Galileans. [Mark 14:70; Luke 13:1; 22:59; 23:6; John 4:45; Acts 2:7]

GALLIO The proconsul of Achaia, appointed by the Emperor Claudius in the year 52, who declined to adjudicate when the Jews brought Paul before the tribunal at Corinth, in the course of his Second Journey.

Lucius Junius Gallio's appointment, which incidentally pinpoints the end of Paul's visit to Corinth and his return via Ephesus and Caesarea to Antioch, is one of the very few certain dates in the apostolic period. This is because Gallio's appointment was included in an inscription discovered at Delphi, in Greece, in 1905.

The Apostle Paul had spent 18 months in Corinth, working with Aquila and Priscilla, both tentmaking and building up the young Christian Church in that very pagan city. No doubt, as elsewhere, the Jewish synagogue had provided both the pulpit and the congregation for Paul's preaching. Certainly, it was the Jews, probably led by their synagogue ruler, Sosthenes, who took Paul up before the tribunal, saying, 'This man is persuading people to worship God contrary to the Law.' Before Paul could even answer the charge, Gallio the proconsul, as the judge, dismissed the case with these words, 'If it were a matter of wrongdoing or vicious crime, I should have reason to bear with you, O Jews; but since it is a matter of questions about words and names and your own law, see to it yourselves; I refuse to be a judge of these things.' (Acts 18:14, 15) And Gallio ordered the court to be cleared.

Gallio's decision was that the prosecution had no case, but the charge against Paul was a cunning one and quite different from that brought by the Jews at Thessalonica. There, they accused Paul and his followers of 'acting against the decrees of Caesar, saying that there is another king, Jesus', at which the magistrates were somewhat disturbed, but must have realized that the accusation was absurd. Here, at Corinth, the Roman proconsul Gallio was asked to decide whether Paul's teaching was contrary to the Law and put him beyond the pale of Judaism, and particularly outside the toleration by the Roman law afforded to Jews. Gallio, however, had the philosophical temperament of his Stoic brother Seneca, and was far too good a lawyer to entertain such a charge. He simply acquitted Paul and cleared the court.

Immediately the Greeks, perhaps even those who had listened to Paul from the God-fearers' courtyard attached to the synagogue, seized Sosthenes the ruler of the synagogue and very possibly Paul's chief prosecutor. They beat Sosthenes in front of the tribunal, but Gallio 'paid no attention' or, as one text put it, 'pretended not to see'.

Gallio was the elder brother of the Stoic philosopher Seneca. [Acts 18:12, 17]

GAMALIEL (Gk. from the Heb. 'reward of God') The great and highly respected Pharisee and doctor of the Law, at whose feet the Apostle Paul claimed to have been educated in Jerusalem, 'according to the strict manner of the Law of our fathers'. Gamaliel was one of the seven rabbis to be honoured with the supreme title of *Rabban*.

Gamaliel was the pupil and grandson of Hillel, who together with his rival Shammai formed the last great 'pair' to hand down the tradition of the Law. Each of them held a distinctive interpretation and had a following or school of interpretation. The school of Hillel, and, of course, Gamaliel, represented the realist, the liberal, and the merciful application of the Law, as exemplified by the outlook of the Pharisees. That of Shammai represented the more rigid, the theoretical and the unimaginative atttitude of the Sadducees to the Law.

When Peter and John, among the apostles in Jerusalem, were arrested in the Temple area for preaching the Messiahship of Jesus, it was the influential Pharisee Gamaliel who took the initiative in securing their release. He prevailed upon the Sadducees in the Sanhedrin, or Council of Justice, by using an argument that was both typically generous and also highly practical: 'Men of Israel, take care what you do with these men'; then Gamaliel proceeded to remind the Council of others whose Messianic claims had perished with them and their followers in the past, and he declared, 'So in the present case I tell you, keep away from these men and let them alone; for if this plan or this undertaking is of men, it will fail; but if it is of God, you will not be able to overthrow them. You might even be found opposing God!' (Acts 5:35-39)

It is perhaps not surprising that the firebrand and persecutor of the early Christian Church, Saul of Tarsus, should have mellowed to the generous wisdom of 'Paul, the aged'. Paul was justifiably proud of being a Jew and a Pharisee, trained in the lecture-room of the great Gamaliel of whom the Talmud says: 'Since the Rabban Gamaliel died, the glory of the Law has ceased.' [Acts 5:34; 22:3]

GAZELLE *see* TABITHA

GENTILES (from the Heb. 'nation', 'people') The Hebrew word *goy* usually implies a non-Israelite people. The Greek *ethnos,* used as a translation for *goy,* indicates 'nation', and as such the word appears mostly in the Revised Standard Version, though in the King James Version the word 'Gentile' is more common. This word 'Gentile' was used of all non-Jews who were considered 'outside the mercy' of the God of Israel.

Jesus and Gentiles

In the 1st century, most Jews believed that the only hope for the Gentiles was for them to accept the Jewish Law. If they did so, being circumcised and making the necessary offering, keeping the Sabbath and food laws and regulations of conduct, they were called 'proselytes'. Other Gentiles were attracted to the Jewish belief in one God and attended worship in the Gentile courtyard of the snyagogues, but were not circumcised. Such were called 'God-fearers', of which one was certainly the centurion at Capernaum, who built the synagogue there. (Luke 7)

Although Galilee of the Gentiles was ringed round (that is the meaning of the word) by Gentile districts, Jesus had remarkably little contact with foreigners during his public ministry. There is record of only one crossing of the border into Phoenicia on the Syria coastline, and a single visit to the Decapolis, the league of ten Greco-Roman colonial cities east of Jordan. Indeed, the more Hebrew Gospel of Matthew specifically describes Jesus's instructions to his disciples, 'Go nowhere among the Gentiles, and enter no town of the Samaritans, but go rather to the lost sheep of the house of Israel.' (Matt. 10:5, 6) At the end of the same Gospel, however, Jesus's final commission to his apostles is all-embracing and universal, 'All authority in heaven and on earth has been given to me. Go therefore and make disciples of all nations, baptizing them in the name of the Father and the Son and of the Holy Spirit.' (Matt. 28:18, 19)

In spite of this, the leaders of the early Christian Church in Jerusalem seem to have been at first rather unwilling to extend their message to the Gentiles. Their early conservatism proved a considerable obstacle to the missionary policy of Paul, though many of the apostles subsequently travelled extensively throughout the Mediterranean and beyond.

In spite of Matthew's portrayal of a rather exclusive ministry, the personal attitude of Jesus to Gentiles seems to have been highly sympathetic and pastoral. (see SYRO-PHOENICIAN, SAMARITAN, CENTURION, LEGION and PILATE) For reasons of practical policy, his immediate mission was to his own people and confined largely to Galilee. There, the climatic conditions and the intensity of the population were ideal for his purpose of selecting and training a group of disciples. The Rift Valley of the lakeside was a trench well dug to receive the Word of God and the humid climate calculated to germinate seeds quickly in a warm emotional soil.

Jewish people, as their scriptures and history reveal, were prepared in a way that no other nation was to expect a saviour or deliverer. Other nations contributed to the preparation by the spread of a common Greek language throughout the Mediterranean, and of the Roman communications-system and security of travel by land and sea. Hence the time, the place and – above all – the people to receive the gospel; the Jewish people were to be 'the sacred school of the knowledge of God and of the spiritual life for all mankind'. Though Jesus's mission was primarily to his own people, it was of vital importance that they should be prepared to share the good news with the Gentile world.

It was necessary to his purpose that his own people

169

should recognize and discharge their mission to their neighbours. The parable of the Good Samaritan, in answer to the question 'Who is my neighbour?', is of great significance to the propagation of the gospel to the world. The priest and the Levite represent the particularist element in the ecclesiastical system, but it was the foreigner who behaved like a neighbour. How much more should the true Israelite behave like a neighbour to his Samaritan cousins, rather than foster a policy of apartheid towards foreigners.

When Jesus cleared the Temple area of the merchants buying and selling, with the words 'Is it not written, "My house shall be called a house of prayer for all the nations"? But you have made it a den of robbers.' (Mark 11:17), only Mark included the important words 'for all nations'. It is Luke, however, possibly the only Gentile evangelist, who brings out the destiny of the Gentiles within the purpose of God. Luke records the words of Simeon at the presentation in the Temple, that the child Jesus is to be 'a light to lighten the Gentiles', as well as to be 'the glory of Israel his people'. Both Luke and Matthew record the words of Jesus: 'You will weep and gnash your teeth, when you see Abraham and Isaac and Jacob and all the prophets in the kingdom of God and you yourselves thrust out. And men will come from east and west, and from north and south, and sit at table in the kingdom of God.' (Luke 13:28-29) Luke alone quotes Jesus as explaining the purpose of his crucifixion and resurrection, 'that repentance and forgiveness of sins should be preached in his name to all nations, beginning from Jerusalem.' (Luke 24:47)

On the day of Pentecost, Peter was crystal-clear in his instructions to potential new recruits to the following of Jesus: ' "Repent, and be baptized every one of you in the name of Jesus Christ for the forgiveness of your sins; and you shall receive the gift of the Holy Spirit. For the promise is to you and to your children and to all that are far off, every one whom the Lord our God calls to him.' And they devoted themselves to the Apostles' teaching and fellowship, to the breaking of bread and the prayers.' (Acts 2:38-39, 42) Thus, in theory baptism replaced circumcision, the Eucharist took the place of the Passover, and the weekly commemoration of the resurrection (the first day of the week) replaced the Sabbath (the seventh day).

Just as Israel had been known as 'the people of God', so this new community thought of itself as 'the Church of the Messiah', bound together by a paschal and personal experience of salvation by the action of Jesus. The young Christian Church felt that it owed allegiance to a new covenant, ratified in the blood of Jesus on the cross, a covenant, however, not restricted to Jews alone but to the world at large. The practical, ritual and social difficulties of extending the membership of the hitherto Judeo-Christian Church to Gentiles were faced and largely solved by the Apostle Paul.

Apostle to the Gentiles

Paul's attitude to the Gentiles sprang from his own conversion, experience, and direct commission as the Apostle to the Gentiles. As he declared to the Galatian Churches: God 'called me through his grace, was pleased to reveal his Son to me, in order that I might preach him among the Gentiles . . .' (Gal. 1:15, 16) In the vision of Ananias, the Lord had said to him, 'Go, for he is a chosen instrument of mine to carry my name before the Gentiles and kings and the sons of Israel; for I will show him how much he must suffer for the sake of my name.' (Acts 9:15, 16)

The Apostles Peter and Barnabas at Antioch, the headquarters of the Gentile Church, were intellectually convinced that there could be no distinction within the Christian Church between Jew and Gentile, but they wavered under the heavy barrage of criticism by Jewish Christians in Jerusalem. The end of Paul's letter to the Galatians reflects the early tensions between the two main parties within the infant Church: those followers of Jesus, who like him had been born and bred Jews, and who felt that one could not be a Christian without also being a Jew; and those followers of Jesus – whether Jew or Greek or Turk – who could not bear the double yoke of being a Jew as well as a Christian. The first are sometimes called Judaizers, the second Hellenists.

On the return of Paul and Barnabas to Antioch from their First Journey in Asia Minor, they found that emissaries from the Jerusalem Church had raised the whole question of the relation of Christian converts from paganism to the Jewish Law. Christian Pharisees put forward the view that since the Christian Church was the direct heir of ancient Israel, converts from paganism should in the ordinary way become Jews by submitting to the rite of circumcision and accepting the obligations of the Law. Antioch took a different view. Paul and Barnabas went up to Jerusalem, and the matter was discussed. Paul's account of the conference is somewhat different from that given in Acts, which perhaps represents the Jerusalem account of the matter. In Paul's view, he was given a perfectly free hand. According to Acts 15, certain minimum restrictions on Gentile converts were laid down. But in any case the issue was in substance a victory for the more liberal party. The demand that converts from paganism should be circumcised and subject themselves to the Mosaic Law was set aside. Paul evidently took this to imply that henceforward Gentile Christians stood on exactly the same footing as Jews, enjoying full rights of intercourse with Jewish Christians.

Following Paul's rebuke to Peter for withdrawing from 'table-fellowship' with Gentile Christians while in Antioch, where Jewish and Gentile Church members seem to have practised 'open communion', Paul defended integration as a vital principle. It may be that his change of missionary partners from Barnabas the Cypriot to the Roman citizen Silas strengthened his hand. His classical statement of 'justification by faith' in the letter to the Christians at Rome explains his reasons. 'For man believes with his heart and so is justified, and he confesses with his lips and so is saved. The scripture says, "No one who believes in him will be put to shame." For there is no distinction between Jew and Greek; the same Lord is Lord of all and bestows his riches upon all who call upon him. For, "everyone who calls upon the name of the Lord will be saved".' (Rom. 10:10-13)

Paul is careful, however, to emphasize the part of his own people in God's plan of salvation and the debt owed to them by Gentiles. 'Now I am speaking to you Gentiles . . . but if some of the branches were broken off, and you, a wild olive shoot, were grafted in their place to share the richness of the olive tree, do not boast over the branches. If you do boast, remember it is not you that support the root, but the root that supports you. . . . You have been cut from what is by nature a wild olive tree, and grafted, contrary to nature, into a cultivated olive tree.' (Rom. 11:13, 17, 18, 24)

The universalism of the Second Isaiah thus finally flourished within the second generation of the Christian Church. 'Here there cannot be Greek and Jew, circumcised and uncircumcised, barbarian, Scythians, slave,

free man, but Christ is all, and in all.' (Col. 3:11)
[Matt. 4:15; 6:32; 10:5, 18; 12:21; 20:19, 25; Mark
10:33; Luke 18:32; 21:24; 22:25; John 7:35; Acts
7:45; 9:15; 10:45; 11:1, 18; 13:46, 48; 14:2, 27;
15:3-23; 18:6; 21:19, 21, 25; 22:21; 26:20, 23; 28:28;
Rom. 1:13; 2:14, 24; 3:29; 9:24, 30; 11:11-25; 15:9-
27; 16:4; 1 Cor. 1:22-24; 10:20, 32; 12:2, 13; Gal.
2:2-15; 3:14; Eph. 2:11; 3:1-8; 4:17; Col. 1:27; 1
Thess. 2:16; 4:5; 1 Tim. 2:7; 1 Pet. 2:12; 4:3; 3 John
7 (in some cases translated as 'Greeks' or 'pagans' in the
RSV)]

GERASENES (Gk. 'inhabitants of Gerasa') *see* GADAR-
ENES

GERGESENES (Gk. 'inhabitants of Gergesa;) *see*
GADARENES

GRECIANS *see* GREEKS

GREEKS The two words for Greeks are used in the
New Testament to indicate three different groups of
people. The word 'Hellenes' is used to describe those of
Greek descent in the narrow sense: Timothy's father
was a Greek. (Acts 16:1, 3) Paul in the synagogue at
Corinth persuaded both Jews and Greeks. (Acts 18:4)
Paul thought himself sent to Greeks and barbarians and
Romans. (Rom. 1:14) The same word 'Hellenes', however, can imply anyone not of Jewish extraction, in a
more general sense: Greeks attending the Jewish Passover asked to see Jesus. (John 12:20) Paul declared
the gospel to be the power for salvation to Jews and
also to Greeks. (Rom. 1:16) For him there was no distinction between Jews and Greeks, for they all had the
same Lord. (Rom. 10:12) There was 'neither Jew nor
Greek . . . slave nor free' for all were 'one in Christ
Jesus'. (Gal. 3:28) (*see* GENTILES)

The word 'Hellenists' was used of Greek-speaking
Jews of the Diaspora. These Hellenists complained that

their widows were neglected in the welfare distributions at Jerusalem, whereas those of the Hebrew-speaking Jews were not neglected. The newly converted Paul disputed hotly with the Hellenist Jews at Jerusalem. (*see* STEPHEN)

The people of Greece

The Greeks of New Testament times were living at least 400 years after the Golden Age of Greece. They were proud, eager, restless and elegant folk with a noble record of art, literature, and philosophy. They had a love of the beautiful and a poetic imagination that peopled Olympus with gods and goddesses. The whole civilized world looks to the ancient Greeks with wonder and gratitude. Never was any nation more rich in culture or more proud of their heritage. (*see* STOICS *and* EPICUREANS)

By the 1st century, however, their best days were over, their political integrity was lost, their religion ineffective, and their mode of life frivolous and corrupt. Though with real piety they kept up their religious rites and their mystery cults held a strong fascination, they had lost their religious belief. Their mythology had become a fairy tale. 'Men had climbed up into Olympus and found no gods there.' The Greeks were lonely and hungry for a faith by which to guide their lives. Their mysteries and philosophy reflected the seriousness and earnestness of spiritual searching.

Despite Paul's disappointing reception at Athens, the Christian gospel secured a strong bridge-head into Europe and established Christian communities in many Greek cities. More than half the letters in the New Testament are written to or from these communities, the fruits of Paul's Second, Third and perhaps subsequent

Journeys. (*see* PAUL, *also* CORINTHIANS, THESSALONIANS, PHILIPPIANS)

The language of Greece

Although Greece became a Roman colony from 146 BC, Greek remained the *lingua franca* of the Mediterranean and the Romans did not enforce the use of Latin outside Italy. Greek was the one language that could carry the traveller from the River Euphrates to Spain. All Roman officials understood and spoke Greek, and it was the commercial language of the Mediterranean world. Thus Christianity was preached in Greek and the New Testament written in Greek, which remained the language of the Christian Church until the middle of the 2nd century.

Jesus, whose mission was primarily to his own people, knew Greek (as we know from his private interrogation by Pilate), but preached and taught in Aramaic, quoting the Old Testament scriptures in Hebrew. Paul, the Apostle to the Gentiles, probably spoke to his Palestinian Jewish hearers in the Hebrew dialect Aramaic, but to those of the dispersion in Greek, quoting the Septuagint translation of the Old Testament. Indeed, these travelling Jews helped to spread the Greek language, and such Jewish authors as Philo and Josephus wrote in Greek.

The colonial cities of Greece

To the east and south of the Lake of Galilee was the Decapolis, a league of ten cities of Greek culture. These were the wealthy, leisure-loving, Greek-speaking, pagan communities – vastly different from the busy Jewish lakeside townships. Each of these had its own territory, stretching in some cases over a considerable area, each with its own constitution, rights and privileges. They

176

were associated by common interests, culture, and obligations. They were mostly founded in the early days of Macedonian conquest, but owed their independence to the Roman general Pompey and came directly under the authority of Rome. A league of Greek cities surrounded by an unsympathetic Jewish population, they were bound together by their common Hellenism in culture, way of life, and religion.

The cities of the Decapolis were Scythopolis, the ancient Beth-shean on the western side of the Jordan, guarding the entrance to the Plain of Esdraelon; on the eastern side Hippos, Gadara and Pella, whose territories were contiguous; on the road which ran south from Pella were Dium, Gerasa, and Philadelphia – the ancient Rabbath Ammon; on the road west from Gadara, Raphana and Kanatha, which lay at the foot of the Jebel Hauran; finally, to the north was Damascus.

The sites of these cities are remarkable at the present day for the striking ruins of the empire that they preserve. Their theatres, their amphitheatres, their temples still stand in ruined magnificence; their aqueducts stretch for miles across the country; their bridges and their roads survive as memorials of the past.

We know of at least one visit of Jesus to the territory of the Ten Towns, on which occasion he cured the man whose name was Legion, gave speech to the deaf mute, and fed the five thousand. [Rom. 1:14, 16; 10:12; Gal. 2:3; 3:28; Col. 3:11; John 12:20; Acts 14:1; 17:4, 12; 18:4; 19:10, 17; 20:21; 21:28; 1 Cor. 1:22, 24]

H

HEBREWS The letter to Hebrew Christians is an eloquent and scholarly homily in classical Greek, addressed to a group of educated Christians of Jewish origin who were possibly in danger of relapsing. It is not likely to have come from the pen of Paul the Apostle, though he may perhaps be responsible for the appendix, a final exhortation which forms the last chapter. The letter is a carefully written thesis with a long-sustained argument step by step for the pre-eminence of Christianity over Judaism.

Who wrote the letter?

The document apppears to come from outside the main stream of primitive Christian theology, but it was already in use by the year 96 and quoted in the letter of Clement of Rome to the Corinthians. It reflects the influence of Paul's earlier letters, particularly those to Corinth and Rome, rather than that of his later letters. This might date it between the years 65 and 95. It was excluded from the first known list of works forming the canon of the New Testament, called the *Muratorian Fragment* and written in Rome about 170. It is, however, to be found in the 3rd-century *Chester Beatty Papyrus* and the great manuscripts of the 4th century, *Codex Sinaiticus* and *Codex Vaticanus*.

In the 2nd and 3rd centuries any possible Pauline authorship was denied, though at Alexandria scholars declared it to be indirectly Pauline; that is, 'translated' by Luke or perhaps 'remembered' by another friend. From the 4th century until the studies of Luther, Erasmus, and Calvin, its Pauline authorship was accepted. Today, it is considered obviously *un*-Pauline in its theology of salvation in Christ, in its literary style, its excellent classical Greek, and deliberate arrangement. The author's declaration (2:3) of his conviction through the witness of early disciples contrasts strangely with Paul's conviction through his direct conversion. As the great Alexandrian scholar of the 3rd century, Origen, remarked, 'Who wrote the epistle? God only knows!'

There are several to whom the authorship has been attributed over the centuries. Luke the physician, whose Greek but not his style showed similarity, obviously shared some parallel ideas on universalism, also found in Stephen's speech (Acts 7). Barnabas was credited by the African scholar Tertullian early in the 3rd century with an epistle to the Hebrews. Priscilla and her husband Aquila have been named as the authors by the German theologian Harnack within this century. Silvanus, secretary to Peter, has been suggested because of the literary similarity of the first letter of Peter and the common use of such illustrative ideas as 'pilgrim', 'shepherd', and 'sprinkling'. Apollos, the Alexandrian Jew 'mighty in the scriptures', has been more plausibly supported by Luther. Apollos, as we know from Acts 18, was 'learned' and 'eloquent', 'for he powerfully confuted the Jews in public', showing by the scriptures that the Messiah was Jesus. (Acts 18:28) Apollos, too, was an orator capable of the conventional rhythm, careful assonance and alliteration to be found in the epistle. Apollos could have shared a knowledge of the wisdom of Solomon and the philosophy of Philo, and he could have been steeped in the Platonic influence and the allegorical interpretation found in the mystical figure of Melchizedek.

The purpose of the letter

The title of this letter 'to the Hebrews' is first found in Tertullian in the early 3rd century. The contents would seem to indicate that it was written to a definite local community of Jewish Christians, perhaps in Asia Minor, the 'home of Gnosticism'. The letter might have fulfilled several purposes. It could have been designed to reconcile Jewish Christians to the destruction of Jerusalem and the Temple in the year 70. It could have been written to prepare them for this event. It could have been meant to prevent them from deserting Christianity. On the other hand, the letter might have been written for Gnostics, who were insisting on the need of some angel mediation, in addition to that of Jesus. Perhaps their contempt for material things had prevented them from appreciating the sacrifice of the man Jesus; and the author wished to emphasize that God's Son had assumed flesh and blood to become the Son of Man.

Whatever his exact intention when he started, the author moves rapidly and imperceptibly from one leading idea to another. The work is full of quotation, allegory and illustration. The main outline of argument is interrupted by frequent digression or emphasis on the practical implication of what he is saying. The value of the work is not in its logical presentation but in its passion for Jesus – as Jesus the Messiah and the Saviour, who deserves devoted service. The writer is concerned to show the sufficiency of Christianity and to give the right place in the scheme of revelation, creation, and world order to Jesus. He is the pre-existent Son of God. He represents the mind, the will and the purpose of God. He is supreme, standing far above the angels, being made perfect through his sufferings and now crowned with glory.

Speaking, as he is, to Christians of Hebrew background, the author works through the ideas of 'priesthood', 'sacrifice', and 'atonement'. He compares the functions of the Aaronic high priest and the sacrificial system of the Old Covenant with the function of Jesus, both priest and victim, of the New Covenant. Like Melchizedek, 'priest of God Most High', Jesus appears without antecedents on the stage of history, as the mediator representing Man to God, and God to Man. The recurrent ceremonial on the Day of Atonement illustrates the need of continuous sacrifice under the old dispensation. In sacrifice, the offerer lays his hand upon the victim, symbolizing its substitution for his life. Jesus used no substitute, but, as the only pure offering once and for all time, he led the way as both victim and human high priest. His was a voluntary substitution of himself for his people; his was a vicarious suffering but not a vicarious punishment. Now, as Man seated at the right hand of God, by his very presence he intercedes for mankind. The writer goes on to appeal for his readers' repentance, for their assurance of forgiveness and for their obedience to God's will, after the example of Jesus.

The author's idealism is shown by his frequent comparison of the Phenomena of human experience with spiritual conceptions of eternal reality. He draws his illustrations from such parallel examples as: the Heavenly and Eternal Jerusalem, as compared with its earthly counterpart; the Tabernacled presence of God within Jesus, as compared with the Tabernacle of Moses; the full revelation of God in Jesus, as compared with a Judaism which does not accept him as Messiah.

Like Mark and John, the author insists that Jesus's

life and death have inaugurated the kingdom, or rule of God. For him, the spiritual world is a present reality, but not yet realized or recognized. So, for him, there are two worlds in the present rather than two ages, one in the present and one in the future.

One of the least attractive features of this letter is its severity, founded perhaps on the Old Testament conception of sacrifice which avails only for sins of ignorance. The writer holds no hope of forgiveness for those who sin after Christian conversion knowing what they are doing, yet purposefully and high-handedly turning their backs on what is right. He offers only an uncompromising warning that such apostasy is tantamount to idolatry, 'seeing they crucify to themselves the Son of God afresh'.

This letter is the first known systematic interpretation of the Old Testament from the Christian point of view. At an early date the Church recognized its worth. Christians of all ages have been inspired by the great chapter on faith (Chapter 11) as well as by the author's profound interpretation of the significance of the person and work of Jesus the Messiah. *see also* ISRAELITES [Heb. 1-13]

HELLENISTS (Gk. 'Greek-speaking Jews') *see* GREEKS

HERMAS The last of a list of five men mentioned in a special greeting from Paul at the close of his letters to the Christian congregation in Rome. Perhaps Hermas, his fellows and 'the brethren who are with them' formed a household or small group within the larger Christian community.

Hermas was a common slave's name. Paul's friend is not to be confused with the writer of the 2nd-century work on penitence and forgiveness called *The Shepherd,* himself a slave in Rome. [Rom. 16:14]

HERMES (Gk. 'messenger') Hermes is the Greek

name for the messenger of the gods, translated some-times as 'Mercury', in Acts 14:12, where the voluble and mercurial character of Paul is contrasted with the dignified appearance and bearing of Barnabas, who was mistaken for Zeus, the father of the gods.

The third of a list of five men, mentioned in a special greeting from Paul at the close of his letter to the Christian congregation in Rome. Perhaps Hermes, his fellows and 'the brethren who are with them' formed a house-hold or small group with the larger Christian community. [Rom. 16:14]

HERMOGENES (Gk. 'born of Hermes') A Christian disciple who, with Phygelus and others in Asia, deserted Paul on his last arrest, perhaps at Troas and through the betrayal of Alexander the coppersmith. The last letter to Timothy conceals the drama of Paul's disastrous departure from Asia and arrival under arrest in Rome where, already convicted, he awaits execution. Many Asian Christians, under the threat of arrest for their association with Paul, simply did not manage to remain loyal. Among these, Paul mentioned by name those whose desertion represented the greatest disappointment, particularly Phygelus and Hermogenes. [2 Tim. 1:15]

HEROD (Gk. 'sprung from a hero') Herod was the family name of the senior officer in the court of the Hasmonean prince Hyrcanus II, called Antipater, in the year 63 BC. He was the military governor of Idumea (called Edom in the Old Testament). The Idumeans had been conquered by John Hyrcanus in about 120 BC and forcibly converted to Judaism. This Antipater was a skilled politician, who established his two sons within the court of Hyrcanus, before being murdered in the year 43 BC. One of these sons, Herod the Great, so successfully courted Roman favour that he was the first to be called 'King of the Jews', and his descendants became the puppet rulers for Rome in Greater Syria throughout the 1st century of the Christian era.

Since the capture of Jerusalem by Pompey in 63 BC, the whole of Syria had become part of the Roman Empire. When Julius Caesar was besieged by the Egyptians at Alexandria, he escaped largely owing to the support of Jewish troops despatched by Antipater. As a reward, Antipater was given Roman citizenship and became procurator of all Jewish territory in Syria. His sons became governors – Phasael in Judea and Herod in Galilee. Despite the murder of Julius Caesar in 44 BC, the rise and fall of Antony, and the shift of power to Octavian, under whose august rule began the golden age of the *Pax Romana,* the family of Antipater remained in power.

1. Herod the Great
2. Herod Archelaus
3. Herod Antipas
4. Herod Philip
5. Herod Agrippa I
6. Herod Agrippa II

1. **Herod the Great** King of the Jews (37-4 BC) Through his political acumen and his consummate diplomacy, Herod extended his authority from Galilee to become ruler of all the Jewish territories and, when in Rome in the year 40 BC, was appointed king of Judea. Although Herod liked to be regarded as a true Jew in spite of his Edomite ancestry, he had much sympathy with Greek culture and literature. He was a great builder, not only of the Temple in Jerusalem and the shrine above the Patriarchal Cave of Machpelah in Hebron, and his many palace-fortresses at Samaria, Jericho, Bethlehem, Masada, Machaerus, and the Antonia

Fortress in Jerusalem, but also of other monuments as far afield as Damascus, Antioch, and Byblos.

Herod was a clever politician consistently backed by the Romans, and an efficient but unpredictable ruler, absolutely unscrupulous where his own interests and security were involved, and absolutely merciless when he felt his own safety was threatened. He executed one of his wives and two of his sons. He has been described as 'an unhappy man with two souls', the one of a modern man of Hellenistic culture, but with a longing to retire into the desert (his castles are all on the borders of the wilderness), and the other soul that of a ruler with Messianic aspirations.

It was perhaps to mitigate his unpopularity that he built the Temple. He died in the year now computed as 4 BC, and we know from the First Gospel that Jesus was born in his reign. Herod is described, on the arrival of the wise men in Jerusalem, as sending them to Bethlehem with instructions to return with news of the child born 'King of the Jews' – the title given by Rome to Herod himself. The murderous massacre of the innocents at Bethlehem, following his discovery of his deception by the wise men, accords well with the character of Herod in his old age. He was in fact buried at his summer palace near Bethlehem, and it would have been surprising if he had not been disturbed at the thought of a rival born so near to his own summer residence.

The Gospel of Matthew depicts the arrival of the 'wise men from the East' at Jerusalem, asking, 'Where is he who had been born king of the Jews? For we have seen his star in the East, and have come to worship him.' The Gospel goes on to describe the disturbing effect of their question upon Herod and his enquiries as to where the Messiah was expected to be born. The chief priests and scribes quoted for him the prophet Micah to the effect that the Messiah is to be born 'in Bethlehem in Judea'. Whereupon Herod summoned the wise men, asked the exact date on which the star had appeared, and sent them on to Bethlehem, saying, 'Go and search diligently for the child, and when you have found him bring me word, that I too may come and worship him.' After visiting the house in Bethlehem and offering their gifts, however, the wise men were warned in a dream to avoid Herod and return home by a different way.

On their departure, Joseph was also warned in a dream of Herod's intention to destroy the child. Joseph's flight to Egypt with Mary and the child was rapidly followed by the massacre of all children of two years old and under within the district and town of Bethlehem. On Herod's death, Matthew records, the holy family returned to Nazareth. Josephus in the *Wars* (1:33-35) gives a grim picture of the physical and mental degeneration of the aging king – deluded, violent, and vicious. The Gospel story of the birth of Jesus falls within Herod's final years, and accords well with the description of Herod's character as recorded by Josephus.

On Herod's death, at his own wish his kingdom was partitioned among three of his surviving sons: Judea, Samaria, and Idumea to Archelaus as ethnarch; Galilee and Perea to Antipas as tetrarch; Iturea, Gaulanitis, and Trachonitis to Philip. None of these had the diplomatic ability of their father. [Matt. 2:1-23; Luke 1:5]

2. Herod Archelaus Ethnarch of Judea, Samaria, and Idumea (4 BC-AD 6) The oldest surviving son of Herod the Great, Archelaus is mentioned in the 'birth stories' of the First Gospel as reigning in Judea on the return of Mary and Joseph from Egypt. It seems that Archelaus inherited all that was worst in the character of his father. He ruled for ten years, before being charged in Rome with misgovernment and banished to Gaul. He was replaced by a Roman procurator, under Augustus a three-year appointment but under Tiberius considerably longer, and in the case of Pontius Pilate ten years. Pilate presided at the trial of Jesus and condemned him to crucifixion. He, too, was recalled to Rome on a charge of oppression, and was convicted and banished in the year 36 to Vienne, and died ten years later. [Matt. 2:22]

3. Herod Antipas Tetrarch of Galilee and Perea (4 BC-AD 39) The second surviving son of Herod the Great, Antipas had John the Baptist imprisoned, and on the request of Herodias, his brother Philip's wife, ordered John's execution. Jesus called Antipas 'that fox' when warned by some Pharisees that Antipas wished to kill him. Antipas is reputed to have been idle, vicious, and extravagant. Luke records that Jesus was taken before Antipas at his trial. Pilate, hearing that Jesus came from Antipas's territory and knowing he was in Jerusalem for the Passover, sent Jesus to him for questioning, but Jesus refused to answer him and was returned to Pilate.

Antipas built the castle and town of Tiberias, his capital, on the north-west coast of the Sea of Galilee. Luke uses his title of tetrarch, literally the 'ruler of a quarter' of the total kingdom of his father. Mark more informally calls him 'king', which title Antipas requested from the Emperor Caligula without success in the year 39. Antipas was summoned to Rome and banished that same year. He married and divorced the daughter of Aretas, king of Arabia, and later married Herodias, the wife of Philip, his half-brother and tetrarch of Iturea, Gaulanitis, and Trachonitis.

The Jewish historian Josephus records that Aretas avenged the divorce of his daughter by defeating Antipas in AD 36. He also records Antipas's execution of

John the Baptist, but does not mention John the Baptist's denunciation of Antipas's marriage to his brother Philip's wife. The Gospels of Mark and Matthew may have been mistaken in linking Herodias with Philip; Josephus says she was first married to an uncle in Rome, and confirms her marriage later to Antipas. [Matt. 14:1-12; Mark 6:14-29; Luke 3:19, 20; 8:3; 9:7-9; 23:7-12; Acts 4:27; 13:1]

4. Herod Philip Tetrarch of Iturea, Gaulanitis, and Trachonitis (4 BC-AD 34) Philip was the youngest and the most efficient of the three sons of Herod the Great, retaining his position until his death in the year 34. It was during a visit to his territory near Caesarea Philippi that Jesus was first recognized and named by his disciples as the Messiah. A strong tradition links the transfiguration of Jesus not only with Mount Tabor but also with Mount Hermon, on whose southern slopes Philip had built a temple in honour of Caesar Augustus, upon the site of an earlier shrine to the god Pan.

Philip is linked in the Gospels of Matthew and Mark with Herodias, before her marriage to Antipas. According to Josephus, Herodias was first married to another member of the Herod family in Rome. Philip is known to have married Salome, his niece, the daughter of Antipas and Herodias. [Matt. 14:3; Mark 6:17-29; Luke 3:19]

5. Herod Agrippa I King of Iturea, Gaulanitis, Trachonitis, and later of Galilee and Perea (AD 37-44) Agrippa, so called after the famous minister and lieutenant of the Emperor Augustus, was the son of Aristobulus, brother of Herodias and grandson of Herod the Great. Educated in Rome and the companion of the young prince Caligula, according to Josephus Agrippa dissuaded Caligula from erecting his imperial statue in the Temple at Jerusalem. On Caligula's accession as emperor, Agrippa inherited the territory of his uncle Philip. On the exile of Antipas and Herodias, Agrippa also ruled Galilee and Perea. He survived the murder of Caligula, and received from Claudius the sovereignty of Judea, Samaria, and Idumea. In fact, he now controlled the whole of what had been his grandfather's kingdom.

Luke, in the Acts of the Apostles, records the first royal persecution of the Christian Church as the work of Agrippa, in which he had James Bar-Zebedee executed and also imprisoned Peter. Luke further describes Agrippa's hideous death (at the age of only 34) at Caesarea, in the act of ratifying a treaty with the cities of Tyre and Sidon. Josephus confirms Luke's account and rates Agrippa as the last great Jewish monarch in the diplomatic tradition of his grandfather Herod the Great. [Acts 12:1-23]

6. Herod Agrippa II King of Chalcis (AD 50-92) The second Agrippa, the young son of the first, and greatgrandson of Herod the Great, was given the Lebanese ethnarchy of Chalcis by the Emperor Claudius. To this was added Galilee, Iturea, Gaulanitis, and Trachonitis in the year 53. In about the year 60, Paul appeared before Agrippa at the request of Festus, the Roman procurator, who wished to draw up the charges against Paul before sending him to Rome.

Luke's account in Acts gives some indication of the respect in which Agrippa was held by both Romans and Jews. Festus lays Paul's case before Agrippa with much deference: 'But I found that he had done nothing deserving death; and as he himself appealed to the emperor, I decided to send him. But I have nothing definite to write to my lord about him. Therefore I have brought him before you, and, especially before you, King Agrippa, that, after we have examined him, I may have something to write.' (Acts 25:25-26) Paul, too, pays tribute to Agrippa in the opening words of his defence: 'I think myself fortunate that it is before you, King Agrippa, I am to make my defence today against all the accusations of the Jews, because you are especially familiar with all customs and controversies of the Jews.' (Acts 26:2, 3) Agrippa's generous reply and Paul's comment reflect the mutual admiration and concern of the two men: 'In a short time you think to make me a Christian!' 'Whether short or long,' Paul replies, 'I would to God that not only you but also all who hear me this day might become such as I am – except for these chains.' (Acts 26:28-29)

Agrippa lived on in Caesarea, surviving the disastrous revolt and destruction of his own people in the years 66-70. With his retirement to Rome and his death there in the year 92, the Herodian dynasty came to an end, having played no little part in the earliest years of the Christian era and the life of the Christian Church. [Acts 25:13-27; 26:1-32]

HERODIANS The political party so named for its support of the Herod family is described by Josephus, the Jewish historian, as wanting to put Herod on the throne instead of the Maccabean Antigonus in 40 BC. The Herodians are mentioned on two occasions in the Gospels; on both they are linked with the Pharisees in opposing Jesus. Evidently the religious leaders wanted to be rid of a popular leader who was challenging the whole system of Jewish religious and social control. Therefore they were willing to join hands with the political forces which wished to maintain the Herodian dynasty and the *Pax Romana*.

On the first occasion that the Herodians are mentioned, Jesus had cured a man with a withered hand, on the Sabbath and within the synagogue at Capernaum. This incident aroused the anger of the Pharisees, for healing was classified as work and Jesus had technically defiled the Sabbath. Mark says that the Pharisees at once began to plot with the Herodians to destroy Jesus.

On the second occasion, within the Temple at Jerusalem, Jesus had just told the provocative and transparently clear parable of the 'Wicked Husbandmen'. This parable was an allegory accusing the leaders of the Jews down the centuries of persecuting the prophets and finally of planning to reject and kill the Messiah himself. In order to trap Jesus into convicting himself of treason, the Herodians and Pharisees again combined, this time to ask his opinion of paying taxes to Caesar. The tax in question was a tribute collected from each inhabitant of Judea, Samaria, and Idumea and much resented by the Jewish population. Its payment would be supported by the Herodians, who were careful to cultivate the Roman favour upon which the Herodian dynasty depended. The tax was paid with a silver denarius which, in contrast to the copper coins put out by the procurator of Judea, bore the name or head of the emperor. Anyone who recommended the payment of so unpopular a tax would have been rejected by the crowds, but to repudiate payment was tantamount to treason, for which Jesus could have been immediately arrested. His answer, however, took the Pharisees and Herodians completely by surprise. ' "Why put me to the test, you hypocrites? Show me the money for the tax." And they brought him a coin. And Jesus said to them, "Whose likeness and inscription is this?" They said, "Caesar's." Then he said to them, "Render therefore to Caesar the things that are Caesar's, and to God the things that God's." ' (Matt. 22:18-21) [Matt. 22:16; Mark 3:6; 12:13]

HERODIAS This granddaughter of Herod the Great is notorious for the sordid scheme by which she secured the execution of John the Baptist.

Both her father, Aristobulus, and her grandmother, Mariamne I, were assassinated by order of Herod, the former in the year 6 BC and the latter in 29 BC. Herodias married her uncle, Herod Beothus, a private citizen in Rome according to Josephus, and they had a daughter called Salome. The Gospel of Mark followed by that of Matthew, indicates that she married Philip, the tetrarch of Iturea, Gaulanitis, and Trachonitis, but this was probably a case of mistaken identity between two different 'Philips'. Certainly, Josephus does not record her association with Philip the Tetrarch, but he does mention her marriage to a member of the Herod family called Philip in Rome, and later to Herod Antipas. In order to marry Herodias, Antipas divorced his own wife, the daughter of the Nabatean King of Arabia, Aretas IV. The latter invaded Antipas's territory in revenge, and inflicted such a crushing defeat on Antipas that he had to seek the help of Roman troops. Popular opinion seems to have regarded this defeat as a divine punishment of Antipas for his execution of John the Baptist a short time before.

The account of the death of John the Baptist in Mark's Gospel reads like a popular legend of the prophet rebuking the king, along the lines of the Old Testament story of Elijah rebuking Ahab for appropriating Naboth's vineyard. John fearlessly condemned Antipas for taking Philip's wife, who was his own niece and consequently by law forbidden to be his wife. No doubt John also condemned Herodias for deserting her first husband to form an adulterous alliance with her uncle Antipas. Certainly, it was Herodias who bore a grudge against John, though her husband Antipas is said to have respected and even to have protected him.

'But an opportunity came when Herod on his birthday gave a banquet for his courtiers and officers and the leading men of Galilee. For when Herodias's daughter came in and danced, she pleased Herod and his guests; and the king said to the girl, "Ask me for whatever you wish, and I will grant it." And he vowed to her, "Whatever you ask me, I will give you, even half of my kingdom." And she went out, and said to her mother, "What shall I ask?" And she said, "The head of John the baptizer." And she came in immediately with haste to the king, and asked, saying, "I want you to give me at once the head of John the Baptist on a platter." And the king was exceedingly sorry; but because of his oaths and his guests he did not want to break his word to her. And immediately the king sent a soldier of the guard and gave orders to bring his head. He went and beheaded him in the prison, and brought his head on a platter, and gave it to the girl; and the girl gave it to her mother.' (Mark 6:21-28)

According to Josephus the execution took place in the fortress of Machaerus beyond Jordan; John's burial is supposed to have been at Samaria, where his tomb was honoured from the 4th century.

Herodias later encouraged Antipas to seek from the emperor the title of 'King', like the newly-crowned Herod Agrippa. The latter, however, reached Rome first and brought charges against Antipas. These led to his exile in Gaul, whither Herodias accompanied him in the year 39. [Matt. 14:3; Mark 6:17, 19, 22; Luke 3:19]

HERODION A Christian greeted by Paul, at the close of his letter to the Church in Rome, as 'my kinsman'. [Rom. 16:11]

HYMENAEUS (Gk. 'pertaining to Hymen, the god of marriage') A heretical teacher within the Christian community, probably at Ephesus or Troas, on the coast of Asia Minor, whom Paul found it necessary to excommunicate, as his teaching represented a real threat to the faith and loyalty of the local congregation. As Paul puts it in his first letter to Timothy, 'By rejecting conscience, certain persons have made shipwreck of their faith, among them Hymenaeus and Alexander, whom I have delivered to Satan that they may learn not to blaspheme.' (1 Tim. 1:19, 20)

In his last letter to Timothy, Paul is even more insistent in his warnings against false teachers. Timothy needs to be a 'sound workman', 'handling the word rightly', avoiding 'what is ignoble', and exercising a strict supervision of his congregation. 'Remind them of this, and charge them before the Lord to avoid disputing about words, which does no good, but only ruins the hearers. Do your best to present yourself to God as one approved, a workman who has no need to be ashamed, rightly handling the word of truth. Avoid such godless chatter, for it will lead people into more and more ungodliness, and their talk will eat its way like gangrene. Among them are Hymenaeus and Philetus, who have swerved from the truth by holding that the resurrection is past already. They are upsetting the faith of some. But God's firm foundation stands.' (2 Tim. 2:14-19)

Exactly what the false teaching of Hymenaeus and Philetus was cannot be exactly or certainly determined. It is likely, however, to have been some early and high-flying Gnosticism, like the Colossian heresy, robbing the resurrection of Jesus of its reality and substituting some allegorical explanation. Paul saw clearly that a purely mystical interpretation of the life and person of Jesus represented a real threat to the Christian faith in the true humanity of the Son of God, who came, lived, died, rose, and returned to God, as 'the first fruits of the human race'. [1 Tim. 1:20; 2 Tim. 2:17]

I

ISRAELITES (Heb. 'who prevails with God') The community of Israel was made up of its clergy, the priests and Levites, and its laity, the Israelites. The social community of Judaism was conscious of its descent and inheritance. Even the simple Israelite knew his immediate ancestors and to which tribe he belonged.

The Apostle Paul was himself a true Israelite, 'a descendant of Abraham, a member of the tribe of Benjamin'. (Rom. 11:1) Paul's threefold description of himself as a Hebrew, an Israelite, and descended from Abraham (2 Cor. 11:22) emphasizes his claim to be a full-blooded Jew.

He perceived, however, that God's promises were made not to Abraham's physical descendants merely as such, but to those whom God should choose. He declared that God's right to choose was not limited to Jews, but that God's promises were extended to apply to those Gentiles who believed; for righteousness is achieved by faith, rather than by inheritance. As a true Israelite, Paul was deeply and emotionally involved in the tragedy of Israel's rejection of the Messiahship of Jesus and that of God's seeming rejection of Israel. (Rom. 9:8-26)

The letters of Paul compare clearly the Old Testament idea of Israel and Paul's own theory of a New Israel, which he illustrates in many different ways.

From creation, the disobedience of the first man, Adam, resulted in mankind's universal expectation of death. Jesus, 'the firstborn among many brethren' (Rom. 8:29), by his obedience to the point of dying, gained for all mankind the promise of life. 'As in Adam all die, so also in Christ shall all be made alive.' (1 Cor. 15:22) In Paul's philosophy of history, Jesus is the pivot and focal point. The old community narrows down to vanishing-point in the death of Jesus. The new community widens out from his resurrection. Both the Apostles Peter and Paul use for Jesus the metaphors of the 'foundation' and the 'cornerstone' on which a new community is to be built. As the twelve patriarchs were the founder-members of the Old Israel, so the twelve apostles were the founder-members of the New Israel. Paul's belief in the special vocation of Israel nevertheless continued; she was like the cultivated olive tree while the Gentiles were like wild olives grafted on to the original tree.

To Paul, however, the real Israel is the responsive 'remnant'. Those who accept Jesus as their Messiah and Lord become the New Israel, by virtue of their response. A person becomes a New Israelite by faith, rather than by descent. Thus Abraham "believed God, and it was reckoned to him as righteousness". So you see that it is men of faith who are the sons of Abraham. And the scripture, foreseeing that God would justify the Gentiles by faith, preached the gospel beforehand to Abraham, saying, "In you shall all the nations be blessed." So then, those who are men of faith are blessed with Abraham who had faith.' (Gal. 3:6-9) A person becomes a New Israelite not by circumcision, but by re-creation. 'For neither circumcision counts for anything, nor uncircumcision, but a new creation. Peace and mercy be upon all who walk by this rule, upon the Israel of God.' (Gal. 6:15, 16) In fact, any who share the faith of Abraham are the New Israelites. 'Therefore remember that at one time you Gentiles in the flesh, called the uncircumcision by what is called the circumcision, which is made in the flesh by hands – remember that you were at that time separated from Christ, alienated from the commonwealth of Israel, and strangers to the covenants of promise, having no hope and without God in the world. But now in Christ Jesus you who once were far off have been brought near in the blood of Christ. For he is our peace, who has made us both one.' (Eph. 2:11-14)

Later writers have extemporized at length on this theme of the Old and the New Israel. The writer of the Book of Revelation, in his vision of a new heaven and a new earth, saw 'the holy city, new Jerusalem, coming down out of heaven from God, prepared as a bride adorned for her husband'. (Rev. 21:2) He continues: 'And I saw no temple in the city, for its temple is the Lord God the Almighty and the Lamb. And the city has no need of sun or moon to shine upon it, for the glory of God is its light, and its lamp is the Lamb. By its light shall the nations walk; and the kings of the earth shall bring their glory into it, and its gates shall never be shut by day – and there shall be no night there; they shall bring into it the glory and honour of the nations.' (Rev. 21:22-26) The same idea of a city of God laid up in heaven occurs in the writings of both Clement and Augustine. Subsequent Christian theologians have likewise tended to bring the future into the present, to project the New Jerusalem into this world and to identify the Christian Church with 'Holy Zion'.

In the earthly city of Jerusalem, from Byzantine times a false tradition transferred the name of Zion from the ancient Davidic city site on Ophel to the Western Hill. The mass of Christian monuments and churches on the Western Hill became loosely and confusingly referred to as on 'Mount Zion'. Thus the Christian Church has appropriated topographically as well as theologically the inheritance and title of Zion, *see also* NATHANAEL, called by Jesus 'an Israelite indeed, in whom is no guile!' [John 1:47; Rom. 9:4; 11:1; 2 Cor. 11:22]

J

JAIRUS (Gk. from the Heb. 'whom Jehovah enlightens') The head of the local sanhedrin or court of elders, supervising the synagogue worship and life of the community at Capernaum, whose little daughter, aged twelve years, Jesus healed or restored to life.

The story of this miracle occurs only in the Synoptic Gospels, where the original account in Mark is abbreviated in Luke, and considerably more abbreviated in Matthew, who omits even the name of Jairus. The account emphasizes the need of faith to release the healing power of Jesus.

The 'ruler' or president of the synagogue came to Jesus in desperate need. His only daughter was dying. He prostrated himself before Jesus and begged him to come back to his house. 'My little daughter is at the point of death. Come and lay your hands on her, so that she may be made well, and live.' (Mark 5:23) Perhaps because Jairus was a well-known and important person, the crowd gathered and followed.

Taking advantage of the press of people, a woman with an incurable haemorrhage – involving probably a ceremonial uncleanness requiring an official expiation – came up behind Jesus and touched the fringe of his robe. She said to herself, 'If I touch even his garments, I shall be made well.' (Mark 5:28) Jesus felt that power had gone out of him, and at once turned round and asked, 'Who touched my garments?' He realized that this was due to no accidental jostling by the crowd, but to someone's longing for healing, and he insisted that they declare their need.

As Jesus looked round, the woman, knowing that she could not escape his notice but that she was now instantly cured, came forward, fell at his feet and owned up. Whereupon Jesus answered: 'Daughter, your faith has made you well; go in peace, and be healed of your disease.' (Mark 5:34)

By now, they were approaching Jairus's house, and while Jairus was still speaking someone arrived to tell Jairus: 'Your daughter is dead. Why trouble the Teacher any further?' (Mark 5:35) Taking no notice, Jesus simply turned to Jairus and said, 'Do not fear, only believe.' When they reached the house to find everyone weeping and wailing, Jesus said, 'Why do you make a tumult and weep? The child is not dead but sleeping.' (Mark 5:36, 39) They scornfully laughed at him, knowing the girl was dead. Jesus then turned them all outside, allowing only the parents and his closest followers, Peter, James and John, to remain. Then in the presence of these five whose faith he could trust, Jesus commanded the child to get up. Mark records his actual words in Aramaic, 'Talitha cumi – Little girl, I say to you, arise.' (Mark 5:41) At once, she rose up and walked, and they were all astonished. Jesus bound them all to silence and told them to give her something to eat.

Nowhere better is the need and power of faith illustrated than in this double miracle story of the woman who believed that just to touch him would cure her, and of the man who went on believing – Jairus, the ruler of the synagogue at Caperaum. *see also* CENTURION [Matt. 9:18-25; Mark 5:22-43; Luke 8:41-55]

JAMBRES (Gk. Iambres) Together with Jannes, according to rabbinical tradition, the names of the magicians at the court of Pharoah, who withstood and reproduced the miracles of Moses and Aaron, trick for trick, as the latter begged Pharaoh to release the Hebrews from Egypt. Although not mentioned by name in the book of Exodus, Paul quoted Jannes and Jambres as the type of men who 'oppose the truth, men of corrupt mind and counterfeit faith; but they will not get very far, for their folly will be plain to all' – as was that of Jannes and Jambres. [2 Tim. 3:8]

JAMES (the English form of 'Jacob' from the Heb. 'heel-catcher' or 'supplanter')

1. James, son of Zebedee (the Great)

2. James, son of Alphaeus

3. James, son of Clopas (the Younger)

4. James, father or brother of Judas (not Iscariot).

5. James, brother of Jesus

6. James, author of the General Letter

1. James, son of Zebedee (the Great) James and John, the two sons of Zebedee, were called by Jesus while mending their fishing-nets by the Lake of Galilee. Luke says that the brothers were partners with Simon and Andrew, sons of John. James is throughout linked with his brother John. Together with Peter, they constituted the innermost circle of Jesus's companions, the eyewitnesses of his life, work, death, and resurrection. They were present at the raising of Jairus's daughter, the transfiguration on the mountain, the agony in the garden. For their zeal and spirit, well-illustrated in their desire to destroy an inhospitable Samaritan village, they were nicknamed 'Boanerges', the 'sons of thunder'.

They were, however, effectually harnessed to Jesus's purpose and his continuing energy and activity within the Church. John, in the early chapters of the Acts (3, 4), is described as the companion of Peter at Jerusalem, in a ministry of preaching and healing, for which they were arrested and taken before the Sanhedrin. Later the same two apostles conducted a preaching mission in the villages of Samaria (Acts 8), after which John is no longer mentioned apart from 'the apostles which were in Jerusalem'.

Barely fifteen years after their calling by the lakeside, James became the political victim of Herod Agrippa I, being executed shortly before Agrippa's own death. 'About that time Herod the king laid violent hands upon some who belonged to the church. He killed James the brother of John with the sword; and when he saw that it pleased the Jews, he proceeded to arrest Peter also.' (Acts 12:1-3) James's martyrdom, described in a single sharp sentence of seven Greek words, is the only absolutely reliable (and the only biblical) record of the death of any one of the twelve apostles. James was also the first to drink his master's cup of death and to be baptized with his master's baptism of suffering, as his master had promised him. (Mark 10:35-40)

According to a 17th-century tradition, without any scriptural support, James is said to have visited Spain before his martyrdom. Another Spanish tradition records the translation of James's body to Santiago de Compostela in north-west Spain, where the shrine is still a centre of pilgrimage. In the Middle Ages, Compostela became the centre of the Christian national movement opposed to the Muslim occupation. The 12th-century Armenian Cathedral of St James, on the Western Hill in the Old City of Jerusalem, encloses the traditional shrine of the head of James, the first apostle-martyr. [Matt. 4:21; 10:2; 17:1; Mark 1:19, 29; 3:17; 5:37; 9:2; 10:35, 41; 13:3; 14:33; Luke 5:10; 6:14; 8:51; 9:28, 54; Acts 1:13; 12:2; Gal. 2:12]

2. James, son of Alphaeus This James, like James son of Zebedee, was one of the twelve apostles appearing in the company listed in the Gospels of Matthew, Mark, and Luke, and was among those present in the Upper Room at Jerusalem after the ascension for the election of a twelfth apostle in place of Judas. In the apostles' rolls recorded in Matthew and Mark, this James is linked with Thaddaeus. Mark also records that Levi — by which name he is referring to Matthew — is a 'son of Alphaeus'. (Mark 2:14) From this it may be inferred that there was a family link between these three members of the twelve — James, Thaddaeus, and Matthew.

Nothing further is known about James, son of Alphaeus, nor is there sufficient evidence to identify him with either James the brother of Jesus, or James the Younger. [Matt. 10:3; Mark 3:18; Luke 6:15; Acts 1:13]

3. James, son of Clopas (the Younger) He is mentioned in only one parallel passage occurring in Matthew, Mark and Luke as the son of that Mary who, with Mary of Magdala and Salome (Luke includes Joanna), witnessed the crucifixion of Jesus. It is Mark who calls him 'the younger', which may refer to his age or his size. The Fourth Gospel does not refer to this Mary as 'Mary, the mother of James', but as 'Mary, the wife of Clopas'. (John 19:25) The context, however, is identical, and this establishes that the parents of James 'the younger' were Clopas and Mary; but there is no further reference to him by name. [Matt. 27:56; Mark 15:40; Luke 24:10]

4. James, father or brother of Judas (not Iscariot) This James was the father of one of the apostles, sometimes called 'Judas', sometimes 'Thaddaeus'. Judas is listed among the twelve apostles only by Luke, both in his Gospel and in the Acts. The corresponding name within the Gospels of Mark and Matthew is that of Thaddaeus, which is omitted by Luke. The Fourth Gospel refers to him as 'Judas, not Iscariot'. It is, therefore, reasonable to identify Thaddaeus and Judas as the same person, with this James as his father. The actual wording in Luke's list is 'Judas son of James', implying either that James was his father or his brother. If this Judas was the writer of the letter of Jude, the last within the New Testament, then he does in fact refer to himself as 'Jude, a servant of Jesus Christ and brother of James'. [Luke 6:16; Acts 1:13]

5. James, brother of Jesus This James was one of four brothers or cousins or half-brothers of Jesus. (For a discussion of their exact relationship *see* JOSEPH **2**.) The conversion of James, 'the brother of the Lord', to belief in Jesus as the Messiah, may well have taken place as a result of the special appearance of Jesus to him after the resurrection, mentioned by Paul. (1 Cor. 15:7) Within ten years he became the acknowledged leader of the Christian Church in Jerusalem. Paul, in the autobiographical chapters of his letter to the Galatian Church, describes how, immediately after his conversion (AD 35-6) and subsequent retreat into the wilderness, he spent a fortnight in Jerusalem with Peter and James. Even Peter himself on his release from imprisonment by Herod Agrippa I (AD 44) asked his friends to 'Tell this to James and to the brethren.' (Acts 12:17) Paul also in his letter to the Galatians narrates how, fourteen years after his conversion, he discussed his mission to the Gentiles with James, Cephas, and John, 'who were reputed to be pillars' of the Church.

Though the initiative of the Christian Church had by now moved from Jerusalem to Antioch, the headquarters of the Church remained at Jerusalem. There, at the centre of Judaism, among the Jewish Christians there existed a powerful party opposed to the welcome of Gentiles who did not observe the Law of Moses. James, however, was held in great respect by both parties for his personal sanctity and his political acumen. Paul and Barnabas had been sent from Jerusalem to plead the case for the welcome of Gentile Christians. Peter also championed their cause, declaring that as all men are saved by their faith in Jesus and by his grace, the Church had no right to impose other restrictions.

James, chairman of the Council and by now regarded as the equivalent of the first bishop of the Church in Jerusalem, gave a ruling. Pagans who turned to God were told only to abstain from food offered to idols, from the meat of strangled animals, and also from fornication. This probably included marriages between near relatives as forbidden by Jewish Law. Thus the Council refused to impose the Law on the Gentiles, only forbidding specific offensive practices. Thus vindicated, Paul and Barnabas continued their work at Antioch. James and other Christians of Jewish origin continued to keep the Law of Moses as their way of life.

When possibly at the close of the year 58 Paul arrived for the last time in Jerusalem, James and the elders of the Christian Church were apprehensive of his coming, for they pointed out, 'You see, brother, how many thousands there are among the Jews of those who have believed; they are all zealous of the Law, and they have been told about you that you teach all the Jews who are among the Gentiles to forsake Moses, telling them not to circumcise their children or observe the customs.' (Acts 21:20-22) At James's suggestion, Paul agreed to undergo a week's ritual purification in the Temple. This, however, only led to Paul's arrest and his long 'Via Dolorosa', from which not even James could rescue him and which took him all the way to Rome.

The Jewish historians Josephus and Hegesippus, both natives of Palestine, record James's execution at the instigation of the high priest and the Sanhedrin, shortly after the death of Festus, the procurator who despatched Paul to Rome in the year 62. James was thrown down into the Kidron ravine from the top of the Temple area wall, and mercifully 'clubbed' out of his misery by a fuller from Siloam, in the valley below.

Before the destruction of the city of Jerusalem in the year 70, the Christian community had left the city and had settled at Pella, beyond the River Jordan. Within a few years they returned, but it was not until early in the 4th century that the vast Byzantine basilica of 'Holy Zion' was built on the site of the Upper Room, which was the first Christian synagogue and headquarters of James, 'the brother of the Lord'. [Matt. 13:55; Mark 6:3; Acts 12:17; 15:13; 21:18; 1 Cor. 15:7; Gal. 1:-19; 2:9]

6. James, author of the General Letter This letter has been called the 'Pastoral Encyclical of James of Jerusalem'. Although traditionally ascribed to James, the brother of Jesus, this homily addressed to the 'twelve tribes in the Dispersion' is perhaps more likely to be the work of an unknown teacher, writing some time shortly before the year 90. The Church to whom he refers is governed by elders. There is no mention of bishops and deacons. Only in the 4th century was this letter included

205

in the canon of the New Testament in the west, and then simply because its address was taken to contain an allusion to James the brother of the Lord – 'James, a servant of God and of the Lord Jesus Christ'.

The writer combines the function of preacher and prophet with a remarkable forcefulness. His message is highly practical and positive, delivered with a wealth of authority. He begins with an exhortation to his readers to treat all trials and persecutions as a privilege, rather than to blame God for them. He is emphatic that true religion must not only be a matter of faith, but of practice: 'But be doers of the word, and not hearers only, deceiving yourselves. For if any one is a hearer of the word and not a doer, he is like a man who observes his natural face in a mirror; for he observes himself and goes away and at once forgets what he was like. But he who looks into the perfect law, the law of liberty, and perseveres, being no hearer that forgets but a doer that acts, he shall be blessed in his doing. . . . Religion that is pure and undefiled before God and the Father is this: to visit orphans and widows in their affliction, and to keep oneself unstained from the world.' (Jas. 1:22-25, 27)

Christians are not to distinguish between classes of people, for the poor have a rich calling from God. The supreme law of scripture is that 'you must love your neighbour as yourself'. To break the law at one point is to be guilty on all counts. What are good wishes without good deeds? 'So faith by itself, if it has no works, is dead. But some one will say, "You have faith and I have works." Show me your faith apart from your works, and I by my works will show you my faith. . . . Was not Abraham our father justified by works, when he offered his son Isaac upon the altar? You see that faith was active along with his works, and faith was completed by works.' (Jas. 2:17, 18, 21, 22)

The writer is swift to condemn uncontrolled language; the tongue, though a tiny part of the body, is vital to its control, as the bit in a bridle or the rudder of a ship. 'So the tongue is a little member and boasts of great things. How great a forest is set ablaze by a small fire! And the tongue is a fire. The tongue is an unrighteous world among our members, staining the whole body, setting on fire the cycle of nature, and set on fire by hell. . . . But no human being can tame the tongue – a restless evil, full of deadly poison. With it we bless the Lord and Father, and with it we curse men, who are made in the likeness of God. From the same mouth come blessing and cursing. [Jas. 3:5, 6, 8-10)

He diagnoses the disunity among his readers: 'What causes wars, and what causes fightings among you? Is it not your passions that are at war in your members? You desire and do not have; so you kill. And you covet and cannot obtain; so you fight and wage war. You do not have, because you do not ask. You ask and do not receive, because you ask wrongly, to spend it on your passions.' (Jas. 4:1-3)

The excellent Greek, forceful style, and facile morality of this letter tend to conceal that it has many parallels with the Sermon on the Mount in its demands for perfection. [Jas. 1-5]

JANNES *see* JAMBRES

JASON (Gk. 'to heal') There are two men of this name mentioned in the New Testament, who may in fact have been one and the same person.

1. A Jewish Christian at Thessalonica, with a Greek name, sheltered Paul and his followers in his house. There, the Jewish community, full of resentment at

Paul's preaching about Jesus as the Messiah, searched Jason's house. Not finding Paul, they dragged Jason and some others before the 'People's Assembly' and accused them of proclaiming Jesus as a rival to the emperor. The City councillors made Jason and the rest give security, before setting them free. [Acts 17:5-9]

2. A Jewish Christian in Rome mentioned at the close of Paul's letter to the Christian community in Rome. Paul describes him as 'my compatriot' – that is, fellow-Jew.

Whether the final chapter of Paul's letter to Rome included messages to Christians at Ephesus or in Rome, the Jason who linked his greetings with that of Paul may well have been the same man of Thessalonica. [Rom. 16:21]

JESUS (Gk., Heb. 'God is salvation') Jesus is universally recognized to have been the Jewish rabbi who, in the period before the destruction of the Temple by the Roman armies, gathered disciples by his teaching and was condemned as a troublesome impostor by priests and other leading men among the Jews of Jerusalem, though his own disciples believed him to be the Messiah. There is little information about him to be found outside the books of the New Testament; but that little is enough to fix the figure of Jesus, the founder of Christianity, in a definite historical setting. The Roman world knew, through a letter of Pliny when he was governor of Bithynia and through an allusion in the works of the historian Tacitus, that Jesus was believed by his followers to be the Messiah of the Jews and the Son of God and also that he was an object of their worship as well as the founder of the Christian community. Jewish traditions recorded in the Talmud depict Jesus as a rabbi, list his disciples and allude to his condemnation for 'practising sorcery and leading Israel astray', as well as his execution on the eve of the Passover feast.

In the books of the New Testament apart from the Four Gospels, there is a considerate amount of evidence about the life of Jesus, particularly in the letters of Paul, who was a personal friend of Peter and other apostles knowing Jesus during his public ministry. In the Acts of the Apostles the speeches of Peter contain an account of the ministry and passion of Jesus, as well as an affirmation of his resurrection. Thus Peter said to Cornelius and others that his message to them was: 'The word which was proclaimed throughout all Judea, beginning from Galilee after the baptism which John preached: how God anointed Jesus of Nazareth with the Holy Spirit and with power; how he went about doing good and healing all that were oppressed by the devil, for God was with him. And we are witnesses to all that he did both in the country of the Jews and in Jerusalem. They put him to death by hanging him on a tree; but God raised him on the third day. . . .' (Acts 10:37-40a)

The Four Gospels

The Gospels, the principal source of our information, are probably the survivors of a considerable body of literature about Jesus which existed in the 1st century AD. They give written form to the oral tradition of the infant Christian Church. This tradition was developed, in the speeches and writings of the Christians of the first generation, in order to present the story of Jesus to those outside the Christian community and also to teach those who followed Jesus to apply his teaching in their lives. This was done not by making a complete biography of Jesus but by a careful selection of episodes in his ministry, with a full and continuous account of his passion and the events which followed it. Each evangelist or writer of a Gospel adapts the tradition to the needs of his particular readers; but it is possible to trace, in each Gospel, the general course of events from the baptism of Jesus by John the Baptist to the resurrection of Jesus. Each Gospel was written by a believer in Jesus and all the writers of the Gospels interpret what they record, having in mind their particular purposes and the needs of their readers.

The Gospel of Mark and the Gospel of John present a notable contrast in their presentations of the life and work of Jesus. Mark's account is generally thought to have been written between 64 and 67 AD, earlier than the other three Gospels. The Gospels of Matthew and Luke seem to have been written later and they contain a great deal of material also found in the Gospel of Mark. This first Gospel to be written in Greek is thought by many scholars to have been composed in Rome, at the time of crisis following the death of the Apostles Peter and Paul and during a persecution of the Christians in Rome. It is thought to contain the recollections of Peter, whose interpreter Mark is said to have been. It was written as a statement of the facts about Jesus for use in the presentation of the message of the Christian community. It forms a group with the Gospels of Matthew and Luke; these three are often called the Synoptic Gospels.

The author of the Gospel of John, often called the Fourth Gospel, wrote for the Christians of the second generation, at a time when almost all those who remembered the life and death of Jesus had died. It has often been said that he assisted Christianity to continue to be a living faith, by proclaiming the Jesus of history and the Jesus of inward experience to be one. In order to do this in a manner which the world of his time could understand, he virtually adapted the story he had to tell to the form of a Greek tragedy. He combined, by the use of his imagination, narrative and symbolism, words and actions of Jesus and his thoughts about their meaning. In another respect he differs from the writers of the Synoptic Gospels. They describe the ministry of Jesus in Galilee, followed by his passion and resurrection in Jerusalem. John lays the scene of a great part of the ministry of Jesus in and near Jerusalem. There are some indications in the Gospels of Mark, Matthew and Luke that Jesus conducted more of his ministry in Judea and Jerusalem than they actually record; in this way they confirm the account given in the Gospel of John. No writer of a Gospel would have claimed to have supplied a complete and accurate biography of Jesus. But Mark, at a time when biography was in vogue in Rome, wrote a coherent life of Jesus the Christ, while the author of the Gospel of John presented to the Greek-speaking world scenes from the life of Jesus the Son of God. (*see* JOHN, LUKE, MARK, MATTHEW)

The birth stories

No account of the circumstances of the birth of Jesus is found either in the Gospel of Mark or in the Gospel of John. According to the Gospels of Matthew and Luke, Jesus was born in Bethlehem before the death of Herod the Great in 4 BC, probably not more than three years earlier. The Gospel of Matthew begins with a genealogy tracing the ancestry of Jesus back to Abraham. Composed in a Hebraic manner, this genealogy consists of three divisions, each containing fourteen generations. The Gospel of Luke has a different genealogy of Jesus, going back to God the universal Father of Mankind, through David, Abraham and Adam. Both include David and both refer to Joseph, the betrothed husband of Mary, rather than to Mary herself.

The belief that Jesus had no human father, but was conceived in the womb of Mary his mother by the action of the Holy Spirit (the Christian doctrine of the Virgin Birth) is clearly stated in both in the Gospel of Matthew and in the Gospel of Luke, where it is expressed in the story of the annunciation of Mary. 'The angel Gabriel was sent from God to a city of Galilee named Nazareth, to a virgin betrothed to a man whose name was Joseph, of the House of David; and the virgin's name was Mary. And he came to her and said, "Hail, O favoured one, the Lord is with you." But she was greatly troubled. . . . And the angel said to her, "Do not be afraid, Mary, for you have found favour with God, and behold you will conceive in your womb and bear a son, and you shall call his name Jesus . . ."' To this Mary replies, ' "How can this be, since I have no husband?" And the angel said to her, "The Holy Spirit will come upon you, and the power of the Most High will overshadow you; therefore the child to be born will be called holy, the Son of God. . . . For with God nothing will be impossible." And Mary said, "Behold, I am the handmaid of the Lord; let it be to me according to your word." And the angel departed from her.' It is noteworthy, however, that the speeches attributed to Peter in the Acts of the Apostles, giving the outlines of the life of Jesus the Christ, make no mention of the Virgin Birth and that the Gospels of Mark and John do not use it in support of the idea of the Messianic function of Jesus. The Christian Church has taken this doctrine from the Gospels of Matthew and Luke. (Matt. 1:18-25; Luke 1:26-38)

Matthew alone describes the dilemma of Joseph finding his spouse to be with child and his reassurance by an angel in a dream. This story could have come from Joseph. Many of the stories in the Gospel of Luke could have come from Mary the mother of Jesus. The Gospel of Matthew is concerned to show the birth of Jesus as the fulfillment of prophecy, in order to prove his Messiahship. He writes for a Christian community having Jews and Gentiles in its membership, so that he shows the child Jesus being welcomed by the Gentile wise men from the east, as King of the Jews. Only secular authority, represented by Herod the Great and his son Archelaus, is seen to reject Jesus. (Matt. 2:3-12, 22) This Gospel quotes Isaiah (7:10-14) to confirm the Virgin Birth, Micah (5:2) to indicate Bethlehem as the place of the birth of the Messiah, Jeremiah (31:15) in connection with the massacre of the children by Herod (Matt. 2:16) and Hosea as predicting the flight of Joseph and Mary with the child to Egypt. They return from Egypt 'to fulfil what the Lord had spoken by the prophet, "Out of Egypt have I called my son"'. The Gospel of Luke alone tells the story of the birth of John the Baptist, the cousin of Jesus, and the announcements by angels of the births of John and Jesus to the father of John, Zechariah, and Mary the mother of Jesus, with the meeting between the two mothers, Mary and Elizabeth. These stories are beautifully told and many believe that the writer of the Greek Gospel of Luke took them from an Aramaic document which he translated. He introduces into his story of the births of John and Jesus three songs, composed in a Hebraic manner. These may have been translations from Hebrew or Aramaic and are known and used in the Christian Church as hymns. In Western Christendom they are called the *Magnificat* (Luke 1:46-55), the *Benedictus* (Luke 1:68-79) and the *Nunc Dimittis* (Luke 2:29-32). In the last of these the old man who blesses the child Jesus in the Temple at Jerusalem says that he is to be 'a light for revelation to the Gentiles and for glory to thy people Israel'.

Both accounts of the birth of Jesus place it in Bethlehem. The Gospel of Luke says that the original home of Mary was at Nazareth in Galilee and that she and Joseph went to Bethlehem in response to the demands of a Roman census. During their stay in Bethlehem the child is born, visited by shepherds who have seen an angelic vision, circumcised on the eighth day after his birth and presented in the Temple at Jerusalem on the fortieth day. His parents, Mary and Joseph, then return with him to Nazareth. However, Luke says that Joseph went to Bethlehem because it was his own city, to which his family belonged. The Gospel of Matthew does not mention Nazareth until the return of the family from their escape into Egypt and seems to imply that they had a house in Bethlehem, into which the wise men from the east brought their gifts. There are some modern critical scholars who consider that the tradition about the birth of Jesus in Bethlehem grew out of the need to prove his Messiahship and that he is more likely to have been born in Nazareth. They draw our attention to a comment recorded in the Gospel of John: 'When they heard these words, some of the people said, "This is really the prophet." Others said, "This is the Christ." But some said, "Is the Christ to come from Galilee? Has not the scripture said that Christ is descended from David, and

comes from Bethlehem, the village where David was?"
So there was a division among the people over him.'

The Bethlehem tradition soon crystallized in the Church and a cave in Bethlehem was pointed out as the birthplace of Christ. This is not mentioned in the Gospels. But about AD 155 Justin Martyr, a Christian whose birthplace was Neapolis in Samaria, wrote in Rome: 'Should anyone desire other proof for the birth of Jesus in Bethlehem . . . let him consider that in harmony with the Gospel story of his birth a cave is shown in Bethlehem where he was born and a manger in the cave where he lay wrapped in swaddling clothes.' The apocryphal Christian Protoevangelium of James, said to have been written during the 2nd century AD, referred to the Cave of the Birth of Jesus. At the close of the 3rd century AD Eusebius, bishop of Caesarea, wrote: 'The inhabitants of the place bear witness of the story that has come down to them from their fathers and they confirm the truth of it and point out the cave in which the Virgin brought forth and laid her child.' The Church of the Holy Nativity was built over this cave in Bethlehem, on the initiative of the Empress Helena, the mother of the Emperor Constantine, in AD 325. From that time forward there is no question of the site being lost, although the church building was destroyed and rebuilt two centuries later.

The boyhood and youth of Jesus

About the childhood of Jesus in Nazareth there is only one story in the Gospels. During a visit made by the family to Jerusalem when he was twelve years old, his parents found him 'in the Temple, sitting among the teachers, listening to them and asking them questions'. His mother said to him, 'your father and I have been looking for you anxiously.' To this Jesus replied, 'Did you not know that I must be in my Father's house?' (An alternative translation is, 'that I must be occupied with my Father's affairs'.) The Gospel of Luke goes on to say, 'Jesus increased in wisdom and in stature and in favour with God and man.' In the Gospel of Mark (and also in the Gospel of Matthew, dependent on Mark at this point in all probability) we are told that Jesus was known as 'the carpenter, the son of Mary, and brother of James and Joses and Judas and Simon', in Nazareth. The Gospel of Matthew says that Jesus was 'the carpenter's son'.

Jesus was educated. Unlike the other religions of the time, the religion of the Jews was essentially recorded in the Book of the Law and the Books of the Prophets, written in a language which people understood and which all children were taught to read. Jewish children were taught to hear, understand and study their sacred books. A synagogue to be found in every village or town and schools attached to the synagogues were attended by all boys. The teachers were the rabbis, from whom the children learned the Law and its meaning, Hebrew history and the Hebrew language.

Nazareth overlooks that great highway and battle-field of history, the Plain of Esdraelon, which is the only flat corridor through the mountain ranges between the Mediterranean and the east. Thus through the plain below the hillside town many armies have marched, from the empires of Egypt, Assyria and Babylon, from Persia and from Macedonia and Rome. The plain continued to be the scene of battles until modern times. Through this plain passed the trade route between Damascus and Egypt, known as 'The Way of the Sea'. In and near Nazareth, a market town of Galilee not far from this great road, caravans of silk and spices passed camels laden with grain and fish. The peasants of Galilee mingled with the merchants and travellers of the east. It has been contended that this made them, or at least some of them, adopt a more or less cosmopolitan outlook. Jesus may have watched the bargains driven in the market-place and listened there to the stories and gossip of the day. It was a rough and ready schooling for the hazards of an itinerant ministry, of open-air preaching and heckling by his opponents in the years of his public life.

The baptism of Jesus by John and his temptation in the desert

It was as a man, 'about thirty years of age' (Luke 3:23), that Jesus came down to the fords of the River Jordan to be baptized by John. He associated himself with the revivalist message of John the Baptist. John, the son of Zechariah and Elizabeth, the cousin of Mary according to the Gospel of Luke, 'came into all the region round about Jordan, preaching a baptism of repentance, for the forgiveness of sins'. According to the Gospel of Matthew his message was 'Repent, for the kingdom of heaven is at hand.' This became the message of Jesus after John was imprisoned by Herod Antipas. The story of the baptism of Jesus by John, as the Gospel of Mark describes it, is much more than an indication of the acceptance by Jesus of the message of John. It is an account of a personal experience of Jesus, a revelation to him both of his Messiahship and of the method of his Messiahship. 'And when he came up out of the water, immediately he saw the heavens opened and the Spirit descending upon him like a dove; and a voice came from heaven, "Thou art my beloved Son; with thee I am well pleased." ' (Mark 1:10, 11) Jesus must have told this story himself and cannot have failed to point out that the words of the voice were quoted from the Psalms and the Book of Isaiah. The first words come from Psalm 2, generally believed to refer to the King-Messiah: 'The Lord hath said unto me, "Thou art my son" ' (cf. Ps. 2:7: 'I will tell of the decree of the Lord; He said to me "You are my son".') The other words of the voice came from the Suffering Servant passages of the Book of Isaiah, which Jesus repeatedly quoted during his ministry. (Isa. 42:1-4: 'Behold my servant, whom I uphold, my chosen, in whom my soul delights.') Jesus constantly used the Suffering Servant passages of the Book of Isaiah to convince his disciples that he had come into the world in order 'to give his life as a ransom for many'. (Mark 10:45 and compare Isa. 53:11, 12)

It would seem that at his baptism Jesus became supremely aware of his Sonship as the Messiah of his people and of the cost in suffering that his calling would demand from him. From that moment, as Peter said in his speech to Cornelius, 'God anointed Jesus of Nazareth with the Holy Spirit and with power'. (Acts 10:38) But the immediate effect of this experience was to drive him into the wilderness, to face the consequences of this new realization. There in an inward mental struggle he rejected various ways of winning the loyalty of men without winning their hearts. These took the form of three temptations. The first was the temptation to bribe a following by the offer of material gain, turning stones into bread to feed the hungry crowds. Another temptation was to astound men by a display of supernatural powers, leaping from the top of the Temple at Jerusalem and floating over the Kidron Valley supported by the angels of God. Thirdly, Jesus was tempted to make a compromise with the forces of evil by imposing his own personal will in opposition to the purpose of God for him; this is expressed in the offer of 'all the kingdoms of the world', in return for an act of prostration before Satan. (Luke 4:1-12; Matt. 4:1-11)

After his temptation, according to the Gospel of Luke, Jesus went back to Galilee, 'in the power of the Spirit . . . and a report concerning him went out through all the surrounding country. And he taught in their synagogues, being glorified by all.'

Whether the setting of the wilderness, the wild beasts, the devil and the angels was symbolical or not, the traditional place of the baptism of Jesus in the Jordan is the ford at Hajlah, not far from the mouth of the river at the north end of the Dead Sea. It is among the lowest points on the earth's surface; on the west of it is the mountainous wilderness of Judea, the traditional site of the temptation of Jesus. It seems that for some time John the Baptist lived on the east bank of the Jordan, perhaps to avoid conflict with the authorities in Judea and Jerusalem and because the regular flow of clean water from the Wadi el-Kharrar into the Jordan facilitated baptisms. Here too was an ideal place, off the road yet accessible from the ford. In the earlier centuries of the history of Christianity tradition seems to have placed the baptism of Jesus on the east bank of the Jordan. But the Greek Orthodox Monastery of St John, on the west bank, contains remains of a Christian shrine of the Byzantine period. Arculf, a pilgrim to the Jordan about 670, describes a small chapel at a lower level than the monastery and a stone bridge from the west bank of the river to a cross in the middle of the stream to indicate the actual place of the baptism of Jesus.

219

For the place of the temptation of Jesus, a tradition indicates a mountain about 820 feet high on the edge of the Jordan valley, overlooking ancient Jericho (Tel es-Sultan). The mountain is called *Sarantarion Horos* in Greek and *Mons Quarantana* in Latin, because of the forty days of the fast kept by Jesus. A pilgrim of the period of the Crusades, named Theodoric, describes a path leading up the mountain, first to a chapel dedicated to St Mary, the mother of Jesus, and then to an altar in the form of a cross, close to which was shown the place, halfway up the mountain, where Jesus sat on the rock. On the summit of the mountain was shown the seat of Satan the tempter. This site commands a magnificent view of the Jordan Valley and of the mountains of Moab, although not of 'all the kingdoms of the world'.

The kingdom of God

This was the opening theme of the teaching and preaching of Jesus. He declared that: 'The time is fulfilled, and the kingdom of God is at hand.' (Mark 1:15) From the beginning of their life as a nation, the Israelites had believed themselves to be under the rule of God. During their history, before and after their exile in Babylon, they came to think of the kingdom of God as including all nations, although the other nations did not acknowledge the rule of God. Over his own people God was the supreme ruler; but he was opposed by the other nations and this opposition would in the end be overcome. During and after the exile of the Jews in Babylon, the recovery of the independence of Israel was expected to be achieved under a prince of David's line, the Anointed of the Lord or the Messiah. Then God would reign in the whole world. The prophets of Israel had foretold a day of judgment and purging by suffering which would precede and usher in the universal rule of God. When the Jews were in the grip of alien occupation and persecution, under the empires of Babylon, Persia, Greece and Rome, they hoped for the triumph of the kingdom or empire of God, after the fall of all these empires, as the result of a supernatural intervention in human history. The writers of the Book of Daniel and the Book of Enoch foretold a 'son of Man', descending through the clouds to establish the kingdom of God in the future, at the end of the period in which the world is dominated by the 'Beasts' which are the Gentile empires. This hope of supernatural deliverance is called 'apocalyptic', as it meant that God would reveal or unveil his purpose for his people ('apocalypse' means 'revelation').

The arrival of Jesus in Galilee, declaring that: 'The time is fulfilled, and the kingdom of God is at hand' (Mark 1:15), had a tremendous impact on the simple people and drew all of them, including the Scribes and Pharisees and Zealots, coming from all directions to hear his message. Jesus believed in the present sovereignty of God and the future universal manifestation of that sovereignty. But he also insisted that the power of the kingdom of God was already at work in the world, through his own coming. Jesus declared that the rule of God comes here and now, insofar as it is acknowledged, and becomes a reality at once to those who accept it. 'But if it is by the Spirit of God that I cast out demons, then the Kingdom of God is come upon you.' (Matt. 12:28) 'But blessed are your eyes, for they see, and your ears, for they hear. Truly I say to you, many prophets and righteous men longed to see what you see, and did not see it, and to hear what you hear, and did not hear it.' (Matt. 13:16, 17) At Nazareth Jesus read a passage from the Book of Isaiah, concerning the Messiah: 'The Spirit of the Lord is upon me, because the Lord has anointed me to bring good tidings to the afflicted; he has sent me to bind up the broken-hearted, to proclaim liberty to the captives, and the opening of the prison to those who are bound: to proclaim the year of the Lord's favour.' (Isa. 61:1-2) (Cf. Luke 4:18-19: 'Because *he* has anointed me to preach good news to the poor. He has sent me to proclaim release to the captives and recovering of sight to the blind, to set at liberty those who are oppressed, to proclaim the acceptable year of the Lord.') He then rolled up the scroll and declared: 'Today has this scripture been fulfilled in your hearing.' (Luke 4:21) When the Pharisees asked him to tell them when the kingdom of God would come, he replied, 'Behold, the kingdom of God is in the midst of you.' (Luke 17:21)

There is no inconsistency in this triple conception of the kingdom or rule of God the Father as eternal, present and also to be fully recognized in the future. According to the Gospel of John, Jesus identified the kingdom of God with eternal life. To accept the rule of God, to enter the kingdom of God and to inherit eternal life are the same. In the Gospel of John, except in the story of Nicodemus, the term 'the kingdom of God' is not used. The term 'eternal life' is constantly used instead of 'the kingdom of God' in John's Gospel, according to some scholars. This may have been because it was more comprehensible to the Greek world and less easily confused with Jewish national aspirations. The Zealots in their battle with Rome may well have said that they fought for the kingdom of God. But it is likely that Jesus used both phrases – with a similar meaning. The word 'kingdom' is found at crucial points in the Gospel of John. The word translated as 'eternal' in that Gospel, the Greek *aionia,* is derived from *aion,* translated 'age' or 'world', which is often found in the other three Gospels. The end of this *aion* and the beginning of the future or coming *aion* signify the time of the Messiah, which is the manifestation of the kingdom of God. Life (in Greek *zoe*) as the object of man's spiritual search and the gift of God is emphasized in all the Four Gospels.

In the Synoptic Gospels, especially in the Gospel of Matthew, many of the parables of Jesus begin with the phrase, 'The kingdom of God is like. . . .' It grows fast like the mustard-seed. It acts like leaven in the lump of God's world. It is like hidden treasure, worth selling everything in order to obtain it. It is like a dragnet full of every kind of fish, from which the contents must ultimately be sorted out. So at the final judgment at the end of the *aion* men will be sorted out. According to the Gospel of Mark, Jesus said to his disciples: 'To you has been given the secret of the kingdom of God, but for those outside everything is in parables.' 'To his own disciples he explained everything.'

The miracles attributed to Jesus in the Gospels are regarded by the writers as signs of the coming of the kingdom of God. In the time of Jesus there was no dispute about the possibility of miracles and the reality of supernatural power was assumed. Two Greek words sometimes translated by the word 'miracle' appear in one sentence of a speech of Peter in Jerusalem, on the feast of Pentecost following the death and resurrection of Jesus. 'Jesus of Nazareth, a man attested to you by God with mighty works [Greek *dynameis*] and portents and signs [Greek *semeia*] which God did through him, as you yourselves know,' is the subject of Peter's speech. The first word used, *dynameis,* meant 'acts of power'; the word translated 'signs' (*semeia*) alluded to the meanings of these acts of power. In modern times miracles are events thought to be beyond the known power of natural causes and therefore attributed to the supernatural by those who believe in it. In the days of Jesus, miracles were also signs of divine power of which the true importance lay in what they might signify. The parables of Jesus were homespun stories of real life with an inner spiritual meaning which could be perceived only by those whose listening and thinking was in tune with the mind of the teacher. The miracles of Jesus seem to have been acted parables; they and the stories about them have a meaning which could not be grasped except by those who believed in Jesus. According to the Gospels the Pharisees still asked Jesus for a sign, after seeing all his miracles. Jesus said to his disciples, 'To you it has been given to know the secrets of the kingdom of heaven, but to them it has not been given.' (Matt. 13:11) The writer of the Gospel of Matthew adds, as a comment, a quotation from the Book of Isaiah: 'You shall indeed hear but never understand, and you shall indeed see but never perceive. For this people's heart has grown dull, and their ears are heavy of hearing, and their eyes they have closed, lest they should perceive with their eyes, and hear with their ears, and understand with their heart, and turn for me to heal them.' (Matt. 13:14, 15; cf. Isa. 6:9, 10) Without faith in Jesus in the minds and hearts of the eye-witnesses, the miracles of Jesus were not an effective means of showing his identity as the Messiah. Mark records that Jesus 'could do no mighty work' at Nazareth, 'because of their unbelief'.

Physical disease was then regarded as the manifestation of evil. Talking about a man who had been born blind, the disciples of Jesus asked him, 'Who sinned, this man or his parents, that he was born blind?' The answer of Jesus is significant: 'It was not that this man sinned, or his parents, but that the work of God might be made manifest in him. We must work. . . .' (John 9:2-4) In other words, we are to cure evils rather than to search for their causes. Among the contemporaries of Jesus the leper was considered to be unclean, spiritually as well as physically; and as such he was rejected. Thus Jesus, by curing the body, showed his power to heal the spirit. As the diseases of body and spirit were thought to be interdependent, those who had faith in Jesus believed him to have power over the bodies and spirits of men.

When Jesus healed the paralytic who was carried to him at Capernaum, seeing the patient on a pallet he said, 'My son, your sins are forgiven.' The scribes then accused him of blasphemy, saying: 'Who can forgive sins, but God alone?' Jesus asked them, 'Which is easier, to say to the paralytic, "Your sins are forgiven", or to say, "Rise, take up your pallet and walk"? But that you may know that the Son of Man has authority on earth to forgive sins.' Jesus then said to the paralytic, 'I say to you, rise, take up your pallet and go home.' (Mark 2:5-11)

A prophecy about the Messiah in the Book of Isaiah (Isa. 61) stated that his coming would be accompanied by the healing of disease and the liberation of men from the power of evil. Mental illness, like physical illness, was regarded as spiritual in origin. It was described as the possession of a person who was ill by evil spirits or demons. The exorcists of the time of Jesus employed magical formulas and spells, of a religious character. Jesus cast out demons by his own authority, ordering them to go out of the person possessed by them. This power was believed to demonstrate his Messiahship. 'If it is by the finger of God that I cast out demons, then the kingdom of God is come upon you,' he said in an argument with his opponents. (Luke 11:20) The demons are represented as recognizing his Messianic power, as they cry out with a loud voice, 'What have you to do with us, O Son of God? Have you come here to torment us before the time?' (Matt. 8:29) On another occasion the evil spirit shouts, 'I know who you are, the Holy One of God.' Jesus orders the demons to be silent. (Mark 1:24, 25)

The miracles of Jesus in raising the dead, as they are found in the Gospels, have the same meaning. Power to restore life to the dead body is symbolical of divine power to give eternal life. The story of the raising of the daughter of Jairus, a ruler of the synagogue at a town in Galilee, comes at the climax of a series of miracles. Delay in the arrival of Jesus results in the death of the child and a message is brought to her father to say that it is too late for the healer to come. But for Jesus death is no ground for despair and he says to the child's father, 'Do not fear, only believe.' (Mark 5:31) In the raising of the daughter of Jairus there is no public display; the faith of the eye-witnesses is essential, so those present are only the parents of the child and his own disciples. The lesson to be learnt by the discerning readers of the Gospels may be that eternal life is not to be found only beyond the grave, but it is to be grasped by a spiritual rebirth, within this present life. Jesus said, in a conversation with Martha, the sister of Lazarus, before the raising of Lazarus in the Gospel of John: 'I am the Resurrection and the Life; he who believes in me, though he die, yet shall he live. . . .' (John 11:25, 26)

The miracles of Jesus within the world of the forces of nature are also reported in the Gospels as signs of the kingdom of God. In many passages of the Hebrew Bible a storm at sea is a symbol of demonic forces, a fearsome monster epitomizing the uncontrollable forces against God. The story of the miracle by which Jesus calmed the stormy water in the Lake of Galilee may have a meaning related to this biblical imagery. The power of God is pre-eminently shown in Jesus's control of the sea. 'A great storm of wind arose, and the waves beat into the boat, so that the boat was already filling. But he was in the stern, asleep on the cushion; and they woke him and said to him, "Teacher, do you not care if we perish?" And he awoke and rebuked the wind, and said to the sea, "Peace! Be still!" And the wind ceased, and there was a great calm. He said to them, "Why are you afraid? Have you no faith?" And they were filled with awe and said to one another, "Who then is this, that even wind and sea obey him?" ' (Mark 4:37-41) Indeed, their own Jewish tradition might have supplied the answer: 'This is God'. After Jesus is seen miraculously walking on the water of the lake, the Gospel of Mark comments that his followers were 'utterly astounded'. (Mark 6:51) The Gospel of Matthew, in giving an account of the same incident, adds that 'Those in the boat worshipped him, saying, "Truly you are the Son of God." ' (Matt. 14:33)

The Suffering Messiah

see CHRIST

The purpose of the passion of Jesus

According to all the Four Gospels, Jesus foretold his own arrest, condemnation and crucifixion and believed that these were required in order that the Messianic purpose of his life might be carried out. The famous German historian of religion Albert Schweitzer thus answered the question: what did Jesus himself believe about his future suffering and death? 'Jesus considered himself the spiritual ruler of mankind and he bent history to his purpose. He cast himself upon the wheel of the world and it crushed him, yet he hangs there still. That is his victory.' This was written by one who did not believe in the resurrection of Christ. Certain historians of religion attribute to the Christian community, as represented by the writers of the Four Gospels, the association between the life of Jesus and the Suffering Servant passages in the Book of Isaiah, together with the purposeful element in the story of the sufferings of Jesus. Schweitzer, disagreeing with them, attributed it to Jesus himself, fully conscious of the consequences of his actions, including his death on the cross, and seeking to fulfil prophecy by forcing events to take place with this purpose in view.

According to the Gospels, Jesus made many references to the Suffering Servant passages in the Book of Isaiah in his teaching. (*see* CHRIST) He asked the disciples James and John this question: 'Are you able to drink the cup that I drink, or to be baptized with the baptism with which I am baptized?' (Mark 10:38) On another occasion he is reported in the Gospel of Luke as saying, 'I came to cast fire upon the earth; and I would that it were already kindled! I have a baptism to be baptized with; and how I am constrained until it is accomplished!' (Luke 12:49, 50)

Jesus went up to Jerusalem on the last journey before his arrest and death, knowing that the kindling of fire on the earth depended on his drinking of the cup of suffering, according to his own belief about himself. The passion was not a martyrdom which he endured passively; it was the accomplishment of his own set purpose, an act of his own will. He need not have gone to Jerusalem and challenged the authorities by his actions there. He need not have stayed in the Garden of Gethsemane to await his arrest; in the Garden his vivid foreknowledge of the end cost him an agony of anticipation. According to the Gospel of John he said, 'For this reason the Father loves me, because I lay down my life, that I may take it again. No one takes it from me, but I lay it down of my own accord. I have power to lay it down, and I have power to take it again. . . .' (John 10:17, 18)

Jesus is represented as knowing himself to be the Messiah, although keeping his conviction a secret, told only to those disciples whom he was certain of not misleading about the nature of his work and purpose. He went to his death in the certainty that it was the will of God, completely aware of what was coming to him, completely accepting it and utterly determined that nothing should prevent the will of God being done.

The passion of Jesus

The Passion narratives, continuous and coherent, occupy a considerable part of each of the Four Gospels. All the Gospels state that there was a meeting of Jewish leaders in which the downfall of Jesus was planned. The Gospel of John describes, in some detail, a meeting of chief priests and leaders of the Pharisees after the raising of Lazarus, at which they discussed the matter in these terms: ' "What are we to do? For this man performs many signs. If we let him go on thus, everyone will believe in him, and the Romans will come and destroy both our holy place and our nation." But one of them, Caiaphas, who was high priest that year, said to them, "You know nothing at all; you do not understand that it is expedient for you that one man should die for the people, and that the whole nation should not perish." . . . So from that day on they took counsel how to put him to death.' (John 11:47-53) There was a real danger of Roman intervention, in the form of a general attack on the Jews, if anyone claiming to be the Messiah had enough support to make him seem to be a danger to the Romans. For the Messianic hope was popularly associated with the end of Roman rule. Certainly there were other motives for an attack on Jesus. The chief priests and the party of the Sadducees might see his expulsion of the traders from the Temple at Jerusalem as a threat to their private interests, as well as to public security. To the party of the Pharisees and the leaders of the scribes and rabbis, his attitude to the traditional interpretation of the Law might appear subversive and dangerous.

The Gospels all give accounts of the treachery of Judas, one of the twelve disciples of Jesus, who betrayed him. The Gospel of Luke implies that the information given by Judas made it possible for the arrest of Jesus to be made secretly, avoiding an uproar among the crowds of people in Jerusalem for the Passover festival. It is also probable that evidence was given by Judas of the Messianic claim of Jesus, at his examination before the chief priests. The motives of Judas were mercenary according to all the Four Gospels. But it is possible that he had simply lost faith in Jesus and wished to provide for his own safety. Some imaginative writers have suggested that he tried to force the hand of Jesus, provoking him by treachery into an open declaration of his Messiahship, without being aware of the fatal consequences.

According to all the Gospels, Jesus ate a last supper with his disciples, on the night before his death. There is a difference between the Gospels about the date of this in the Jewish calendar. The Synoptic Gospels appear to identify the Last Supper with the Passover feast. The Gospel of John represents Jesus as crucified on the day of the Passover feast and places the Last Supper on the previous evening. However, the description of the Last Supper in the Gospels of Mark and Matthew may suggest that it is not the Passover feast, although the name of the Passover is given to it. A hymn is mentioned; but Mark and Matthew put the breaking of the bread before the cup is passed round. In the Gospel of Luke the cup comes before the breaking of the bread; this may indicate the Passover feast. John's account of the date is considered by many to be historical; a man with a group of followers who might be expected to defend him would not be arrested on the night of the Passover. The Synoptic Gospels seem to imply that the arrest was not intended to be on the feast of the Passover (which includes the previous evening). 'They said, "Not during the feast, lest there be a tumult of the people." ' (Mark 14:2; Matt. 26:5) The Jewish leaders are described in the Gospel of John as fearing to be defiled, if they entered the Roman governor's headquarters for the trial of

231

Jesus before Pilate. The Passover feast was still in the future at that point. The bodies of Jesus and of the thieves crucified with him were removed from the crosses late in the afternoon, before sunset, on the day of the crucifixion, so that there would be no evidence of the execution when the Sabbath of the Passover festival began. The symbolical significance of the date of the crucifixion, according to the Gospel of John, is remarkable. At noon, as the crucifixion took place, the Passover lambs were killed in the Temple. The resurrection, on the first day of the week, coincided with the offering of the first-fruits in the Temple. So in the letter of Paul to the Corinthian Christians he can write 'Christ, our paschal lamb, has been sacrificed' and 'Christ has been raised from the dead, the first fruits of those who have fallen asleep.' (1 Cor. 5:7; 15:20)

The atmosphere at the Last Supper must have been heavy with a sense of the impending passion of Jesus combined with all the sacrificial associations of the Passover. The Gospel of John does not describe the supper itself, for the writer has already included in his Gospel, in the passage after the feeding of the five thousand (John 6:25-59), a long account of the teaching of the Church about Jesus as 'the bread of life'. He, however, tells the wonderful story of Jesus washing the feet of his disciples after the supper, giving a last example of loving humility. The writers of the Synoptic Gospels relate the actions of Jesus, as they described them in their accounts of the feeding of the five thousand and other similar happenings during the ministry of Jesus in Galilee. 'Taking the loaves . . . he looked up to heaven, and blessed and broke the loaves and gave them to the disciples.' (Mark 6:41) But this time the actual words of Jesus are given. 'Take; this is my body,' he said, as he gave the bread. 'This is my blood of the covenant which is poured out for many,' he said, giving the cup of wine. To his followers, the bread was a sign and more than a sign; like the live coal from the altar brought to the prophet Isaiah at his call, it was to purge them, that they might share his atoning power. Nor could they fail to remember the blood sprinkled by Moses, first upon the altar and then upon the people of Israel, 'the blood of the covenant which the Lord has made with you', at the foot of Mount Sinai. Thus Jesus is said to have instituted what became in the Christian community the Holy Eucharist, the sacrifice of the New Testament, the means of communion between him and his followers. For this purpose he had evaded arrest until then. As the Gospel of Luke records his words, he said at the Last Supper: 'I have earnestly desired to eat this Passover with you before I suffer.'

The arrest and trials of Jesus

Judas had already slipped out into the darkness when, with a sense of foreboding, Jesus and his remaining disciples went down into the Kidron Valley and crossed the brook to reach the Garden of Gethsemane. It is probable that this was their regular resting-place and their meeting-place, before they came into the city together or returned from the city to their lodgings at Bethany or elsewhere for the night. The Gospel of Luke indicates that on occasions they used to spend the night on the Mount of Olives. The Gospel of John says 'across the Kidron valley . . . there was a garden, which he and his disciples entered. Now Judas, who betrayed him, also knew the place; for Jesus often met there with his disciples.' Although no doubt he could have returned over the hill to Bethany, Jesus remained there, purposefully, to await his arrest. In a final human agony of anticipation, he submitted himself to the divine will. On the arrival of Judas with those who were sent to arrest Jesus, he was identified and apprehended and his disciples fled. From the Garden of Gethsemane the prisoner and his escort returned to the Western Hill of Jerusalem, passing down the Kidron, in at the Fountain Gate and up the ancient stairway that led from the Pool of Siloam to the palace of the high priest, in which the scribes and elders were assembled.

At a place which many believe to have been the site of the house of Caiaphas the high priest, there are striking remains of ancient buildings that illustrate the story of the trial of Jesus there. On this site, under the Church of St Peter, there are remains of buildings at several levels, cut into the rocky face of the hill. Above is the courtroom, with a raised dock at one end and the bottle-neck of a cell for the condemned in the centre of the rock floor. Below this is the guardroom, with whipping-block and with staples for the prisoners' chains. Further down is the cell for the condemned, where Jesus may have spent the night before his crucifixion in the darkness, remembering the words of Psalm 88: 'I am reckoned among those who go down to the pit . . . in the regions dark and deep . . . afflicted and close to death . . . I am helpless. . . .'

The descriptions in the Gospels of the trial or examination before the religious authorities vary considerably. The Gospels of Mark and Matthew agree closely; the Gospels of Luke and John give different accounts. The Gospel of Mark, followed by that of Matthew, describes the trial of Jesus before the 'whole Council' (the Sanhedrin) as taking place on the night of his arrest. The first charge of blasphemy was that he had said that he would destroy the Temple. The witnesses did not agree and the charge was not proved. The next charge was that he had claimed to be the Messiah. Judas could have given evidence on this charge and perhaps did so. Peter was sitting within earshot and could have been pressed into giving evidence. Perhaps that is why he was asked three times and denied three times that he knew anything about Jesus. Jesus, when directly questioned on this charge by the high priest, said 'I am,' according to the Gospel of Mark, and 'You have said so,' according to the Gospels of Matthew and Luke. According to the Gospel of John he refused to answer about his disciples and his teaching. But in the three other Gospels his answer to the question of the high priest about his Messianic claim includes a reference to 'the Son of Man sitting at the right hand of power and coming with the clouds of heaven'. This brought about his conviction for blasphemy. According to the Gospels of Matthew and Mark, 'they all condemned him as deserving death'. The Council met early on the following morning to formulate the charges which they were to present before Pilate the Roman governor. He was waiting for the prisoner and his accusers at the Praetorium. According to the somewhat different account in the Gospel of Luke the trial at the house of the high priest was not held until the morning after the arrest of Jesus. This would be lawful, whereas it was unlawful to hold a trial during the night. Peter denies that he knows Jesus, not during his trial, but in the course of the night before it. At the trial there is no mention of the charge that Jesus said he would destroy the Temple. The Council does not condemn Jesus to death on the charge of claiming to be the Messiah, the one charge mentioned. Jesus is mocked before the trial by the servants of the high priest, in the

235

account given by Luke; in the Gospels of Matthew and Mark the members of the Council appear to mock him during the trial.

The Praetorium was probably within the Antonia Fortress. This is described thus by the great Dominican scholar Vincent: 'This gigantic quadrilateral, cut almost entirely out of the rocky hill, covered an area of 150 metres east to west, by 80 meters north to south. It was protected by powerful corner towers and enclosed installations as complex and diverse as a palace and camp. The outstanding but characteristic feature of this complex was, without doubt, the courtyard, about 2,500 metres square, serving as a place of meeting between the city and the Antonia. Extending over deep water cisterns, covered with a massive polished pavement, surrounded by tall cloisters, this courtyard was really the heart of the fortress whose activity it regulated. . . . Pilate had his tribunal set up within the courtyard, transformed for the occasion into the Praetorium, called indeed the "Pavement" *par excellence*. Where could one find more appropriate a setting for the place where Pilate pronounced the sentence which sent Jesus on his way to Calvary? On to this Pavement the prisoner and his escort proceeded, while the crowd of those not entering the castle for fear of ceremonial defilement on the day of the Passover were left standing in and around the double gateway. Pilate, seated in his curial chair at the head of a stairway, may well have gazed down on the Pavement in disgust.

According to the Gospels of Mark and Matthew, Jesus was accused by the chief priests of treason against the Roman authority in declaring himself to be the King of the Jews. The description is one of a perfunctory routine. The Gospel of Luke, however, gives detailed and specific charges: 'We found this man perverting our nation, and forbidding us to give tribute to Caesar, and saying that he himself is Christ a king. . . . He stirs up the people, teaching throughout all Judea, from Galilee even to this place.' The high priest intends to place the responsibility for the death of Jesus on the shoulders of Pilate, claiming that he himself is a loyal supporter of the Roman administration. He wants to make the case of Jesus seem to be similar to that of any other self-appointed leader of an uprising against authority. In the Gospel of Luke the crowd, incited by the chief priests, demands the release of Barabbas, 'a man who had been thrown into prison for an insurrection started in the city, and for murder'. According to the other Synoptic Gospels and the Gospel of John, Pilate offered to release either of the two prisoners, Barabbas or Jesus, as it was customary to release a prisoner on the day of the Passover feast. The assembled crowd, no doubt under the influence of the priests and the Council, demanded the release of Barabbas and the crucifixion of Jesus. After making a feeble gesture of protest, Pilate condemned Jesus to the customary sequence of execution: scourging, mocking and crucifixion. Luke seems particularly anxious to show that the Roman governor did not want to crucify Jesus. Pilate believes in his innocence and declares it three times. An attempt is made to pass Jesus over to the jurisdiction of Herod, to whom Pilate sends him; but Herod, after ridiculing him, returns him to Pilate. Luke mentions no mocking by the soldiers in the Praetorium, described in the Gospels of Mark and Matthew. Pilate finally offers to flog Jesus and then to release him; but he is faced with something like a riot among the crowd and so releases Barabbas and condemns Jesus to death.

The Gospels were written, in all cases, either shortly before the war between the Jews and the Roman Empire of AD 66-70 or during the period after the war. The Romans associated the Christians with the Jews, although recognizing a difference between the two communities. The conviction of Jesus by a Roman governor and his death by a Roman form of capital punishment, crucifixion, were facts about the account of Jesus given by the Christians. They were an embarrassment to those who sought to stop the Roman persecution of Christianity. This may well have influenced the way in which the trials of Jesus were presented to the readers of the Gospels. The Council of the Jews, the Sanhedrin, was described as morally responsible for the sentence of death pronounced by the Roman governor. But Pilate may well have been influenced by the stories of the cleansing of the Temple by Jesus and his alleged intention to destroy the Temple. Though aware of the lack of evidence for any charge of treason, he must have been afraid of Messianic claims, since all associated the coming of the Messiah with the end of the Roman rule. He could not dismiss the charge of treason, if Jesus refused to refute it and remained silent. Having secured his own conviction for blasphemy, before Caiaphas, Jesus did nothing to secure his own release, before Pilate. The Gospel of John gives an account of a conversation between Jesus and Pilate, about the nature of the kingship of Jesus. It is not possible to know how such a conversation could have been recorded. It may well have been meant by the writer of the Gospel to explain the situation to his readers a generation later. Jesus declared, 'My kingship is not of this world; if my kingship were of this world, my servants would fight . . . but my kingship is not from the world. . . . You say that I am a king. For this I was born and for this I have come into the world, to bear witness to the truth. Everyone who is of the truth hears my voice.' (John 18:36, 37)

The crucifixion of Jesus

The crowd continued to call for the crucifixion of Jesus until Pilate pronounced the desired judgment, washed his hands publicly and returned to his quarters. After the necessary preparations three prisoners, Jesus and two bandits or robbers, formed a procession on the Pavement with their escort and passed out of the Antonia Fortress through the great double gate with its two guardrooms, one on each side, the prisoners carrying their huge crosses along the way to Calvary, known later among Christians as the Via Dolorosa.

The Gospels of Mark and Matthew agree in their accounts of the crucifixion, although Matthew adds the earthquake in which 'the rocks were split'. A remarkable fissure in the whole height of what now remains of a great rock has been treated since c.350 as evidence for the truth of this story in the Gospels and for the authenticity of the traditional site of the place which local Christian tradition regards as Cavalry. The description of the crucifixion in the Gospel of Mark is a stark and grim account of the death of the strong and silent Son of God, the Master still in control of the situation, 'bending history to his purpose'. It is unrelieved by the pity and sympathy shown in the Gospel of Luke. Jesus is too weak to carry his cross. He refuses the drugged wine, choosing to remain conscious. The soldiers strip him, crucify him and then share out his clothing. The passers-by jeer at him, taunt him, and tell him to get down from the cross, if he has miraculous powers. Those crucified with him revile him. The only words he is heard to utter are 'My God, my God, why hast thou forsaken me?' But supernatural events accompany his death, the sudden descent of the darkness and the split in the curtain in the Temple, which should hide but then reveals the Holy of Holies. The only man to recognize Jesus as the Son of God at the moment of his death is the Roman centurion in charge of his execution.

The account of the Gospel of Luke has been contrasted with the other accounts of the crucifixion, as an appeal to the pity of the readers. Crowds follow Jesus to his crucifixion, including wailing women and sympathetic watchers. One of the bandits who are crucified with Jesus is penitent and confesses his own guilt, recognizing the innocence of Jesus. The Roman centurion says that 'Certainly this man was innocent'. This description has been characterized as that of a martyr's death, surrounded by sympathy. The Gospel of Mark tells the story of a man willing to die. Mark's story carries with it a Christian interpretation. For every event a prediction is found in the Psalms and the Prophets of Israel. The words ascribed to Jesus are taken from the beginning of Psalm 22, which he may be thought to have been saying in prayer. The end of that Psalm is a picture of the universal reign of God: 'Yea, to him shall all the proud of the earth bow down . . . men shall tell of the Lord to the coming generation, and proclaim his deliverance to a people yet unborn, that he hath wrought it.'

The burial regulations of the Book of Deuteronomy (21:23) demanded that crucified criminals – or indeed any executed criminals – should be buried before sunset. This may have been especially important when the Passover Sabbath began in the evening, and the Romans respected local laws and customs in such matters.

If the body of Jesus had not been claimed, it might have been buried in a common grave. But Joseph of Arimathea begged the permission of Pilate to bury Jesus in his own tomb cut in the rock. Mark says: 'Joseph of Arimathea, a respected member of the Council, who was also himself looking for the kingdom of God, took courage and went to Pilate and asked for the body of Jesus.' The Gospel of Matthew describes Joseph of Arimathea as 'a rich man . . . and a disciple of Jesus'. Luke says that he was 'a member of the Council, a good and righteous man, who had not consented to their purpose and deed'. John calls him 'a disciple of Jesus, but secretly', who, together with Nicodemus, another secret friend of Jesus, anointed the body of Jesus, and buried it in a new tomb very near the place of his crucifixion.

The tomb was in a garden or grove of trees, presumably the private property of Joseph of Arimathea. Even if Herod Agrippa, at the building of the 'Third Wall' in the year 43, enclosed the garden within the walled city, it would have been untouched as a place of burial and the Christians, even if they did not own it, could have pointed it out to one another. Even the destruction of Jerusalem in the year 70 would not cause tombs cut in the rock or rocks split by earthquakes to disappear. When the city was rebuilt by the Romans in the year 138, after the Bar-Kokhba rebellion of 135, it is certain that the traditional site of the death and burial of Jesus Christ was covered by a terrace on which a Roman forum and temples of the deities of Rome were built. Recent archaeological investigation seems to show that the place which Christian tradition regards as Calvary was in a deep quarry, probably used for the defence of the 'Second Wall'. In this quarry the rock split by an earthquake is 32 feet higher than the level of the natural rock on all sides of it. What remains of it is 14 feet square. There were several tombs cut in the rock in the sides of the quarry. The Roman builders in the year 138 filled this trench with earth and built upon it, as their walled city was to be on both sides of the line of the 'Second Wall'. They may well have done this without intending the desecration of a holy place, belonging to a new community of which they knew little or nothing. But it was said by Christians in later centuries that the Emperor Hadrian felt it to be necessary thus to desecrate, systematically and thoroughly, the sites of the crucifixion and resurrection of Jesus Christ. In this way he marked the sites for the Christian excavations in 323-5, when the first Church of the Holy Resurrection of Christ was built, by the orders of the first Christian Roman emperor, Constantine the Great. The shrines then built included the rock split by an earthquake at Calvary (still to be seen in the church) and the tomb identified as the Holy Sepulchre of Jesus Christ. The traditional tomb was destroyed to a very great extent in the 11th century; the shrine contains remains of it. This is the central shrine in the church which Western Christians call the Church of the Holy Sepulchre, known to local Christians and to Eastern Christendom as the Church of the Holy Resurrection.

The resurrection

The followers of Jesus of Nazareth believed that he had shown himself to be alive. In the New Testament we find three ways of presenting the resurrection of Jesus Christ. First of all the Christian community or Church exists and the life of that community is the continuation of the life of Jesus of Nazareth. Secondly, followers of Jesus of Nazareth say and write that on the first day of the week, the day after the Sabbath which followed his death, his tomb was found to be empty. Thirdly, many of the followers of Jesus state in the books of the New Testament that during the six weeks after his death he appeared to them and showed them that he was alive.

All the Four Gospels record visits made to the tomb of Jesus by his disciples, who found it to be empty. The Gospels of Luke, Matthew and John, as well as the Acts of the Apostles and the First Letter of Paul to the Corinthians, record appearances of Jesus after the resurrection. The Gospel of Mark says that women who were disciples of Jesus bought spices after sunset on the Sabbath day following the crucifixion, in order to anoint his body. Very early in the morning on the first day of the week they came to the tomb of Jesus. They found that the stone in the entrance of the tomb was rolled back. 'And on entering the tomb, they saw a young man sitting on the right side, dressed in a white robe; and they were amazed. And he said to them, "Do not be amazed; you seek Jesus of Nazareth, who was crucified. He has risen, he is not here; see the place where they laid him. But go, tell his disciples and Peter that he is going before you to Galilee; there you will see him, as he told you." And they went out and fled from the tomb, for trembling and astonishment had come upon them; and they said nothing to anyone, for they were afraid.' (Mark 16:5-8) At this point the Gospel of Mark ends. It is universally recognized that the verses which follow are a later addition, an attempt to finish an unfinished work which appears differently in various manuscripts. The writer of the Gospel of Mark may have stopped at that point, with the words 'they were afraid', or may have added something now lost.

The Gospel of Matthew says that the Council of the

243

Jews asked Pilate to put a guard on the tomb of Jesus, that he told them to send their own men as guards. This they did and sealed the entrance of the tomb. There was an earthquake during the night, 'For an angel of the Lord descended from heaven and came and rolled back the stone, and sat upon it. . . . And for fear of him the guards trembled and became like dead men.' When the women who were disciples of Jesus came early next morning, it was this angel who gave them the message recorded in the Gospel of Mark as given by 'a young man'. As they went away, 'Behold, Jesus met them and said, "Hail". And they came up and took hold of his feet and worshipped him.' Jesus repeats the command of the angel: 'Go and tell my brethren to go to Galilee.' The guards report the matter to the chief priests, who instruct them to say that while they were asleep the disciples of Jesus stole his body. The disciples then meet Jesus at an appointed place in Galilee.

In the Gospel of Luke, when the women enter the tomb and are perplexed to find that the body of Jesus is not there, two men suddenly appear beside them. 'The men said to them, "Why do you seek the living among the dead? Remember how he told you, while he was still in Galilee, that the Son of Man must be delivered into the hands of sinful men, and be crucified, and on the third day rise." And they remembered his words. . . .' When the Gospel of Luke describes appearances of Jesus after his resurrection, they occur in Judea, first on the road to Emmaus and then at Jerusalem in the Upper Room. He shows the scars of his crucifixion and eats with his disciples.

The Gospel of John gives an account coming from the women, and particularly from Mary of Magdala, together with the recollections of the Apostle Peter and of another disciple, 'the one whom Jesus loved'. The women went to the tomb early in the morning, found it empty and ran to summon the men. When Peter and the other disciple came to the tomb, they looked into it. Peter went into the tomb, in which he had seen that there was no dead body, and it is reported that 'he saw the linen cloths lying, and the napkin, which had been on his head, not lying with the linen cloths, but rolled up in a place by itself.' The disciple other than Peter, 'the one whom Jesus loved', grasped what had happened, as soon as he went in: 'he saw and believed'. But Peter did not grasp it, 'for as yet they did not know the scripture, that he must rise from the dead'. They went home. Meanwhile Mary of Magdala saw two angels in white sitting in the tomb. When they asked her why she was weeping, she said that some people had taken the dead body of Jesus away and had hidden it in some unknown place. Turning round outside the tomb, she suddenly saw through her tears the figure of someone whom she imagined to be the gardener and begged him to tell her where the body of Jesus could be found. It was Jesus and he called her by her name, 'Mary'. She fell at his feet and said to him in Hebrew, 'Rabboni' (Master). 'Jesus said to her, "Do not hold me, for I have not yet ascended to the Father; but go to my brethren and say to them, I am ascending to my Father and your Father, to my God and your God." '

On the evening of that day and also a week later Jesus appeared to his disciples in Jerusalem. He showed them the marks of the nails in his hands and in his side, where the lance of a soldier had pierced his body. He is reported as saying to one of them, Thomas, who needed proof, 'do not be faithless, but believing. . . . Have

245

you believed because you have seen me? Blessed are those that have not seen and yet believe.'

In the last chapter of the Gospel of John, which many scholars regard as a kind of appendix, coming after the original end of the book, there is the story of the appearance of Jesus on the shore of the Sea of Galilee. After a fruitless night of fishing in deep water, Peter and seven other disciples of Jesus were approaching the shore at dawn when a voice hailed them, saying, 'Children, have you any fish?' They answered, 'No.' The voice then said, 'Cast the net on the right side of the boat, and you will find some.' They did so and there were so many fish in the net that they could not haul it into the boat. It was then that the disciple, 'the one whom Jesus loved,' recognized the voice of Jesus and said, 'It is the Lord'. Peter jumped into the water, while the others brought the boat to the land, dragging with it the net full of fish. On the beach Jesus gave them bread and fish and ate with them. 'They saw a charcoal fire, with fish lying on it, and bread. . . . Jesus came and took the bread and gave it to them and . . . the fish.' Afterwards he questioned Peter three times and three times ordered him to take care of the other disciples. 'Simon, son of John, do you love me more than these? . . . Feed my lambs. . . . Do you love me? . . . Tend my sheep. . . . Do you love me? . . . Feed my sheep.' It seems that Jesus is regarded by the authors of the Gospel of John as thus making Peter the leader of the Church. The fact that Peter had three times denied all knowledge of Jesus at the time of his trial before the chief priests is overlooked. The promise given to Peter according to the Gospel of Matthew is confirmed.

The Book of the Acts of the Apostles is a sequel to the Gospel of Luke, written by the same author. It is said there that Jesus presented himself alive (to the apostles whom he had chosen) 'after his passion by many proofs, appearing to them during forty days'. In the same book, in the speech of Peter to Cornelius, he says that God raised Jesus from the dead 'and made him manifest, not to all the people but to us who were chosen by God as witnesses, who ate and drank with him after he rose from the dead'.

The ascension

Only the author of the Gospel of Luke relates the story of the ascension of Jesus Christ into heaven from the Mount of Olives. In the Gospel he writes, 'Then he led them out as far as Bethany, and lifting up his hand he blessed them. While he blessed them, he parted from them.' In the Acts of the Apostles there is more description, 'And when he had said this, as they were looking on, he was lifted up, and a cloud took him from their sight . . . they were gazing up into heaven as he went. . . . Then they returned to Jerusalem from the mount called Olivet. . . .'

The Gospel of John, however, used the word 'ascend'. Jesus in that Gospel says to Mary of Magdala, 'I am ascending.' And on an earlier occasion asks, 'What if you were to see the Son of Man ascending where he was before?' Paul in his letter to the Ephesians writes, about the risen Jesus Christ, 'he also ascended far above all the heavens, that he might fill all things. And his gifts were that some should be apostles, some prophets, some evangelists, some pastors and teachers.'

According to the Gospels there is a great difference between the appearance of Jesus Christ during the six weeks after his crucifixion and all later visions of him seen by his followers. After the time which may be

247

called his ascension, he is seen, 'sitting at the right hand of God', in a state which is outside earthly space and time. Before the ascension, he is in Judea or in Galilee, and he is present in a bodily form. He is not a spirit, in the sense of a vision. Yet he promises that he will be with his followers. As he says in the Gospel of Matthew, 'Lo I am with you always, to the close of the age.' [Matt., Mark, Luke, John, and all books of the New Testament]

JESUS JUSTUS *see* JUSTUS

JESUS BARABBAS *see* BARABBAS This name is not to be found in any extant manuscript, though the great biblical scholar Origen records having seen the name in the first half of the 3rd century.

JOANNA The wife of Chuza, the steward or domestic administrator of Herod Antipas, Joanna was among the women who helped Jesus financially in Galilee. She was also a witness of the empty tomb on Easter morning. *see* CHUZA [Luke 8:3; 24:10]

JOHN (Gk. from the Heb. 'God has been gracious') The various men who are thought to have been called 'John' are dealt with separately. John the Evangelist may also have been the author of at least one, if not all three, of the Letters. John, son of Zebedee, might also have been the beloved disciple.

1. John the Baptist
2. John, son of Zebedee
3. John, the beloved disciple
4. John the Evangelist
5. John the Elder
6. John, father of Peter
7. John, relative of Annas
8. John Mark, the Evangelist
9. John the Divine

1. John the Baptist John was the cousin and forerunner of Jesus. In the prophetic tradition he appeared out of the wilderness, heralding the coming of the Messiah and proclaiming the baptism of repentance for the forgiveness of sins. At the River Jordan, he recognized Jesus as the Messiah, baptized him, and pointed him out to his own disciples as 'the Lamb of God'. The story of John the Baptist is the drama of a man aware of his own mission and greatness, yet willing to step aside and act as a signpost to one even greater than himself. John was imprisoned and executed by Herod Antipas in about the year 30.

Miraculous birth

Born in the hill-country of Judea, John was the son of elderly parents, Zechariah, a priest, and Elizabeth, daughter of a priestly family and a relative of Mary, the mother of Jesus. Luke tells the story of John's birth. Both his parents were worthy in the sight of God, but they were childless. When it was Zechariah's turn to serve in the Temple at Jerusalem, he was attending to the altar of incense in the sanctuary when he had a vision of an angel. The angel announced that his prayer had been heard and that Elizabeth was going to have a son, whose name was to be John. 'And you will have joy and gladness, and many will rejoice at his birth; for he will be great before the Lord . . . and he will go before him in the spirit and power of Elijah, to turn the hearts of the fathers to the children, and the disobedient to the wisdom of the just, to make ready for the Lord a people prepared.'

When the old priest asked, 'How shall I know this?' the angel replied, 'I am Gabriel, who stand in the presence of God; and I was sent to speak to you, and to bring you this good news. And behold, you will be silent and unable to speak until the day that these things come to pass, because you did not believe my words, which will be fulfilled in their time.' When he returned home at the end of his duties, his wife Elizabeth conceived. Six months later, the angel was sent to Mary in Nazareth to make a similar announcement of the birth of Jesus. Mary set out at once to visit Elizabeth over the hills of Judea, and stayed with her some three months before returning to Nazareth. Meanwhile, Elizabeth's baby arrived, was circumcised, and named 'John'.

His father recovered his power of speech and blessed God, saying, 'And you, child, will be called the prophet of the Most High; for you will go before the Lord to prepare his ways.'

The two boys were born within six months of each other, in towns within sight of each other. Joseph and Mary had come to Bethlehem for the census; the home of the priest Zechariah and Elizabeth was below Mount Orah in Ein Karem, the 'Gracious Spring'. Before the time of the Russian pilgrim Daniel, in 1107, the birthplace of John was located, within the village, in a cave that is now shown within the Franciscan Church of St John. On the other side of the valley is the Fransciscan Church of the Visitation, in the crypt of which is shown the spring that according to tradition appeared at the meeting-place of Mary with Elizabeth. This is the spring which gives a name to the town today. The life of the young John was hidden for nearly thirty years in the wilderness, from which he emerged to fulfil his vocation.

Luke carefully states that it was in the year 28 that John began his public ministry of baptizing in the River Jordan, and preaching the baptism of repentance for the forgiveness of sins. Mark includes the prophecy of Isaiah, 'Behold, I send my messenger before thy face, who shall prepare thy way.' All four evangelists see John's coming as a fulfilment of Isaiah's prophecy: 'The voice of one crying in the wilderness: Prepare the way of the Lord, make his paths straight . . .', but only the first three Gospels describe the power of John's message, which drew all Judea and all the people of Jerusalem. They describe his dress of camel-skin and his diet of locust-beans and wild honey, in the pattern of the Bedouin today. The theme of John's teaching was revivalist: the Messiah is coming, people need the spiritual preparation of repentance. Baptism was the traditional Jewish symbolism for cleansing from sins; the Greek word for 'repentance' means 'a change of heart'. John's baptism by water was to prepare people for the Messiah's baptism by the Spirit of God; with the coming of the Messiah, his work was done.

Matthew and Mark tell the story of John's imprisonment and death retrospectively, as though they occurred before the public ministry of Jesus. They tell how John was imprisoned by Herod Antipas for denouncing Herod's marriage with Herodias, his brother Philip's wife. John's courage rivalled that of the prophet Elijah in his denunciation of Ahab and Jezebel. Biblical prophecy depends on the human acceptance of God's terms for its fulfilment. Since John's message was to be accepted – which generally it was – then his ministry became that

251

foretold in the name of Elijah. Both of them were fore-runners, and both of them concentrated their courage on the spot where it could witness most dramatically for righteousness – the royal palace.

When in prison, John sent his disciples to Jesus with the question, 'Are you he who is to come?' His question may have indicated his doubt, but more likely his hope that he was to have a successor and that he had not been a failure after all. Jesus's answer, mentioning his performance of the works predicted for the Messiah, should have reassured him. Matthew and Mark describe John's execution, at Herod's command, to fulfill a rash promise to Herodias's daughter, Salome. This took place, according to Josephus, the Jewish historian of the 1st century, in Herod's fortress of Machaerus, an isolated Hasmonean outpost east of the Dead Sea.

John's disciples

A rather different picture of John the Baptist is given in the Fourth Gospel. John is shown as the witness and forerunner of the Messiah, whom he recognizes by the descent of God's Spirit in the form of a dove. As John said, 'He who sent me to baptize with water said to me, "He on whom you see the Spirit descend and remain, this is he who baptizes with the Holy Spirit." And I have seen and have borne witness that this is the Son of God.' (John 1:33, 34)

The Fourth Gospel has only this account of Jesus's baptism by John, and omits the fact that Jesus began to preach only after John's imprisonment. In this Gospel, the ministry of the two men is simultaneous, until Jesus attracts the most disciples and John withdraws. As John himself put it, 'He who has the bride is the bridegroom; the friend of the bridegroom, who stands and hears him, rejoices greatly at the bridegroom's voice; therefore this joy of mine is now full. He must increase, but I must decrease.' (John 3:29, 30)

The reason for this deliberate subordination of John in the Fourth Gospel is likely to be that, even at the end of the 1st century when this Gospel was written, there were still some disciples of John who considered John more important than Jesus himself. The writer of this Gospel describes John the Baptist from the first as surrounded by disciples, who were soon to become the core of Jesus's own band of followers. The evangelist shows clearly that they did so at the suggestion of John himself, who pointed them to Jesus as 'the Christ', and 'the Lamb of God'. Luke tells us that John had taught his disciples how to pray. Matthew describes how they fasted. We know, too, something of their loyalty to John as their leader, through his imprisonment and execution to his burial. Twenty years later, there were still disciples of John, among them the learned Alexandrian Jew Apollos, who met Paul in Ephesus and later became the first bishop of Corinth.

The place of baptism

John the Baptist's activities were based on at least two points on the River Jordan, one accessible to the people of Samaria, one to the people of Judea. The former is likely to have been in the area of Salem (John 3:23), Tel er-Ricra, probably at the five wells of Aenon ('the place of the spring'), located at Ed-Der. The southern place of baptism, described by St John as at Bethabara (meaning 'ford-house' or 'ferry-house'), is probably less than a mile from the accepted place of baptism today. It is unlikely that there was a proper village there, but rather a few huts for those operating the ferry, the cus-

253

toms, and the frontier business between Judea and Perea. There would probably have been a lodging-house or caravanserai. The Madeba mosaic shows the ferry above the place of baptism, with a house standing on piles, presumably designed with a view to floods.

Early tradition has always represented the place where Jesus was baptized by his cousin John as being the spot shown today: the ford at Hajlah. It seems that John lived for some time beyond Jordan, perhaps to avoid the authorities of Judea or Jerusalem, perhaps because of the regular and clean flow of the Wadi el-Kharrar from the east into the Jordan. It was an ideal place for his purpose, off the road yet easily approached from the ford. In 1902, at the outlet of the Wadi el-Kharrar two small buildings dating back to Byzantine times stood on arches, presumably at one time in the water – one of them nearly 33 feet square. The pilgrim Theodosius, in the year 530, found a Church of John the Baptist, built by order of the Emperor Anastasius, at this point on the east bank. This church apparently rested on arches built out over the water. A cross on a marble pillar stood in the river to mark the place of baptism. Antoninus, forty years later, found only the pillar. Perhaps the floods had carried away the foundations of the little church. The coming of the Persians put an end to other shrines on the east bank of the Jordan.

On the west bank, a monastery of St John had existed since the time of Justinian, if not before. This, too, appears on the Madeba mosaic and in the writings of Antoninus and Arculf. For centuries, this was the focus of Christian pilgrimage from Jerusalem. The present church, erected in 1882 on this site, includes Byzantine remains. Arculf, in 670, described a small chapel under the monastery and a stone bridge leading out over the water to a cross at the place of baptism.

John and Qumran

Many scholars have wished to establish a direct connection between John the Baptist and the monastic community at Qumran, whose scrolls have been found in caves near the Dead Sea. It is possible that John was one of the Essenes, who pursued the ideal of purity and holiness in the isolation of the desert. It is probable that John was influenced, directly or indirectly, by their practices – particularly by their ritual washing and cleansings, not to mention their formation of a company of disciples seeking to 'fly from the retribution that is coming'. (*see* ESSENES)

Certainly, Jesus himself adopted and prescribed the practice of baptism as the means of Christian initiation. Jesus also proclaimed much the same gospel as John: 'The time has come. The kingdom of God is close at hand. Repent and believe.' Yet for Jesus, John was the last of the prophets and forerunners of the *old* world, which had given place to the *new* order with the coming of the Christ. Hence Jesus's final appraisal of John: 'I tell you, among those born of women none is greater than John; yet he who is least in the kingdom of God is greater than he.' (Luke 7:28) [Matt. 3; 4:12; 9:14; 11:2-18; 14:2-10; 16:14; 17:13; 21:25-32; Mark 1:4-14; 2:18; 6:14-29; 11:27-32; Luke 1:13-80; 3:2-20; 7:18-35; 9:7, 19; 11:1; 16:16; 20:4-6; John 1:6-40; 3:23-36; 4:1; 5:33-36; 10:40, 41; Acts 1:5, 22; 10:37; 11:16; 13:24, 25; 19:3, 4]

2. John, son of Zebedee John was the son of Zebedee, the Galilean fisherman possibly from Bethsaida, and of Salome, whom some traditions describe as the sister of

Mary, the mother of Jesus. John and his brother James were fishermen, whom Luke describes as partners with Peter and Andrew. John, his brother James, and Peter formed the inner circle of the disciples of Jesus. John is mentioned twice in the Acts as accompanying Peter, both in healing and confirming the faith of the primitive Church. He is also one of the three 'pillars of the Church' whom Paul met at Jerusalem.

John may have been one of the unnamed disciples of John the Baptist at the Jordan who, together with Andrew and Peter, later became disciples of Jesus. Jesus called John and his brother while they were in their boat mending their nets. They promptly left their father Zebedee in the boat with the men he employed. Salome is listed as one of the women who 'looked after' Jesus in Galilee. It seems, therefore, that Zebedee's family was of some substance. John appears to have been sufficiently acquainted with the high priest's palace in Jerusalem to know the girl portress and to be able to persuade her to admit Peter at the time of the trial of Jesus. Perhaps the tradition, expressed in the building by the Crusaders in Jerusalem of a small chapel dedicated in the name of 'Zebedee's fish-shop', indicates the presence in Jerusalem of members of his family. It is not impossible that they might have been purveyors of Galilean fish to the high priest's household. Certainly, the disciples of Jesus were men of varying means.

The lists of the disciples of Jesus reveal the nickname given to John and his brother James as 'Boanerges', 'sons of thunder', presumably because of their angry temperaments, or glowering faces. 'Son of' implies 'having the quality of' thunder. Whether the nickname implies humour or rebuke, it is certain that John and his brother were reproved by Jesus. John once said to Jesus

at Capernaum, ' "Master, we saw a man casting out demons in your name, and we forbade him because he does not follow with us." But Jesus said to him, "Do not forbid him, for he that is not against you is for you." '
When James and John asked Jesus to reserve for them the seats of honour on either side of him at his Messianic banquet in heaven, Jesus replied, 'You do not know what you are asking.' And he went on to ask if they could share his destiny. They confidently affirmed that they could, whereupon Jesus answered, 'The cup that I drink you will drink . . . but to sit at my right hand or at my left, is not mine to grant . . .' James was in fact the first of Jesus's apostles to suffer martyrdom, at the command of Herod Agrippa, and a writer of the 5th century records the martyrdom of John as early as AD 44. John and James received a further rebuke from Jesus when his messengers were not welcome in a Samaritan village, and the 'sons of thunder' suggested, 'Lord, do you want us to bid fire come down from heaven and consume them up?' Jesus and his disciples shared the rigours of his itinerant ministry often without shelter: 'The Son of Man has nowhere to lay his head.'

Despite their temperament and Jesus's frank rebukes, the two brothers, James and John, together with Peter, formed an inner circle within the group of disciples, and it is these three whom Jesus takes with him on at least three important occasions. They accompany him into the house for the raising of Jairus's daughter; they are permitted to witness the glory of Jesus's transfiguration on the mountain; they are chosen to support him and to witness his agony in the Garden of Gethsemane. Apart from one question to Jesus asking when his prophecy of the destruction of the Temple was going to be fulfilled, John is not further mentioned by name throughout the story of the Passion. It is possible, however, that he may have been the person referred to in the Fourth Gospel as 'the beloved disciple'. If so, then a very great deal is to be known of his character and the important part played by him in the Upper Room, at Calvary, at the empty tomb, and in Galilee. *see also* JOHN 3. *and* JOHN 4. [Matt. 4:21; 10:2; 17:1; Mark 1:19, 29; 3:17; 5:37; 9:2, 38; 10:35, 41; 13:3; 14:33; Luke 5:10; 6:14; 9:28, 49, 54; 22:8; Gospel of John; Acts 1:13; 3:1, 11; 4:13, 19; 8:14; 12:2; Gal. 2:9; 1, 2, and 3 John; Revelation to John]

3. John, the beloved disciple The term 'the disciple Jesus loved' is used only by the writer of the Fourth Gospel and on only four occasions, all during or following the Passion of Jesus. The first scene is set in the Upper Room on the night of the Last Supper, after the meal. Jesus, having washed the disciples' feet, sat down with them and warned them of his forthcoming betrayal, 'Truly, truly, I say to you, one of you will betray me.' The disciples looked at each other wondering who it could be. 'The disciple whom Jesus loved' was reclining next to Jesus. Simon Peter signed to him and said, 'Tell us who it is of whom he speaks'; so leaning back on Jesus's breast he said, 'Lord who is it?' 'It is he to whom I shall give this morsel when I have dipped it.' He dipped the piece of bread and gave it to Judas.'

The second occasion is on Calvary when the crucifixion is completed and the long agony has begun. 'When Jesus saw his mother, and the disciple whom he loved standing near, he said to his mother, "Woman, behold, your son!" Then he said to the disciple, "Behold, your mother!" And from that hour the disciple took her to his own home.'

The third occasion when the term was used is early

on Easter morning when Mary of Magdala has been to the tomb only to find it empty and the stone rolled away. 'So she ran, and went to Simon Peter and the other disciple, the one whom Jesus loved, and said to them "They have taken the Lord out of the tomb. . . ." ' So Peter set out with the other disciple. They ran together, but the other disciple, running faster than Peter, reached the tomb first; he bent down and saw the linen cloths lying on the ground but did not go in. Peter who was following now came up, went right into the tomb, saw the linen cloths on the ground and also the cloth that had been over his head rolled up in a place by itself: 'Then the other disciple, who reached the tomb first, also went in, and he saw and believed. . . .'

The final scene is some time later on the Lake of Galilee after a fruitless night's fishing with Peter and the others. As they bring the boat into the north shore, a voice calls, 'Cast the net on the right side.' They do so and enclose so vast a haul of fish that they cannot even land it. At that moment 'the disciple whom Jesus loved' said to Peter: 'It is the Lord!' After landing the catch and eating breakfast on the beach, Peter is solemnly thrice commissioned by Jesus to feed his sheep. Then Jesus predicts Peter's own destiny of crucifixion: ' "When you are old, you will stretch out your hands, and another will gird you and carry you where you do not wish to go." And after this he said to him, "Follow me." Peter turned and saw following them the disciple whom Jesus loved, who had lain close to his breast at the supper . . . and said to Jesus, "Lord, what about this man?" Jesus said to him, "If it is my will that he remain until I come, what is that to you? Follow me?" '

The closing verses or epilogue of the Gospel state: 'This is the disciple who is bearing witness to these things, and who has written these things; and we know that his testimony is true.'

From these four scenes it seems inconceivable that this intimate friend should have been outside the twelve, if even outside the inner circle of Peter, James and John. Apart from the list of fishermen on this final expedition in the last chapter of the Gospel, there is not a single reference to John, son of Zebedee. It is unlikely that a disciple so often mentioned within the other three Gospels should be unconsciously omitted from the Fourth Gospel, even though he was often rebuked! It is likely that John, son of Zebedee, was the 'disciple Jesus loved', even if the Gospel of John was written by another hand.

It must have been the work of someone whose affection and respect for John, son of Zebedee, was considerable and who was willing to undersign all he said. In fact the authority for the Gospel is that of John, son of Zebedee, even if the authorship is not. *see also* JOHN **2.** *and* JOHN **4.**

4. John the Evangelist Whoever the actual author of the Fourth Gospel was, the depth and the effect of his work places him second in importance only to Paul among the members of the primitive Christian Church. It was this man who, writing in the very last years of the 1st century when all eye-witnesses to the life of Jesus were dead, expressed a wonderful union between the belief in an historical outward act of God and a living inward experience of the risen Jesus. His book is a meditation in the manner of the Jewish Midrash, but in Christian form. In parts, it is very early indeed, especially the narrative of the passion of Jesus. It has affinities too with the Qumran literature of the Dead Sea Scrolls and may perhaps have been based on a Palestinian Aramaic original, now lost.

From the internal evidence, already discussed in the two preceding articles concerning John, son of Zebedee, and the beloved disciple, together with the external evidence of the early Church Fathers, we may draw some conclusions about the authorship of the Fourth Gospel. Then turning to the content and matter of the Gospel, we can examine the purpose and method of its writing, its relationship to other Gospels, its presentation of Jesus and its effect upon the Christian Church.

Who wrote the Fourth Gospel?

Internal evidence appears to identify the author with John, son of Zebedee, particularly the four passages concerning 'the disciple Jesus loved'. By a process of elimination it can be confirmed that this phrase refers to John, son of Zebedee, who is not otherwise mentioned in the Gospel, except perhaps as the companion of Peter and the disciple of John the Baptist. If John, son of Zebedee, is the author, however, 'the disciple Jesus loved' is a strangely immodest title for an author to apply to himself. If, however, the Gospel had been dictated to scribes, in the first person, they could have replaced the words 'I, John' with 'the disciple whom Jesus loved'. Were the actual author to be other than John, son of Zebedee, from whom, however, the information was received, such a title would be possible. Were the actual author to have respected John, son of Zebedee, as being loved by Jesus more openly than the other disciples, such a title would be understandable. Now, the final appendix to the Gospel specifically identifies the authority of the Gospel with the 'disciple Jesus loved' and therefore with John, son of Zebedee. These verses also imply that the actual author was himself a disciple of John, son of Zebedee. Of course, these verses might have been added some years afterwards, but they appear in all extant manuscripts of this Gospel.

The external evidence at first appears conflicting; some of the early Fathers of the Church, such as Irenaeus of Lyons (130-200) and Clement of Rome (*c.* 100), argued for John, son of Zebedee, as the author when at Ephesus. However, Papias, bishop of Hieropolis (60-130), said that there were *two* Johns, the apostle who was dead and the elder who was still alive. Dionysius, a later bishop of Ephesus, confirmed that there were two tombs at Ephesus, both ascribed to a John. In any case, a strong tradition connected the Gospel with Ephesus. The conclusion seems to be again that the authority for this Gospel was that of John, son of Zebedee, but that it was either written or edited by an elder, also living at Ephesus and also called John. The 2nd and 3rd Letters of John are both addressed from 'the Elder' and are probably entirely the work of this second John. The First Letter resembles, more than the 2nd and 3rd, the style and content of the Gospel and may therefore be the work of John, son of Zebedee. *see also* JOHN **2.** *and* JOHN **3.**

Need for a written record

It may help to compare the backgrounds of the Gospels of Mark and John, the first and the last Gospels within the New Testament to be written. Both Gospels were written during periods of crisis and emergency. Both were written for specific and vital purposes. Without both, the course of Christianity might have been rather different. Mark was faced with the death of the two great pillars of the apostolic Church. Peter and Paul had made the events and teaching live before their cosmopolitan congregations – as only inspired eye-witnesses and men with personal experience and knowledge can. Upon their death, it was essential that some written record – based upon their teaching – should be made available for the work of the Church. Who was better equipped to undertake the task than the man who had been a travelling companion to Paul and a secretary to Peter – the task of writing 'the beginning of the good news of Jesus Christ, the Son of God'. Mark must have been saturated with the apostolic preaching and tradition and with what was most required.

After some 70 or 80 years the apostolic age was at an end and the eye-witnesses of the Word made Flesh no longer among men to inspire and proclaim. The primitive hopes and momentum were spent; moreover Christianity had to be adapted to the needs of the Hellenistic world. Christianity had to unite her belief in an historical act of God with her present inward experience. John set out to fulfill two objects – one purely religious, the other practical.

First he set out to impress the belief that Jesus was not only the Messiah and the Son of Man of Jewish tradition, but also the Son of God – a title more understandable and far more significant to the Gentile world. Men must 'believe' in the actual historic person of Jesus and 'have life' by a realization of the purpose of his life, which is not merely a thing of the past, but an ever-living fact of the present. Jesus's life on earth was but the beginning of a larger and ever-enduring life open to all believers; for the historical person of Jesus can be revealed to any true believer, now and always. Secondly John had a practical object – to meet some of the questions and accusations levelled at Christianity by his

Gentile contemporaries and to support and build up the idea of the Christian Church.

John himself had a strong and certain conception of both the person and life of Christ, and not unnaturally interpreted facts accordingly. To him, facts were valuable because they supported or illustrated the beliefs he wished to impress. He therefore selected and concentrated upon a few episodes which bear witness to the divinity of Christ. Similarly, he adapted and modified his selected material, reading a meaning into words and incidents independent of their actual circumstances. To him the outward event was often a mere shell, covering a hidden message, which was only apparent to the believer.

Consequently John did not, like Mark, record by narrative and dialogue events as they happened – but he adapted and matched narrative to dialogue, and vice-versa, to achieve his purpose. Therefore, both narrative and dialogue are in the same style and it is sometimes impossible to distinguish editorial comment from narrative or dialogue. The teaching of Jesus, combined with editorial comment, makes up long discourses. Through the calculated combination of narratives and discourses, John adapted to the needs of his readers the Gospel message, as it was recorded by Mark or as he, John, had seen and heard it.

John sought to interpret the Jewish ideas of the 'Messiah' and the 'kingdom' in such terms as 'truth' and 'eternal life'. This is well illustrated in the private conversation at the trial in which Pilate asked Jesus, 'Are you King of the Jews?' [the Messiah]. 'Jesus answered, "My kingship is not of this world. . . ." Pilate said to him, "So you are a king?" Jesus answered, "You say that I am a king. For this I have come into the world, to bear witness to the truth. Every one who is of the truth hears my voice." '

The Word of God

The prologue – the first eighteen verses of the Fourth Gospel – is a poem about the 'Word' of God. John opens his prologue as the book of Genesis. The Greek words 'In the beginning' can equally mean 'In principle' or 'At the root of the Universe' – thus implying not just an event in time, but also an eternal reality: 'In the beginning was the Word, and the Word was with God, and the Word was God. He was in the beginning with God; all things were made through him, and without him was not anything made that was made. In him was life, and the life was the light of men. The light shines in the darkness, and the darkness has not overcome it.'

The Greek term *Logos* or 'Word' has a long history. As early as the 6th century BC an Ephesian philosopher, Heraclitus, had used it to explain the order and sense within the world. 'Though this "Word" – this fundamental law – exists from all time, yet mankind is unaware of it, both before they hear it and in the moment that they hear it.' For him, the Logos was the pantheistic principle of reason within the universe, which explained its logic or sense. Later, the Stoics took over the idea and popularized it as the dynamic principle of reason operating within the world. Greek and Roman philosophers developed the idea that the *Logos* was the mind of God, the means of communion between God and man. Philo, the Jewish philosopher of Alexandria, born about 20 BC, made the *Logos* a bridge between the God of Israel and the Gentile world. The *Logos* or 'Word' of God is responsible for the creation of the world, as well as being the inspiration of the prophets

265

and the means of covenant and continued communication between God and his people. Philo almost personified the *Logos* as the image and instrument of God, referring to the *Logos* as the 'firstborn son' or the 'Wisdom' of God.

The writer of the Fourth Gospel does not use the term 'Wisdom', but identifies Jesus with the *Logos* or 'Word' of God. Mark began his Gospel with John the Baptist. John began the Fourth Gospel with the Creation. The gospel was uttered in the 'Word' of God, but Jesus is the gospel and the 'Word' that began the creation of the Word itself. The *Logos* was no new thing. It existed before creation. The world in its entirety was his creation. The Psalmist wrote: 'By the word of the Lord the heavens were made and all their hosts'. (Ps. 33) So the gospel concerns all men. It is the light of all men. It is identical with the author of life, but it was rejected and the darkness did not understand it, nor indeed quench it.

The exception to that darkness was the witness of John the Baptist, who was typical of the prophets. 'There was a man sent from God, whose name was John. He came for testimony, to bear witness to the light, that all might believe through him. He was not the light, but came to bear witness to the light.' The Light was there to be seen, yet man did not see it. Even his own people did not recognize or receive him. There were some, however, who accepted the *Logos* and underwent a new birth as 'sons of God'. This new creation, like the old, was brought about by the *Logos*. To Jesus was owed both creation and re-creation. He was and is both the creative 'Word' and the sacramental presence of God with us.

'The true light that enlightens every man was coming

into the world. He was in the world, and the world was made through him, yet the world knew him not. He came to his own home, and his own people received him not. But to all who received him, who believed in his name, he gave power to become children of God; who were born, not of blood nor of the will of the flesh nor of the will of man, but of God. And the Word became flesh and dwelt among us, full of grace and truth; we have beheld his glory, glory as of the only Son from the Father.'

For the writer of the Fourth Gospel, the 'grace and truth' of Jesus even replaced the covenant of the Law. (Exod. 34:27) This record of John was confirmed by the apostles and all Christians who received 'grace upon grace'. 'And from his fullness have we all received grace upon grace. For the law was given through Moses; grace and truth came through Jesus Christ. No one has ever seen God; the only Son, who is in the bosom of the Father, he has made him known.'

The presentation of Christianity in the Fourth Gospel is seen most clearly when contrasted with that of the first three Gospels – as typified by the Gospel of Mark.

The most striking difference in the teaching of Jesus, as recorded in these two Gospels, is in what is said about Jesus himself. Mark's Jesus did not demand any opinion of himself, or belief in himself. His message was similar to that of John the Baptist (as Mark records him). He preached repentance, a change of heart and conduct. He hid his Messiahship until Peter's confession at Caesarea Philippi, and even then forbade his disciples to tell it to others. His disciples gradually grew to recognize him as the Son of Man, the Messiah, who would come in glory to judge the world – his verdict depending upon the conduct of men, not upon the belief of men and certainly not upon their recognition of him. Jesus does not openly admit his Messiahship until standing before the high priest. Even then, there is no question of his divinity; his disciples acknowledge his Messiahship, as Enoch's supernatural or Daniel's human 'Son of Man', but not as the Son of God. That is left to the Gentile Roman centurion.

The disciples' recognition of Jesus as Son of God must have taken place some time between his resurrection and Peter's first recorded sermon in Jerusalem (Acts 2), perhaps on the occasion, recorded in John, of Thomas's confession 'My Lord and my God'. Even so, the conviction of the apostles of Jesus's divinity must also have been a process accelerated by the action of the Holy Spirit among them at Pentecost.

John's portrait of Jesus is very different from that of Mark. Mark, except in his prologue, does not himself call Jesus 'Son of God'. He may continually hint at it to his readers as though to say, 'But you and I know that only God can do such miracles,' but he does not represent Jesus or his disciples referring to Jesus as Son of God. John represents Jesus as openly admitting his Messiahship, from his meeting with John the Baptist onwards. John the Baptist immediately recognized him. Jesus did not simply preach repentance and good conduct; he preached himself as the Son of God. He openly claimed a unique relationship with God. Salvation was not a matter of conduct, but of belief in himself. (John 3:16) The disciples were not fully convinced till after the resurrection – perhaps at the confession of the most practical, if obstinate, member of the party, Thomas. John, anxious to present Jesus both as an historical personality and as the Son of God, both flesh and *Logos,* emphasized his true humanity as 'the Word made flesh'.

Jesus is tired, hungry and thirsty at the well, where the Samaritan woman, seeing him without rope and tackle, 'pulls his leg' – before drawing water for him. He weeps at Lazarus's tomb. Simultaneously, John emphasized his divinity, for he is miraculously satisfied when the disciples bring him food to the well, and John implies that he wept at their lack of faith.

Both Mark and John regard miracles as signs or evidence of God's power and presence in Jesus, whether expressed as acts of power or as signs. Both show Jesus apparently unwilling to do unnecessary miracles. Both indicate that the faith is essential – Mark at Nazareth; John at Bethany. In Mark, sheer compassion appears to prompt Jesus, as in the case of the feeding of the five thousand, yet he uses every miracle to point a lesson – even though on most occasions only the spiritually-minded or believing witnesses can grasp the real significance of the event. In John, the purposes of all miracles recorded are the glory of God and the production of faith in men.

Mark records Jesus doing miracles, as far as possible, in the presence of a few eye-witnesses. John does not hesitate to portray Jesus calling out to Lazarus 'in a loud voice', for the benefit of bystanders and the glory of God. John, however, does not include more than six miracles: Changing water itno wine at Cana, healing the officer's son at Capernaum and the paralytic at the public baths of Bethesda, feeding the five thousand, giving sight to the blind man, and the raising of Lazarus. He has carefully chosen these miracles to exclude the more common practice of exorcism. John has included the more striking and unique miracles, emphasizing them accordingly: 'Thou hast kept the good wine until now', 'Born blind', and 'Four days in the tomb'.

In one other respect, John has contributed information – not forthcoming from the Synoptic Gospels – about the locality of Jesus's teaching. John lays nearly the whole scene of the ministry in the Jerusalem district and not up in Galilee. There are indications in the Synoptic Gospels that Jesus did conduct more of his ministry in Judea than they in fact record. Scribes and Pharisees from Jerusalem (Luke 5:17; Mark 3:7; 7:1) went up to Galilee to hear Jesus. Judas was a native of Kerioth in Judea. Jesus's friendship with Mary, Martha, and even with Joseph of Arimathea must have been the result of more than one or two previous visits. Jesus's lamentation over Jerusalem implies that he had on many occasions preached there. Perhaps the chronological order of Mark may be more accurate than that of John, but it is probable that Jesus did spend a great deal more of his life and ministry in Judea than Mark records. Neither of the evangelists would have claimed to have written a complete and accurate biography of Jesus. The material was not available, but Mark – writing at a time when biography was in vogue in Rome – arranged his material into as coherent a 'life of Christ' as he could. John preferred to write 'Scenes from the life of Jesus, the Son of God'.

Mark's account – in spite of its slightly pro-Roman outlook – is generally thought to be remarkable for its utter simplicity, honesty, and fidelity to tradition. The incorporation of so much of Mark's material in later Gospels is ample proof of its worth. Its value and usefulness, at the time of crisis following the death of the apostolic leaders and amid the persecutions of Christians in Rome, must have been incalculable – not only for devotional purposes as the sacred memoirs of the earliest leader of the apostles, but also as a balanced and clear statement of the facts for evangelistic use.

John, however, writing long after the events in the life of Jesus and aware of the mistakes made by clinging to such reminiscences as Mark's Gospel contained, without any real inward impulse or spiritual reality, assisted Christianity to continue as a *living* faith. He transplanted Christianity before the roots had time to wither, proclaiming the Jesus of history and the Jesus of inward experience to be *one*. In order to do so in such a manner as the Hellenistic world could understand, he had virtually to adapt the gospel story to that of a Greek tragedy. He had to combine, by means of a reverent use of his imagination both historicity and symbolism, both the words and actions of Jesus, and also the very thoughts. [Gospels of John]

5. John the Elder This John was author of at least one of the letters attributed to John. He was an anonymous and venerable father of the Christian Church at Ephesus in the first half of the 2nd century AD.

Links with the Fourth Gospel

From the 2nd century onwards, the traditional view of the authorship of the writings in the New Testament attributed to John was that they were all the work of the Apostle John, son of Zebedee. Many modern scholars still support his authorship of the Letters of John on the following grounds: Most of the themes in the Letters have a place also in the Gospel. There is a general affinity of theological outlook, both insisting on the necessity of Jesus's coming 'in the flesh', both speaking of judgment, forgiveness, God's love for mankind, the mutual love and obedience enjoined upon men, together with God's promise of the gift of his Spirit to men. The styles of the

Gospel and of the First Letter are similar. A list has been compiled of at least fifty phrases in the First Letter which have close parallels in the Gospel. Both use the method of antithesis, or contrast, of darkness and light, flesh and spirit, truth and falsehood. The First Letter of John claims to have been written by an eyewitness who has 'seen, heard, and handled' Jesus the 'Word' of God. If we assume the author of the Gospel was the Apostle John, this is just the sort of claim we might expect him to make. Even if we decide that the Gospel was not written by the apostle, we can still claim apostolic authorship for the First Letter of John.

Within the last thirty years, however, this assumption of the traditional view has been strongly criticized and the identification of authorship challenged. In the matter of the styles of the Gospel and Letters, while there is a certain similarity, the differences are shown to be great. In the Gospel, there are thirty key words, closely related to the central ideas and constantly recurring — these do not occur in the Letters.

As compared with the rest of the New Testament, there is a decided affinity of thought and standpoint, but there are fundamental divergencies of outlook between the Gospel and the Letters of John. The Gospel has many quotations and many implicit allusions to the Old Testament. Its author displays an acquaintance with Jewish ideas and practices and his work reflects the strong influences of Judaism, both Rabbinic and Hellenistic. The Letters, on the other hand, have no quotations from the Old Testament and one single reference to it. (1 John 3:12) There are no other books in the New Testament which have so little mention of the Hebrew Bible as the Letters of John.

In the Gospel, Hellenistic and Hebraic ideas are

united, but in the Letters, the Hellenistic element has freer play. There are various points where the Letters represent a theological outlook nearer to primitive Christianity than that of the Gospel. The Letters hold out the prospect of a near second coming of Jesus and of the end of the world. They take no account of the re-interpretation of the coming again of Jesus, in the Holy Spirit and in the Church at Pentecost, as is so clearly implied in the Gospel. The ideas within the Letters, about the effects of Jesus's death and the theology of man's redemption, resemble the proclamation of the very primitive Christian Church, rather than the cosmic significance of the 'Word' the *Logos,* the 'Mind' of God made flesh – expressed so clearly in the prologue of the Gospel. The conception of the 'Spirit of God' within the Letters remains too much within the limits of rather primitive Christian belief.

So, in regard to their ideas of eschatology, atonement, and the Spirit, the outlook of the Letters is very different from that of the Gospel. It might be possible to hold that the same man wrote the First Letter, first, and the Gospel much later – but the Gospel is presupposed within the Letter. Without the Gospel the Letters would hardly be intelligible and the Gospel provides the necessary background to the Letters. Such differences combine to show that the First Letter is the work of an admiring disciple of the evangelist, who has absorbed much but not all of his theology. It is a strange coincidence, however, that two contemporary writers, living in the same area, should share such similarities of style, outlook, theology, and purpose.

Who was John?

The writer of the Letters was not named in the text, but since the Letters were known to Polycarp, bishop of Smyrna, Papias, bishop of Hieropolis, and Irenaeus, a native of Smyrna who became bishop of Lyons – all of whom lived in the first half of the 2nd century AD – the Letters were certainly known in Asia Minor by that time. Since the Letters presuppose a situation within the Churches to which they were written similar to that at Corinth in the year 96 in the time of Clement, the third bishop of Rome after Peter, and whose own letters tackle the same sort of problems, the Letters of John were probably written at the turn of the 1st century. The Church was no longer being persecuted, following the succession of Nerva, also in the year 96; so the Church emerged to face a new set of conditions, including a spirit of unrest and development.

In the Second and Third Letters, the author describes himself as the 'elder'. Literally, this just meant 'old man'. It also bore a technical sense in the early Church after Jewish custom, as the title of one of the board of 'elders' who ministered to a local congregation. The authority with which this elder speaks, however, is more than local. There seems to have been another quasi-technical use of the term 'elder' current for a short time in Asia. Christians in this province seem to have spoken of 'elders' when they referred to a group of teachers, who formed a link between the apostles and the next generation. Apparently they were a small group, and it was quite possible for one of these teachers to be spoken of as *'the* Elder'. Irenaeus several times referred to things he had learned from 'the Elder' and 'the Elder the disciple of the Apostles'. It is unlikely that 'the

Elder' is to be identified with the Apostle John, for why refer to himself as 'elder' rather than 'apostle'?

The argument in the Third Letter turns altogether on the question of the writer's authority. If he were an apostle would he not have silenced his opponent Diotrephes by claiming the authority of an apostle? Papias talks of 'John the Elder'. Irenaeus quotes the First and Second Letters, over the name of 'John the Apostle'. It is, therefore, likely that the true author of the First and Second Letters was 'John the Elder', whose grave along with that of 'John the Apostle' was shown at Ephesus in the 3rd century.

Papias called the Elder 'a disciple of the Lord', that is, a survivor of the group who had known and followed Jesus in his lifetime. Irenaeus says that this 'disciple of the Lord' survived until the time of Trajan and was known to other elders in Asia. Irenaeus thought that this disciple was also in fact the apostle, but it seems more likely that this disciple John was not an apostle so much as one of the elders. He must have been nearly ninety if he had been a disciple of Jesus – but that is the claim of the opening verse of the First Letter.

The message of the First Letter

The Letter opens with a similar sort of preface to that of the Gospel, using similar words such as 'the beginning' and the *Logos*. In this preface the writer declares the purpose of his letter. The body of the letter consists of three clear and simple expositions: on the nature of Christianity, life in the family of God, and the certainty of the Christian faith. The letter ends with a brief postscript and encouragement to prayer.

On the nature of Christianity, the writer severely criticizes false ideas of religious experience and stresses the need for repentance: 'If we say we have no sin, we deceive ourselves', but 'the blood of Jesus Christ cleanses us from all sin'. The writer declares the following: Jesus intercedes for his followers in heaven, as perfect man he is the ideal advocate. Love is the essence of Christianity and distinguishes it from paganism. The Antichrist is coming soon. The time is short. Men must act now. Christians must not be perverted by teaching which denies the divinity of Jesus, but they may be assured that the gospel story is true and no lie.

Concerning life within the family of God, Christians are the children of God, the Father. The writer stresses the gravity of sin and declares the incompatibility of sin with God. Love is the bond of the family: 'We know that we have passed out of death into life, because we love the brethren.' That is his love for us through Jesus, and man's love for his fellow-men. True love demands action. The writer stresses the dangers of false teaching, which denies the reality of the incarnation, the fact that the 'Word' or 'Mind' of God became flesh in the person of Jesus. God himself is love; through love he sent his son to die for man, who should respond with love to God and to his fellow-men.

Concerning the certainty of the Christian faith, the writer declares that there are three signs of God's indwelling: the Spirit, confession that Jesus is the son of God, and love: 'God is love, and he who abides in love abides in God, and God abides in him.' Love is that attitude of mind which should pervade all Christian conduct. By far the greatest contribution to theology of the First Letter is its unprecedented and unequalled expression of the true nature of Christian love, and the perception of the all-important truth that God himself is love personified. This love is the bond that binds the family of God to each other and to the Father.

The Second and Third Letters

The Second Letter, thinly disguised in the form of a private letter, is a pastoral message addressed to a single Christian congregation, by a person who calls himself 'The Elder'. The writer encourages his readers against those who spread propaganda for a false doctrine which denies the reality of the incarnation of God in Jesus. This heretical teaching seems to present a real threat to the local Christian Church.

The Third Letter is a genuine piece of personal correspondence, giving a vivid glimpse into the life of the local Church and full of human interest. The Elder seems to be responsible for a circuit of local churches. His representatives carry the gospel to the pagan population, with the financial and moral support of the Christian communities in the neighbourhood. In one church, his agents have met with opposition and a very divided reception. The opposition was led by one Diotrephes, who carried the day and drove out his agents; they returned to the Elder to report. In this situation the Third Letter was written. The Elder plans a personal visit to the offending community; he writes to a loyal supporter, Gaius, and entrusts the letter to one Demetrius, who is universally respected within the circuit of churches. The agents return with this letter to resume their interrupted mission, under the loyal protection of Gaius and duly warned against Diotrephes. The outcome of the Letter and the success or failure of the Elder's agents is not known. [1st, 2nd and 3rd Letters of John]

6. John, father of Peter Simon Peter's father was sometimes called by the Greek form of his Hebrew name, Jona(h). (Matt. 16:17) He was the father of at least two sons, Andrew and Peter, and his home was at Bethsaida, the 'fisher home', to the north of the Lake of Galilee. Perhaps, like his sons, he was a man of piety and of skill in deep-water fishing.

This John is mentioned three times in the Gospels, on each occasion linked with his son Peter. On the first occasion, recorded in the first chapter of the Fourth Gospel, the scene was the ministry of John the Baptist, by the River Jordan, when the Baptist told his own disciples, who included the two fishermen brothers, and Philip of Cana, that the man from Nazareth was Jesus, 'the Chosen One of God'. Early the following morning, Andrew met his brother Peter and said to him, 'We have found the Messiah' and he introduced Peter to Jesus. 'Jesus looked at him, and said, "So you are Simon the son of John? You shall be called Caphas" (which means Peter).'

On the second occasion, Jesus had taken his followers into the quiet and lovely mountainous scenery on the southern slopes of Mount Hermon, in the neighbourhood of the source of the River Jordan at Caesarea Philippi, the shrine and city of Pan. There, in retreat from the bustle of the lakeside, Jesus had asked his followers, 'Who do the people say that I am?' Peter had answered for his companions, 'You are the Christ, the Son of the living God.' In response to this profession of faith, Jesus proclaimed Peter's per-eminence among his followers, 'Blessed are you, Simon Bar-Jona! For flesh and blood has not revealed this to you, but my Father who is in heaven. And I tell you, you are Peter, and on this rock I will build my Church.' So this John's son was to become the leader of the apostles and the first bishop of Rome.

On the last occasion, recorded in the final chapter of the Fourth Gospel, the scene is by the lakeside, after the resurrection of Jesus, when seven of his followers have discovered him on the beach, along the north shore, when they returned from a night's fishing. They have had breakfast together, cooked on a charcoal fire, and Jesus has called Peter over to test and to commission him. 'Simon, son of John, do you love me more than these?' to which Peter replied, 'Yes, Lord; you know that I love you.' Jesus then said to him, 'Feed my lambs.' A second time Jesus said to him, 'Simon, son of John, do you love me?' and Peter had given him the same answer and been told 'Tend my sheep.' Then Jesus said to him a third time, 'Simon, son of John, do you love me?' Peter was upset at this third question – perhaps corresponding to his threefold denial of Jesus during the trial at the house of Caiaphas – and again declared, ' "Lord, you know everything; you know that I love you." Jesus said to him, "Feed my sheep." '

These three occasions, on which Jesus described Peter formally as the son of his father John, were the landmarks in the gospel narratives of Peter, his naming as the Rock, his appointment as the Rock on which the Church was to be built, and finally his threefold testing and commission to feed and care for the flock of Christ. This last event has been commemorated by successive chapels of the Primacy on the rocks of the north shore of Galilee. The column-bases of a medieval church are visible in the clear water offshore; they enclose an enormous rock which projects out over the water, as well as the modern little basalt chapel of the Primacy. This great rock was known to medieval pilgrims as the

Mensa Christi, the 'Table of the Lord'. It still stands in its striking simplicity, a silent witness to the Galilee resurrection tradition. [Matt. 16:17; John 1:42, 43; John 21:15-17]

7. John, relative of Annas This John is only mentioned once among the members of high-priestly families, within the Sanhedrin. The Supreme Council was, on this occasion, convened in emergency to deal with the situation caused by the powerful preaching of the apostles in Jerusalem. Peter and others were arrested and detained overnight, possibly in the guardroom at the high priest's palace where Jesus himself had been imprisoned overnight. The modern church of St Peter in Gallicantu possibly covers the site of this house of Caiaphas and, on a series of levels cut into the rock of the cliff face, enshrines the courtroom of the Council, the guardroom complete with the whipping block and staples for prisoners' chains and a bottleneck condemned cell.

This John is reported to have met with the rulers, elders, and scribes, together with Annas, Caiaphas, Alexander, and other Sadducees. Their decision was to warn the apostles and forbid them to preach in the name of Jesus, but for fear of the people they dared not punish them. [Acts 4:6]

8. John Mark, the Evangelist *see* MARK

9. John the Divine Author of the Book of Revelation. Of all the preceding Johns who might or might not have been the writer of the Fourth Gospel and one or more of the Letters, there can be remarkably little certainty of authorship. St John 'the Divine', as the Authorized Version of the Bible calls him, cannot perhaps be identified with John the Apostle and son of Zebedee with any greater certainty. If, however, John Bar-Zebedee lived for any length of time into the reign of the Roman

Emperor Domitian (AD 81-96), it is possible that he was the 'Seer of Patmos' whose visions the Book of Revelation records.

Patmos and Ephesus

It is possible with some imagination to reconstruct the events which led to the revelation of such visions to such a man and their remarkable record in writing. Towards the end of the 1st century, a Roman quinquereme – a large galley with five banks of oars – slipped through the surf and spray into the harbour of the rocky island of Patmos. Patmos is one of a number of small islands off the Turkish coast and yet from its rocky heights one can pick out the approximate direction of each of the seven parishes to which the writer of Revelation sent messages. While the galley-slaves lay exhausted across their oars, a long chain of convicts bound for the penal settlement threaded its way up the rocks to the sound of the lash. These men were deported for life to work in the stone quarries, to sleep in the caves, and live in the confines of the island of Patmos. Among them was one John, condemned as a Christian agitator for his activities in the seven cities of the mainland, of which the chief was Ephesus.

John had made his home at Ephesus and loved his adopted city, having come to speak its language and think in terms of its mentality. He was in heart but not in soul a citizen of Ephesus, the cathedral city of paganism in Asia.

To the worship of Artemis at Ephesus, immensely old and mystical, was added the modern emperor worship, as a political expedient in an age that was frankly sceptical of the old gods. To give divine honour to the emperor, however, and admit the claim of the state upon

281

the soul was impossible for the Christian and the Jew, bound by the commandment 'Thou shalt have none other gods but me'. Thus, the sacrifice to the emperor became the passport of the loyal citizen, but to refuse this sacrificial homage meant death. The more Christians resisted, the more they were feared and the more cruelly they were persecuted. Nevertheless, from the earliest visits of Paul, in the fifties, to the time of John, Asia became the nursery of Christendom. Indeed, in the year 431 Ephesus was the place of a great Council of the Christian Church.

Towards the end of the 1st century, this John, having spent his life for his seven precious parishes whose Christian communities he may have helped to found, had had to leave them to struggle for survival against the fanatical pagan cults. There on Patmos, where today the huge Orthodox Monastery of St John crowns the rocky hilltop, John, inspired by the skyscrapes, wrote the message of God's denunciation of evil, sending his love, his longing and his encouragement to his beloved 'Churches of Asia'. It is not surprising that his visions of a 'new heaven and a new earth' have 'no more sea' and 'no more thirst'. He ends, 'He who testifies to these things says, "Surely I am coming soon." Amen. Come, Lord Jesus!'

The record of visions

One of the most striking features of the book is the oddness and crudity of its Greek style, completely obscured in the Authorized Version. The spasmodic lack of regard for syntax and grammar in the Book of Revelation is in marked contrast with the smoothness and correctness of the Greek of the Fourth Gospel. Perhaps the only possible explanation is that John wrote a record of his ecstatic experiences during his visions. Only this, says one translator, could account for the incoherence, the repetition, and the incredible piling up of words. It seems that the Gospel and the Revelation are the works of different Johns.

The Revelation has been described as an inspired picture-book which, by an accumulation of magnificent poetic imagery, makes a powerful appeal to the reader's imagination. Many of the strange beasts, symbols, and apocalyptic figures of the visions would have been much better understood by Christians for whom the book was first written than they are for us today, but some are still clear. In the prologue, the writer declares that he is 'John, who bore witness to the word of God and to the testimony of Jesus Christ, even to all that he saw.' The first three chapters consist of John's greetings to his beloved Seven Churches of Ephesus, Smyrna, Pergamum, Thyatira, Sardis, Philadelphia, and Laodicea. His messages are inspired by a vision of seven golden lamp-stands surrounding a figure of Jesus, who says, 'Fear not, I am the first and the last, and the living one; I died, and behold I am alive for evermore, and I have the keys of Death and Hades. Now write what you see . . .' And to each Church, the message of God flows to encourage or to reproach.

Then follows a series of prophetic visions. The first describes the preparations for the Day of Judgment. God entrusts the future of the world to the Lamb, who is worthy to break the seven seals of the scroll of the book of life. God's servants are to be preserved and rewarded; their prayers bring the Great Day nearer. The great battle between good and evil is symbolized by a struggle between the woman and the dragon. The soverignty of God is absolute and his ultimate purpose is to destroy all forms of evil. He is in control of history.

The second of the prophetic visions shows the coming punishment of evil, epitomized in all that is Roman – pagan cults and the idolatrous emperor-worship – while the songs of victory are sung in heaven. The third prophetic vision reveals the coming destruction of the pagan nations, the chaining up of Satan for a thousand years before the final battle of the End. The last of the visions is of the heavenly, Messianic Jerusalem, through the centre of which flows the river of life of which all the thirsty are invited to drink. Over and over again, the nearness of the End is proclaimed, 'The time is close . . . very soon now, I shall be with you again'.

So, John the convict among the stone quarries of Patmos, aware of the vast forces of evil ranged against Christianity in his time, at one moment opened a door in heaven and at another lifted the cover off the bottomless pit. For he lived in the age of blood and fire. He was not a vindictive man, but he wrote 'in the spirit' with a frightening sense of the reality of good and evil, a reality whose bitterness burned, but whose sweetness was inexpressible. [Revelation to John]

JOSEPH (Gk. from the Heb. 'may God add [children]') This much-used Jewish name was that of five different persons in the New Testament.

1. Joseph, father of Jesus
2. Joseph, brother of Jesus
3. Joseph of Arimathea
4. Joseph Barsabbas
5. Joseph Barnabas

1. Joseph, father of Jesus This Joseph was the spouse of the virgin Mary at the time of the annunciation of the angel Gabriel and the conception of Jesus. Joseph subsequently married Mary and, on the birth of the child, adopted him as his son. The few references within the Gospels suggest that he was a humble, kindly, generous, and conscientious parent who probably taught Jesus the carpenter's trade. Perhaps Jesus's respect for Joseph is, in some measure, reflected in his deliberate adoption of the affectionate title of *Abba* – 'Daddy' – for God, and in his deep personal apprehension of the fatherhood of God.

Joseph's dilemma

Matthew describes how Joseph discovered that his espoused Mary was pregnant, and the dilemma in which this placed Joseph. 'Being a just man and unwilling to put her to shame', he had already made up his mind to put her away informally, when in a dream he was reassured by an angel. 'Joseph, son of David, do not fear to take Mary your wife, for that which is conceived in her is of the Holy Spirit: she will bear a son, and you shall call his name Jesus, for he will save his people from their sins.' Thus reassured of her virginal conception, Joseph took Mary to his home and, when the child was born, duly named him 'Jesus'. Matthew adds as a credential to his account the prophecy of Isaiah (7:14): 'Behold, a virgin shall conceive and bear a son, and his name shall be called Emmanuel', which Matthew explains means 'God with us'.

The child was born in Bethlehem in Judea, during the reign of Herod the Great (perhaps in what is known as the year 6 BC). Some time later (anything up to two years) some wise men came to Jerusalem from the east (probably astrologers from Persia or Arabia). On their arrival they asked, 'Where is he who has been born king

285

of the Jews? For we have seen his star in the East, and have come to worship him.' (Matt. 2:2) After a somewhat guarded reception by Herod, and again guided by the star which for them had portended the birth of a king, the wise men came 'into the house' in Bethlehem where the family lived, offered their gifts, and returned without further contact with Herod.

After the wise men had left, Joseph was warned by the angel to 'Rise, take the child and his mother, and flee to Egypt, and remain there till I tell you; for Herod is about to search for the child, to destroy him.' (Matt. 2:13) Again Matthew adds a prophetic credential to the story, quoting Hosea (11:1) – 'Out of Egypt have I called my son'. Joseph's escape was amply justified by Herod's massacre of the children in Bethlehem. Only after Herod's death did Joseph – guided again by the angel – return with his family to Israel. Distrusting Herod's successor Archelaus, Joseph took his family up to Galilee and settled in the town of Nazareth. Matthew again adds the prophetic 'He shall be called a Nazarene.' This is indeed the first mention of Nazareth by Matthew.

Considerably later in his narrative, and perhaps some thirty years later in time, Matthew describes Jesus's return to Nazareth in the course of his public ministry. Surprised at his wisdom and power, the members of the synagogue congregation exclaim, 'Is not this the carpenter's son? Is not his mother called Mary? And are not his brothers James and Joseph and Simon and Judas? And are not all his sisters with us? Where then did this man get all this?' (Matt. 13:55, 56) The Greek word for carpenter can be applied to the trade of building and repairing in wood, stone, or metal. No further mention of Joseph appears in Matthew's Gospel.

Luke's version: the cares of fatherhood

Luke describes Mary at the time of the annunciation as 'a virgin betrothed to a man whose name was Joseph, of the house of David'. Unlike Matthew, Luke describes Mary and Joseph as living in Nazareth. Only the census, for which everyone went to his own town for registration, took them to Bethlehem, because Joseph 'was of the house and lineage of David'. So it was in Bethlehem that Mary gave birth to her son, 'and wrapped him in swaddling cloths, and laid him in a manger, because there was no place for them in the inn'. Here the shepherds hurried in to find 'Mary and Joseph, and the babe lying in a manger'. At the child's circumcision, 'he was called Jesus, the name given by the angel before he was conceived in the womb'.

Forty days after the birth, both parents are described as taking the child to the Temple for him to be presented and redeemed by sacrifice. Both the 'father' and mother are described standing there, wondering at what was said about him by the old priest Simeon. When the ceremony was completed and the Law fulfilled, they 'returned into Galilee, to their own city, Nazareth'.

Luke further describes the regular Passover visits of the parents to Jerusalem, with particular reference to the visit when the boy Jesus was twelve years old (perhaps to celebrate his 'confirmation' as a 'son of the Law'). When they had mislaid the boy on the first day of the return journey, and had discovered him among the doctors in the Temple, his mother said, 'Son, why have you treated us so? Behold, your father and I have been looking for you anxiously.' 'How is it that you sought me?' he replied. 'Did you not know that I must be in my Father's house?' But they did not understand what he meant. 'And he went down with them and came to Nazareth, and was obedient to them; and his mother kept all these things in her heart.' (Luke 2:48-51)

Luke's account of Jesus's later visit to the synagogue at Nazareth evokes the comment 'Is this not the carpenter's son?' But there is no gospel mention of the survival of Joseph after the Jerusalem Passover visit, when Jesus was twelve years old. In John's Gospel, both Philip (talking to Nathanael) and the Jews at Capernaum identify Jesus as the 'son of Joseph', and at Capernaum they claim to know his father and mother. (John 6:42)

Certainly, the accounts of Matthew and Luke disagree as to the original home of Joseph, and even, in their genealogies, as to his father's name. But in most other respects their accounts can be considered complementary rather than contradictory. It has been suggested that this may be because Matthew's primary source of information for his birth narrative was the person or family of Joseph, whereas Luke's account certainly reflects the thoughts and feelings of Mary.

Was there a family partnership?

The apocryphal infancy gospel called after James, the brother of Jesus, but likely to have been written in the 2nd century, declares Joseph to have been elderly at the time of his marriage to Mary. His comparatively early death might account for there being no mention of him at the crucifixion, and it would certainly help to explain why the public ministry of Jesus did not begin until he was nearly thirty years old, if he was needed for family and business reasons within his own home.

In the 4th and 5th centuries, an apocryphal History of Joseph the Carpenter accounted for a growing veneration of Joseph within the Eastern Churches, as the pattern of domestic holiness. His feast was introduced into the Roman calendar in 1479 and his name inserted in the Litany of the Saints in 1729. He is usually represented in art, staff in hand, with the boy Jesus. [Matt. 1:16-24; 2:13; Luke 1:27; 2:4-51; 3:23; 4:22; John 1:45; 6:42]

2. Joseph (also Joses, or Joset), brother of Jesus When Jesus returned to Nazareth in the course of his public ministry, and spoke in the synagogue there, the congregation recognized him as the 'carpenter's son' and claimed to know his family, naming four brothers and mentioning his sisters. Luke in the birth stories refers to Jesus as Mary's 'first-born son' (2:7). Some of the Church Fathers, wishing to uphold the perpetual virginity of Mary, suggested that these brothers and sisters were the children of a previous marriage of Joseph. Others, including the 4th-century biblical scholar Jerome, have suggested that the normal Greek words used for 'brothers' and 'sisters' could be intended to include 'cousins'. It must be admitted that oriental customs can be quoted to support this. However, we may see a purpose in the selection of the words used.

Mark, no doubt followed by Matthew and Luke, describes Jesus teaching at Capernaum and, hearing that his mother and brothers have arrived and are asking for him, he replied, ' "Who are my mother and my brothers?" Looking around on those who sat about him, he said, "Here are my mother and my brothers! Whoever does the will of God is my brother, and sister, and mother." ' (Mark 3:33-35) John describes how, at the feast of Tabernacles when the Jews were out to kill Jesus and he had to remain in Galilee, his brothers failed to understand his purpose and message, saying to him,

' "Leave here and go to Judea, that your disciples may see the works you are doing. For no man works in secret if he seeks to be known openly. If you do these things, show yourself to the world." For even his brothers did not believe in him.' (John 7:3-5) Luke, however, relates how Mary the mother of Jesus 'with his brothers' remained loyal in their prayers along with the apostles in Jerusalem after the ascension of Jesus.

Of this brother Joseph – unlike Jesus's brother James, whom we know to have become the first bishop in Jerusalem – there is no further mention. [Matt. 13:55; 27:56; Mark 6:3; 15:40, 47]

3. Joseph of Arimathea Each of the Gospels contributes to the picture of Joseph of Arimathea. Mark describes him as 'a respected member of the council' (that is, the Sanhedrin), 'who was also himself looking for the kingdom of God'. Matthew simply calls him 'a rich man'. Luke vouches for him as 'a good and righteous man', and adds that he had 'not consented to their [the members of the Sanhedrin] purpose and deed'. John calls him 'a disciple of Jesus, but secretly, for fear of the Jews'.

All four Gospels record that after the crucifixion of Jesus, Joseph went to Pilate and asked for the body of Jesus, obtained permission, took it down, wrapped it in a linen cloth, and laid it in a tomb. Mark adds that Pilate 'granted the body to Joseph. And he bought a linen shroud', and finally 'rolled a stone against the door of the tomb'. Matthew adds that it was Joseph's own personal tomb. Luke adds that no one had ever been laid in the tomb till then. He also adds that the women returned home to prepare spices and ointments, which they later took to the tomb on the first day of the week, after the Sabbath.

It is interesting, however, that Paul makes no mention of Joseph of Arimathea in his speech at Pisidian Antioch, during his First Journey. He says that it was the Jews who 'took him down from the tree, and laid him in a tomb'. (Acts 13:29) The traditional site of Joseph's home town Arimathea is Ramlah, near Lydda, on the coastal plain south-west of Jerusalem. According to the apocryphal *Gospel of Nicodemus,* Joseph helped to found the first Christian community at Lydda.

In 1135 the Englishman William of Malmesbury, in a history of the ancient church of Glastonbury in Somerset, recorded the legend of Joseph of Arimathea's voyage to England, bringing the holy chalice, or grail, used at the Last Supper. A number of legends surround the 'Holy Grail' and the 'Glastonbury Thorn', a species of Levantine hawthorn flowering twice a year and still to be seen today. [Matt. 27:57, 59; Mark 15:43, 45; Luke 23:50; John 19:38]

4. Joseph Barsabbas, nicknamed Justus *see* BARSABBAS *and* MATTHIAS

5. Joseph Barnabas *see* BARNABAS

JOSES (Gk. form of 'Joseph') **1.** The brother of Jesus *see* JOSEPH **2.**

2. 'Surnamed by the apostles "Barnabas" ' *see* BARNABAS

JUDAS (Gk. from the Heb. 'praised', 'celebrated')

1. Judas Iscariot

2. Judas Barsabbas

3. Judas of Damascus

4. Judas of Galilee

5. Judas, brother of Jesus

6. Judas, son of James

1. Judas Iscariot The traitor disciple, who betrayed and enabled the arrest of his master, Jesus.

Owing to the lapse of time between the events of the

gospel story and their recording, the story of Judas gathered accretions and interpretations. It is not possible with any certainty to draw from the Gospels a single and concurrent account of Judas's place among the twelve. Therefore, the events in which he was involved will be mentioned with reference to the comments of each evangelist, then his possible motives will be discussed, and finally certain obvious misconceptions will be disposed of.

Always an outsider?

On lists in all three Synoptic Gospels, Judas appears last with the epithet 'who betrayed him'. He is described as 'Iscariot', which might possibly be an Aramaic adaption of *Sicarius*, the Latin for 'dagger-man', implying that Judas was a Zealot partisan. 'Iscariot' is more likely, however, to mean simply *Ish* ('man') *Kerioth*, from Kerioth, a town in southern Judea. In which case, Judas would have been the only non-Galilean among the twelve and, therefore, the 'odd man out'; certainly he seems to have been essentially lonely and misunderstood.

John frankly calls him 'a thief' or 'betrayer', 'possessed by the devil', or 'the son of perdition'. It is as though the evangelists could not paint him black enough in retrospect. After all, they had all at one time or another denied or deserted their master and the blackness of Judas might make their own greyness less noticeable. Jesus himself, however, is acknowledged to have been a clear reader of personality and he must have first called Judas, and then have appointed him as the treasurer or accountant of the little company. Jesus is hardly likely to have given Judas the job if it was to be a source of temptation to him, nor is Judas likely to have joined a band of intinerant and penniless preachers if he was a greedy and petty pilferer.

Jesus must have seen in Judas a potentially useful member of his team, and Judas must have seen in Jesus the potential fulfilment of Messianic prophecy. Christians, particularly in the west, have long speculated on the reasons for the original choice of Judas, his suicide, his motives and the relatively small amount of blood-money paid to him. One theory is that Judas was probably the most passionate nationalist of the group, of shrewder stuff than the rustic Galileans swift to recognize the potential of Jesus, 'mighty in works and deeds', to be the Messiah long awaited by such as he.

Judas, more than the others perhaps, seems to have misunderstood or disregarded Jesus's interpretation of his own Messiahship. Faced with a slow and steady process of disillusionment and disappointment, at what so many of Jesus's followers considered to be lost opportunities (John says they wanted to make him 'King'), Judas's impatience seems to have grown until he himself grasped the initiative.

Whether intending perhaps to force Jesus into declaring himself Messiah, at the height of the Passover feast, when support was ready to hand – or whether driven to a pathetic revenge for his deep personal disappointment and frustration, Judas acted the traitor. Three years' close acquaintance with Jesus may well have convinced Judas of Jesus's Messiahship, but also of a genuine inability to declare himself. Judas, by pushing Jesus at the tactical moment, may well have felt that he was acting for Jesus's own good; for Judas's ideal of Messiahship did not include Jesus actually allowing himself to be killed. Once, however, the plot was under way, there was no brake to apply.

The betrayal

All three Synoptic Gospels declare that Judas himself approached the chief priests 'in order to betray Jesus to them'. They were glad and promised to reward him. Matthew adds that they gave him thirty silver pieces, the equivalent of under ten dollars or four pounds sterling – that is, the purchase-value of a foreign slave in Old Testament times, or the amount claimed by a Jewish slave if his master drew blood in New Testament times. If Judas was as greedy as is often supposed, he could have extorted far more from the high priests.

At the Last Supper with his disciples, the night before the Passover feast, Jesus gave a clear warning of his impending betrayal: 'And as they were at table eating, Jesus said, "Truly, I say to you, one of you will betray me, one who is eating with me." They began to be sorrowful, and to say to him one after another, "Is it I?" He said to them, "It is one of the twelve, who is dipping bread in the same dish with me. For the Son of Man goes as it is written of him, but woe to that man by whom the Son of Man is betrayed! It would have been better for that man if he had not been born."' (Mark 14:18-21) Matthew adds that Jesus identified Judas as his betrayer. 'Judas, who betrayed him, said, "Is it I, Master?" He said to him, "You have said so."' (Matt. 26:25)

The Fourth Gospel, substituting the story of the feet-washing for that of the Last Supper, describes the conversation that followed in considerable detail. The warning is all the more poignant, following the lesson in humility illustrated by Jesus's washing of his disciples' feet, including those of Judas. 'Truly, truly, I say to you, a servant is not greater than his master; nor is he who is sent greater than he who sent him. If you know these things, blessed are you if you do them. I am not speaking of you all; I know whom I have chosen; it is that the scripture may be fulfilled, "He who ate my bread has lifted his heel against me".' (John 13:16-18)

Now the betrayer must be dissuaded or dismissed, but first Jesus gives Judas the place of honour next to himself and hands him a chosen morsel of food, concealing his treachery from all but the 'beloved disciple' seated on Jesus's other side. 'The disciples looked at one another, uncertain of whom he spoke. One of his disciples, whom Jesus loved, was lying close to the breast of Jesus; so Simon Peter beckoned to him and said, "Tell us who it is of whom he speaks." So lying thus, close to the breast of Jesus, he said to him, "Lord, who is it?" Jesus answered, "It is he to whom I shall give this morsel when I have dipped it." So when he had dipped the morsel, he gave it to Judas, the son of Simon Iscariot.' (John 13:22-26)

Judas seems to have rejected Jesus's last gesture of friendship, for, as John says, 'Satan entered into him'. So Jesus said, 'What you are going to do, do quickly,' and Judas went out literally and figuratively into the dark, for 'it was night'.

The Synoptic Gospel go on to describe the walk down to Gethsemane, the agony in the Garden, and then the arrival of Judas with the Temple police. Judas had given them a sign by which they would recognize Jesus – ' "The one I shall kiss is the man; seize him and lead him away safely." And when he came, he went up to him at once, and said, "Master!" And he kissed him. And they laid hands on him and seized him.' (Mark 14:44-46) The description of the arrest in the Fourth Gospel is rather one of purposeful surrender. 'Then Jesus, knowing all that was to befall him, came forward and said to them, "Whom do you seek?" They answered him, "Jesus of Nazareth." Jesus said to them, "I am he." Judas, who betrayed him, was standing with them. When he said to them, "I am he," they drew back and fell to the ground. Again he asked them, "Whom do you seek?" And they said, "Jesus of Nazareth." Jesus answered, "I told you that I am he; so, if you seek me, let these men go." ' (John 18:4-8)

Judas is not mentioned at the trial before the Council, though undoubtedly he must have given his evidence, probably of Jesus's acceptance of the title of Messiah from Peter at Caesarea Philippi: 'Thou art the Christ'. But it required two witnesses to convict and Peter himself contrived to remain out of sight in the gallery, partially recognized by his Galilean accent in spite of his denial. Again Judas is mercifully not mentioned at the later trial before Pilate, or at the crucifixion, though his presence and his feelings are all too clearly revealed in the events that followed.

Matthew's account of Judas's pathetic remorse and suicide is based on the Old Testament prophecy of Zechariah (11:12, 13): 'When Judas, his betrayer, saw that he was condemned, he repented and brought back the thirty pieces of silver to the chief priests and the elders, saying, "I have sinned in betraying innocent blood." They said, "What is that to us? See to it yourself." And throwing down the pieces of silver in the temple, he departed; and he went and hanged himself.' (Matt. 27:3-5) Luke's account in Acts of an accidental death, known to all the people in Jerusalem, seems more likely to be accurate. Both accounts, however, link the death of Judas with a cemetery for foreigners in Jerusalem, called Akeldama, 'The Field of Blood', the site of which is today still to be seen south of the Western Hill, across the Valley of Hinnom.

What was his motive?

The synoptists made no effort to analyse the motive of Judas. The Fourth Gospel, rather unworthily perhaps, simply accuses him of greed and theft, quoting Judas's reaction to the anointing of Jesus by Mary and Bethany with precious ointment – ' "Why was this ointment not sold for three hundred denarii and given to the poor?" This he said, not that he cared for the poor but because he was a thief, and as he had the money-box he used to take what was put into it.' (John 12:5-6) This motive does not seem to fit the facts of Judas's selection by Jesus as a disciple, nor his appointment as treasurer, presumably for his business acumen. This is not to deny the evil inspiration which, as John says, was the basic cause of Judas's treachery. Whether he was misguidedly trying to force Jesus's hand to declare his Messiahship, for nationalistic motives, or was simply jealous, as a shrewd southerner, of his rustic Galilean rivals, such as Peter and John, we may never know. We may be sure, however, that Judas was no puppet predestined to play a necessary part in the betrayal of Jesus. Judas was essentially a free agent, acting from his own motives at any given moment.

Another enigma of the story is not why but what Judas actually betrayed. Was it just a convenient place of arrest away from the Passover crowds? Was it Jesus's secret admission to his Messianic identity? This alone could and did result in his conviction, but it came from his own lips 'I am' with all the purposefulness of the 'Son of Man who came to give his life a ransom for many'. [Matt. 10:4; 26:14, 25, 47; 27:3; Mark 3:19;

14:10, 43; Luke 6:16; 22:3, 47; John 6:71; 12:4; 13:2, 26-29; 18:2-5; Acts 1:16, 25]

2. Judas Barsabbas *see* BARSABBAS

3. Judas of Damascus The owner of the house, in the street called Straight, where Ananias was told to enquire for Saul of Tarsus, following his conversion on the road to Damascus.

'The Lord said to him in a vision, "Ananias." And he said, "Here I am, Lord," ' and the Lord directed him to find Saul in the house of Judas, saying that Saul also had had a vision – but of Ananias entering and laying hands upon him to restore his sight. It was not surprising that Ananias timidly demurred, saying, 'Lord, I have heard from many about this man, how much evil he has done to thy saints at Jerusalem; and here he has authority from the chief priests to bind all who call upon thy name.' (Acts 9:13, 14) But the Lord reassured him and Ananias departed, and entered the house and, laying his hands on him, said, ' "Brother Saul, the Lord Jesus who appeared to you on the road by which you came, has sent me that you may regain your sight and be filled with the Holy Spirit." And immediately something like scales fell from his eyes and he regained his sight.' (Acts 9:17, 18)

Judas, the Jewish host of Saul, the future Christian apostle, played no small part in the critical days following Saul's conversion. [Acts 9:11]

4. Judas of Galilee A Galilean patriot from Gamala who raised a revolt in bitter opposition to the census, or enrolment, ordered by the Roman Emperor Augustus, during the governorship of Quirinius in AD 6. It was on the occasion of the incorporation of Judea into the Roman province of Syria and it was probably the first Roman provincial census, by Roman methods, to be held in

Judea. The Galilean uprising was cruelly suppressed by the Romans, its leader Judas killed, and 2,000 of his followers were crucified. The momentum, however, survived underground in the form of a constant guerrilla movement, whose members were known as Zealots.

The great rabbi and Pharisee Gamaliel cited the suppression of Judas and his followers to persuade the Sanhedrin that false Messiahs and their followers would similarly perish, without the direct action of the Council. It was wiser to leave the apostles of the early Christian Church, for if that movement was of God, it would survive and prosper, regardless of any intervention by the Council. [Acts 5:37]

5. Judas, brother of Jesus Writer of the General Letter of Jude. This Judas is among the family of Jesus mentioned by the congregation of the synagogue at Nazareth, when they were impressed by the wisdom and works of Jesus. ' "Is not this the carpenter, the son of Mary and the brother of James and Joses and Judas and Simon and are not his sisters here with us?" And they took offence at him.' (Mark 6:3) John commented on the fact that in the last year of Jesus's life, his own brothers did not believe in him. Of the four brothers, nothing certain is known further about Joseph or Simon, but James became the leader and first bishop of the Christian Church in Jerusalem, and Judas the author of a brief letter, which survives within the New Testament.

This letter was written round about the year 80, as a warning against false teachers in the Church. The writer calls himself 'Jude, a servant of Jesus Christ, and brother of James'. James, leader of the Church at Jerusalem for some twenty years, was obviously known to his readers. There seems little reason to doubt the author's claim to his relationship. The destination of the letter cannot be determined, but it appears to have been somewhere where the interpretation of the gospel and Christian life was far too free and undisciplined. The writer had to encourage his readers to 'contend for the faith which was once for all delivered to the saints. For admission has been secretly gained by some who long ago were designated for this condemnation, ungodly persons who pervert the grace of our God into licentiousness and deny our only Master and Lord, Jesus Christ.' (Jude 4)

Jude's warning is remarkably clear: these false teachers are immoral, covetous, anti-authority, 'Wordly people, devoid of the Spirit'. 'These are grumblers, malcontents, following their own passions, loud-mouthed boasters, flattering people to gain advantage. But you must remember, beloved, the predictions of the apostles of our Lord Jesus Christ; they said to you, "In the last time there will be scoffers, following their own ungodly passions." It is these who set up divisions, worldly people, devoid of the Spirit.' (Jude 16-19) Then the writer presses home his own advice, 'But you, beloved, build yourselves up on your most holy faith; pray in the Holy Spirit; keep yourselves in the love of God; wait for the mercy of our Lord Jesus Christ unto eternal life.' (Jude 20-21)

Finally the letter ends quite beautifully with this farewell: 'Now to him who is able to keep you from falling and to present you without blemish before the presence of his glory with rejoicing, to the only God, our Saviour through Jesus Christ our Lord, be glory, majesty, dominion, and authority, before all time and now and for ever.' (Jude 24-25)

This letter is particularly interesting because it shows

the strength of Old Testament Jewish traditions within the faith and life of the Church. Both Jude and his brother James were zealous observers of the Law, as well as leaders of Christian thinking. Jude speaks in terms of disobedient angels 'in eternal chains in the nether gloom until the judgment of the great day'. 'But when the archangel Michael, contending with the devil, disputed about the body of Moses, he did not presume to pronounce a reviling judgment upon him, but said, "The Lord rebuke you." But these men revile whatever they do not understand, and by those things that they know by instinct as rational animals do, they are destroyed. Woe to them! For they walk in the way of Cain, and abandon themselves for the sake of gain to Balaam's error, and perish in Korah's rebellion.' Such passages seem very far from the central themes of the Christian gospel, but show how very Jewish in their thinking some of the early Christian writers (such as the author of 2 Peter also) must have been.

For those concerned with the exact relationship of Jude to Jesus, *see* JOSEPH **2.** [Letter of Jude]

6. Judas, son of James One of the twelve, but not Iscariot. Judas is listed among the twelve apostles only by Luke, both in his Gospel and in the Acts. The corresponding name in the Gospels of Mark and Matthew is that of Thaddaeus, which is omitted by Luke. The Fourth Gospel refers to him as 'Judas, not Iscariot', when at the Last Supper he asks Jesus: 'Lord, how is it that you will manifest yourself to us, and not to the world?' It is, therefore, reasonable to identify Thaddaeus and Judas as the same person, with James as their father. (The name Lebbaeus is included as an alternative to Thaddaeus only in some minor manuscripts at Matt. 10:3, and also in the Western Text only at

Mark 3:18, but Lebbaeus is not to be found in the Revised Standard Version.) The actual wording in Luke's list is 'Judas, son of James', implying either that James was his father or his brother. If this Judas was the writer of the Letter of Jude, the last in the New Testament, then he does in fact refer to himself as 'Jude, servant ot Jesus Christ and brother of James'. [Luke 6:16; John 14:22; Acts 1:13. Thaddaeus: Matt. 10:3; Mark 3:18]

JUDE *see* JUDAS **5.** AND **6.**

JULIA One of the Christians greeted by Paul at the close of his letter to the Church in Rome. Julia is linked with the name of Philologus, perhaps her husband, in a group or household of five, 'and the saints that are with them'. Both names were common among Roman slaves. [Rom. 16:15]

JULIUS Julius was a centurion in the Augustan cohort, a corps of officer-couriers. He was in charge of Paul and other political prisoners sailing for Rome from Caesarea.

Julius was considerate enough to allow Paul to go ashore at Sidon to visit friends, but he disregarded Paul's warning not to sail from Crete so late in the year, instead taking the advice of both the captain and the ship's owner. Driven before a storm for fourteen days, the ship was virtually out of control when at last soundings indicated that land was near. The crew attempted to escape in the ship's boat, but at Paul's suggestion Julius made the soldiers cut the ropes and let the boat drop away. When the ship finally ran aground, the soldiers prepared to kill the prisoners, lest they escape. Julius, however, 'wishing to save Paul', would not let them, and ordered all who could swim to jump overboard and the rest to follow on planks and wreckage. In this way all came safe and sound to land.

Paul, indeed, knew only too well what a shipwreck was like (2 Cor. 11:25), and Luke, who was with him on this occasion, describes Paul's constant initiative and encouragement in emergency. Certainly, Julius may well have recognized the experience of Paul and, by accepting Paul's advice to jettison the ship's boat, ensured that the crew remained on board to beach the ship. Thus without Julius the centurion's respect for Paul's judgment, Paul might have perished before reaching Rome; and, indeed, all the centurions of Paul's acquaintance protected him. [Acts 27:1-44]

JUNIA(S) One of the Christians greeted by Paul at the end of his letter to the Christian Church in Rome. Junias is linked with Andronicus. Paul refers to them as his 'kinsmen', probably meaning that at least they were fellow-Jews, if not blood-relatives. Paul also calls them his 'fellow-prisoners', though during which of his imprisonments is uncertain. Paul goes on: 'They are men of note among the apostles. They were in Christ before me.' This immediately places their conversion within five years of the crucifixion of Jesus and connects them with the Church at Jerusalem rather than at Antioch. In fact, they may well have been associated with the Stephen group of Hellenized Jews who dispersed to found branches of the Church in Antioch, Cyprus, and elsewhere in the eastern Mediterranean. It is just possible that Junias should be read as 'Junia', in the feminine, which would then suggest the wife of Andronicus and a woman apostle. [Rom. 16:7]

JUPITER (Lat. *Jupiter*, Gk. *Zeus*) *see* ZEUS

JUSTUS (Gk. 'just') **1.** The surname of Joseph Barsabbas *see* BARSABBAS

2. The surname of Titius, a devout proselyte at Corinth, to whose house, next to the Jewish synagogue, Paul removed when virtually ejected from the synagogue by the opposition of the Jews. It was essential that Paul had somewhere to preach his message that Jesus was the Messiah, and the violent opposition of the Corinthian Jews provoked him to a change of policy, marked by his declaration, 'Your blood be upon your heads! I am innocent. From now on I will go to the Gentiles.' And from that moment, he moved into the house of the Gentile – and possibly Roman – convert Titius Justus. [Acts 18:7]

3. The surname of Jesus, one of Paul's companions at Rome during his first imprisonment at the time of his writing to the Christian community at Colossae. [Col. 4:11]

L

LAODICEANS (Gk. *Laodikeis*) Laodicea, together with Hierapolis and Colossae, was one of the three cities within the fertile valley of the River Lycus, about 100 miles east and inland from Ephesus. All three cities were probably evangelized by Epaphras, a convert of Paul from Ephesus. He was probably trained within a missionary team during Paul's long and systematic period of teaching at Ephesus, in the course of his Third Journey. Some forty years later, the writer of the Book of the Revelation of John the Divine reprimands the Laodiceans for their 'lukewarmness' and lack of enthusiasm for the cause of the Seven Christian Churches in Asia.

Laodicea was a wealthy city founded in the middle of the 3rd century BC. Within the Lycus Valley, Laodicea was on one of the trade-routes of Asia, which ensured its commercial prosperity. The city was a leading banking centre, where Cicero cashed drafts in 51 BC, and which no doubt financed the reconstruction following the great earthquake of AD 60. Laodicea's refusal of relief from the senatorial earthquake fund may be quoted in John's comments in the book of Revelation. 'To the angel of the church in Laodicea write . . . I know your works: you are neither cold or hot . . . for you say, I am rich, I have prospered, and I need nothing; not knowing that you are wretched, pitiable, poor, blind, and naked.' (Rev. 3:14-17) The Lycus Valley also produced a glossy black wool for cloaks and carpets. Laodicea had a famous medical school, which pioneered the use of collyrium as an eye-ointment. 'The words of the Amen, the faithful and true witness' in the Book of Revelation says, ' "because you are lukewarm. . . . I will spew you out of my mouth" ', a reference to the emetic qualities of warm soda-water from the springs of Hierapolis. By the time of John of Patmos, under the Emperor Domitian, Laodicea had become the capital of the province of Phrygia.

Some thirty years earlier Paul, writing from his imprisonment in Rome to the Christian community at Colossae, sent his affectionate greetings and encouragement to the Christian community at Laodicea. 'Paul, an apostle of Christ Jesus by the will of God, and Timothy our brother, To the saints and faithful brethren in Christ at Colossae: Grace to you and peace from God our Father. We always thank God, the Father of our Lord Jesus Christ, when we pray for you, because we have heard of your faith in Christ Jesus and of the love which you have for all the saints, because of the hope laid up for you in heaven. Of this you have heard before in the word of the truth.' (Col. 1:1-5) This letter continued with a magnificent statement, calculated to deal with a local heresy diluting Christian theology with pagan and Jewish philosophy. Paul roundly declared Jesus the Messiah as the supreme power for salvation, the ultimate reality and all-sufficient redeemer, and intermediary between God and man.

At the end of the letter to Colossae, Paul wrote, 'And when this letter has been read among you, have it read also in the church of the Laodiceans; and see that you read also the letter from Laodicea.' (Col. 4:16) The letter to the Laodiceans does not appear to have survived within the New Testament. It has, however, been suggested that the Letter to the Ephesians may supply the clue. The destination of this letter is perhaps less certain than its authorship. At least three of the most ancient manuscripts omit the address 'at Ephesus' in the opening verse. In the year 140, the scholar Marcion substitutes the address 'to the Laodiceans'. We know from Paul's letter to the Colossians (4:16) that he did in fact write a letter to the Laodiceans, and that he suggested that the congregations at Colossae and Laodicea exchange letters after they had read their own. Both letters were sent by the hand of Tychicus and his route would inevitably take him to many other Asian congregations during the course of his journey. It may well be, therefore, that what we know as the letter to the Ephesians was a circular letter of which, perhaps, half a dozen copies were carried by Tychicus. The bearer may have been instructed to fill in the blank address before delivering each copy of the letter, but probably failed to do so on at least one copy, of which the letter to the

Laodiceans may have been one. [Col. 21:1; 4:13-16; Rev. 3:14]

LAZARUS (Gk. from the Heb. 'helped by God')

1. The beggar in the parable of the Rich Man and Lazarus. He is the only character in all the parables of Jesus to be given a name. This parable may or may not allude to some contemporary incident, known to Jesus's hearers. It is one of a whole sequence of parables recorded only in Luke's Gospel and for the most part addressed to the Pharisees and Scribes, illustrating God's fatherly care for every kind of person. In the parable of the Marriage Feast, it is the poor, the maimed, the blind and the lame who are the guests. The Lost Sheep and the Lost Coin reflect his care for the very last, lost sinner. The Prodigal Son demonstrates the longing of the father to forgive. The story of the Judge and the Widow shows his care for the deprived and oppressed, that of the Pharisee and the Publican his mercy on the outcast and rejected.

Jesus insisted that it was impossible to serve two masters in this life. 'You cannot serve God and mammon.' When the Pharisees scoffed at him, he answered, 'You are those who justify yourselves before men, but God knows your hearts; for what is exalted among men is an abomination in the sight of God.' (Luke 16:13, 15) It was then that he told them the parable of the Rich Man and Lazarus.

It is the tragedy in three acts, with two chief characters: the Rich Man, often called for convenience by the Latin word *Dives,* meaning 'wealthy', and the beggar called Lazarus, a Hebrew word meaning 'he whom God helps'.

In the first act, the scene is the home of Dives, a well-to-do man of the world and a respectable pillar of society. Neither his character nor his means of income are questioned. At his gate, however, lies Lazarus the beggar, a mass of sores, ill-clad and hungry. Every now and then he is given the leavings of the rich household, but even then his claims are disputed by the dogs, who add to his misery and degradation. To Dives, this familiar figure of Lazarus had come to be accepted as part of the street scenery, and he simply does not *see* the beggar at his gate. There is no bitterness, but only blindness. And so the first act closes.

In the second act, the scene is the next world, described in terms of popular Jewish thought. There is Paradise and Hades within sight of hearing of each other, but separated by a deep gorge. Dives has been buried in a manner appropriate to his status. Lazarus's burial is not mentioned, but his soul had an escort of angels. In Paradise Abraham presides at the feast; reclining on the couch next to him in the place of honour is the one-time beggar Lazarus; while Dives in Hades on the other side of the gorge is in torment and begs for water. Abraham reminds him that he has had *his* good time and now it is the turn of Lazarus; nothing can be done about it. The gulf that separated them both on earth seems to be still there in the next world, but now it is eternal.

In the third act, the scene is the same. Dives now accepts his position, but pleads for others in danger of sharing his fate. They like him have not been properly warned. Abraham, however, does not agree. People have all the warning they need. If they do not listen now, they will not be persuaded even by a resurrection or return from the next world. There the parable ends without comment, explanation, or judgment.

The Fourth Gospel, however, may be said to provide

an epilogue. It shows that Lazarus *of Bethany* was in fact raised from the dead, but the Pharisees and Scribes to whom the parable was told did not believe or repent, and nor apparently did they do so following the resurrection of Jesus himself. [Luke 16:19-31]

2. The brother of Martha and Mary in Bethany, an intimate friend of Jesus whose 'home from home' was their house whenever he came up to Jerusalem, particularly for the Passover festival. Lazarus was raised from the dead by Jesus and became a walking witness of the divine power and calling of Jesus, which represented such a threat to the vested interests and security of the high priests and their Council.

The story to be found within the Fourth Gospel has been variously described as the true account either of an actual miracle, or of an historical event which has been later elaborated into the reason for the decision of the Jewish leaders to kill Jesus. Finally the story has also been assessed as an entirely fictitious tale used as a vehicle for introducing some particular points of Christian teaching, not unconnected with the parable in Luke's Gospel. There are some to whom the Fourth Gospel, written perhaps as much as thirty years after the Synoptic Gospels, appears to be a meditation on, rather than a record of, historical events. On the other hand the chronology of the ministry and particularly the passion of Jesus within the Fourth Gospel are presented in a convincing sequence and timetable.

The story in John's Gospel, therefore, may best be regarded as that of an actual miracle, not recorded by the synoptists, but typically adapted to the teaching purposes of the writer. The synoptists clearly see the driving of the merchants from the Temple as the final cause for the plot to kill Jesus, but they describe Jesus lodging in Bethany during the earlier part of that Passover week. In the Fourth Gospel, the 'cleansing of the Temple' is associated with an earlier visit of Jesus to Jerusalem, and the person and household of Lazarus play a key role in the events that lead to the Passover plot.

The story opens with the illness of Lazarus, whose sisters at once send for Jesus, saying, 'Lord, he whom you love is ill.' Jesus is apparently on the far side of the River Jordan and comments: 'This illness is not unto death; it is for the glory of God, so that the Son of God may be glorified by means of it.' Jesus remains there two more days before suggesting a return to Judea. The disciples question his wisdom: 'Rabbi, the Jews were but now seeking to stone you, and you are going there again?' Jesus answers, 'Our friend Lazarus has fallen asleep, but I go to awake him out of sleep.' To talk of 'sleep' was a recognized euphemism for 'death' and Jesus makes the situation very clear: 'Lazarus is dead; and for your sake I am glad that I was not there, so that you may believe.'

On his arrival, Jesus finds that Lazarus died four days ago and that many Jewish friends have come to comfort the two sisters. Martha, leaving Mary at home, comes to meet Jesus with the words, 'Lord, if you had been here, my brother would not have died. And now I know that whatever you ask from God, God will give you.' Jesus answers, 'Your brother will rise again.' 'I know that he will rise again,' returns Martha, 'in the resurrection at the last day.' 'Jesus said to her, "I am the resurrection and the life; he who believes in me, though he die, yet shall he live, and whoever lives and believes in me shall never die. Do you believe this?" She said to him, "Yes, Lord; I believe that you are the Christ, the Son of God, he who is coming into the world." ' (John 11:21-27) (This passage forms the first gospel for the Requiem Mass in the Catholic Church of the Latin Rite today.)

Martha then went to call her sister and Mary greeted him with exactly the same first words as those of her sister Martha. Jesus, seeing her weeping and her Jewish friends with her, was deeply moved and asked, 'Where have you laid him?' Seeing Jesus weep too, some of the friends asked, 'Could not he who opened the eyes of the blind man have kept this man from dying?' Jesus came to the tomb and told them to take away the stone. Martha reminded him that after four days there would be a smell, but they did so; and Jesus began to pray, ' "Father, I thank thee that thou hast heard me. I knew that thou hearest me always, but I have said this on account of the people standing by, that they may believe that thou didst send me." When he had said this, he cried with a loud voice, "Lazarus, come out." The dead man came out, his hands and feet bound with bandages, and his face wrapped with a cloth. Jesus said to them, "Unbind him, and let him go." ' (John 11:41-44)

Many of the Jews present are reported to have believed in Jesus as the Messiah, but others went and reported the matter to the Pharisees, who with the chief priests immediately called together the Council to plan his downfall. Jesus himself escaped to the town of Ephraim overlooking the wilderness.

Not a week later, however, Jesus had returned to Bethany for the Passover week, and the writer of the Fourth Gospel adds, 'When the great crowd of the Jews learned that he was there, they came not only on account of Jesus but also to see Lazarus, whom he had raised from the dead. So the chief priests planned to put Lazarus also to death, because on account of him many of the

Jews were going away and believing in Jesus.' (John 12:9-11) The following day the crowds came out from Jerusalem to greet his triumphant entry with palm branches, and the evangelist again comments, 'The crowd that had been with him when he called Lazarus out of the tomb and raised him from the dead bore witness. The reason why the crowd went to meet him was that they heard he had done this sign.' (John 12:17, 18)

Today the village of El-Azariah (the Arabic form of Lazarion, the House of Lazarus), nestles under the Mount of Olives, facing east towards the wilderness and the Jordan Valley. It was above the now empty spur that the village of Bethany stood in the time of Jesus. Today, there are two new churches, one Greek Orthodox, the other Franciscan. The latter covers the remains of 4th-century church built over the tomb of Lazarus, then within the cemetery of Bethany. The village has since grown up around the church of the tomb. Jerome tells us that already at the beginning of the 4th century a church had been built over it. In the 11th century the site was covered by a mosque, and a little later the Latin custodian of the holy places in the Holy Land obtained permission to open a new entrance into the tomb.

It is strange that there is no further mention of Lazarus and his family in the history of the early Christian Church at Jerusalem. According to an Eastern tradition, he and his sisters were put in a leaking boat, on the Mediterranean, but reached the island of Cyprus, where Lazarus became bishop of Kitium. In the year 890, his supposed relics were transferred to Constantinople. In Crusader times, pilgrimage to the house of Mary, Martha, and Lazarus at Bethany was revived and a legend became popular in the west that Lazarus had been bishop of Marseilles and was martyred under Domitian. [John 11:1-44; 12:2, 9, 10, 17]

LEBBAEUS (Gk. 'hearty'). The name Lebbaeus is included as an alternative to Thaddaeus only in some minor manuscripts at Matt. 10:3, and also in the Western Text only at Mark 3:18, but Lebbaeus is not to be found in the Revised Standard Version. *see* THADDAEUS [Matt. 10:3]

LEGION This Latin word, used for a regimental unit of 6,000 soldiers in the Roman army, was adopted as his name by the demoniac living on the east shore of Galilee and possessed by unclean spirits, for, said he, 'we are many'. The actual name occurs only in the Mark and Luke Gospels, though the story is told in all the three Synoptic Gospels.

Jesus and his disciples crossed to the 'other side'. (*see* GADARENES) As they disembarked, they were met by a savage demoniac possessed by many unclean spirits, who lived within the tombs on the hillside. Mark's account is particularly vivid of a wild figure whom no one could bind, not even with chains and fetters. 'For he had often been bound with fetters and chains, but the chains he wrenched apart, and the fetters he broke in pieces; and no one had the strength to subdue him. Night and day among the tombs and on the mountains he was always crying out, and bruising himself with stones. And when he saw Jesus from afar, he ran and worshipped him; and crying out with a loud voice, he said, "What have you to do with me, Jesus, Son of the Most High God? I adjure you by God, do not torment me." For he had said to him, "Come out of the man, you unclean spirit!" And Jesus asked him, "What is your name?" He replied, "My name is Legion; for we are many." ' (Mark 5:4-9)

In primitive communities, mental illness is naturally interpreted as possession by evil spirits who need to be tamed by force. The use of chains for this purpose was common in medieval Europe to restrain the evil in the person, which appeared to reduce him to the level of a savage animal. In the primitive thinking of 1st-century Palestine, the power to suppress evil spirits could only come from God, the all-good. Therefore anyone able to exercise such power over evil received his power from God, and the miracles of Jesus were consequently interpreted as proofs of his Messiahship and divine commission. It is interesting, if ironical, that his Messiahship, in the Synoptic Gospels, is never publicly recognized and proclaimed except by the handicapped members of the community, whether blind or possessed. It is blind Bartimaeus at Jericho who begs, 'Jesus, Son of David, have mercy.' It is the demented 'Legion' who begs, 'Jesus, Son of the Most High God, I adjure you by God, do not torment me.' Matthew adds the significant words, 'Have you come here to torment us before the time?', meaning before the prophesied coming of the Messiah.

Jesus then said, 'Come out of the man, you unclean spirit,' and he asked him, 'What is your name?' for the knowledge of the name of a person enabled control over him (Jacob at Penuel). The man replied, 'My name is Legion; for we are many,' and the word 'legion' is still used to indicate a vast number. The psychologist can infer much from this story, for the man was cut off from the community by his own choice, a schizophrenic whose multiple personalities were well described by the name of 'Legion'.

The man begged Jesus eagerly not to send his many spirits 'out of the country', and as there was a large herd of pigs feeding on the hillside, the spirits begged Jesus,

'Send us to the swine, let us enter them.' So Jesus agreed, and the story continues, 'And the unclean spirits came out, and entered the swine; and the herd, numbering about two thousand, rushed down the steep bank into the sea, and were drowned in the sea.' (Mark 5:-13)

The story is a conflation of both what people thought they saw was happening and of their current ideas about what should happen. They believed in the existence of evil spirits and in their need to be transplanted to animals, if driven out of men – rather like bacteria needing to feed on flesh in order to survive. The actual reason behind the headlong flight of the pigs over the cliff may well have been a combination of the neglectful curiosity of their herdsmen, the shouting of the man, and the sudden movement of the people from the nearby township. The result was the same. 'The herdsmen fled, and told it in the city and in the country. And people came to see what it was that had happened. And they came to Jesus, and saw the demoniac sitting there, clothed and in his right mind, the man who had had the legion; and they were afraid. And those who had seen it told what had happened to the demoniac and to the swine. And they began to beg Jesus to depart from their neighbourhood.' (Mark 5:14-17)

As Jesus was getting into the boat, the man who had been possessed begged Jesus that he might come with him, but Jesus refused, saying, 'Go home to your friends, and tell them how much the Lord has done for you, and how he has had mercy on you.' (Mark 5:19) And the man went off and began to tell in the Ten Cities how much Jesus had done for him. [Mark 5:9; Luke 8:30]

LEVI (Gk. from the Heb. 'joined'). **1.** Son of Alphaeus, mentioned by the name of Levi in the story of his call by Jesus, in Mark and Luke. Though both Matthew and Luke followed the Marcan version of the story almost verbatim, yet Matthew changes the name of 'Levi' to that of 'Matthew'. When, however, the three synoptists list the twelve apostles, all three omit the name of 'Levi', but include the name of 'Matthew'. In Matthew's Gospel, 'Matthew' is called 'the publican'. Furthermore, in the list of apostles present at Pentecost, there is no mention of the name 'Levi', but only of 'Matthew'. Therefore, it is sound to assume that 'Levi' became known as 'Matthew' and that the two names refer to one and the same tax-collector, called by Jesus from his desk at the frontier town of Capernaum. *see* MATTHEW [Mark 2:14; Luke 5:27, 29]

2. Son of Jacob, the Patriarch mentioned in the letter to Hebrew Christians as the father of the priestly tribe. [Heb. 7:9]

3. Son of Melchi and father of Matthat mentioned by Luke within the genealogy of Jesus. [Luke 3:24]

LEVITE(S) The Levites were the descendants of the priests of the high places deposed by the religious reformers of the 8th century BC, whose views are expressed in the Book of Deuteronomy. By the 1st century, the Levites were an inferior clergy, lower in rank than the priests and fulfilling the mass of minor tasks essential to the maintenance of worship in the Temple. In theory, the Levites were the descendants of Levi, one of the twelve patriarchs and sons of Jacob. The tribe of Levi appears early to have lost favour and even perhaps its tribal distinction. Moses was a Levite and used his own tribe to purge the people of Israel after the 'golden calf' incident. Later, the Levites became known as pro-

316

fessional priests. They were not allocated a tribal territory, but lived in the cities of other tribes.

In the 1st century, from among the descendants of Levi, the priesthood were the descendants of Aaron, and the high priests – a privileged class within the priesthood – were the descendants of Zadok, the high priest who anointed Solomon king. The lowest strata of this ecclesiastical hierarchy was that of the Levites, who were limited to the inferior duties, taking no part in the offering of sacrifice and forbidden access to the central Temple building.

Divided into twenty-four weekly courses, they served the needs of the Temple in their turns, there being some 10,000 Levites in all. Some performed the instrumental music of the Temple, others formed the choir, others were doorkeepers; others acted as servers, dressing the high priest in his vestments, assembling the scrolls, and cleaning such parts of the Temple as they were allowed to enter. The Temple police and guards were provided from among the Levites; these patrolled the courts of the Temple by day and night, enforcing the discipline of admission to the correct courts and exacting punishment from offenders.

There were of course many sons of Levi who did not wish to fulfill the traditional functions of Levites within the Temple and followed other pursuits, crafts and trades, even as Scribes and Pharisees.

The Levite in the parable of the Good Samaritan Jesus told the story in answer to the lawyer's quibble, 'Who is my neighbour?' The story described the reaction of three travellers to seeing a wounded man by the roadside. 'Now by chance a priest was going down that road; and when he saw him he passed by on the other side. So likewise a Levite, when he came to the place and saw him, passed by on the other side.' At this point, the hearers, who thought of their community in terms of Priests, Levites, and Israelites – as perhaps Christians today of bishops, clergy, and lay people – might have been confident that the hero would be an Israelite. Their shock and consternation when the hero turned out to be a hated Samaritan – one publicly cursed in the synagogue and whose evidence was unacceptable in the court of law – can be easily imagined. The parable did not exactly answer the question of the lawyer, 'Who is my neighbour?' but it illustrated graphically that neighbourhood was unlimited, by race or religion. The only criterion for neighbourliness is need. [Luke 10:32]

The Levites sent to interrogate John the Baptist

'And this is the testimony of John, when the Jews sent priests and Levites from Jerusalem to ask him, "Who are you?" He confessed, he did not deny, but confessed, "I am not the Christ." And they asked him, "What then? Are you Elijah?" He said "I am not." "Are you the prophet?" And he answered, "No." They said to him then, "Who are you? Let us have an answer for those who sent us. What do you say about yourself?" He said, "I am the voice of one crying in the wilderness, 'Make straight the way of the Lord,' as the prophet Isaiah said." ' [John 1:19-23]

The Levitical priesthood compared with that of Jesus

The writer of the letter to Hebrew Christians argued for the superiority of the priesthood of Jesus, as descended from Melchizedek, to that of the Levites descended from Aaron. The writer points out that Abraham the

318

forefather of Levi paid tithes to Melchizedek, whose order was therefore superior to that of Levi. [Heb. 6:20; 7:11]

LINUS One of the four who sent their personal greetings at the close of Paul's final letter to Timothy in Ephesus, perhaps the last he ever wrote. From the grouping of the names, Linus may well have been the son of Pudens and Claudia. Paul is writing from prison, presumably in Rome, after his conviction and expecting execution. This family, not elsewhere mentioned in the New Testament, may have ministered to the final needs of Paul, along with the 'beloved physician', Luke, Paul's fellow-prisoner to the end. [2 Tim. 4:21]

LOIS The grandmother of Timothy, a lieutenant of Paul destined to become bishop of Ephesus. Eunice was a Christian Jewess married to a Greek (Acts 16:1) and living with her family at Lystra. Paul may well have persuaded Timothy, his mother Eunice, and his grandmother Lois to become Christians, on the very first visit to Lystra with Barnabas in the year 46 (Acts 14:8-20). Certainly Timothy knew of Paul's stoning by the Jews on that occasion (2 Tim. 3:11). When Paul passed through Lystra again, on his Second Journey some four years later, he collected Timothy from his home and family. Because he wanted to use Timothy for evangelism among the Jews, who knew that his father was a Greek, Paul personally took Timothy and circumcised him, to convince them of his adherence to the Jewish Law.

Paul, in his correspondence with Timothy, acknowledges generously the careful training of Timothy in the Jewish faith and scriptures within his own home and family. 'I am reminded of your sincere faith, a faith that dwelt first in your grandmother Lois and your mother

Eunice and now, I am sure, dwells in you.' (2 Tim. 1:5) And again, 'Continue in what you have learned and have firmly believed, knowing from whom you learned it and how from childhood you have been acquainted with the sacred writings which are able to instruct you for salvation through faith in Christ Jesus.' (2 Tim. 3:14, 15)

Possibly Lois had died, or Eunice remained with her at Lystra, for Paul did not send her greetings in his letters to Timothy at Ephesus. [2 Tim. 1:5]

LUCAS see LUKE

LUCIUS There are two men of this name mentioned in the New Testament, who may in fact have been one and the same person. The first is listed among the leaders of the progressive Christian Church in Antioch as prophet and teacher. These also included Barnabas, Simeon Niger, Manaen, a member of the court of Herod the tetrarch, and Saul. This Lucius came from Cyrene, on the north coast of Africa.

The second reference to Lucius comes in the final greetings at the close of Paul's letter to the Christian community in Rome. Paul describes him as 'My kinsman'.

Whether the final chapter of Paul's letter to Rome included messages to Christians at Ephesus or at Rome, the Lucius who linked his greetings with those of Paul may well have been the same man of Cyrene. [Acts 13:1; Rom. 16:21]

LUKE Although Luke is mentioned only twice by name within the New Testament, by the year 170 he was acknowledged as author of both the Third Gospel and the Acts of the Apostles. His character emerges very clearly from these writings as that of a highly sensitive and sympathetic person of wide interests and perception. He was possibly an early Gentile convert to Christianity, who may himself have met Jesus. He became the loyal and indefatigable secretary, doctor, and companion of the Apostle Paul. Luke was perhaps a Syrian by birth, hailing from the city of Antioch on the Mediterranean. He was possibly a slave, educated, and trained in medicine within some Greco-Roman household in an eastern Mediterranean country. Some recent scholarship has suggested, however, that Luke was a Jew, whose writings were translated from a Semitic language.

From the 'we' sections of the Acts (16:10-17; 20:5-15; 27:1-37; 28:1-14) which describe his adventures with Paul (and which may be parts of Luke's own travel diary), we can deduce some biographical details about him. He accompanied Paul on his Second Journey across the Aegean from Troas in Asia Minor to Philippi in Greece. On Paul's Third Journey, six years later, he returned with Paul from Philippi to Jerusalem. And he accompanied Paul on his final journey from Caesarea, seat of the procurator of Judea, all the way to Rome. There he loyally remained with Paul throughout his captivity.

Much of the early history of the development of Christianity, as recorded in the Acts, revolves round the Church at Antioch, where Luke was an early member of the Christian community. Antioch also had the honour of being both the birthplace of the name 'Christian' and the headquarters of the mission to the Gentiles. Indeed, Antioch was second only to Jerusalem in the early history of Christianity. Of the glories of this one-time capital of Syria which straddled the River Orontes, few remain today. There are some massive sections of ancient city walling, some arches of Trajan's aqueduct, and the rather scanty remains of a theatre and stadium. The ancient city, in the time of Paul and Luke, extended over the slopes and plateau of Mount Silpius to the south of the smaller modern town.

In other documents Luke is referred to as being unmarried, writing his Gospel in Greece, and dying at the age of 84. In 356, Constantine II had his relics translated from Thebes in Boeotia to Constantinople, where they were later preserved in the Church of the Apostles. Later legends describe Luke variously as one of the seventy disciples sent out by Jesus, as living in Bithynia, Alexandria, and Achaia, as dying a natural death, and as being martyred in the time of Domitian. Luke is the patron saint of both doctors and artists. In the Middle Ages, pictures of Mary, the mother of Jesus, were ascribed to him, both at the Syrian Church in Jerusalem, at Santa Maria Maggiore in Rome and in several other places.

Luke's Gospel

Luke's writings form at least a quarter of the New Testament. In a two-volume work, he tells the story of Christianity from the birth of Jesus until the gospel reached the whole of the Mediterranean world. As there is no reference in his writings to the martydom of Paul, both the Gospel and Acts might well have been completed before that event (AD 64). However, Luke's description of the fall of Jerusalem – in 70 – is less likely to be simply a prediction than those in the other Gospels. This may indicate a date after 70. The authorship of Luke has not been seriously disputed, being supported by Justin Martyr and a succession of bishops and scholars, including Polycarp, Papias, Clement, Irenaeus, and Tertullian. The author of the Gospel sets out his purpose in a brief prologue addressed to 'Theophilus' (which means 'God-lover') – probably a Roman nobleman, identified by some as Flavius Clemens, fourth cousin of the Emperor Domitian.

The writer of both Luke and Acts appealed to the Romans, emphasizing the universal elements in Jesus's actions and teachings. His genealogy attempts to trace the ancestry of Jesus back to Adam, whereas Matthew begins with Abraham. Luke's description of the passion of Jesus is more generous to the Roman authorities than those of Matthew and Mark. He translates carefully into Greek all Hebrew terms, laying less stress on the fulfilment of Old Testament prophecy in the life of Jesus, which he tells as a message of universal salvation for all men. Much of the teaching of Jesus he describes as given over the supper-table, full of compassion, kindness, and self-identification with the needs of the people concerned.

The parables included in Luke's Gospel lay stress on these characteristics in the personality of Jesus and in the conduct subsequently required in his followers. In fact, Luke's portrait of Jesus may reflect the colours to be found in the artist himself. These include – as in the parable of the Prodigal Son and the conversation with the penitent thief on the cross – forgiveness and affection towards sinners. Luke shows clearly Jesus's neighbourliness and his respect for foreigners in the parable of the Good Samaritan, and his concern for the outcasts and the poor in the parable of the Rich Man and Lazarus, the healing of the Ten Lepers, the story of Zacchaeus, and the parable of the Pharisee and the Publican.

Luke's Gospel records – as none of the others do – Jesus's sensitivity towards women and children. He gives the names of many women concerned with the gospel story, including Mary, Elizabeth, Anne, Mary Magdalene and Susanna. Luke has a great interest in children. He tells us about the birth of Jesus in great detail, about the child whom Jesus took and 'put him by his side' before the disciples as an example of simple faith, and about the children brought to Jesus. If Luke was a slave, that might account for his surprisingly uncompromising presentation of Jesus's teaching about the dangers of wealth. For Luke, poverty was a virtue; where Matthew records Jesus's words, 'Blessed are the poor in spirit,' Luke unequivocally records, 'Blessed are *you* poor.' Where Matthew records, 'Blessed are those who hunger and thirst for righteousness,' Luke records, 'Blessed are you that hunger now.' Luke even describes Jesus as demanding total renunciation of a man's family as a condition of discipleship.

Luke is also the evangelist of prayer. He tells us about Jesus's prayers; how he taught men to pray, and that he prayed before he chose his disciples. Jesus, we are told, prayed at his baptism, and the transfiguration, in Luke, takes place during prayer. Luke makes it very plain that the Holy Spirit is ruling and guiding the disciples. He alone gives the full story of the nativity of John the Baptist and of the conception of Jesus as the action of the Spirit of God. A strong sense of the supernatural alongside a gracious humanity lends great charm to his Gospel, and to his portrayal of Jesus. The Gospel of Luke has been called 'the most beautiful book in the world'.

'The reign of Christ'

The theme of the Gospel has been summed up as 'the reign of Christ, how it is established and how it must be maintained'. Luke, with supreme literary skill and artistry, puts a Jewish story in a world-wide setting: the hero of the story is not just the Jewish Messiah but the king of the universe.

Luke claims to be – and is – carefully systematic in his presentation of the facts. Nowhere else does any New Testament writer so clearly declare his aims or marshal his evidence in favour of the world-wide significance of Jesus the Messiah. The Messiah comes as God's answer to the faith and expectation of the people. Luke alone places the lovely hymns which reflect the Messianic expectation of the Jews in the mouths of Zechariah, Mary, and Simeon. These hymns now form canticles within the liturgy of the Christian Church, as the *Benedictus* – 'Blessed be the Lord God of Israel, for he is visited and redeemed his people' – the *Magnificat* – 'My soul magnifies the Lord, and my spirit rejoices in God my Saviour' – and the *Nunc Dimittis* – 'Lord, now lettest thou thy servant depart in peace, according to thy word; for mine eyes have seen thy salvation'.

The prayer of the old priest Zechariah is heard: he is the father of John the Baptist, the forerunner of the Christ, and in the Benedictus he proclaims that the saviour of the House of David, promised of old, is at hand. The prayer of Mary is heard: she has found favour with God and is the mother of the Saviour, and in the *Magnificat* she declares that the promise to Abraham is to be fulfilled. And Simeon proclaims in the *Nunc Dimittis* that the infant Messiah is to be a 'light for revelation to the Gentiles, and for glory to thy people Israel'.

Luke himself quotes the prophet Isaiah: 'All flesh shall see the salvation of God'. The first sermon which Jesus preaches in Nazareth after his baptism shows that even in the time of Elijah and Elisha God was not to be confined within the bounds of any narrow Jewish nationalism. Jesus finds greater faith in a Roman centurion than he has found in any Jew. He prophesies the rejection of the Jews and the call of the Gentiles: 'And men will come from east and west, and from north and south, and sit at table in the kingdom of God.' Repentance for the forgiveness of sins will be preached to all the nations. Indeed, Luke's universalism is clearly seen in every page of his Gospel.

It is therefore on the canvas of universalism that Luke paints the figure of Christ as King and his claims to the throne. 'Of his kingdom there will be no end,' said the angel to Mary. 'I must preach the good news of the kingdom of God to the other cities also,' said Jesus in Capernaum. On Palm Sunday, Jesus entered Jerusalem as a king, refusing to check his disciples for exclaiming, 'Blessed is the King who comes in the name of the Lord!' At the Last Supper, he promised a reward for his apostles: 'You are those who have continued with me in my trials . . . so do I appoint for you that you may eat and drink at my table in my kingdom.'

Before Pilate, Jesus was accused by elders of claiming to be 'Christ a king'. Pilate asked him, 'Are you the King of the Jews?' The soldiers mocked him on his cross with the words, 'If you are the King of the Jews, save yourself!' The penitent thief on the nearby cross appealed to him, 'Jesus, remember me when you come in your kingly power.' After the resurrection and on the road to Emmaus, Jesus explained that the Christ had to suffer in order to enter into his glory. The Gospel of Luke is the record of his royal progress and the fulfilment of prophecy, through his passion and resurrection, to his ascension and enthronement.

The Acts – Christianity's first chronicle

Of all the writings of the New Testament, the Acts of the Apostles, Luke's second volume, most closely resembles a work of secular history, being provided with constant indications of time and place. The Acts is a selection of events illustrating the first encounter of the kingdom of God in Jesus with the Roman Empire. Drawing upon all kinds of sources and information besides his own personal experience, Luke describes how the gospel – the good news of Jesus and the universal kingdom of God – spread from Jerusalem all over the Roman Empire and finally reached Rome itself. It is a masterly summary of the preaching and movements of the early Christian teachers, under the guidance and power of the Holy Spirit. The letters of Paul reveal the Acts as a very skilled selection of events illustrating the growth of the early Church.

According to a commentary on Luke written about 160-80, the Acts was written in Achaia after the death of Paul, about 64-5. Eusebius argued for an earlier date – perhaps 62 – following Paul's first Roman captivity. Some contemporary scholars suggest a date after the publication of the works of the Jewish historian Josephus, which they find reflected in both the Gospel and the Acts, perhaps 90-5. Both works may include eyewitness accounts by the author, particularly the 'we' passages in Acts, but Luke also had access to oral and written traditions.

These last possibly included a manuscript in Aramaic or Hebrew, which Luke seems to have translated word by word into Greek to form the basis of the first two chapters of the Gospel. He certainly used Mark's Gospel, half of which he includes almost word for word, though excluding any reference to almost three chapters of that Gospel – a remarkable omission (Mark 6:45-8:28). Luke also probably used some 200-250 verses of a 'Sayings' collection – given the name of 'Q' for Quelle, German for 'source'. There is also a considerable corpus of gospel parables and stories, peculiar to Luke.

The Acts is a literary masterpiece as much as is the Gospel. The birth of the early Church and the career of Paul are related with great skill and efficiency. The speeches of Peter, Stephen, and Paul are magnificent, and though there is less beauty in the Acts, some passages are incomparable – particularly the conversions of Cornelius, Paul, and the elders of Miletus – and, of course, the description of the shipwreck at Malta.

As Luke, 'the beloved physician', is one of the most attractive personalities in the New Testament, so his two-volume work must have provided effective Christian 'propaganda' within the Roman patrician circle for whom he wrote. His own particular contribution to the gospel and the presentation of the character of Jesus is best seen in the beautiful parables which only Luke records. Luke is, however, first and foremost the evangelist of the incarnation, which is to him not a theological conception, but a reality. He presents the Jewish background, birth and childhood of Jesus. In places, his Gospel is more Jewish than the others. For Luke, Jerusalem is the centre of the story and the scene of the triumphs of Jesus, whether as a child of twelve years in the Temple or at his Messianic entry into the Temple on Palm Sunday, the establishment of his Kingdom by the cross of Calvary or the commission of his followers in the Upper Room and on Olivet. [Gospel of Luke; Acts of the Apostles; Col. 4:14; 2 Tim. 4:11]

LYCAONIAN The local dialect of the people of Lystra

and Derbe, spoken by the people of Lystra when they mistook Barnabas and Paul for the gods Zeus and Hermes, during Paul's First Journey through Anatolia. *see* ZEUS [Acts 14:11]

LYDIA The rich lady from Thyatira who met Paul by the little River Ganga, outside Philippi, a Roman colony and city founded by Alexander the Great in Macedonia. Lydia's household was the first in Europe known to have been converted and baptized.

Paul found few Jews at Philippi and no synagogue. He probably waited some days until the Sabbath and then went to the river, where he might expect any local Jews to be at prayer. There, he met a few women who gathered regularly for prayer; among these was Lydia, who was in the purple-dye trade and came from the city of Thyatira, 100 miles or more north of Ephesus in Asia Minor. Paul and his companions sat down and talked to the women who had gathered; Lydia listened and opened her heart to what Paul said; she was herself a pagan and only loosely attached to the little Jewish community. She insisted on being baptized by Paul, together with her household, and begged the three visitors, Paul, Timothy, and Silas, to accept hospitality. 'If you have judged me to be faithful to the Lord, come to my house and stay.'

On the way from Lydia's house to the prayer-meeting, a fortune-telling slave-girl called out after Paul and the others, 'These men are servants of the Most High God, who proclaim to you the way of salvation.' She did this each day, until Paul lost his temper and ordered the fortune-telling spirit to leave the woman. But when her owners realized that they would not make any more money out of her, they seized and dragged Paul and Silas into the market-place, where they charged them before the magistrates with causing a disturbance. The crowd joined in, and the magistrates had them stripped and flogged. After many lashes, they were thrown into prison and committed to the safe-keeping of the gaoler, who put them in the inner prison and fastened their feet in the stocks.

That night, while Paul and Silas were praying and singing, there was an earthquake, which opened the cells and released the prisoners. The gaoler, presuming his charges had escaped, was only just prevented by Paul from committing suicide. In gratitude the gaoler took Paul and Silas to his home, where they preached to, converted and baptized his whole family – who, in turn, fed them and washed their wounds.

At daylight, the magistrates sent the order for their release, to which Paul typically replied, 'They have beaten us publicly, uncondemned, men who are Roman citizens, and have thrown us into prison; and do they now cast us out secretly? No! Let them come themselves and take us out.' (Acts 16:37) The magistrates duly arrived, and begged them to leave the town.

As soon as they left the prison, they went to the house of Lydia to meet and encourage the newly-formed Christian congregation, then left on their way to Thessalonica. It was to this little Christian community at Philippi, based on the house of Lydia, that Paul wrote later, when in prison in Rome or perhaps Ephesus, a letter full of happiness, gratitude, affection and reassurance. Lydia was certainly a key person in the foundation of the Christian Church at Philippi. [Acts 16:14, 40]

LYSANIAS One of the rulers in power at the beginning of the ministry of John the Baptist, the non-Jewish Lysanias is included as tetrarch of Abilene, a district in

Syria north of Herod Philip's territory and between the cities of Chalchis and Damascus. The Jewish historian, Josephus, records that the territories of both Philip and Lysanias were given to Herod Agrippa in AD 37 by the Roman Emperor Caligula. Luke did his best to date the events of his Gospel by reference to current political affairs. [Luke 3:1]

LYSIAS *see* CLAUDIUS LYSIAS

M

MACEDONIAN The mysterious man of Macedonia in Paul's vision at Troas, during his Second Journey, who encouraged Paul to cross the Aegean into Europe, with the words 'Come over to Macedonia and help us.'

The narrative of Luke, within the Acts, from this moment onwards is written in the first person plural, '*We* sought to go on into Macedonia, concluding that God had called *us* to preach the gospel to them.' (Acts 16:10) As this is the first of the 'we' passages, indicating the presence of Luke himself, it has often been thought that Luke first joined Paul either at Troas or at Philippi in Macedonia. In which case, it is just possible that the Macedonian in Paul's dream or vision might have been Luke himself, but Paul had many Macedonian friends including Gaius, Aristarchus, Secundus, Sopater, Epaphroditus, and also Lydia.

Macedonia, an insignificant Greek kingdom constantly involved in tribal war, was unified by Philip II (359-36 BC), whose son Alexander led the conquering armies of Macedonia as far as the Ganges and overthrew the Persian Empire. Macedonia had become part of the Roman Empire in 167 BC. [Acts 16:9]

MAGDALENE (Gk. from Heb. 'tower of God') *see* MARY OF MAGDALA

MAGI (Gk. 'wise men', 'sages') The wise men were the first Gentiles to worship the child Jesus as the Messiah or 'King of the Jews'. Following a star, they came from the east to Bethlehem with gifts of gold, frankincense, and myrrh. The Greek word used in Matthew's Gospel is that for 'wise men' (R.S.V.), translated 'astrologers' in the New English Bible. The Arabic *Gospel of the Infancy,* one of the many apocryphal Gospels, starts the birth narrative with the words:

'And it happened when the Lord Jesus was born in Bethlehem of Judea at the time of King Herod, the Magicians arrived from the east in Jerusalem, as Zoroaster had predicted: and they had offerings with them – gold, frankincense, and myrrh, so they worshipped Him and offered their offerings.'

Some early legends linked the wise men with Zoroaster, and this association still persisted when in AD 614 Persian invaders spared the Justinian Church of the Nativity because there was a frieze, over the great triple doorway entrance, of the wise men, of whom one was in Persian costume. Certainly Persia and Mesopotamia were famous for their magical practices.

The 2nd-century theologian Tertullian refers to the wise men as 'almost kings', and by the 6th century the tradition of their kingship was widespread. The 3rd-century theologian Origen declared that they were three wise men, probably because of their three gifts. Again, by the 6th century they had been given the names 'Caspar, Melchior, and Balthasar'. In the Middle Ages, they were venerated as saints and their relics were said to have been taken by Frederick Barbarossa to Cologne Cathedral in the year 1162.

It has been suggested that gold, frankincense, and myrrh could well have come from Arabia and that there had been Jews there since the fall of Samaria and Jerusalem. The text 'wise men from the East came to Jerusalem' does not clearly reveal whether they were oriental astrologers or whether they arrived from east of Jerusalem. Both Tertullian and the Palestinian martyr Justin, early in the 2nd century, thought the Magi came from Arabia, like the 'kings of Arabia and Saba' bringing gifts, in the prophecy of Isaiah (Isa. 60:6). Certainly they were Arab tribes called after the stars, and one tribe called 'Planeteers' who claimed that it was their ancestors who visited 'the prophet Jesus the Messiah'.

However legendary the origin of Matthew's account and whatever accretions it may have gathered, the story is well told and true to life, and accounts for Herod's unsuccessful attempt to kill the child Jesus. Many had their stars and other men saw their risings. The observation of a particular star heralding the birth of a unique personality may have coincided with the conjunction of the planets Saturn and Jupiter in the year 7 BC, or (less likely) the appearance of Halley's Comet in 11 BC. Neither, however, would be likely to 'come to rest over the place where the child was'!

The personality of Herod the Great seen in the story exactly coincides with his historical character. On the arrival of the Magi, asking, 'Where is he who has been born King of the Jews?', Herod was 'troubled and all Jerusalem with him', as well they might be from previous experience of their elderly, morose, cruel, and suspicious ruler. Herod's ruse to send the wise men to discover the whereabouts of the child and to call for their report, just in order that he could assassinate a potential rival 'king of the Jews', was typical of the tyrant. 'Then Herod summoned the wise men secretly and ascertained from them what time the star appeared; and he sent them to Bethlehem, saying, "Go and search diligently for the child, and when you have found him bring me word, that I too may come and worship him."' (Matt. 2:7, 8)

Herod's summer palace was on a hilltop within a mile or so of Bethlehem; he is unlikely to have relished the advent of a rival in the nearest town. His fury at the evasion of the Magi, and their return to their own country 'by another way', rather than passing through Jerusalem, was also characteristic of him. His subsequent massacre of the innocents, the male children of 'two years old and under' (perhaps the wise men had first seen the star some time before) was also absolutely in accordance with his known character and practice.

The significance of the coming of the wise men, to the writer of Matthew's Gospel, was that they were the vanguard of the Gentile worshippers of Jesus the Messiah. It is on the theme of Jesus's world-wide commission to his disciples that this Gospel ends: 'Go therefore and make disciples of all nations, baptizing them in the name of the Father and of the Son and of the Holy Spirit . . .' (Matt. 28:19) [Matt. 2:1-11]

MALCHUS The slave of the high priest, whose right ear Peter cut off with a sword during the skirmish that took place at the arrest of Jesus in the Garden of Gethsemane. Malchus must have been one of the party of Temple police and others, armed with swords and staves, detailed to execute the arrest.

Only the Fourth Gospel gives the names both of the slave 'Malchus' and his assailant 'Peter', although all three Synoptic Gospels describe the event. In the Fourth Gospel the story of the arrest is rather that of a surrender, and Jesus's words to Peter are, 'Put your sword into its sheath; shall I not drink the cup which the Father has given me?' Luke the doctor's account mentions the fact that Jesus 'touched his ear and healed him'. [John 18:10, also by implication Matt. 26:51; Mark 14:47; Luke 22:50]

MANAEN (Gk. from the Heb. 'comforter') This man is listed among the prophets and teachers of the Christian Church in Antioch, who were 'guided by the Spirit' to select and despatch Paul and Barnabas on the First Journey, to Cyprus and Galatia. These leaders at the headquarters of the Christian Church included Barnabas, himself a Cypriot Jew, Simeon, Lucius from Cyrene, and Manaen, a one-time companion of Herod Antipas.

Luke describes Manaen as literally 'nourished together' with Herod the Tetrarch, implying that he was a foster-brother or child-companion at the court of Herod. His link with the family of Herod may well be due to the fact that an older Manaen, who was a well-known Essene, had been befriended by Herod the Great, having predicted, when Herod was only a child, that he would become 'king of the Jews'. The young Manaen of Antioch known to Luke may well have been a grandson of the Essene Manaen, brought up with Herod's children and later, perhaps, a particular friend of Herod Antipas.

Luke seems to have been remarkably well-informed about the Herod family, even mentioning Joanna, the wife of the steward of Herod Antipas, who helped Jesus and his disciples in Galilee. Perhaps Manaen was the source of Luke's information; they certainly shared a

considerable acquaintance with Antioch. [Acts 13:1]
MARK *or* **JOHN MARK** (Gk. from the Lat. 'large hammer') Mark, a young man in his early teens during the ministry of Jesus, became a friend and companion of the Apostle Paul, and later of the Apostle Peter. After their martyrdom in Rome, Mark wrote his Gospel, which is said to reflect the mind and memory of Peter.

Mark's Jewish name was John and his adopted Roman surname was Marcus – just as the Jew Saul adopted the Roman name of Paulus. Mark is mentioned at least ten times in the New Testament, in three different groups of passages. First he appears as the son of Mary, a leading Christian woman in Jerusalem, at whose house the early Church met for prayer. Here was the natural meeting-place of the apostles and disciples in Jerusalem, and Peter went there on his escape from prison. A tradition links this house with the Upper Room, in which Jesus ate the Last Supper, and regards Mark as the son of the 'good man of the house'. Some have suggested that he was the 'young man' who fled naked from the Garden of Gethsemane at the time of Jesus's arrest. It is possible that Judas, having left the disciples at the Last Supper in the Upper Room, returned there to arrest Jesus, only to find him gone to Gethsemane; and that young Mark heard the knocking at the door and slipped out of bed to go and warn Jesus in Gethsemane.

In about the year 46 Paul and Barnabas took the Palestinian John Mark, then a young man, on their First Journey, from Antioch to Cyprus and Perga in Pamphylia, where Mark decided to return home to Jerusalem. Paul and Barnabas, an older cousin to Mark, had taken him 'to assist them'; the same word in Luke 4:20

is translated as 'attendant'; no motive is given for his return, and his reasons clearly failed to satisfy Paul. In 49 a violent disagreement took place between Barnabas and Paul as to whether they should take Mark with them on their Second Journey. This resulted in Paul and Barnabas separating, Paul taking Silas overland through Syria and Cilicia on his long journey of three years' duration, while Barnabas sailed with Mark for the island of Cyprus.

We next hear of Mark some ten years later, reconciled to Paul, a 'fellow-worker', a comfort to Paul in his imprisonment, and a useful assistant. We hear of a possible visit of Mark to the Church at Colossae (Col. 4:10), but do not know whether it materialized. The final reference to Mark comes in the closing greeting of the first letter of Peter from Rome, who entrusts his letter to the hand of Silvanus and adds the greetings of 'my son Mark', rather as Paul refers to Timothy. It is possible that Mark was the companion and spiritual 'son' of Peter, before and after his attendance on Peter in Rome.

Certainly the key to the origins of the Second Gospel may lie in this relationship, and Papias (60-130), bishop of Hierapolis in Asia Minor, states that 'Mark, having become the interpreter of Peter, set down accurately though not in order, everything that Peter remembered of the words and actions of the Lord'. Irenaeus, in about 185, wrote: 'After the deaths of Peter and Paul, Mark, the disciple and interpreter of Peter, himself handed down to us in writing the things that Peter had proclaimed.' At the time of the martyrdom of Peter and Paul, during the persecutions of Nero, Mark must still have been in his early fifties. Eusebius states that he went to Alexandria and became its first bishop.

337

From there, as a prize of war, his relics were taken to Venice and transferred to the Doges' Chapel, now the cathedral of St. Mark's. The Egyptian Church assigns its principal liturgy to his name, but among the Alexandrian Christian writers both Clement and Origen make no reference to Mark's residence in Egypt.

Author of the Second Gospel

The internal evidence of his Gospel confirms the other historical evidence about the man. He was certainly a Jew. He knew his scriptures, and he knew how to use them. He knew Aramaic, the colloquial language of Palestine. He understood Jewish life and thought, and was well aware of the political and geographical divisions of the age. He used such terms as Pharisees, Sadducees, Scribes, elders, priests, Temple, and synagogue with ease and accuracy. On the other hand, though a Jew by birth, he worked for the Church among the Gentiles. The version of the scriptures which he quoted is the Greek Septuagint. It has been said that 'while the cloth which he used came from Galilee and Judea, the threads with which the garment was sewn, and the pattern which was followed, were those of the great Hellenistic world of the 1st century'.

We can guess the motives which led to the composition of a 'Gospel of Jesus Christ' – the title is found in the very first verse – in the reign of terror for Christians after their condemnation for the great fire in Rome during the winter of the year 64-5. Christians needed to be reminded of the sufferings of Jesus as an example and inspiration to them in their own persecution. The Gospel has been called 'a Gospel for Martyrs'. When the last eye-witnesses to the life of Jesus were being killed or were dying, it was essential that the facts of his life should be set down in writing for the benefit of the early Church. It seems that Mark's Gospel was the first published account of the life, work, and death of Jesus – and it soon became an accepted work, forming the basis of the Gospels of both Matthew and Luke, and was also known to the writer of the Fourth Gospel.

Of the 660 verses in Mark's Gospel, 600 are to be found in Matthew's Gospel, and 350 in Luke's Gospel, and only 60 in neither. The verbal agreement between Mark's and the other two Gospels is striking, though at times Matthew and Luke adjust the language of Mark for reasons of reverence, accuracy, brevity, or propriety. Matthew and Luke, however, never combine to contradict the order of events as recorded by Mark. Such similarities in substance, language, style, grammar, and chronological order are easily explained by the priority of Mark's Gospel.

Compared with the later Gospels, Mark's is shorter, more direct and informal, written in the simple Greek used throughout the Mediterranean world. At first sight, this Gospel appears to consist of a series of events loosely strung together. There is little continuous biographical narrative; some stories are full of vivid dramatic detail, while others are abrupt in their brevity. The episodes gradually combine to present a clear picture of the public life of Jesus. There is no account of the birth of Jesus, only a brief introduction about the 'forerunner' or 'herald', John the Baptist, before the hero Jesus arrives from Nazareth full-grown to be baptized by his cousin in the River Jordan.

Within 20 verses, Jesus has begun to select his team of disciples and to preach, teach, and heal in the synagogues of Galilee. At once he makes friends and enemies. Controversy with the Scribes and Pharisees

(Chapter 3) is followed by a group of parables (Chapter 4), which in turn is followed by a series of miracles (Chapter 5). A careful ordering of the episodes presents a sequence of stages which lead steadily up to a climax. The opposition grows, and Jesus retires from the lakeside, crossing the border into a foreign land, to complete the teaching and training of the twelve. At last they grasp his real identity as the expected Messiah, and from that moment Jesus is able to tell them of the real purpose of his life and of the ordeals, both for him and for them, which lie ahead. 'The Son of Man came not to be served but to serve, and to give his life as a ransom for many.' It is as though the whole Gospel hinges on their recognition of Jesus as the Christ, and the last half of the Gospel is the fulfilment of his purpose in the final journey to Jerusalem and the events which follow there.

Mark's portrait of Jesus

The personality of Jesus comes through clearly to the reader – from his words and actions, and the response they arouse in others; his great energy, firmness, and friendliness, his power of command, his severity, his sympathy, and his tremendous courage. Against the background of a ruthless Roman occupation, of a priestly and privileged aristocracy, a religious leadership based on a legal code and tradition – amid political firebrands, religious fanatics, a depressed people, and wild hopes of deliverance – the whole story becomes vivid and its outcome inevitable.

The last three chapters, unlike the earlier ones, tell in continuous narrative and much detail how Jesus was arrested, tried, and executed. It is the tale of a good man, progressively encircled by his opponents, betrayed by a friend, denied and deserted by his disciples, trapped by plotting priests, condemned by a weak judge, and executed with all the shame and agony of crucifixion. Yet through all the grim details, the purpose, dignity, and royalty of the central figure would seem to justify the assessment of Albert Schweitzer that 'Jesus bent history to his purpose, flung himself upon the wheel of the world. It crushed him, yet he hangs there still. That is his victory.'

One of the intriguing features of Mark's Gospel is that in it, though the conscious fulfilment of Messianic prophecy and the forcing of events to that end may be traced throughout, the secret of Jesus's identity as Messiah is concealed almost until the end. The reader is taken into the author's confidence with the title, 'The gospel of Jesus Christ, the Son of God'. Jesus himself is told by the divine voice at his baptism, 'Thou art my beloved Son,' but all the characters in the story are left to draw their own conclusions. The disciples do so only shortly before the crucifixion. The centurion in charge of the execution squad recognizes Jesus—but by then Jesus has admitted his identity to the high priest at his trial before the Sanhedrin; indeed, he admitted it in order to secure his own conviction.

Such is the dramatic irony of this Gospel that the readers can share the knowledge of the identity of its hero with the writer, because they know the answer to such questions as 'Who can forgive sins but God alone?' or 'Who then is this, that even wind and sea obey him?' Yet even at the crucifixion it is only the supernatural events – the darkness and the rending of the veil of the Temple – that witness to the identity of Jesus as the strong, silent, and purposeful 'Son of God'. [Acts 12:12, 25; 15:37-39; Col. 4:10; Philem. 24]

MARTHA (Gk. from the Aram. 'lady', 'mistress') One of two sisters of Lazarus of Bethany, intimate friends of Jesus, whose 'home from home' was their house whenever he came up to Jerusalem, particularly for the Passover festival.

Only Luke and John mention the sisters by name, but both Gospels give the same impression of their respective characters, as may be seen in this very perceptive and sensitive passage from the pen of Luke, 'the beloved physician'. 'Now as they went on their way, he entered a village; and a woman named Martha received him into her house. And she had a sister called Mary, who sat at the Lord's feet and listened to his teaching. But Martha was distracted with much serving; and she went to him and said, "Lord, do you not care that my sister has left me to serve alone? Tell her then to help me." But the Lord answered her, "Martha, Martha, you are anxious and troubled about many things; one thing is needful. Mary has chosen the good portion, which shall not be taken away from her." ' (Luke 10:38-42) The name of Martha still epitomizes the practical and efficient but over-busy and intolerant housekeeper. The hospitality of the Orient indeed requires the housekeeper to be over-busy.

For the significance of the household of Mary, Martha, and Lazarus to the story of the passion of Jesus, and for the story of the raising of Lazarus, *see* LAZARUS [Luke 10:38-42; John 11:1-44]
Mary, mother of Jesus
MARY (Gk. from the Heb. 'obstinacy')
1. Mary, mother of Jesus
2. Mary of Magdala
3. Mary, mother of James and Joses
4. Mary, wife of Clopas

5. Mary of Bethany
6. Mary, mother of John Mark
7. Mary, member of the Christian Church at Rome

1. Mary, mother of Jesus A devout Jewish girl perhaps in her mid-teens betrothed to Joseph, a carpenter in Nazareth of Galilee, she was chosen by God to be the mother of Jesus. Through her willing obedience to God's will and purpose of redemption, she has come to be regarded as foremost among the Christian saints.

According to the Acts of the Apostles Mary, mother of Jesus, shared with the apostles the events of Pentecost, after the ascension of Jesus. Mary occupies a unique place in the affection and devotion of many Christians, both in the East and the West. Mary is to them what Abraham is to both Jews and Moslems: the person whose obedience to and acceptance of God's call and commission brought blessing to his people. To Christians also, Mary was the ark by which God became present among his people, in the person of Jesus. Consequently, the place of her birth, traditionally a cave beneath the Church of St Anne, her mother, and the tomb in which she rested in the Kidron ravine at Gethsemane before her assumption into heaven are greatly venerated in Jerusalem.

Mary's background

According to a 2nd-century apocryphal infancy narrative, called the *Protoevangelium* (literally 'first gospel') of James, Mary was the child of elderly parents, Joachim and Anna, in Jerusalem. This would accord with her priestly family connections noted by Luke (1:36). The 6th-century Roman emperor, Justinian, built a basilica at Constantinople in honour of her mother; both her parents were, and are, commemorated

343

in Eastern Christendom from medieval times. There is another tradition, supported by two references in early apocryphal Christian writings to 'Mary the Galilean', that her birthplace was at Sepphoris in Galilee.

At Jerusalem the history of the Church of St Anne is closely linked with that of the Pool of Bethesda (John 5). Both in Aramaic and Hebrew the word 'Bethesda' means 'House of Mercy'. St Jerome and Bishop Eusebius interpreted it as 'House of Effusion', which is also the meaning of the word 'Anna'. A large Byzantine basilica appears on the Madeba mosaic map of Jerusalem. The site of the pool is still under excavation, beside the surviving Crusader church of St Anne.

It would seem that Mary went from Jerusalem to live at Nazareth, as indicated in the Gospel of Luke. Beneath the new Latin Church of the Annunciation, as late as March 1960, have been found Greek *graffiti* of 'Hail Mary', dating back to the 2nd century. This enormous church covers the site of Crusader, Byzantine, and even earlier synagogue-style churches, all in their turn built to venerate the visit of the angel to the peasant girl Mary.

The Orthodox Church has a tradition that the annunciation took place not only at the site of the present Latin basilica, but also at Mary's Well over which it has built its own church.

This tradition comes from the apocryphal *Gospel of St James,* which has of course no sort of canonical authority. In that Gospel, we are told: 'One day when the Virgin Mary was found as usual at the fountain to draw water, there, where the young woman of the Orient cannot elsewhere be seen in public, an angel appeared and saluted her. She was afraid and fled to her house where she started to spin, when suddenly the angel appeared

344

to her again to announce the divine message.' It is likely enough that Mary went to the present well to draw her water, since it was the city's only water supply.

'*Hail, O favoured one!*'

Luke relates the story of the visit of the angel to the peasant girl Mary with consummate artistry. 'In the sixth month the angel Gabriel was sent from God to a city of Galilee named Nazareth, to a virgin betrothed to a man whose name was Joseph, of the house of David; and the virgin's name was Mary.' (Luke 1:26-27) In a single sentence, the sender, the messenger and the receiver are introduced: God Almighty, the angel Gabriel, and the girl betrothed to the village carpenter. 'And he came to her and said, "Hail, O favoured one, the Lord is with you!" But she was greatly troubled at the saying, and considered in her mind what sort of greeting this might be. And the angel said to her, "Do not be afraid, Mary, for you have found favour with God." ' (Luke 1:28-30)

The divine choice of Mary implies her utter devotion and dedication; even the angel delivers his message with reverence and humility, 'Hail Mary, full of grace within the presence and favour of the Lord God'; she is disturbed and ashamed at such an extravagant greeting.

Then comes the burden of the message (is it a command or an invitation?): 'And behold, you will conceive in your womb and bear a son, and you shall call his name Jesus. He will be great, and will be called the Son of the Most High; and the Lord God will give to him the throne of his father David, and he will reign over the house of Jacob for ever; and of his kingdom there will be no end.' (Luke 1:32-33) Mary's reply is no refusal, but only an enquiry as to how she is to accept. 'And Mary said to the angel, "How can this be, since I have no husband?"' (Luke 1:34) It is only then that the messenger can unfold the divine plan of the sender. 'And the angel said to her, "The Holy Spirit will come upon you, and the power of the Most High will overshadow you; therefore the child to be born will be called holy, the Son of God."' (Luke 1:35) Momentarily, the divine plan for the redemption of mankind waited upon the consent of this little Jewish girl, before she sealed her acceptance with that stupendously humble fiat: 'And Mary said, "Behold, I am the handmaid of the Lord; let it be to me according to your word". And the angel departed from her.' (Luke 1:38) God's plan had already been transformed into action.

Mary is the personification of the part of Israel which was ready to 'hear the word of God and do it'. Thus she became the 'brother, sister and mother' of the Messiah.

The virgin birth

see JESUS

The visitation

By way of encouragement, the angel Gabriel had announced to Mary the news of her cousin Elizabeth. 'And behold, your kinswoman Elizabeth in her old age has also conceived a son; and this is the sixth month with her who was called barren. For with God nothing will be impossible.' (Luke 1:36) Mary promptly set out to visit her cousin Elizabeth at her home in the 'hill country of Judea'. Elizabeth met her with the words, 'Blessed are you among women, and blessed is the fruit of your womb! And why is this granted me, that the mother of my Lord should come to me? For behold, when the voice of your greeting came to my ears, the babe in my womb leaped for joy.' (Luke 1:42-44)

It is at this point that Luke includes the paean of praise that has come to be included in the liturgies of all the Christian Churches as the *Magnificat*. In nearly every manuscript it is put into the mouth of Mary, but in a few it is attributed to Elizabeth. It is still to-day the custom of the oriental woman to sing, about her work.

The feast of the Visitation, kept within the Eastern and Western Churches, is a commemoration of the significant role of these two women in God's plan of redemption, as perceived by Luke, who emphasizes the agency of the Holy Spirit in the life of Elizabeth as well as of Mary. The visitation would have been the most natural event, for Mary would have welcomed an opportunity to escape from prying eyes and malicious tongues in Nazareth. The three months' rest with her cousin would have been the most welcome retreat. The older woman, Elizabeth, herself going through the same experience, would have been of great comfort and support to the young peasant girl, Mary, plunged so unexpectedly though so willingly into pregnancy.

These considerations are on the most ordinary level of personal relations. But in this case there was something far removed from the ordinary that would give each an added incentive to seek the society of the other. Each knew that there was something altogether exceptional about the promise of her child. Elizabeth's age, quite apart from her husband's visions, had alerted her to the marvel that was happening to her. Mary's virginity, combined with the angelic annunciation, had left her in no doubt that she was being used as a willing agent in the hand of God.

It is impossible to say how they understood so

347

quickly the respective roles they had to play and what would be the relative positions of their children. It is, of course, possible that some communication had already passed between Mary and Elizabeth, so that the older women knew already of the wonderful circumstances attending the pregnancy of Mary. In any case, Elizabeth had no hesitation in joyfully accepting the minor role for her own child, and so establishing even before their birth the position of John as the forerunner of Jesus the Messiah.

When the time came, the two boys were born within six months of each other, in towns within sight of each other. Joseph and Mary had come to Bethlehem for the census; the home of the priest Zechariah and Elizabeth was below Mount Orah in Ein Karem, the 'Gracious Spring'. This is the spring that according to medieval tradition appeared at the meeting-place of Mary with Elizabeth, and it gives its name to the town today.

The birth stories

According to the Gospels of Matthew and Luke, Jesus was born in Bethlehem before the death of Herod the Great (4 BC) but probably not more than three years earlier. The birth stories have been described as 'too manifestly legendary in character to contain any reliable data' and there is a division of opinion as to whether these stories are contradictory or complementary, perhaps as a result of the lapse in time before their recording.

Luke alone relates the promise of the birth of Jesus's cousin, John the Baptist, the annunciation by the Angel Gabriel to Mary in Nazareth of the birth of Jesus, followed by the visitation by Mary to her cousin Elizabeth in Judea, and the birth of John the Baptist. These stories are beautifully told either from oral tradition in the Greek style, or possibly from an Aramaic document, which would account for their Hebrew phraseology translated into Greek.

Both Matthew and Luke record the birth of Jesus in Bethlehem but give different reasons for doing so. Luke says that the original home of Mary and Joseph was at Nazareth in Galilee, and that they came to Bethlehem in response to the demands of a Roman census because Joseph was of David's family and therefore had to report to the City of David. Luke describes the visit of the shepherds, the circumcision on the eighth day, and the presentation after forty days, followed by their return home to Nazareth. Matthew, however, does not mention Nazareth until their return from Egypt to settle there for the first time. Matthew seems to imply that Joseph and Mary already lived in Bethlehem; he describes the visit of the wise men taking place in their 'house'. 'When they saw the star, they rejoiced exceedingly with great joy; and going into the house they saw the child with Mary his mother, and they fell down and worshipped him. Then, opening their treasures, they offered him gifts, gold and frankincense and myrrh. . . . Now when they had departed, behold, an angel of the Lord appeared to Joseph in a dream. . . . And he rose and took the child and his mother by night, and departed to Egypt. . . . But when Herod died, behold, an angel of the Lord appeared in a dream to Joseph in Egypt, saying, "Rise, take the child and his mother, and go to the land of Israel, for those who sought the child's life are dead." ' 'And he went and dwelt in a city called Nazareth.' (Matt. 2:10, 11, 13, 14, 19, 20, 23)

There are some who consider that the tradition of the birth of Jesus in Bethlehem grew out of the need for credentials to prove his Messiahship and that he was more likely to have been born in Nazareth. 'Would the Christ be from Galilee? Does not scripture say that the Christ must be descended from David and come from the town of Bethlehem?'

Certainly, the Bethlehem tradition very soon crystalized within the early Church. Justin Martyr of Nablus and Rome wrote in AD 155: 'Should anyone desire other proof for the birth of Jesus in Bethlehem, according to Micah's prophecy and the history described by the disciples in the Gospels, let him consider that in harmony with the gospel story of his birth, a cave is shown in Bethlehem where he was born and a manger in the cave where he lay wrapped in swaddling clothes.' So, too, the early apocryphal *Protoevangelium* of James referred to the cave. At the close of the 3rd century Eusebius, bishop of Caesarea, writes: 'The inhabitants of the place bear witness of the story that has come down to them from their fathers, and they confirm the truth of it and point out the cave in which the Virgin brought forth and laid her child.' The first Church of the Nativity was built over this cave on the initiative of the Empress Helena, mother of the Emperor Constantine, in 325. From then onwards, there is no real question of the site having been lost. There is a continuous chain of evidence from the building of the first church to the present day.

The purification and presentation

As Mary and Joseph had fulfilled the Law of Moses by the circumcision and naming of the child Jesus on the eighth day, so Mary, in dutiful patience and obedience, fulfilled the forty days of her purification, before coming up to Jerusalem to make her thanksgiving. 'And when the time came for their purification according to the law of Moses, they brought him up to Jerusalem to present him to the Lord (as it is written in the law of the Lord, "Every male that opens the womb shall be called holy to the Lord") and to offer a sacrifice according to what is said in the law of the Lord, "a pair of turtledoves, or two young pigeons." ' (Luke 2:22-24)

The first-born son of every Jewish family had to be presented within the Temple at Jerusalem forty days after birth. In pagan times, the first son was sacrificed to the tribal god, as the first-fruit of the family. Now, the Mosaic Law had altered this primitive custom by demanding the offering of five shekels, in order to 'redeem' or buy back the child from God, to whom his life was owed.

So it was that the parents of Jesus took him up to Jerusalem to present him to the Lord, as is demanded in the Book of Exodus (13:2): 'Every first-born male must be consecrated to the Lord'. Mary and Joseph took with them the poor man's offering demanded in the Book of Leviticus (5:7) at purification: 'a pair of turtledoves or two young pigeons'.

On this occasion, an upright and devout Jew called Simeon who looked forward to the deliverance of Israel met them in the Temple. He had been shown that he would not die without seeing 'the anointed one of God'. Taking the child Jesus in his arms, he blessed God, saying, 'Lord, now lettest thou thy servant depart in peace, according to thy word, for mine eyes have seen thy salvation which thou hast prepared in the presence of all peoples a light for revelation to the Gentiles, and for glory to the people Israel.' (Luke 2:29-32)

As Simeon gave the child Jesus back into the arms of his mother and blessed the parents, he uttered the

351

rather enigmatic prophecy, 'Behold, this child is set for the fall and rising of many in Israel, and for a sign that is spoken against (and a sword will pierce through your own soul also), that thoughts out of many hearts may be revealed.' (Luke 2:34-35) This has generally been taken to refer to the anguish caused to Mary the mother of Jesus at his crucifixion.

The visit to Jerusalem

When her son was twelve years old and ready to be initiated as a 'Son of the Law', Mary and Joseph took him up to Jerusalem for the feast of Passover. 'And when the feast was ended, as they were returning, the boy Jesus stayed behind in Jerusalem. His parents did not know it, but supposing him to be in the company they went a day's journey, and they sought him among their kinsfolk and acquaintances; and when they did not find him, they returned to Jerusalem, seeking him. After three days they found him in the temple, sitting among the teachers, listening to them and asking them questions; and all who heard him were amazed at his understanding and his answers. And when they saw him they were astonished; and his mother said to him, "Son, why have you treated us so? Behold, your father and I have been looking for you anxiously." And he said to them, "How is it that you sought me? Did you not know that I must be in my Father's house?" And they did not understand the saying which he spoke to them. And he went down with them and came to Nazareth, and was obedient to them; and his mother kept all these things in her heart.' (Luke 2:43-51)

His reply did not hurt her so much as perplex her. She did not understand, but once again, she took it to her heart. Over and over again, Mary was to feel she

352

had lost her son, in the Temple, in his crowded Galilean ministry, on the cross, even perhaps after the ascension, and there were times when she simply could not reach or understand him. Such humbling grief, loss, and love are well expressed in Michelangelo's *Pietà* in St. Peter's, Rome.

Mary's home and family

Nazareth, the market-town of southern Galilee, was also a religious centre, and surrounded by scenery recalling the Old Testament judges, prophets, and kings. It overlooked the 'Way of the Sea', one of the main trade-routes between Damascus and Egypt. Here, caravans of silks and spices passed camels laden with grain and fish. Here, the rough and rustic Galilean peasant mingled with the merchants and travellers of the east in a truly cosmopolitan community. The living-conditions of the Holy Family in this hillside town of Nazareth are best illustrated by the so-called 'Workshop of St Joseph', a Franciscan church built on the site of a Byzantine church, whose baptistry and cave-crypts are still to be seen.

Here would have been the home of the Holy Family: a single-roomed cottage used as a workshop by day and as a bedroom by night. Up above on the flat roof, a booth of green branches would have given shade or shelter on summer evenings. Underneath, in a cave-basement, formed between the limestone strata of the rising hillside, was the living-room. Here, in the centre of the cave, a flat raised surface provided the low table. Round this, reclining or squatting on the floor, the family may have eaten its simple meals. In the centre of the wall was a small niche, once blackened by the oil lamp for which it was designed. In the floor were the round openings down into the grain silos, carved out of the rock below floor-level. Above each silo, carved in the cave wall, are still the staples through which the rope passed to lower a basket or bucket into the silo below.

The exact composition of the family that occupied such accommodation has been a matter either of doubt or of dogma among Christians.

When Jesus returned to Nazareth in the course of his public ministry and spoke in their synagogue, the congregation recognized him as the 'carpenter's son' and claimed to know his family, naming four brothers and mentioning his sisters. Luke in the birth stories refers to Jesus as 'Mary's first-born' (2:7). Some of the Fathers of the Church, wishing to uphold the perpetual virginity of Mary the mother of Jesus, have suggested that the normal Greek words used for 'brothers' and 'sisters' could be extended to include 'cousins'. Oriental customs can be quoted to support this. Other Christians, however, have seen a purpose in the selection of the Greek words used.

Certainly, the Catholic and Orthodox attitude to Mary, as a symbol of human sanctity and purity, has some roots in the mentality of religious people in the Near East – when the books of the New Testament were written. This attitude is not simply and solely an import from the Greek or European world.

The great majority of Christians, however, believe that Jesus was the only son of Mary. This view is perhaps supported by three pieces of evidence in the New Testament: (1) Luke 1:34: If Mary is going to have children by her husband, why is she astonished at being told that she will have a son? The dialogue is written, in its Greek form, by Luke; but it is written on the assumption that Mary and Joseph are known to have had

354

no children. (2) John 19:25-27: Mary is placed in the charge of the beloved disciple, on the assumption that she is a widow without children other than Jesus. (3) John 19:25 read with Matthew 27:56, Mark 15:40 and Luke 24:10: James the younger and Joses are sons of Clopas and of Mary the sister of Mary the mother of Jesus. But James and Joses are among the 'brothers' of Jesus in Mark 6. The *Protoevangelium* of James, supposed to be written about AD 150, makes James the son of Joseph by a wife who died before he was betrothed to Mary. The theological importance of Jesus having 'brothers and sisters' is not affected by their exact relationship to him.

Mark, no doubt followed by Matthew and Luke, describes Jesus teaching at Capernaum and hearing that his mother and brothers have arrived and are asking for him. He replied, 'Who are my mother and my brothers?' And looking at those sitting in a circle about him, he said, 'Here are my mother and my brothers! Whoever does the will of God is my brother, and sister, and mother.' (Mark 3:33-35) John describes how, at the feast of Tabernacles when the Jews were out to kill Jesus and he had to remain in Galilee, his brothers failed to understand his purpose and message – saying to him, ' "Leave here and go to Judea, that your disciples may see the works you are doing. For no man works in secret if he seeks to be known openly. If you do these things, show yourself to the world." For even his brothers did not believe in him.' (John 7:3-5) Luke, however, relates how Mary the mother of Jesus 'with his brothers' remained loyal in their prayers along with the apostles in Jerusalem, following the ascension of Jesus.

355

The miracle at Cana

This is the first of the seven signs or miracles upon which the writer of the Fourth Gospel allegorizes and extemporizes to compare the new gospel of Jesus with the dispensation of the Old Testament. Although the historical reliability of the events and conversations within the story may be questioned, somewhere behind John's account there was probably an actual historical incident involving Jesus and his mother Mary at a wedding. In any case, as a 1st-century reconstruction or illustration of the relationship between mother and son, it is important.

'On the third day there was a marriage at Cana in Galilee, and the mother of Jesus was there; Jesus also was invited to the marriage, with his disciples.' (John 2:1, 2) Mary was already at the wedding, perhaps in some position of responsibility, when Jesus and six of his friends turned up, no doubt straining the planned provision of food and drink. She was quick to draw his attention to the fact, but he had already noticed it.

'When the wine failed, the mother of Jesus said to him, "They have no wine." And Jesus said to her, "O woman, what have you to do with me? My hour is not yet come." ' (John 2:3, 4) His answer is not rude, but in the Greek is perfectly respectful and can be even tender. He used the same word to her from the cross: 'Woman, behold thy son.' So, too, his seeming refusal includes an implicit understanding and assurance: 'It is all right. It is not my time yet.' Mary at once understood and knew that he would do what might be needed.

'His mother said to the servants, "Do whatever he tells you".' (John 2:5) Seeing the large water-pots which supplied water for both washing up and toilet facilities, Jesus said to the servants, 'Fill the jars with water.' 'Now draw some out, and take it to the steward of the feast.' When the water reached the tables, it had become wine; so the bride's family was saved from disgrace and Mary's trust was justified. There were to be many times during his intense, intinerant ministry when her confidence in him would be sorely strained. She was not likely to grasp the full purport of his life and work perhaps until after his crucifixion and resurrection.

At the cross of Jesus

Of the four evangelists, only John mentions Mary at the crucifixion. Certainly she must have shared Jesus's disgrace and degradation, his pain and thirst. Her anguish was part of the tragedy and must have contributed to the sufferings of her son. Consequently he did not want her to see the agony of death itself, so he commended her to the care of the beloved disciple. 'But standing by the cross of Jesus were his mother, and his mother's sister, Mary the wife of Clopas, and Mary Magdalene. When Jesus saw his mother, and the disciple whom he loved standing near, he said to his mother, "Woman, behold, your son!" Then he said to the disciple, "Behold, your mother!" And from that hour the disciple took her to his own home.' (John 19:25-27)

If, as the story tells us, she went with that disciple to his own home and left the scene of crucifixion, she would have been spared the memory of the end and she would have spared him the added anguish of knowing that she was there watching his final agony. At this moment, if not many times before, the prophecy of the old priest Simeon at the presentation in the Temple was ful-

357

filled: 'A sword shall pierce thine own soul.' And inevitably it was her own son who held the sword.

Mary in later life

There are two clearly contrary theories or traditions as to where Mary lived her last years. One is that she remained in Jerusalem to live in the house of John Bar-Zebedee, traditionally on Mount Zion. The other is that she accompanied John on a journey to Ephesus, where she lived to the end of her life. Both theories are supported by local tradition.

In Jerusalem, Mary is venerated by Christians and Muslims and respected by Jews. The eastern gate into the Old City is called in Arabic the *Bab Sit Miriam,* the 'Gate of the Lady Mary'. The area inside and outside that part of the city has long been associated with Mary.

East of the viaduct on which the Jericho road crosses the Kidron is an ancient church, now almost buried by the accumulation of centuries of rubble in the bottom of the ravine. A tradition records how the body of Mary, the mother of Jesus, was brought here from the house of St John on Mount Zion for burial. An extension of this same tradition records how from here she was carried bodily into heaven, three days after her burial. As in the case of the Holy Sepulchre, her rock tomb was isolated and left standing within a basilica, built about the year 440. It is perhaps this basilica that is to be seen on the Madeba mosaic, outside the eastern wall, in the Kidron Valley.

The Church in the Byzantine Empire, including Ephesus, seems to have accepted this tradition before 787 and Ephesus as the place of Mary's burial has very little traditional support. The Church of the Tomb of Mary is an integral part of Gethsemane. It was used by

Christians of many different nations and rites in the 15th, 16th and 17th centuries, and there is a Muslim *mihrab* in the building, showing the direction of Mecca. This is in honour of Mary, but also because of the Islamic tradition that Jesus was taken up into heaven from Gethsemane, his arrest, suffering, trial and death being illusionary. The building was, for some time before 1757, under Latin control, and Latins at various times before 1757 used the tomb itself as an altar. The Eastern communities, before 1757, had the use of various altars in the building. After 1757 the building came under the joint control of the Greek Orthodox and Armenian Patriarchates and the tomb is used as an altar, daily, by both these communities. The Copts and the Syrian Orthodox officiate on altars in the building regularly; but these altars are in the posession of the Armenians. It is the Latins on the other hand who hold the Cave of the Agony, just outside the door of the church.

From Byzantine times, a large church on the Western Hill, called 'Christian Zion', was said to cover several sites. These included the Upper Room and place of feet-washing, later to become the headquarters and first synagogue of the Christian community, the house of John, and later also the place of the supposed 'falling asleep' of Mary.

The history of the Zion Church is hard to unravel. Bishop Epiphanius, a native of Palestine in the 4th century, referring to documents of the 2nd century, wrote: 'Hadrian . . . found the whole city razed to the ground and the Temple of God destroyed and trodden underfoot. There were only a few houses standing and the House of God, a little building in the place where the disciples on their return from the Mount of Olives, after the Saviour's ascension, assembled in the Upper

Room'. It was the 'little building', mentioned by Epiphanius and restored by Bishop Maximus, that was transformed into the great basilica called 'Holy Zion' by Archbishop John early in the 5th century. Burned down by the Persians in 614, the 'mother of all churches' was restored by Modestus, the Christian patriarch of Jerusalem, 20 years later. We know also that the patriarchs of the 7th century venerated within the same church a stone, on which tradition related that the mother of Jesus 'fell asleep'.

In 685, Bishop Arculf made a drawing or plan of the church on a wax tablet, showing in this one building, facing east, the cenacle or supper-room on the south-east side (once within the house of St Mark) and the rock of the dormition on the north-west side (once within the house of St John). This accords exactly with the location of the cenacle and the dormition shrines today. The Crusaders built, over the remains of the earlier church, a large church with three aisles and dedicated it to 'St Mary of Mount Zion'.

Today a great modern church and the Benedictine Monastery of the Dormition stand on part of this traditional site, while remains of a shrine of the cenacle or room of the Last Supper are nearby, on top of the shrine of the 'Tomb of David'.

The Ephesian theory is that, following the early persecutions, the Diaspora of Hellenistic Christians, and Peter's departure from Jerusalem, John took Mary the mother of Jesus to Anatolia, on the west coast of Asia Minor. Paul's failure to mention John or Mary's presence in Ephesus is sometimes put forward as an objection to this theory, but it must be pointed out that he also made no mention of Peter's mission to Rome, although Peter died there before Paul.

In the 5th century, Pope Celestine I referred to Ephesus as the home of Mary the mother of Jesus and of John. Hippolytus of Thebes in the 7th century mentioned that Mary had lived for eleven years at Ephesus before her death. This tradition survived the Muslim occupation of Ephesus in 1090 and thrived among the scattered Christian community in surrounding villages. Since the end of the last century, a small shrine in the Byzantine style, some miles to the south of the ruins of Ephesus, has been a place of Latin pilgrimage and devotion, as symbolizing a home of Mary in Ephesus. The preponderance of scholarly opinion and archaeological evidence supports the 3rd-century tradition of Mary's life and death in Jerusalem, rather than in Ephesus.

The gentle saint

Homage, but not worship, is rightly accorded to the mother of Jesus. She was the willing and obedient instrument of the purpose of God. She made a home for God, in the person of Jesus, first within her own body and then in the cottage at Nazareth. She carried him and gave him birth. She fed, cleaned, and clothed him over his helpless years. She cared for and cultivated his character through a formative decade of years. Under her influence he 'increased in wisdom and in stature, and in favour with God and man'. (Luke 2:52)

Unlike some other members of his family, Mary maintained her love and confidence in him, under seemingly impossible strains. She was found among the twelve at Pentecost, a totally reconciled and responsible leader within his Church, dedicated to continue his work.

She never dominated him, but enabled him to be himself, even though there were times when she felt 'He is beside himself' (Mark 3:21). Though constantly puzzled and driven to ponder and treasure up her problems in her own heart, she never thwarted his divine progress. Though at times he appeared to go his own way, yet she maintained the unity of her family until the end. If Jesus's tremendous sense and experience of the loving fatherhood of God was the basic theme of all his teaching, what must his respect have been for his human mother? 'Hail Mary! full of grace, the Lord is with thee. Blessed art thou among women.'

Perhaps the last to be written about Mary the mother of Jesus is to be found in the vision of John the Divine of Ephesus. 'A woman clothed with the sun, with the moon under her feet, and on her head a crown of twelve stars; she was with child . . . and the dragon stood before the woman . . . that he might devour her child when she brought it forth. She brought forth a male child, one who is to rule all the nations with a rod of iron, but her child was caught up to God and to his throne, and the woman fled into the wilderness, where she has a place prepared by God.' (Rev. 12:1-6) [Matt. 1; 2; 13:55; Mark 6:3; Luke 1:26-56; Acts 1:14]

2. Mary of Magdala The Synoptic Gospels describe Mary of Magdala as one of the women from Galilee who gave financial help and domestic service to Jesus and his disciples, and who was present at the crucifixion and burial of Jesus. The Fourth Gospel gives Mary of Magdala pride of place as the first witness of the resurrection and the risen Christ.

The lakeside town of Magdala, whose excavated ruins and water-conduits border the west shore of Galilee north of Tiberias, is approximately marked by its successor, Megdel or Magdal. It was the largest of some ten sizeable towns round the lake in the time of Jesus.

The first three Gospels give little evidence of Mary's character. Only Luke comments that 'seven demons had gone out' of her, but there is no evidence that Jesus had exercised her and she was probably an epileptic, for epilepsy was commonly attributed to possession by evil spirits. This reference in Luke's Gospel immediately follows the story of a sinful woman who anointed the feet of Jesus during a meal at the house of Simon the Pharisee. The tradition of the Church has from early times identified Mary of Magdala with the woman living an immoral life in the city. Rightly or wrongly, Mary has become for all Christians the type of passionate penitent.

The story of Simon the Pharisee recorded by Luke has many distinctive features. The scene is set in Galilee, not Bethany. The woman is locally notorious, with a bad name in the town. She comes purposefully to make an act of penitence to Jesus: 'and standing behind him at his feet, weeping, she began to wet his feet with her tears, and wiped them with the hair of her head, and kissed his feet, and anointed them with the ointment'. (Luke 7:38)

Simon the Pharisee condescendingly looks on, assuming that a prophet like this rabbi Jesus would at least have the insight to perceive the sort of woman she was and therefore drive her away. When both the woman herself and Simon have waited long enough for their true motives to be tested, Jesus, reading their minds, says to the Pharisee, ' "Simon, I have something to say to you." And he answered, "What is it, Teacher?"

"A certain creditor had two debtors; one owed five hundred denarii, and the other fifty. When they could not pay, he forgave them both. Now which of them will love him more?" Simon answered, "The one, I suppose, to whom he forgave more." And he said, "You have judged rightly." ' (Luke 7:40-43) Then turning to the woman whose uninhibited penitence and emotional abandon contrasted clearly with the veiled criticism and discourteous condescension of the Pharisee, Jesus said, ' "Do you see this woman? I entered your house, you gave me no water for my feet, but she has wet my feet with her tears, and wiped them with her hair. You gave me no kiss, but from the time I came in she has not ceased to kiss my feet. You did not anoint my head with oil, but she has anointed my feet with ointment. Therefore I tell you, her sins, which are many, are forgiven, for she loved much; but he who is forgiven little, loves little." And he said to her, "Your sins are forgiven . . . your faith has saved you; go in peace." ' (Luke 7:44-50)

Luke is not slow to perceive and to compare the passion of penitence and the coldness of reason. With his deep sensitivity, Luke well knows that the basis of all forgiveness is love, and that the spring of love is often just this sense of forgiveness.

Again, and not surprisingly perhaps, Mary of Magdala has also been identified with Mary of Bethany, the sister of Martha and Lazarus. The Fourth Gospel describes Jesus at supper in the household at Bethany during the Passover week, following the raising of Lazarus. 'There they made him a supper; Martha served, and Lazarus was one of those at table with him. Mary took a pound of costly ointment of pure nard and anointed the feet of Jesus and wiped his feet with her hair; and the house was filled with the fragrance of the ointment.' (John 12:2, 3) Certainly these two Marys were very similar in temperament.

Yet again, Mary of Magdala has been identified with the woman with the alabaster cruse who anointed Jesus in the house of Simon the Leper at Bethany, as recorded in Mark's and copied in Matthew's Gospel. All these anointings have their variations on the theme of the reformed sinner or passionate penitent, yet not one of them can be linked with the slightest degree of certainty with Mary of Magdala. They may indeed refer to different women on different occasions. Whereas the Western Church, in the feast of Mary of Magdala on 22 July, makes no distinction between the three women, the Eastern Church regards each as a different person.

Both Mark and Matthew describe her, together with Mary the mother of James and Joses, and with Salome, 'looking on from afar' at the crucifixion, then attending the entombment in the rock-hewn sepulchre belonging to Joseph of Arimathea. All three Synoptic Gospels mention the two Marys arriving at the tomb early on the Easter morning. 'And when the sabbath was past, Mary Magdalene, and Mary the mother of James, and Salome, bought spices, so that they might go and anoint him. And very early on the first day of the week they went to the tomb when the sun had risen. And they were saying to one another, "Who will roll away the stone for us from the door of the tomb?" And looking up, they saw that the stone was rolled back; for it was very large. And entering the tomb, they saw a young man sitting on the right side, dressed in a white robe; and they were amazed. And he said to them, "Do not be amazed; you seek Jesus of Nazareth, who was crucified. He has risen, he is not here; see the place where they laid him. But go, tell his disciples and Peter that he is going before you to Galilee; there you will see him, as he told you." And they went out and fled from the tomb; for trembling and astonishment had come upon them; and they said nothing to any one, for they were afraid.' (Mark 16:1-8)

Only John, however, tells the story of Mary's meeting with the risen Jesus in the garden. John does not mention the other women, but only Mary of Magdala's dawn visit to the empty tomb, and her summoning of Peter and John. They confirmed her story and went home. 'But Mary stood weeping outside the tomb, and as she wept she stooped to look into the tomb; and she saw two angels in white, sitting where the body of Jesus had lain, one at the head and one at the feet. They said to her, "Woman, why are you weeping?" She said to them, "Because they have taken away my Lord, and I do not know where they have laid him." Saying this, she turned round and saw Jesus standing, but she did not know that it was Jesus. Jesus said to her, "Woman, why are you weeping? Whom do you seek?" Supposing him to be the gardener, she said to him, "Sir, if you have carried him away, tell me where you have laid him, and I will take him away." Jesus said to her, "Mary." She turned and said to him in Hebrew, "*Rabboni!*" (which means Teacher). Jesus said to her, "Do not hold me, for I have not yet ascended to the Father; but go to my brethren and say to them, I am ascending to my Father and your Father, to my God and your God." Mary Magdalene went and said to the disciples, "I have seen the Lord"; and she told them that he had said these things to her.' (John 20:11-18)

Although Mary may not in fact have been the woman who anointed Jesus in a passion of penitence, or from a realization of forgiveness, yet John's story of her meeting with Jesus tends to confirm this aspect of her character. She passes from the depths of despair in her loss of her master to the height of ecstasy in her recognition of his risen presence. Jesus has affectionately to rebuke her with words which mean 'Stop clinging to me!' She was clearly as uninhibited and reckless in her devotion to Jesus as any of the women in the 'anointing' stories.

Among the legends that surround the person of Mary of Magdala, two are of particular interest. According to an early tradition within the Greek Orthodox Church, she accompanied John to Ephesus, where she died and her body was taken later to Constantinople. A groundless 9th-century tradition links her with the journey of Martha and Lazarus by sea to the south of France, where in the Middle Ages her tomb was claimed to be at Aix-en-Provence. [Matt. 27:56-61; 28:1; Mark 15:40-47; 16:1-9; Luke 8:2; 24:10; John 19:25; 20:1-18]

3. Mary, mother of James and Joses This Mary was the constant companion of Mary of Magdala, in the first three Gospels being linked with Mary Magdalene both in Galilee and in Jerusalem.

Mary, the mother of James the younger and of Joses, was one of the women who gave Jesus and his group of disciples both financial assistance and domestic care, during their arduous intinerant ministry. With them also, she was a witness at the crucifixion and entombment of Jesus; she shared with them the surprise and shock of finding the stone rolled away from the tomb on the first day of the week. 'And when the sabbath was past, Mary Magdalene, and Mary the mother of James, and Salome, bought spices, so that they might go and anoint him. And very early on the first day of the week they went to the tomb when the sun had risen. And they were saying to one another, "Who will roll away the

367

stone for us from the door of the tomb?" And looking up, they saw that the stone was rolled back, for it was very large. And entering the tomb, they saw a young man sitting on the right side, dressed in a white robe; and they were amazed.' (Mark 16:1-5) She heard the message of the 'young man' within the tomb: 'And he said to them, "Do not be amazed; you seek Jesus of Nazareth, who was crucified. He has risen, he is not here; see the place where they laid him. But go, tell his disciples and Peter that he is going before you to Galilee; there you will see him, as he told you."' (Mark 16:6, 7) The reaction of the women is variously reported, Mark saying that they were too frightened to tell anyone, Matthew recording their meeting with Jesus on their way home, Luke including their delivery of the message to the apostles, who simply did not believe them! 'And they remembered his words, and returning from the tomb they told all this to the eleven and to all the rest. Now it was Mary Magdalene and Joanna and Mary the mother of James and the other women with them who told this to the apostles; but these words seemed to them an idle tale, and they did not believe them.' (Luke 24:8-11)

The Fourth Gospel mentions Mary of Magdala as the only woman visiting the tomb on the Easter morning, but specifically mentions among the watchers by the cross of Jesus 'his mother, and his mother's sister, Mary the wife of Clopas, and Mary Magdalene'. If the characters in this account can be identified with those at the crucifixion as recorded in the Synoptic Gospels, then this 'Mary, the mother of James and Joses' was also the wife of Clopas. [Matt. 27:56; 28:1; Mark 15:40, 47; 16:1; Luke 24:10; John 19:25; 20:1]

4. Mary, the wife of Clopas This Mary is only mentioned in the Fourth Gospel, as present at the crucifixion of Jesus, together with his mother and her sister and Mary of Magdala. The equivalent person mentioned in the Synoptic Gospels is Mary, the mother of James. If these two characters are identical, then this Mary and her husband Clopas were the parents of James the Younger and of Joses. *see* MARY 3. [Matt. 27:56; 28:1; Mark 15:40, 47; 16:1, 8; Luke 24:10; John 19:25]

5. Mary of Bethany One of two sisters of Lazarus of Bethany, intimate friends of Jesus, whose 'home from home' was their house whenever he came up to Jerusalem, particularly for the Passover festival.

Only Luke and John mention the sisters by name, but both Gospels give the same impression of their respective characters as may be seen in this very perceptive and sensitive passage from the pen of Luke, 'the beloved physician'. 'Now as they went on their way, he entered a village; and a woman named Martha received him into her house. And she had a sister called Mary, who sat at the Lord's feet and listened to his teaching. But Martha was distracted with much serving; and she went to him and said, "Lord, do you not care that my sister has left me to serve alone? Tell her then to help me." But the Lord answered her, "Martha, Martha, you are anxious and troubled about many things; one thing is needful. Mary has chosen the good portion, which shall not be taken away from her." ' (Luke 10:38-42) The name of Martha still epitomizes the practical and efficient but over-busy and intolerant housekeeper, as opposed to that of Mary the contemplative who has chosen the better part.

For the significance of the household of Mary, Martha, and Lazarus to the story of the Passion of Jesus and for the story of the raising of Lazarus *see* LAZARUS 2.

Later in the week following the raising of Lazarus, John describes Mary anointing the feet of Jesus with oil at a supper at which Martha served and Lazarus was at table. John's account appears to be a conflation of Mark's story of the anointing at the house of Simon the Leper, in Bethany, and Luke's story of the anointing at the house of Simon the Pharisee, in Galilee. Tradition has linked Mary of Magdala with the woman 'with a poor reputation in the city' in Luke's story, at the house of Simon the Pharisee. [Luke 10:38-42; John 11:1-44; 12:1-8]

6. Mary, mother of John Mark This Mary was the owner of the house which became the first Christian synagogue, or meeting-place, in Jerusalem. Very probably tradition is right in identifying the Upper Room as the scene of both the Last Supper and the first meeting of the apostles of Jesus, following the ascension. The instructions of Jesus on Maundy Thursday clearly indicate a sizeable and suitable room at a secret rendezvous. 'And he sent two disciples, and said to them, "Go into the city, and a man carrying a jar of water will meet you; follow him, and wherever he enters, say to the householder, 'The Teacher says, Where is my guest-room, where I am to eat the passover with my disciples?' And he will show you a large upper room furnished and ready; there prepare for us." And the disciples set out and went to the city, and found it as he had told them; and they prepared the passover.' (Mark 14:13-16) Again, after the ascension 'they returned to Jerusalem from the mount called Olivet, which is near Jerusalem, a sabbath day's journey away; and when they had entered, they went up to the upper room, where they were staying. . . . All these with one accord devoted themselves to prayer, together with the women and Mary the mother of Jesus, and with his brothers.' (Acts 1:12-14)

It is not surprising, therefore, that Peter, after his escape from prison, should make his way at once to this secret headquarters of the early Church. 'He went to the house of Mary, the mother of John whose other name was Mark, where many were gathered together and were praying. And when he knocked at the door of the gateway, a maid named Rhoda came to answer.' (Acts 12:12, 13) Peter's first thought would have been to report to James, the leader of the Judeo-Christian community, and he seems to have expected to find James at Mary's house. She seems to have been a widow of some substance, for the house was in her name and she had servants. Again, Peter's voice was well known to the girl Rhoda, so he was probably a frequent caller.

If the Apostle Barnabas was an uncle or cousin to John Mark, then this Mary of Jerusalem may have been a sister or aunt to Barnabas. As he was a Cypriot Jew and appointed leader of the early Church in Antioch, Mary would probably have had connections far beyond the Jerusalem Church and would have been known at least by name in Syria and Cyprus.

One traditional site of the house of Mary, the mother of John Mark, on the Western Hill of Jerusalem within the Old City walls, is today occupied by the Syrian Orthodox Bishopric headquarters, church and convent. The attraction of this church for Christian pilgrims is that its Syrian liturgy is a form of Aramaic, the language spoken by Jesus and his disciples.

According to the strongest tradition, however, the cenacle or supper-room was on the very top of this Western Hill and in the immediate vicinity of the Tomb of David. Subsequent Christian monuments and churches in this area are somewhat confusingly referred to, from Byzantine times onwards, as being on 'Mount Zion'. Christians came to regard their 4th-century 'Zion Church' as the 'mother of all churches', because they cherished on this site memories of the Last Supper, the washing of the feet, the resurrection appearances of Jesus to his followers, and the outpouring of his spirit at Pentecost. Bishop Epiphanius, a native of Palestine in the 4th century, and referring to documents of the 2nd century, wrote: 'Hadrian . . . found the whole city razed to the ground and the Temple of God destroyed and trodden underfoot. There were only a few houses standing and the House of God, a little building in the place where the disciples on their return from the Mount of Olives, after the Saviour's Ascension, assembled in the Upper Room. This [church] was built in the part of Zion which had escaped destruction, together with some buildings round about and seven synagogues that stood alone on Zion like cottages, one of which remained standing down to the time of . . . the Emperor Constantine.'

St Cyril of Jerusalem, in 348, refers to the 'Upper Church of the Apostles where the Holy Spirit descended upon them'. The Spanish nun Aetheria, in 385, identified the site as the scene of both the Easter appearances of Jesus and of the events at Pentecost. She described the special services held in this church on these great festivals. The pilgrim Theodosius, in 530, adds the fact that the Upper Room was in the house of Mark the Evangelist. This was the first synagogue of the Church and their headquarters in Jerusalem. [Acts 12:12]

7. Mary, member of the Christian Church at Rome This Mary was mentioned early in Paul's list of greetings and picked for particular comment, along with Persis, as a hard worker within the Christian community at Rome. [Rom. 16:6]

MATTHEW (Gk from Heb. 'gift of God') Matthew was the tax-collector who was called by Jesus from his desk at the frontier-town of Capernaum. He became one of the twelve apostles and was, by tradition, the author of the First Gospel, written for Jews by a Jew to present Jesus as the Messiah. Very little about Matthew the man can be discovered from the New Testament, unless he is the author of the First Gospel. Apart from his call, all other references to Matthew are found only within lists of apostles. The Gospel attributed to Matthew is in fact carefully compiled from at least three sources. Matthew the tax-collector may have been responsible for one source, or for their skilful collation.

The calling of Matthew

The call of Matthew is related in each of the first three Gospels, though the name given him in Mark and Luke is 'Levi'. As Simon was called Peter, 'the Rock', and Thomas called Didymus, 'the Twin', so probably Levi became known as Matthew, 'the gift of God'. He was called by Jesus rather later than the fishermen Peter, Andrew, James, and John, although his immediate response and following would indicate some previous acquaintance with and confidence in Jesus. Jesus's choice of Matthew was an unexpected one, for he was one of the tax-collectors or publicans, so-called from the Latin *publicani*, referring to people employed in collecting the state, or public, revenue. (*see* TAX-COLLECTORS) Perhaps by the quayside or the roadside, the shadow of Jesus fell across the customs ledger of Matthew, the publican. In the words of Matthew's Gospel, 'He said to

him, "Follow me." And he rose and followed him.'
(Matt. 9:9)

The Gospel story goes on to describe a supper held at
Matthew's house, attended by many publicans and others, with Jesus as the guest of honour. Luke's Gospel
points out that this party was particularly for Jesus, and
held at Matthew's house. At once the Pharisees and
Scribes rebuked Jesus to his disciples, accusing him of
eating and drinking with publicans and sinners. To
which Jesus replied, 'Those who are well have no need
of a physician, but those who are sick. Go and learn
what this means, "I desire mercy, and not sacrifice."
For I came not to call the righteous, but sinners.'
(Matt. 9:12-13)

According to Papias (c. 60-130), the bishop of Hieropolis in Asia Minor, Matthew made a collection of the
sayings of Jesus in Hebrew. According to Eusebius (c.
260-340), bishop of Caesarea, Matthew preached to
the Hebrews. Various traditions record his martyrdom —
in Ethiopia, in Persia, or in Pontus on the Black Sea.

The Gospel

This is in part a manual of Christian teaching, in which
Jesus the Messiah is shown to be both the fulfilment of
God's purpose revealed in the Hebrew Scriptures and
the Lord of the Christian Church in the New Testament. It is an account of the ministry of Jesus from the
pen of a rabbi, completed in the last quarter of the 1st
century. It was traditionally held to be the oldest of the
four Gospels, and consequently is placed first in the
New Testament. From the beginning of the 4th century
it was consistently attributed to Matthew. But its contents seem to show it to be the work neither of an apostle nor of an eye-witness. The narrative of the life of

374

Jesus in it is based on the Gospel of Mark, into which has been inserted much material, mostly about the teaching of Jesus, in five long discourses. For example, Chapters 3 and 4, being narrative largely from Mark, are followed by Chapters 5, 6, and 7 of the 'long discourse' or the Sermon on the Mount. Chapters 8 and part of 9, taken from Mark, are followed by more chapters of teaching.

The Gospel is a skilfully compiled and comprehensive work, combining at least two other written documents, of which one, containing an account of the teaching of Jesus, may be the record made by Matthew himself, and the reason behind the attribution of the whole Gospel to him. Matthew's training in accountancy and record-keeping may have been very useful to Jesus and the twelve. In this Gospel, the teaching of Jesus is carefully collected, divided according to subjects, and inserted at appropriate points in Mark's narrative. Ninety-five per cent of Mark's Gospel in included in that of Matthew. The incidents recorded by Mark are sometimes shortened in Matthew, with some loss of vividness and graphic description. Matthew consciously adjusts Mark's bluntness, for the sake of reverence and propriety, on many occasions. For example, in this Gospel, it is the disciples and not Jesus who forget to take food when they cross over the lake. Jesus did no miracles in Nazareth, according to Matthew, because of the people's lack of faith. Mark had written 'he could do no mighty work there'. Matthew does not include the terrified cry of the disciples to Jesus in the storm on the lake: 'Do you not care if we perish?'

This Gospel has certain specific points of interest with regard to the character of Jesus as the Messiah, the teacher, and the lawgiver of the Church. It was written after the controversy within the early Christian Church about the admission of Gentile Christians, resolved in the year 42 by the first Council of Jerusalem. Before that time, the Judeo-Christian Church was divided into two parties, clashing over their attitudes to the observance by the Gentiles of the Law of Moses. A 'circumcision party' held that all Christians must keep the Jewish Law and be circumcised. The other party among the Judeo-Christians considered the Law of Christ sufficient for the Gentiles. The Gospel-writers seem to reflect this division of opinion in their presentation of the Law of Moses as taught by the Pharisees, and of its interpretation and fulfilment by Jesus.

The writer of the First Gospel sought to prove that Christianity was the fulfilment of Judaism, and that Jesus's mission was primarily to the Jews, whose failure to respond to it had been followed by its extension to the Gentiles. He sought to show the teaching of Jesus to be the new Law, and the Christian Church of Jews and Gentiles to be the new Israel. There is a recurring emphasis on the fulfilment of the Old Testament in the person of Jesus, the 'son of David'. Mark often alluded to the Old Testament prophecies; Matthew used them independently of their original context in what may seem to be a somewhat artificial fashion, showing their fulfilment in Jesus. Perhaps these Messianic 'proof-texts' were part of a collection in circulation within the early Church and this collection was the work of Matthew himself, mentioned by Papias in the 2nd century.

Unlike Mark, Matthew does not say that the Messiahship of Jesus was hidden. The voice at his baptism proclaims to all, 'This is my beloved Son.' The disciples, seeing Jesus walking on the water, declare 'Truly you are the Son of God,' long before Peter confesses, 'You are the Christ.' Matthew adds to the story of Peter's confession given in Mark, the words spoken by Jesus, 'And on this rock [Peter] I will build my church,' implying that the secret of Jesus's identity and of his victory through suffering is to be enshrined in the community of his followers, the Church.

The great contribution of Matthew to the total picture of Jesus in the Gospels is his careful record of the teaching of Jesus about the principles upon which life is to be lived under the rule of God. The teaching of Jesus about these principles is carefully grouped into five discourses – a sort of Christian Pentateuch – as follows: the Sermon on the Mount (Chapters 5, 6 and 7); the Instructions to the Apostles (Chapter 10:5-42); a Collection of Parables (Chapter 13:1-52); Relationships within the Church (Chapter 18:1-35); the Discourse on the End of the World (Chapters 24 and 25). This account of the teaching of Jesus Christ was a source of guidance to the early Church; it can still be read as one continuous instruction, set within the story of the life, death and resurrection of Jesus.

The Sermon on the Mount

The Sermon on the Mount has won universal recognition as a supreme statement of the ethical duties of man. It is a statement of the Christian standard of life, but makes a general appeal to the human conscience of all men. It does not, at first sight, seem to vary from what is best in the ethics of Confucius, of the Buddha, or indeed of the Pharisees of Jesus's own day. The Sermon is not so much a detailed statement of principles as a series of illustrations of the way in which those principles work in actual living. The principles are twofold.

The first is self-renunciation: 'If any man would

come after me, let him deny himself and take up his cross and follow me. For whoever would save his life will lose it, and whoever loses his life for my sake will find it.' (Matt. 16:24-25) The second is service: 'Whoever would be great among you must be your servant, and whoever would be first among you must be your slave.' (Matt. 20:26-27) Jesus offers himself as the supreme illustration: '. . . The Son of Man came not to be served but to serve, and to give his life as a ransom for many.'

The Sermon on the Mount begins with a list of spiritual qualities and the rewards that accompany them: 'Blessed are the poor in spirit, for theirs is the kingdom of heaven . . .' The task of the disciples in the world is illustrated by the metaphors of salt and light. Their true piety can be seen in *secret* giving, praying and fasting. Their trust in God's providence is to be that of the birds and the flowers. They are to go on asking from God, who loves to give to those who ask him. They are not to criticize, like a man with a log in his own eye seeing a splinter in that of his neighbour.

The 'golden rule' is given: 'Whatever you wish that men would do to you, do so to them; for this is the law and the prophets.' And the Sermon ends with a terrifyingly simple story of the man who builds his house on the rock of obedience and action, contrasted with the man who builds his house on the sands of apathy and inaction. 'And when Jesus finished these sayings, the crowds were astonished at his teaching, for he taught them as one who had authority, and not as their scribes.' As Moses on Mount Sinai gave the Ten Commandments, so Jesus on the mountain in Galilee gave the new law, not commandments so much as ideals. The existence of the Law of Moses made the Tradition of the Scribes necessary, for it was only by a traditional interpretation of the Law that it could be applied to any particular day and circumstance. For instance, if keeping the Sabbath involved not working, it was necessary for tradition to define what constituted work in that day and age.

For Jesus, the Law was to be obeyed by willing assent to principles. For a system of written law, he substituted a law of the heart. 'You have heard that it was said to the men of old, "You shall not kill: and whoever kills shall be liable to judgment." ' And again, 'You have heard that it was said, "You shall not commit adultery." But I say to you that every one who looks at a woman lustfully has already committed adultery with her in his heart.' The old Law sought to cure the disease of sin by treating its symptoms as seen in the outward action. Jesus tried rather to prevent sin at the stage of intention, and to deal with evil in the heart before it reached the hand.

The ethical teaching of Jesus in the Sermon on the Mount is unique. Matthew's careful record and selection is invaluable, not only to the Christian but to all people of faith and for all time. As Matthew, at the beginning of his Gospel, tells the story of the wise men from the east coming to the king and saviour of mankind, so he ends with Jesus's commission to his apostles to 'Go therefore and make disciples of all nations.' [Matt. 9:9; 10:3; Mark 3:18; Luke 6:15; Acts 1:13]

MATTHIAS (Gk. from Heb. 'gift of Jehovah'). The twelfth apostle of Jesus elected to fill the gap left by the death of the traitor Judas.

In the presence of some 120 disciples of Jesus, the Apostle Peter outlined the brief ministry of Judas Iscariot among the twelve and recorded his violent death.

Peter then called for the replacement of Judas from among the men who had been associated with the first disciples, from the baptism of John to the ascension of Jesus. It was important that there should be twelve apostles, to witness to the fact of the resurrection of Jesus. There had to be twelve to correspond to the twelve tribes of Israel. Indeed, in some ancient manuscripts, a tribe is assigned to each apostle. The necessary qualifications were his human witness of the resurrection of his divine selection, so two certain witnesses were proposed of which one was chosen by lot, after earnest prayer for the guidance of the Holy Spirit. This method had been used for the selection of Saul as the first king of Israel, a thousand years previously. Now, for the two candidates Justus Barsabbas and Matthias, 'They cast lots for them, and the lot fell on Matthias; and he was enrolled with the eleven apostles.'

Tradition numbers both candidates among the seventy disciples sent out by two, during the early ministry of Jesus, but neither of them are mentioned elsewhere in the New Testament, nor is there any knowledge of their subsequent ministries. [Acts 1:23, 26]

MEDES *see* ARABIANS

MERCURY *see* HERMES

MICHAEL (Heb. 'who is like God') The greatest of the archangels and guardian of Israel. In early Hebrew thinking, angels were the agents and instruments of the will of God upon earth. They executed his will and delivered his messages. (*see* ANGEL) During their exile in Babylon (586-36 BC), the Jews were influenced by Babylonian and Persian ideas of a transcendent God working within his creation through a host of angelic intermediaries. By the 2nd century BC, Michael and the archangels were attributed with great supernatural powers.

The Book of Daniel refers to Michael as the 'Prince', protector of God. The letter of Jude (verse 9) refers to him as the 'archangel contending with the devil' and declares that Michael 'disputed about the body of Moses'. Jude was referring to a Jewish tradition of the 'Assumption of Moses', according to which Michael, though provoked to anger by Satan who had charged that Moses being a murderer was not worthy of burial, yet did not condemn Satan but gently rebuked him. In the warlike vision of John the Divine Michael is depicted as the champion of Israel who has conquered the devil and his angels and driven them out of heaven and down to earth. 'Now war arose in heaven, Michael and his angels fighting against the dragon; and the dragon and his angels fought, but they were defeated and there was no longer any place for them in heaven. And the great dragon was thrown down, the ancient serpent, who is called the Devil and Satan, the deceiver of the whole world – he was thrown down to the earth, and his angels were thrown down with him.' (Rev. 12:7-9)

Within the Christian Church, the festival of Michaelmas Day embraces Michael and all the angels. Michael is always represented with a sword, standing over the dragon. [Jude 9; Rev. 12:7-9]

MNASON A wealthy Cypriot Jew of the Diaspora, with whom Paul and some of his party stayed on their arrival in Jerusalem, at the close of his Third Journey. Paul, with the representatives of many Christian communities in the eastern Mediterranean, planned to hand over personally to the leaders of the Church in Jerusalem the very considerable fund of money collected for the poverty-stricken congregation in the Holy City. Accommodation was arranged for them with one of the earliest Christian converts, Mnason, rather than with any of the elders of the Church, perhaps because these latter anticipated the reception that awaited Paul. [Acts 21:16]

N

NARCISSUS (Gk. 'daffodil') 'Greet those in the Lord who belong to the family of Narcissus,' says Paul in his final greetings at the close of his letter to the Christian congregation in Rome.

There was in fact a certain freedman, Tiberius Claudius Narcissus, who exercised considerable authority under the Emperor Claudius, but who was put to death on the accession of Nero. The custom was that his property and slaves would pass into the hands of the emperor, though his slaves would retain the name of their previous master. This seems to have been confirmed in this case by inscriptions referring to 'Narcissiani'. It seems that the household slaves of Narcissus may indeed have been among the 'saints of Caesar's household' to whom Paul refers in his letter to the Church at Philippi. (Phil. 4:22) [Rom. 16:11]

NATHANAEL (Heb. 'God has given') The personal name of Bartholomew, one of the twelve apostles. Nathanael is mentioned by his personal name only in the Fourth Gospel, where he is shown to have been introduced to Jesus by Philip and where he is said to have come from Cana in Galilee. Under the name of Bartholomew, meaning 'son of Tolmai', he is listed among the apostles together with Philip in the Gospels of Matthew,

Mark, and Luke, and also as being present at the election of a substitute apostle for the traitor Judas, in the opening chapter of Acts. The identification of Bartholomew and Nathanael has been widely accepted by biblical scholars from the 9th century to the present day.

The Fourth Gospel describes how Jesus was on the way back to Galilee from his own baptism by John the Baptist in the Jordan Valley. On his way, he passed through the village of Cana, where Nathanael lived. His friend Philip, who had himself been a disciple of John the Baptist, called in to see Nathanael and to say, 'We have found him of whom Moses in the law and also the prophets wrote, Jesus of Nazareth, the son of Joseph.' Nathanael thought of Nazareth, the next place up the road from Cana, as a rather insignificant and uncouth little town. So he asked with some scepticism, ' "Can anything good come out of Nazareth?" Philip said to him, "Come and see." '

In the quaint little village of Cana, Nathanael was an earnest and sincere Jew, who was looking forward to the coming of the Messiah. It was his custom, as it was of many orthodox Jews to sit under the family fig-tree whenever he wished to be quiet and pray.

Now it so happened that the day Philip went to bring him to Jesus, this is exactly what he had been doing. He had been reading about the patriarch Jacob and his cunning. He had been reading about the dream of the ladder and the angels going up and down between heaven and earth. Perhaps, too, he had read of Jacob wrestling with the angel and winning the name of 'Israel', which means 'who prevails with God'. At any rate, he, Nathanael, had begun to wrestle with the idea that this new teacher from Nazareth could be the long-expected Messiah, for whom Philip and he had been waiting. So he said, 'Not from Nazareth, surely?' and Philip answered, 'Come and see,' and so they went. As Nathanael approached, Jesus read his thoughts and said to him, 'Behold, an Israelite indeed, in whom is no guile!' Nathanael was absolutely stunned and said, 'How do you know me?' Jesus answered, 'Before Philip called you, when you were under the fig-tree, I saw you.' That is, 'My sympathy had reached you, before your friend broke in with the news that confirmed your thoughts and prayers'. Nathanael could only exclaim, 'Rabbi, you are the Son of God! You are the King of Israel!'

It is as though Jesus, called by the title that would be nailed to his cross, again addressed Nathanael along these lines: 'Are you believing because I saw you under the fig-tree? Is that why you believe? No, of course not! It is because of your honest wrestling with your doubts. You are a true son of Jacob. Now I promise you greater things. Jacob saw a ladder set up to heaven and the "angels of God ascending and descending on it". You will see heaven opened and the angels of God ascending and descending upon the Son of Man. Now you are looking at him of whom that ladder is just a picture. You see him who is the link between heaven and earth.'

The final reference to Nathanael in the Fourth Gospel relates that, after the resurrection of Jesus and together with six others, he was fishing in the Lake of Galilee, when the risen Jesus appeared to them. They had been out all night on the lake and returned at dawn to find Jesus standing on the beach, though they did not at first recognize him. He called out to them, ' "Children, have you any fish?" They answered him, "No." He said to them, "Cast the net on the right side of the boat, and you will find some." So they cast it, and now they were not able to haul it in, for the quantity of fish. . . . But the other disciples came in the boat, dragging the net full of fish, for they were not far from the land, but about a hundred yards off. . . . Jesus said to them, "Come and have breakfast." Now none of the disciples dared ask him, "Who are you?" They knew it was the Lord. Jesus came and took the bread and gave it to them, and so with the fish. This was now the third time that Jesus was revealed to the disciples after he was raised from the dead.' (John 21:5, 6, 8, 12-14)

Nathanael, the orthodox Jew from Cana of Galilee, traditionally carried his apostolic witness of the resurrection of Jesus as far as India and was finally flayed alive at Albanopolis in Armenia. He is often depicted with his skin over his arm and the knife in his hand. [John 1:45-51; 21:2]

NAZARENE(S) (Gk 'sprung from Nazareth', a patrial name applied to Jesus) Literally inhabitants of Nazareth, a town in Galilee, which was the home of Jesus and his family from his birth, traditionally at Bethlehem, until the start of his lakeside ministry, based on Capernaum. Matthew's Gospel, unlike that of Luke, makes no reference to Nazareth until the death of Herod the Great and his succession by Archelaus, ruler of Judea in 4 BC. Matthew then declares that Joseph, being warned in a dream, did not return to Bethlehem but withdrew to the district of Galilee. 'And he went and dwelt in a city called Nazareth, that what was spoken by the prophets might be fulfilled, "He shall be called a Nazarene".' (Matt. 2:23) The writer thus justifies the choice of Nazareth by a prophecy that is to be found nowhere in the Bible.

The town of Nazareth is not mentioned in the Old

Testament, but it may be that Matthew had in mind a Hebrew phrase in the prophecies of Isaiah (9:1) and wished to show that Jesus was the *Nezer*, or 'branch', which was to spring from the stump of the fallen tree of Jesse. Naturally, however, the name 'Nazarene' was linked with the town of Nazareth.

Nazareth ranks with Jerusalem as one of the three main Christian holy cities of Palestine. Yet Nazareth's standing is very different from that of the two other towns. They were from the first marked out as Christianity's most important centres, and as such the victims of hostility towards it. Pagan temples were built over their holy places, though these had, in fact, the unintentional consequence of preserving and pinpointing their sites. Nazareth, on the other hand, was in the first centuries of Christianity strangely neglected by its friends and enemies alike. Origen, for instance, in the 3rd century lived for several years at Caesarea – only some thirty miles away – but never, it seems, took the trouble to visit Nazareth.

Thereafter, Jesus is referred to as 'of Nazareth' by friends and foes alike. The crowd tell blind Bartimaeus: 'Jesus of Nazareth is passing by.' The maid in the high priest's palace at the trial of Jesus points to Peter, saying, 'This man was with Jesus of Nazareth.' (Matt. 26:71) Peter at Pentecost declares: 'Jesus of Nazareth, a man attested to you by God with mighty works and wonders and signs.' (Acts 2:22) Healing the lame man at the Beautiful Gate of the Temple, Peter orders, 'In the name of Jesus Christ of Nazareth, walk!' (Acts 3:6) Stephen's accusers say: 'We have heard him say that this Jesus of Nazareth will destroy this place [the Temple] and will change the customs which Moses delivered to us.'

Finally, the hired prosecutor of Paul, the Roman orator Tertullus, charged Paul before Felix at Caesarea, 'For we have found this man a pestilent fellow, an agitator among all the Jews throughout the world and a ringleader of the sect of the Nazarenes.' (Acts 24:5) The new sect had early received the popular nickname of 'the Nazarenes', a term of reproach like the word 'Christians'.

Nazareth became in the years after Jesus's death a predominantly Jewish town, unlike Bethlehem which became Christian at an early date. When in 614 the Jews joined with the Persians in attacking the Christians, the Jews of Nazareth provided one of the largest contingents in that force.

Until recently it used to be thought that there were no Christians at all in Nazareth in these early years; certainly it was assumed that there was no Christian church there up to the time of Constantine, when one was built by Joseph of Tiberias at Constantine's command. Recent excavation, however, has shown that this was not so. In March 1960, when workmen were preparing to lift a mosaic pavement for preservation from the south wing of the Byzantine convent which had just then been uncovered, they came upon some bases, columns and a beautifully worked double arch which were all clearly of pre-Byzantine date. On some of these were graffiti of which one included the invocation 'XE MARIA', the Greek for 'Ave Maria'. There is now no doubt that though Christians in Nazareth in these early years were few, yet they did exist and did erect a Christian church there of a synagogue type. The only member of this community whose name has come down to us is that of Conon, who suffered martyrdom in the middle of the 3rd century. During the persecution of Decius,

Conon is reported to have said to his judges in Phrygia: 'I am of Nazareth, a relative of the Lord whom I serve, as did my ancestors'.

Successive Byzantine, Crusader and Franciscan churches on the traditional site of the annunciation have now been succeeded by a vast modern church. In this are preserved the remains of the 'Ave Maria' graffiti and the synagogue churches, and the traditional cave of the annunciation. Elsewhere are shown the traditional Latin site of the 'Workshop of Joseph', over cave-basements purporting to have been the home of the Holy Family, also the Greek churches over the sites of Mary's Well and of the synagogue. *see* MARY **1.** [Matt. 2:23; Acts 24:5]

NEREUS This man and his sister are included in a long list to whom Paul sent greetings in the final chapter of his letter to the Church in Rome. It is possible that these greetings may have been addressed also to the Church in Ephesus. Perhaps 'Philologus and Julia, Nereus and his sister, Olympas, and all the saints who are with them' may refer to a single household.

A 4th-century tradition of the Roman Church associates Nereus and Achilleus with the Roman princess Domitilla, the Emperor Vespasian's niece. Domitilla was burnt, as a Christian, by order of her cousin, the Emperor Domitian. The apocryphal *Acts of Nereus and Achilleus* describe the deportation of Domitilla and two eunuchs of her household, Nereus and Achilleus, to the island of Terracina, where the princess was burnt and the other two were beheaded. Their remains are believed to be in the cemetery of St. Domitilla, at Rome on the Via Ardeatina. The inscription on their tomb indicated that they were soldiers. [Rom. 16:15]

388

NICANOR (Gk. 'conqueror') *see* NICOLAUS

NICODEMUS (Gk. 'victor over the people') The Pharisee, ' ruler of the Jews' and a member of the Sanhedrin or Great Council, who first came to Jesus by night. Later, he defended Jesus in the Council, protesting against their judgment of him without a hearing. Finally he, together with Joseph of Arimathea, administered the last rites to the body of Jesus before burial. Only the Fourth Gospel mentions Nicodemus.

On the first occasion John begins to describe a meeting and conversation between Nicodemus and Jesus, but the conversation soon develops into a discourse by Jesus without record of any response from Nicodemus. It is hard also to assess where the discourse ends and John's own comment begins, but the reappearance later of Nicodemus in the Gospel reveals the impact of their meeting on Nicodemus.

The meeting was at Jerusalem and by night, possibly in the Garden of Gethsemane, Jesus's regular meeting-place with his disciples on the Mount of Olives overlooking the city. Nicodemus, the highly-placed ecclesiastic, was typically cautious and diplomatic. He knew Jesus at least by reputation, he was genuinely impressed; he recognized that this new movement was from God. He was unwilling to commit himself and openly lend his support, because he would then lose influence in the Council and among the Pharisees. So he came by night, secretly, introducing his enquiry by a sincere but diplomatic compliment, 'Rabbi, we know that you are a teacher come from God; for no one can do these signs that you do, unless God is with him.' (John 3:2)

Jesus promptly cut him short, sweeping his compliment aside and striking at the root of Nicodemus's problem. Diplomacy and sympathy are out of place; so is an admiration for Jesus's powerful signs and teaching. Only one thing matters, and that is a new start, for anyone longing for the kingdom of God. 'Truly, truly, I say to you, unless one is born anew, he cannot see the kingdom of God.' (John 3:3)

The Greek words mean both 'born anew' and 'born from above'. New birth can only come from above, it is not something a man can do for himself, as Nicodemus is quick to point out. 'How can a man be born when he is old? Can he enter a second time into his mother's womb and be born?' (John 3:4) After all, Nicodemus had inherited a long tradition as a Pharisee. He had tested his tradition in a long life of experience, disciplining his conduct, speech and thinking. How could he now break away from all this to begin again?

Jesus, however, was adamant and Nicodemus must have grasped what he meant when he insisted, 'Truly, truly, I say to you, unless one is born of water and the Spirit, he cannot enter the kingdom of God. That which is born of the flesh is flesh, and that which is born of the Spirit is spirit. Do not marvel that I said to you, "You must be born anew." The wind blows where it wills, and you hear the sound of it, but you do not know whence it comes or whither it goes; so it is with every one who is born of the Spirit.' (John 3:5-8) To Nicodemus, the words 'born of water' must have implied the baptism of John the Baptist in the River Jordan.

The words 'born of the Spirit' should have recalled John's promise of the baptism 'by spirit and fire' to be administered by his successor. New birth, new life could only be gained by the baptism of repentance, and then discipleship with Jesus among those in whom the birth and life were already stirring with the Spirit of God.

The Spirit was like the desert wind, a powerful unseen force, no one knowing from where it came, or whither it would go next.

For the Pharisee, this made things even more difficult. God had given the Law; devout men had drawn up in great detail its application. God had made a covenant with his people, to be carefully kept. Any talk of an unpredictable wind was destructive of institutional religion, so Nicodemus said to Jesus, 'How can this be?' And Jesus answered: 'Truly, truly I say to you, we speak of what we know, and bear witness to what we have seen; but you do not receive our testimony. If I have told you earthly things and you do not believe, how can you believe if I tell you heavenly things? And as Moses lifted up the serpent in the wilderness, so must the Son of man be lifted up.' (John 3:9, 11, 12, 14) And with this first prediction of the passion, the account of the meeting with Nicodemus with Jesus fades into the meditations of the writer.

As Jesus's ministry proceeded. His credentials as Messiah were constantly questioned, his place of birth, his ancestry, and his message. The officers of the Council brought back reports of his teaching and signs, much impressed by him. 'No man ever spoke like this man.' The Pharisees and priests, however, poured scorn upon them as deceived and the crowds as credulous and ignorant of the Law. 'Are you led astray, you also? Have any of the authorities or of the Pharisees believed in him? But this crowd, who do not know the law, are accused.' (John 7:46, 47-49) It was at this point that Nicodemus, still concealing his loyalties, postpones judgment on a matter of legal principle. 'Does our law judge a man without first giving him a hearing and learning what he does?' (John 7:51) At which his fellow Pharisees asked whether he was also a Galilean because he sympathized with this Galilean upstart.

Finally, Nocidemus appears with Joseph of Arimathea at the burial of Jesus. Joseph had bravely begged the body from Pilate to ensure a decent burial. Nicodemus came bringing a hundred pounds weight of myrrh and aloes to embalm his body. These two 'took the body of Jesus, and bound it in linen cloths with the spices, as is the burial custom of the Jews. Now in the place where he was crucified there was a garden, and in the garden a new tomb where no one had ever been laid. So because of the Jewish day of Preparation, as the tomb was close at hand, they laid Jesus there.' (John 19:40-42)

It is not possible to know the extent and depth of Nicodemus's discipleship, though many traditions credit him with becoming a faithful follower of Jesus in later years. [John 3:1-9; 7:50; 19:39]

NICOLAUS (Gk. 'conqueror of the people') Nicolaus, Nicanor, Parmenas, Prochorus and Timon were men 'of good repute, full of the Spirit and of wisdom', selected by the Hellenists to be some of the seven deacons, most of whom were Hellenistic Greek-speaking Jews, and commissioned by the apostles with prayer and the laying-on of hands; they supervised the daily distribution of bread to the Hellenist widows and poor in Jerusalem.

The earliest members of the Christian Church in Jerusalem had been mostly pious Jews, who had continued to visit the Temple and to observe the Jewish Law. The original disciples of Jesus, perhaps from Galilee or from the neighbourhood of Jerusalem, were Aramaic-speaking. Now, as others, both Jews and foreigners, had come to settle in the city, sometimes residing near the

Temple, the Christian Church had acquired new members from these newcomers. Christian evangelism had been particularly successful among the Hellenistic Jews, who spoke Greek instead of Aramaic. Consequently, there developed in Jerusalem two classes of Christian believers, the Hebrews and the Hellenists, both accepting the Messiahship of Jesus.

The welfare and relief of the needy have always been a characteristic of Judaism and the Law insists on providing for the fatherless and the widow, the slave and the stranger. The Christian community gladly accepted such obligations, as may be seen from the very considerable fund for poor-relief that Paul brought back to Jerusalem from his Mediterranean congregations. There developed, however, a sense of resentment among the Hellenists that their widows were being neglected in the daily distribution at Jerusalem. This threatened to cause some friction between these two groups, the Hebrews and the Hellenists.

The twelve apostles immediately took action, summoning the community as a whole body and ruling, 'It is not right that we should give up preaching the word of God to serve tables. Therefore, brethren, pick out from among you seven men of good repute, full of the Spirit and of wisdom, whom we may appoint to this duty. But we will devote ourselves to prayer and to the ministry of the word.' (Acts 6:2-4) The whole Christian community approved this course of action and they chose seven men to undertake the domestic and financial administration of the poor-relief. These seven deacons, as they later came to be called, were apostles commissioned by prayer and the laying-on of their hands. Whatever the terms of their commission, certain of them are known to have been heavily involved in evangelistic work, particularly Stephen and Philip.

The names of the seven – Stephen, Philip, Prochorus, Nicanor, Timon, Parmenas, and Nicolaus – all indicate a Greek background, though most of them must have been of Jewish birth.

Nicanor, Parmenas and Timon are not mentioned elsewhere in the New Testament, nor has any legend or tradition concerning them survived, except that they were among the seventy disciples with Jesus in Galilee. Prochorus has been named as the writer of a late and apocryphal *History of the Apostle John*. According to a medieval legend, John dictated his Gospel to Prochorus.

The last, Nicolaus, Luke specifically describes as a 'proselyte of Antioch', meaning that he was born a pagan but had accepted the Jewish faith before being converted to Christianity by his new belief in the Messiahship of Jesus.

The Nicolaus of Antioch is not likely to have been responsible for the heretical doctrines of the Nicolatians, hated within the Christian community at Ephesus and held by some also in the congregation at Pergamum at the close of the 1st century. (Rev. 2:6, 15) The Nicolatians taught that Christians were free to eat food offered to idols and to practise immorality in the name of religion. They survived into the 3rd century and are mentioned by Irenaeus, bishop of Lyons, *c.* 200, by Clement, a theologian of Alexandria, *c.* 215, and by Tertullian, a Father of the African Church, *c.* 220. [Acts 6:5]

NIGER (Lat. 'black') *see* SIMEON

NYMPHA(S) A wealthy matron, or man, of the city of Laodicea in the Lycus Valley, east of Ephesus (*see* LAODICEA), whose house was large enough to serve as the meeting-place of one of the groups into which the Church in a large city was divided. Paul sends his greetings to 'the brothers at Laodicea, and to Nympha and the church in her house'. It is not certain from the manuscripts whether the person here named is Nympha, a woman, or Nymphas, a man. [Col. 4:15]

O

OLYMPAS One of the Christian converts greeted by Paul, at the close of his letter to the Christian congregation at Rome. Olympas is listed within a group, which includes Philologus and Julia, Nereus and his sister, 'and all the saints that are with them'. [Rom. 16:15]

ONESIMUS (Gk. 'useful') The runaway slave from Colossae, converted by Paul in Rome and returned to his master Philemon with a 'converting letter' (the most personal one from the pen of Paul to survive), begging the welcome in Christ Jesus of 'my child, Onesimus'.

During his captivity Paul was approached by an escaped slave called Onesimus. The Greek name means 'useful'. This slave had run away from his master Philemon in Colossae and had made his way to the vast cosmopolitan city of Rome, a notorious hide-out for fugitive slaves. There, in destitution and danger, the hunted man had sought out the imprisoned Apostle Paul and had attached himself to him as his personal attendant. Paul came to know Onesimus's story, his unsatisfactory record as a slave to Philemon, whom he had robbed as well as deserted and to whom now his very life was forfeit on both accounts. Useless as Onesimus had been to Philemon, he became invaluable to Paul and had apparently matured considerably in Christian commitment, for he was prepared to return, at risk of his life, to his deserted master Philemon.

The sole purpose of Paul's 'covering letter' is to return Philemon's property with a plea not only for his forgiveness of Onesimus but for his reception now in the status of a brother in Christ Jesus. Paul's letter is amazing in its tact, its tenderness, and utter charm. It presumes to seek the pardon of a slave for the most serious and the most easily identified offences against the common law, both theft and escape. Speaking as a Christian apostle to one for whose conversion he is indirectly responsible, he does not begin to dictate, but delicately touches on their mutual obligations.

He gently poses his petition for Onesimus as an old man might for his son. He even implies that he would have wished Philemon to return Onesimus to Rome in order to serve him in prison on behalf of Philemon. 'Accordingly, though I am bold enough in Christ to command you to do what is required, yet for love's sake I prefer to appeal to you – I, Paul, an ambassador and now a prisoner also for Christ Jesus – I appeal to you for my child, Onesimus, whose father I have become in my imprisonment. (Formerly he was useless to you, but now he is indeed useful to you and to me.) I am sending him back to you, sending my very heart. I would have been glad to keep him with me, in order that he might serve me on your behalf during my imprisonment for the gospel; but I preferred to do nothing without your consent in order that your goodness might not be by compulsion but of your own free will.' (Philem. 8-14)

Paul proceeds next to his daring request not only for Onesimus's forgiveness, but that he should be welcomed back as a brother. Then Paul underwrites whatever sum of money Onesimus owes to his master; taking the pen from his secretary – probably Timothy – Paul himself writes his own bond in the required legal terms: 'I, Paul, ... will repay it ...' but adds, 'to say nothing of your owing me even your own self.' [Col. 4:9; Philem. 10]

ONESIPHORUS (Gk. 'profit-bringer') A hospitable and loyal friend of Paul, who rendered him good service at Ephesus and who eagerly searched out Paul during his last imprisonment in Rome. Onesiphorus and his household were not ashamed of Paul's chains and constantly brought him food, drink, news, and encouragement. Paul in his last letter to Timothy blesses Onesiphorus: 'May the Lord grant him to find mercy from the Lord on that Day [of Judgment] and you well know all the service he rendered at Ephesus.'

When in prison at Caesarea, in Rome, and probably at Ephesus also, Paul was often allowed visitors. Indeed, in Rome, Christian companions seem to have taken in turn the privilege of sharing his cell as fellow-prisoners. The emotional temperance of parts of that final letter indicate the strain under which Paul spent the delay, perhaps years, between his probable betrayal by Alexander the coppersmith at Troas, his trial and sentence to death, and his final execution in Rome. At the very close of his letter Paul sends his farewell greetings not to Onesiphorus, but to his family and household in Ephesus, as though perhaps Onesiphorus is still visiting Paul and his constant attendant, Luke, in Rome, if indeed Onesiphorus was still alive. [2 Tim. 1:16; 4:19]

P

PARACLETE(Gk. literally 'called to one's side', hence 'advocate') *see* SPIRIT OF GOD

PARMENAS (Gk. 'constant') *see* NICOLAUS

PARTHIANS *see* ARABIANS

PATROBAS The fourth of a list of five men, mentioned in a special greeting from Paul at the close of his letter to the Church in Rome. Perhaps Patrobas, his fellows and 'the brethren who are with them' formed a household or small group within the larger Christian community. The historian Tacitus describes the freeing of a Patrobas, one of Nero's slaves, and his execution under Galba. [Rom. 16:14]

PAUL (Gk. from Lat. 'little') It was through the driving energy and unshakeable faith of Paul, the great Apostle to the Gentiles, that the Christian Church became an organized and established force within the Roman Empire. He hardly looked the part. 'A man rather small in size, bald-headed, bow-legged, with meeting eyebrows, a large, red and somewhat hooked nose,' he was described by a writer in the 2nd century, Onesiphoros, in the apocryphal *Acts of Paul and Thecla*.

Yet the power of the man was unmistakable. 'Strongly-built,' the account ran on, 'he was full of grace, for at times he looked like a man, at times like an angel.' The frescoes on Roman catacombs seen to confirm this description. Such was the apostle who inspired courage and brotherhood into the early, struggling Christian communities in Palestine, Syria, and the Greek cities of the eastern Mediterranean provinces.

By the time of his martyrdom in Rome in AD 67, Paul had helped to create a world-wide Church in the space of a mere thirty-seven years after the crucifixion of Christ. And perhaps the two most remarkable facts about this remarkable man are that he was a citizen of the Roman Empire, and that his first contact with Christianity was as one of its most ferocious persecutors. Not for him the unique, personal faith of the apostles who had known Jesus: dazzled and blinded in a searing vision on the Damascus road, he became a Christian only after a shattering experience which transformed his entire mental outlook and way of life.

Roman citizen, Hellenized Jew

Paul's story is known to us from the account in the Acts of the Apostles supplemented by his own letters, but there must have been many events in his life which are unrecorded. It is possible that Luke's second volume, the Acts, was written as an apologia for Paul before his trial in Rome – indeed, Luke begins his narrative in Jerusalem and ends in Rome, with Paul still under house-arrest. Of Paul's letters, the writer of the 2nd-century letter attributed to Peter said, "Some things in Paul's letters are hard to understand.' Without some knowledge of the circumstances, the motives, and the addresses, this is very true. But once the situation in which the letter was written is understood, the warmth of Paul's message is immediately felt.

With the Acts, Paul is called by his Hebrew name, Saul, until his clash on the island of Cyprus with the wizard Bar-Jesus. Then Luke writes, 'Saul, who is also called Paul, filled with the Holy Spirit, looked intently at him. . . .' In the letters, he always calls himself 'Paul'. As a Roman citizen, he was probably called by both names from birth, for double names were common among Jews of the dispersion. The change from 'Saul' to 'Paul' – from the Hebrew to the Greco-Roman – was particularly appropriate at the time he began to be apostle to the Gentiles.

Everything Paul achieved was the result of his threefold background. He was of Roman citizenship, of Greek culture, and of Jewish faith. Born in Tarsus in the first years of the Christian era, he inherited his Roman citizenship from his Jewish father, and always showed distinct pride in his birthplace. It was, as he said, 'no mean city'. Tarsus was a Hellenized city, famous for its university, its gymnasium, theatre, art school, and stadium. It was, however, in a strategical position to the north-east of the Mediterranean, between the Cilician Gates and the coast, and often suffered siege and destruction. Within this environment of typically Greek institutions, Paul grew up to speak and think in the colloquial Greek of the eastern Mediterranean.

Tarsus was a provincial capital of the Roman Empire, and Roman citizenship and a sense of identification with Rome played a decisive part in Paul's life. It gave him the right to vote, and a dignity which in a number of emergencies he was quick to claim. He was exempt from degrading punishments, even down to the manner of his martyrdom: whereas Peter was crucified, Paul was beheaded with the sword. A Roman citizen also had the right to appeal to the emperor himself, and when Paul felt that he could not retain security or obtain justice by other means, he could and did 'appeal to Caesar'.

Yet Paul was above all a Jew. To the end of his life he retained a deep and abiding love for his 'brethren, my kinsmen by race'. 'For I could wish that I myself were accursed and cut off from Christ for [their] sake . . . to them belong the patriarchs, and of their race, according to the flesh, is the Christ. God who is over all be blessed for ever. Amen.' The son of a devout Jew, Paul proclaimed himself to be of pure Jewish blood, 'a Hebrew born of Hebrews'. He was originally named Saul, and like his namesake King Saul he was a member of the tribe of Benjamin and acutely aware of his Jewish religious and cultural heritage.

Early years: the scourge of the Christians

A Pharisee and the son of a Pharisee, destined for the Rabbinate, Paul had a strict upbringing in the synagogue school, his education based almost entirely on the Old Testament scriptures. From the age of thirteen, as a 'Son of the Law', he would have joined together with his father in the adult worship in the synagogue at Tarsus. About AD 28, at something over the age of eighteen, Paul went to Jerusalem to study theology under Gamaliel, a member of the Sanhedrin of much wisdom and moderation. He must have been a keen student of the scriptures and Rabbinate learning: his letters include some two hundred scriptural quotations.

When in Jerusalem, Paul probably lived with his sister. By the age of about thirty, he was an acknowledged defender of Judaism. It was about this time that the Greek-speaking element in the Jewish-Christian community at Jerusalem provoked considerable persecution from the Jewish authorities. Stephen, foremost among these Hellenized Jewish-Christians, was using scripture to support the Messiahship of Jesus and to indict the authorities for their reliance upon the Temple. Stephen's teaching particularly incensed Paul, who entered whole-heartedly into the persecution which followed.

Stephen's martyrdom – he was stoned publicly, without procuratorial consent – possibly indicates the interregnum following Pilate's resignation, and may therefore have been in AD 36. The fact of an Arabian governor ruling in Damascus at the time of Paul's conversion indicates a period of hostility between Herod Antipas and King Aretas of Petra – also in the year 36. It was at this time that there was a brief persecution of Christians in Jerusalem, followed by a dispersal of Hellenized Jewish-Christians to Antioch and Damascus – in the Gentile world. The high priest at Jerusalem, whose authority appears to have at that time extended as far as Antioch and Damascus, willingly commissioned Paul to travel north and arrest any followers of 'The Way' that he could find. And Paul, refusing even to consider the Messiahship of Jesus, whose followers claimed that he had 'risen from the dead', set out for Damascus, filled with a fanatical determination to defend the honour of God and to destroy this heresy.

Paul's blinding vision

Riding over the spine of Judea and Samaria, perhaps Paul may have passed through Nazareth, the home of the prophet-Messiah whose claims he rejected, through Capernaum, up the Jordan Valley on the road to Damascus. Then suddenly, outside the city, he was blinded by a light from heaven and fell to the ground, hearing a voice saying, 'Saul, why do you persecute me? I am Jesus, whom you are persecuting; but rise and enter the city, and you will be told what you are to do.' His companions led him, blind and helpless, into Damascus, where he fasted for three days. By a vision, a Christian disciple, Ananias, was instructed to visit him at the house of Judas in Straight Street, there to welcome and baptize him, and then to unfold and complete the divine commission of the Apostle to the Gentiles. Paul tells the story of his conversion both before the Sanhedrin in Jerusalem and before Herod Agrippa at Caesarea; he clearly records the words of Ananias: 'Brother Saul . . . the God of our fathers appointed you to know his will, to see the Just One and to hear a voice from his mouth; for you will be a witness for him to all men of what you have seen and heard.' (Acts 22:14, 15)

Paul's acceptance of Jesus as the Messiah was very different from that of the other apostles. They had already known Jesus, as disciples, as their master and teacher. They claimed apostolic authority as witnesses of Jesus's resurrection. Paul, however, probably never saw Jesus in the flesh; he became a Christian and an apostle, without ever having been a disciple. In fact, Paul hardly mentions the earthly life and teaching of Jesus, but he is fascinated by the significance of his death and resurrection. For he, Paul, had come face to face with Jesus, 'whom God has raised up', as Peter proclaimed.

Paul's conversion was remarkable for the *total* reversal that it involved in his thinking and the complete redirection of his whole life. In the very act of bitter persecution, he was called and commissioned as Apostle to the Gentiles, and called by the very person whose followers he was persecuting. It is not surprising that the grace and mercy of God towards all men forms the keystone of Paul's teaching. If anyone had experienced the totally undeserved and unconditional mercy of God, it was Paul on the road to Damascus. He discovered that the Christians were right in their recognition of the

Messiah. He recognized the agent of his conversion as the risen Jesus, who identified himself to the Pharisee Paul with the words, 'I am Jesus, whom you are persecuting.'

In Paul's conversion are to be found the seeds of his very distinctive Christian teachings: justification by faith rather than by works, and salvation through the mercy of God in Jesus. His interpretation of the cross of Jesus was that it is the glory of God and the means of man's redemption, and – above all – the reconciliation of all men. All this was developed through his personal experience and living with the Christian community, to which he brought all his loyalty, intellect, and skill as a Pharisee. It was Paul who developed and applied a full theology of the sacraments, baptism, and communion by which members of the Christian Church were to be initiated, nourished, and governed by the Spirit of God. And the Spirit was inseparable from the continued presence of Jesus among his followers.

The new apostle

Paul's movements after his conversion are in some doubt, for Luke's narrative in the Acts of the Apostles does not include Paul's retirement or retreat into the desert, mentioned in the beginning of his letter to the Church in Galatia. There Paul says: 'I did not confer with flesh and blood, nor did I go up to Jerusalem to those who were apostles before me, but I went away into Arabia; and again I returned to Damascus.'

When Paul did return to Damascus, the essentials of his teaching and message were already crystal-clear: God's promise to Abraham has been fulfilled in the resurrection of Jesus. The risen Jesus is the climax of history, for he is both Messiah and God. God comes to all people, as he came to Paul, in the person of Jesus. This aggressive preaching provoked fury and consternation among Jews at Damascus; they enlisted the support of Aretas, whose Nabatean kingdom then included Damascus, to secure Paul's arrest. Luke describes his escape: 'His disciples took him by night and let him down over the wall, lowering him in a basket.' (Acts 9:25) The date of his escape must have been before AD 40, because King Aretas died in that year.

The ancient city of Damascus lies to the south-east of the modern city. The street called Straight was the old east-west main traffic artery. The Roman-period east gate has been recently excavated, at the end of Straight Street. The overhanging perimeter walls, though of much later date, give a vivid impression of the possibility and method of Paul's escape, as he described it: 'At Damascus, the governor under King Aretas guarded the city of Damascus in order to seize me, but I was let down in a basket through a window in the wall and escaped his hands.' (2 Cor. 11:32, 33)

Three years after his conversion, Paul sent up to Jerusalem to meet Peter, and stayed with him for fifteen days. 'But I saw none of the other apostles,' he wrote to the Galatians, 'except James the Lord's brother. . . . Then I went into the regions of Syria and Cilicia. And I was still not known by sight to the Churches of Christ in Judea.' (Gal. 1:19-22) Luke describes the cold reception and suspicion with which the Church leaders in Jerusalem greeted Paul, and relates that it was Barnabas who secured Paul's acceptance. Luke also declares that Paul's own preaching provoked such opposition that the Church leaders persuaded him to leave Jerusalem and, taking him to Caesarea, put him on a ship going to Tarsus.

Not till fourteen years later did Paul return to Jerusalem.

Luke's narrative in the Acts now turns to the activities of Peter and his conversion of the Roman centurion Cornelius and his household. Paul says that he 'went into' Syria and Cilicia. If he did attempt some unrecorded work at that time, it might well explain some of the punishments and perils of which we have no other account. 'Five times I have received at the hands of the Jews the forty lashes less one,' he wrote to the Corinthians. 'Three times I have been beaten with rods; once I was stoned. Three times I have been shipwrecked; a night and a day I have been adrift at sea; on frequent journeys, in danger from rivers, danger from robbers, danger from my own people, danger from Gentiles, danger in the city, danger in the wilderness, danger at sea, danger from false brethren.' (2 Cor. 11:24-27)

The capital of Syria was Antioch, third city in the world after Rome and Alexandria. Whether through the teaching work of the Hellenized Christians from Cyprus and Jerusalem, or of Paul himself, or of both, the Christian Church was firmly established at Antioch and the city was to become the headquarters of Paul's future journeys. The Church leaders in Jerusalem sent Barnabas to superintend the Church at Antioch, and Barnabas in turn chose Paul as his assistant, collecting him from Tarsus. For a whole year, they taught together. It was at that time that the derisive title of 'Christians' was first given to the members of the Church at Antioch — and gladly accepted.

Of the glories of the one-time capital of Syria which straddled the River Orontes, little remains. There are some massive sections of ancient city walling, some arches of Trajan's aqueduct, and the rather scanty remains of a theatre and stadium. The ancient city extended over the slopes and plateau of Mount Silpius, to the south of the smaller modern town.

Warned of famine by visitors from Jerusalem, the Church at Antioch held a collection for the Christians at Jerusalem and sent it by the hands of Barnabas and Paul.

It is difficult to reconcile Paul's account and Luke's account (Acts 11) of Paul's visit to Jerusalem. If, in fact, the letter to the Galatians was written before the Council, then the task of putting his case in writing in his letter to the Galatians may have helped to crystallize the issues and conclusions in Paul's thinking. Shortly afterward, Paul and Barnabas, together with the other delegates from the Church at Antioch, set out for a conference with the leaders of the Church in Jerusalem (Gal. 2). It seems likely that this informal conference took place at the time of the visit of Paul and Barnabas to present the offering from Antioch (Acts 11). The Acts account makes no mention of this discussion, but perhaps the author has passed over in silence a dispute that was not settled until later, preferring instead to give a full account at the time of the settlement (Acts 15). This would be in keeping with his tendency in Acts, to minimize the controversies that developed within the community, and to give the impression that the harmony of the fellowship was never disturbed more than briefly. But since this conference with the apostles was of prime importance for Paul's side of the argument in the Galatian letter, he related it there in some detail.

In his letter to the Church in Galatia, Paul implies that he discussed with the Church leaders in Jerusalem the adaptation of the creed and teaching to the need of the Gentile Christians in Antioch. As a result, Paul declared, his own work was approved and the *universal* significance of Jesus's life and teaching was recognized. On their return to Antioch, the spontaneous success of the young Christian Church generated a new enterprise. Under the guidance of the Holy Spirit, we are told, Paul embarked on the first of his great journeys, accompanied by Barnabas – their destination being the island of Cyprus.

The wizard of Cyprus

On a journey that was to cover 1,400 miles, they set off down the Orontes Valley to sail from the port of Seleucia to Salamis, the eastern harbour of Cyprus. There were many Jews working in the copper-mines of Cyprus, and a number of Hellenized Jewish-Christians had come to the island after the persecution in Jerusalem in the year 36. Now, ten years later, Paul and Barnabas arrived, and they made direct for Paphos, seat of the Roman proconsul Sergius Paulus, who may have been a God-fearing attendant at the local synagogue. One of the proconsul's household was a magician called Elymas Bar-Jesus, who attempted to bar from his master the preaching of the Christian gospel. Paul very quickly and mercilessly exposed him, and the proconsul accepted Paul's message about Jesus.

From this moment Paul was recognized as the leader of the venture. His Jewish name Saul was replaced by his Greco-Roman name of Paul – which may or may not reflect his physical appearance as short of stature. Certainly the Latin word *paulis* can describe the 'runt' of a litter!

Crossing to the south coast of Asia Minor, Paul and Barnabas landed at Attalia and headed inland, crossing the western spurs of the Taurus Mountains, infested with robbers and other dangers. A few miles inland, John Mark (*see* MARK) left them and returned to Jerusalem. The others arrived at Antioch, the capital of Pisidia (not of Syria), 100 miles inland, an important centre with a large Jewish community. In their synagogue, Paul delivered an address (fully recorded in Acts 13) to both Jews and Gentiles: 'Men of Israel, and you that fear God, listen . . . brethren, sons of the family of Abraham, and those among you that fear God, to us has been sent the message of this salvation.' (Acts 13:16, 26) It would seem that the pattern of Paul's work was immediately established. On arrival, he went straight to the synagogue, if there was one; there in the prayer-hall he spoke loud enough to be heard in the God-fearers' court. Afterwards he adjourned to a friendly household to answer questions. But after one night in Pisidian Antioch, opposition had crystallized. Paul and Barnabas were expelled from the city – but not before Paul had convinced many Gentiles, who were later to form the core of the Christian community in that place. It seems clear that they were accepted as followers of the Messiah, without undertaking all the obligations of the Law, by the apostolic decision of Paul.

Paul and Barnabas now turned east, and after nearly 100 miles of rough travelling reached Iconium (modern-day Konya). Here again their visit followed the same pattern, and a Church was formed before Paul and Barnabas were forced to move on under threat of being stoned. They reached Lystra, 25 miles towards the coast. Here there was no synagogue, so Paul spoke in the open and healed a cripple. When the crowd realized what had happened, they declared Paul and Barnabas to be gods and attempted to offer them sacrifices, considering the tall and dignified figure of Barnabas to be Zeus, father of the gods, and Paul, the shorter, mercurial character, to be Hermes, messenger of the gods. Very soon, however, hostile Jews arrived from Iconium and Antioch and turned the mob against them. Paul was stoned and dragged outside the town. He recovered, however, and ventured back into the town for the night before escaping next morning along the road to Derbe.

There, after a useful and unmolested visit, Paul and Barnabas decided very bravely not to cut down to the coast, but to return by the same route, appointing elders to report progress within these new Christian communities, and encouraging them all to persevere in their newfound faith. Paul's letter to the Church in Galatia (if it is directed to the Church in Lystra, Derbe and Iconium) reflects the bitter issues left to be settled within these communities – particularly those between Jewish-Christians and Christians of Gentile origin.

Having sailed from Attalia, Paul and Barnabas returned to Syrian Antioch, to find the Christian community there divided by the insistence on the part of a deputation from the Church in Jerusalem that circumcision was necessary for salvation. Once again, the Church at Antioch despatched Paul and Barnabas to Jerusalem, this time to present the case for the Gentile Christians. James, the brother of Jesus and the first bishop of Jerusalem, gave a ruling. The pagans who turned to God were told merely to abstain from food offered to idols, from blood from the meat of strangled animals, and from fornication. Thus the Council of Jerusalem refused to impose the Law on the Gentiles, only forbidding certain specific practices, which still continue to be forbidden by the Canons of Eastern

Christendom. The Council's delegates Judas and Silas conveyed the decision to the Church at Antioch, accompanying Paul and Barnabas on their return.

Thus vindicated, Paul and Barnabas continued their work at Antioch. However, they as Jewish-Christians continued to keep the Law of Moses as their own rule of life. When on one occasion Peter withdrew from table-fellowship with Gentiles, fearing to offend the 'circumcision' party, he was corrected by Paul for undermining the equal status of all the Christians.

Westward to Europe

The probable date of the Jerusalem Council was AD 49-50, and next spring Paul and Barnabas planned to revisit together the young Churches in Cyprus and Galatia. They disagreed, however, on whether or not John Mark, Barnabas's nephew, should accompany them and finally they divided forces, Barnabas sailing with Mark for Cyprus while Paul took Silas to encourage the Galatian Churches.

Paul and Silas travelled by road, round the coast and over the pass of the Cilician Gates to Derbe and Lystra, where Timothy was added to the team. Because Timothy was the son of a Greek married to a Jewess, Paul did insist on his circumcision in order to remove obstacles to his working among Jews. They revisited Iconium and Antioch, but this time, driven by some positive spiritual guidance, they did not turn south to the coast. They made their way through Phrygia to Troas, on the north-west coast of Asia Minor – and there, guided by the vision of a Macedonian calling for help, Paul took ship across the Aegean, sailing via Samothrace to Europe.

Taking to the Via Egnatia, that great military highway which linked Rome to the East, the party moved inland to Philippi, a Roman colony and city founded by the father of Alexander the Great. There being few Jews and no synagogue, Paul stayed with a devout Jewess named Lydia, a dealer in dyed cloth, whose household was the first in Europe to be converted and baptized. Paul was enabled to conduct house-meetings near the River Ganga – but soon an unpleasant incident cut short their stay in Philippi. A soothsaying slave-girl with an evil spirit began following them, and Paul commanded the spirit to leave her. Her employers, who made considerable profits from her fortune-telling, had Paul and Silas arrested.

Under pressure from the mob, the magistrates had Paul and Silas stripped, flogged, thrown into gaol, and put in the stocks. That night, however, an earthquake released all the prisoners. The unfortunate gaoler was about to commit suicide when Paul called him and told him about Jesus. He and his family were converted; they took their prisoners home to feed them before returning them to the prison. When the order of release arrived the following morning, Paul insisted on the magistrates themselves freeing them. Although Paul never forgot his degradation and suffering at Philippi, his letter to the Church there is full of affection and thanksgiving.

The party then travelled seventy miles westward along the Via Egnatia to Thessalonica, chief port of the northern Aegean. For three consecutive Sabbaths Paul preached in the synagogue, proving Jesus to be the Messiah, and enjoyed some success among both Jews and Gentiles. With the help, however, of a market-place mob his Jewish opponents stormed the house of one Jason, a Jew of the dispersion with whom Paul was staying, and charged Paul with proclaiming Jesus as a rival emperor. Finding only Jason himself, they dragged him before the city council, who made Jason pay security before releasing him. This Jason may well be the relation of Paul mentioned in his letter to the Romans.

Under cover of dark, Paul and Silas escaped to Beroea, again travelling westward along the highway. Perhaps the fact that Paul's stay among the Thessalonians was cut short to a bare three weeks may explain their wrong ideas about the return of Jesus, corrected by Paul in his correspondence to them from Corinth. At Beroea they were welcomed in the synagogue, but were once again hounded by trouble-makers, this time from Thessalonica. Silas and Timothy remained at Beroea for some time before turning back, Timothy to Thessalonica, Silas to Philippi.

Paul now made a journey to Athens, which three centuries before had been the intellectual centre of the world. There, stirred by the idolatry of the Athenians, Paul preached in the synagogue and the market-place. At the request of Epicurean and Stoic philosophers, Paul gave an exposition of his teaching before the Council of the Areopagus on Mars Hill. It was a masterpiece of tact, insight and condensation but practically it was a complete failure. His message conflicted with the Greek conception of the human body as a tomb imprisoning the spirit of man, and his audience repudiated the idea of the resurrection of the body. Paul made few converts in Athens. Filled with disappointment, he travelled across the isthmus in fear and trembling for his reception at Corinth.

Corinth was a city of great commerce, wealth, and squalor, renowned for its culture and notorious for its immorality. Here Paul remained for eighteen months, working as a tentmaker with Aquila and his wife Priscilla, Jews expelled from Rome by the edict of Claudius in the year 49. On the arrival of Timothy and Silas, they taught both Jews and Greeks, in the synagogue and then in a private house. As a result, a large Church was formed at Corinth, mostly from the poor and slave classes. During that time Paul, hearing Timothy's report from Thessalonica, sent his first letter to that Church about the second coming of Jesus. After further reports he sent them his second letter, warning the Thessalonians against misconceptions about the End and urging them not to use the teaching of justification by faith as an excuse for lawlessness, but rather to persevere in faith and good works. Both these letters convey Paul's intensity and affection, and reveal the power of his personality.

With the arrival in the year 51 of a new proconsul of Achaia, named Gallio, certain members of the Jewish community accused Paul of teaching religion 'in a way that breaks the Law'. Gallio refused to adjudicate, but the time had come for Paul and his party to move on. He reached Ephesus, on the west coast of Asia Minor, made a brief visit to the synagogue, and after promising to return on his next journey, sailed for Caesarea, where he greeted the Church on his way north to return to Antioch.

This Second Journey of 2,800 miles must have taken three years – probably AD 50-2, the greater part of which was spent at Corinth.

Mission to Ephesus

After a short stay at Antioch Paul was on his travels again, heading up through the Cilician Gates, through Cilicia and Galatia, encouraging the young Christian communities, until he reached Ephesus – a journey of some 500 miles over rugged country. About this time an Alexandrian Jew, Apollos, and a dozen others arrived in Ephesus. They were disciples of John the Baptist, but they had never received the Holy Spirit or been baptized in the name of Jesus. After their instruction by Aquila and Priscilla, Paul baptized them and laid his hands on them, and they 'spoke with tongues and prophesied'.

For the next three years – perhaps between 54 and 57 – Paul was involved in a concentrated mission at Ephesus, the chief city of paganism in Asia, whose temple of Artemis – 'Diana of the Ephesians' – was a great centre of paganism in the Mediterranean world. To the small Christian communities founded along the coastline of Asia, the Temple of Diana (*see* ARTEMIS) at Ephesus was an infernal counterpart to the Temple at Jerusalem. (*see* EPHESIANS) Paul spent the first three months of his ministry teaching in the synagogue. When the inevitable break within the Jewish community occurred, he moved to the lecture-room of Tyrannus. There he remained in teaching and discussion with both Jews and Greeks, for a period of two whole years, in the siesta hours of noon to four in the afternoon.

Remarkable progress followed his systematic instruction, which was also accompanied by a ministry of healing. Both Jews and Greeks came to respect the name of Jesus, rather than the magical arts of Diana. From Ephesus, Paul sent well-trained teachers to Colossae and Macedonia, and it was at this time also that some of the Seven Churches of Asia, mentioned by John in the Book of Revelation, were founded. (*see* JOHN THE DIVINE)

Soon, however, the Christian success provoked fierce

opposition, particularly from the commercial, pleasure-loving pagans of the fertility-cult of Diana. This culminated in the financially-prompted riot – raised by Demetrius the silversmith and other craftsmen whose trade in silver shrines and trinkets of Diana was threatened by a slump brought about by the teaching of Paul. These merchants took their grievance to the market-place, stirred the crowd into seizing two of Paul's Macedonian companions, and dragged them into the nearby theatre. In the uproar that followed, the situation was only saved by the tact of the town clerk, who had the men released and dispersed the crowd; but relations were now so strained that Paul decided to close his ministry in Asia Minor. He sent Timothy and Erastus on to Macedonia, and planned to follow them.

Rebukes for the Corinthians

During his time in Ephesus, Paul had heard news from Corinth that made it necessary for him to write a letter of warning (2 Cor. 6:14; 7:1) to that Christian community against immorality. Shortly afterwards, he received an official letter from the Corinthians asking advice on specific matters of doctrine, which Paul answered in a letter now known as 1 Corinthians. This he sent by sea, while Timothy took the land route to deal with the situation in person.

Neither the letter nor Timothy's visit achieved the desired effect, and Paul himself sailed for Corinth. Even he failed to reform the Corinthian Church, and after being grossly insulted he sailed back to Ephesus. From there, he wrote a 'severe letter', his third (possibly 2 Cor. 10-13), which was carried by Titus, an older and more experienced man than Timothy. This letter demanded a proper respect both for Christian morality

416

and for Paul himself, as the founder of the Christian Church in Corinth.

When Paul finally closed his ministry in Ephesus, he travelled overland north to Troas, whence he sailed once again for Macedonia to visit Philippi, Thessalonica, and Beroea. Somewhere en route, he met Titus who at last brought him the good news that the Corinthian Church was ready to conform, and that they had already by a majority vote censured the culprit. Paul immediately wrote his fourth letter to Corinth (possibly to be found in 2 Cor. 1-9) omitting the content of his previous letter. In this last letter he forgave his antagonist, closed the controversy, and arranged for a collection to be taken for the poor Christians at Jerusalem. Paul seems then to have travelled overland to Corinth, where he spent the winter months, in which time he wrote his letter to the Church in Rome, to prepare them for his coming and to secure their support for a journey to Spain.

Paul's plan to sail directly from Corinth for Jerusalem, taking his poor-relief collection, was thwarted by some threat of ambush. Consequently he returned overland to Macedonia, perhaps collecting Luke in Macedonia and meeting his other escorts in Troas, whence he had first sailed for Europe some eight years before. Luke describes a Saturday or Sunday evening Eucharist in a first-floor room, at which Paul preached so long that a boy called Eutychus (the name means 'lucky') dozed off and fell out of the upper window, but was picked up and restored by Paul.

Wishing to reach Jerusalem by Pentecost, Paul summoned the elders of the Church of Ephesus to meet him on the coast at Miletus, where he bade them a fond farewell, sharing with them his apprehension of the fate

417

that awaited him in Jerusalem. At Patara, on the southern tip of Asia Minor, they boarded a cargo vessel bound for Tyre. They sailed down the Phoenician coast, stopping a day at Acre (Ptolemais), and then on to Caesarea, where they enjoyed the hospitality of Philip the Evangelist. Once again, Paul received a prophetic warning of the sufferings in store for him in Jerusalem, but he proclaimed himself ready not only for arrest but for death 'for the name of the Lord Jesus'. On arrival in Jerusalem, Paul lodged at the home of a Cypriot Christian called Mnason.

Burning faith and energy

Paul's journeys can be traced in his letters, as well as in the Acts of the Apostles. From the early letters to the Christian communities in Thessalonica, Galatia, Corinth, and Rome, his very distinct personality emerges, under every kind of physical and emotional strain, sometimes beyond his endurance. Often the briefest references are the most revealing of his perseverance. For two years, day by day, he taught right through the four long, hot hours of the siesta at Ephesus. Later, at Caesarea, he was to remain two whole years in prison, awaiting trial, through the idle and greedy procrastination of the Roman procurator, Felix, who expected a bribe.

Only in his last letter to the Church at Corinth does Paul himself hint at the cost of his calling. 'I know a man in Christ who fourteen years ago was caught up to the third heaven – whether in the body or out of the body I do not know, God knows. . . . And to keep me from being too elated by the abundance of revelations, a thorn was given me in the flesh, a messenger of Satan, to harass me, to keep me from being too elated. Three times I besought the Lord about this, that it should leave me; but he said to me, "My grace is sufficient for you, for my power is made perfect in weakness." I will all the more gladly boast of my weaknesses, that the power of Christ may rest upon me. For the sake of Christ, then, I am content with weaknesses, insults, hardships, persecutions, and calamities; for when I am weak, then I am strong.' (2 Cor. 12:2, 7-10)

What Paul's 'thorn in the flesh' was we may never know, whether physical, such as malaria or dysentery, or some particular source of personal temptation. How true, however, of himself were Paul's words: 'But we have this treasure in earthen vessels, to show that the transcendent power belongs to God and not to us. We are afflicted in every way, but not crushed; perplexed, but not driven to despair; persecuted, but not forsaken; struck down, but not destroyed; always carrying in the body the death of Jesus, so that the life of Jesus may also be manifested in our bodies. For while we live we are always being given up to death for Jesus's sake, so that the life of Jesus may be manifested in our mortal flesh.' (2 Cor. 4:7-11)

Prisoner for Christ

On his arrival in Jerusalem, towards the close of the year 58, and nearly 30 years after the passion of Jesus, Paul began his own Via Dolorosa, amid the fickle fury of the crowds, the same feebleness of the Roman procurator, and the same fertile cunning of the religious authorities. Even James and the elders of the Christian Church were apprehensive of his coming, for they pointed out, 'You see, brother, how many thousands there are among the Jews of those who have believed; they are all zealous for the law, and they have been told

419

about you that you teach all the Jews who are among the Gentiles to forsake Moses, telling them not to circumcise their children or observe the customs.' Paul agreed to undergo a week's ritual purification in the Temple, with four other men under a vow for whose expenses he paid, to show that he personally kept the Law. When the week's ritual was almost completed, some Asian Jews recognized Paul and, stirring up the crowd, accused him of bringing Greeks into the Temple. They would have lynched Paul if the guard had not turned out to protect him and hustle him up the steps of the Antonia Fortress. Paul, speaking in Greek and declaring his Roman citizenship, requested a final opportunity to address the mob, which he did in Hebrew.

When he described his own conversion, all listened in silence, but when he declared his mission to the Gentiles he was shouted down. Taken into the fortress for flogging, in preparation for his interrogation, Paul claimed exemption by his citizenship, was taken into protective custody, and appeared before the Sanhedrin the following day.

Within the Council, Paul skilfully divided the Pharisees from the Sadducees by claiming to be a Pharisee and basing his claims to be a Pharisee on the resurrection of the dead, a doctrine unacceptable to the Sadducees. Paul was withdrawn from the debate that followed and returned to the fortress. Some forty men vowed to fast until they had killed Paul. Information of their plot reached the Roman commander and he sent Paul, under both an infantry and a calvary escort, that night down to Antipatris, a Roman staging-post on the way to the coast. The next morning, after travelling all through the night, the infantry returned to Jerusalem, and the cavalry took Paul on to Caesarea to present him to the procurator Felix. When his accusers from Jerusalem brought a prosecutor called Tertullus down to Caesarea, Felix heard the case. Paul successfully challenged the charge of disturbance and profanation of the Temple, but he was retained in custody for the two remaining years of Felix's term of office. Felix, anxious to gain favour with the leaders of the Jews, left Paul in close confinement.

The new procurator, Festus, was approached on the matter by the Jewish chief priests, who demanded Paul's transfer for trial before the Council in Jerusalem. Festus, however, invited the accusers to Caesarea, and during the hearing asked Paul if he was willing to return to Jerusalem for trial. That left Paul with only one alternative: as a Roman citizen to appeal to the emperor himself. Festus had no choice but to accept his appeal and send him, under escort, to Rome. In order to arraign the charges, he took the opportunity to present Paul to Herod Agrippa II, the secular head of the Jewish people. Paul's eloquent speech evoked Agrippa's comment, 'In a short time you think to make me a Christian! . . . this man could have been set free if he had not appealed to Caesar.'

Probably in the autumn of the year 60, Paul and other prisoners in the charge of a centurion called Julius (*see* JULIUS) boarded a coaster which sailed round the eastern Mediterranean, calling in at Tyre and Myra on the south coast of Asia Minor. There they transferred to a larger ship of the grain fleet based on Alexandria, which took them along the south coast of Crete to the small port of Fair Havens. Though it was late autumn and the time of rough weather, the captain, supported by the centurion and ignoring a warning from Paul, decided to run for the larger harbour of Phoenix, further west along the Cretan coast. The ship was driven hopelessly off course by a hurricane 'north-easter', passing the island of Cauda and scudding south-west towards the coast of Africa. After a fortnight's running helplessly before the wind, the ship was wrecked on the island of Malta. Largely owing to the initiative and common-sense of Paul, whose fourth experience of shipwreck this was, all hands were saved. For three months they enjoyed the hospitality of the Maltese, before sailing in another Alexandrian vessel for Puteoli, via Syracuse in Sicily, Rhegium on the toe of Italy, and through the Straits of Messina. After a week at Puteoli they went on to Rome on foot. Christians came out to meet the party at the Appian Market, to accompany and encourage them on the final stage of their journey. On arrival in Rome, Paul was allowed to rent a house and receive visitors, though constantly guarded for two years under house-arrest.

Letters from captivity

During this time, Paul wrote what have come to be called the 'captivity letters'. The first of these was probably to the Church at Colossae, about 100 miles inland from Ephesus and founded during Paul's long stay in that city. This letter is in the nature of a denouncement of heresy with a scholarly defence of Paul's teaching of the Atonement – that Jesus is the only mediator necessary between man and God. A second letter addressed to the Church at Ephesus, following rather the same theme, may in fact have been originally written to the Laodiceans, a Christian community on the road between Ephesus and Colossae (mentioned in Col. 4:16). Both these letters were sent by the hand of Tychicus, as was the personal letter to Philemon begging the life of his runaway slave Onesimus, who had been so 'useful' (a pun on the meaning of the slave's name) to Paul in his captivity. This last letter gives the impression that Paul expected his release and planned to revisit Asia.

Whether Paul was released, and whether he fulfilled his ambition to visit Spain, as expressed in his letter to the Romans (15:24), and implied by Clement some forty years later, we cannot be certain, nor do we know whether he returned to the eastern Mediterranean. The so-called 'pastoral epistles' of 1 and 2 Timothy and Titus provide the only possible clues, being probably written after the first term of imprisonment, if they are the work of Paul. From them it would appear that Paul *did* revisit Asia, Achaia, and Macedonia. His final paragraph of advice in his second letter to Timothy could imply that he was finally arrested at Troas, for Timothy is asked to bring the cloak and scrolls left there.

A final betrayal?

It could also imply that his arrest was due to the treachery of one 'Alexander, the coppersmith', who 'did me great harm'. Certainly this letter indicates that the end is near: 'No one took my part; all deserted me. May it not be charged against them! But the Lord stood by me and gave me strength to proclaim the word fully, that all the Gentiles might hear it. So I was rescued from the lion's mouth.'

Eusebius, the 'Father of Church History', and 4th-century bishop of Caesarea, records that Paul was again taken to Rome and killed in Nero's persecution in the year 67. Tertullian, the 'Father of the African Church' in the 2nd century, records that he was beheaded. St Gregory the Great and later writers site his execution on the left bank of the Tiber, some three miles from

Rome on the road to the port of Ostia. The place became known as the 'Three Fountains', following the legend that where Paul's head bounced three times, three fountains appeared. His body was traditionally believed to be buried in a cemetery nearer Rome, by the Ostia Way, on the site of which now stands the Basilica of St Paul Outside the Walls – dedicated to the most powerful personality in the history of the Christian Church. [Under the name of SAUL: Acts 8:1; 9:1-30; 13:1-12. Under the name of PAUL: Acts 13:13-28; Letter to the Romans; 1 Cor. 1:12, 13; 3:4, 5, 22; 16:21; 1 Thess. 2:18; 2 Thess. 3:17; 1st and 2nd Letters to Timothy; Titus; Philem. 9; 2 Peter 3:15]

PAULUS *see* SERGIUS PAULUS

PERSIS (Gk. 'Persian woman') One of the women warmly greeted by Paul at the close of his letter to the Christian congregation in Rome, as 'beloved' and 'one who had worked hard in the Lord'. Her name was common among female slaves. [Rom. 16:12]

PETER (Gk. from the Aram. 'rock'; original name in Gk. *Simon,* 'hearing') Simon called Peter was a master fisherman on the Lake of Galilee, who became one of the earliest disciples of Jesus. He became one of Jesus's closest friends and was the first to recognize Jesus as the Messiah. He is particularly remembered for his threefold denial of Jesus, his repentance, and his threefold commission by Jesus to 'feed my sheep'. This rustic Galilean fisherman, whose character resembled shifting sand rather than the rock from which Jesus named him 'Peter', did in fact become the natural leader of the twelve apostles. Later, his leadership seems to have been superseded by Paul, but Peter is the traditional first bishop of Rome, and his tomb is reputed to have been excavated below the high altar of the basilica of St Peter at Rome.

A wealth of human qualities

Of all the personalities in the New Testament, perhaps we know most about the character of Peter. He is the more attractive for his constant mistakes and forgiveness, his boisterous and impetuous enthusiasm, and for his good intentions and self-confidence that so soon seemed to disappear. At first he seems to have been a surprising choice as the 'Rock' upon which Jesus was to found his Church, but he justified his choice by an example, that has inspired and encouraged Christians down the centuries.

The sources of information about Peter include the Gospels, Acts, Galatians, and tradition. He was the son of a certain John, or more probably Jonah. He was a native of Bethsaida, literally a 'fisher home', near the Lake of Galilee. He was living at Capernaum, however, at the beginning of the ministry of Jesus, together with his wife and her family, reasonably near the synagogue. Living in the district of Galilee (*Galil* in Hebrew means a region or encircled area) surrounded by Gentiles, Peter may have spoken colloquial Greek, but his native language would be Aramaic and his Galilean accent was quite obvious in Jerusalem at the trial of Jesus. When Peter and John were described by the Sanhedrin, the supreme Council, as 'uneducated, common men', this applied to their lack of Rabbinic training.

Peter and Andrew his brother were fishermen by trade and in partnership with Zebedee and his sons. Jesus drew his disciples from the fishermen of Galilee, whose best fishing-grounds were at the north-east of the lake, where the Jordan River deposited its silt. He drew his followers from the hardy men who braved the west wind's sudden squalls, funnelled down through the Gulf of Pigeons above Magdala. In a highly-concentrated population, often inflamed by a spirit of nationalism, Jesus went to a trade which had no private wrongs. He called men, not from their dreams, but from work they were content to do from day to day, till something higher should touch them. And so it has come to pass that not the jargon of fanatics and brigands, but the speech of the fishermen and their simple craft has become the language and symbolism of Christianity.

In the Gospels, Peter's character appears to be at variance with the nickname of the 'Rock', given to him by Jesus. Whether his name was to describe his physique or his temperament, that name was prophetically confirmed by Jesus at Caesarea Philippi and amply justified by his granite-like leadership of the apostles from Pentecost onwards. He was always a man of action, but from his calling by Jesus to his denial of Jesus he was a man of impulse and aggressive energy, of childlike simplicity and daring, alternating with a weak and cowardly instability.

The turning-points in Peter's life were the appearance of Jesus to him after the resurrection, and Jesus's three-fold questions and commission to him to 'feed my sheep'. Certainly from Pentecost onwards he was the true and undoubted leader of the Church, facing without fear the consequent persecution and punishment, and doing so with an inspiring courage and humility. This humility is strikingly illustrated in the Gospel of Mark, which shows him in a far less favourable light than do the other three Gospels! This is striking when it is remembered that Mark's Gospel has been said by Irenaeus, as early as the year 85, to have been based on the reminiscences of Peter, the 'mind behind' the Second Gospel. (*see also* MARK)

A sincere pupil

The word 'disciple' means a 'pupil', and Peter was certainly prepared to learn and was deeply concerned about his faith. Peter and his brother Andrew were probably both disciples of John the Baptist during his ministry of teaching and baptism by the River Jordan. Peter was introduced to Jesus by Andrew, and Jesus greeted him, 'So you are Simon the son of John? You shall be called Cephas' – the Aramaic equivalent of the Greek 'Peter', meaning 'rock'. The evangelists used the Greek name 'Peter', which became his personal name and was applied to no one else in the New Testament. It is probable that Peter, Andrew, and Philip – all from the same town, Bethsaida – returned with Jesus to Galilee, attending the wedding at Cana, and were impressed by the miracle of the changing of the water into wine (John 2:11), before resuming their fishing on the lake. When Jesus himself arrived at Capernaum to begin his lakeside ministry, on leaving the synagogue with James and John he went straight to the house of Peter and Andrew, where he cured Peter's mother-in-law of a fever.

Some time later, Jesus used Peter's boat from which to speak to the crowds on shore. There are little bays on the north coast of the lake which form natural auditoria, with the water of the lake acting as a sounding-board. On this occasion Jesus prevailed upon Peter's greater experience, persuading him to shoot his nets in daylight after a fruitless night's fishing. The two pairs of brothers, James and John, Andrew and Peter, were completely overcome by the remarkable catch which they then made, and they were called by Jesus to follow him in full-time training to become 'fishers of men'.

From then onwards, Peter's house at Capernaum became the headquarters of Jesus's lakeside ministry, and Peter's boat was always at his disposal. The selection of the team of twelve disciples was completed, and Peter was always included at the head of the list. Perhaps this was not so much because he was acknowledged as leader by the other disciples, as the result of the fact that his household was the headquarters of the group and that he and Andrew were its first members.

With James and John, Peter formed an inner circle of three, who alone were allowed to accompany Jesus into the house for the raising of Jairus's daughter, to witness the transfiguration, and to share the agony in the Garden of Gethsemane. Peter was often the spokesman of the twelve, and was their natural leader. He walked on the water. He spoke loyally for the others when Jesus's teaching about the 'Bread of Life' scandalized them. He expressed the conviction of the twelve when he made his great confession at Caesarea Philippi: 'You are the Christ, the Son of the living God.' At once Jesus replied, 'You are Peter, and on this rock I will build my church, and the powers of death shall not prevail against it. I will give you the keys of the kingdom of heaven . . .' Peter's confession of faith, however, was followed by a sharp rebuke, because he refused to listen to Jesus's first prediction of his passion. In his capacity as leader, Peter was approached by the tax-collectors for the Temple tribute due from Jesus and his disciples. He was constantly voicing the questions of the twelve about the limits of forgiveness, and about the destruction of the Temple.

Peter's role in the passion story was considerable.

428

Together with John, he was entrusted with the preparations for the Last Supper, in which Jesus clearly confirmed his leadership 'when you have turned again', and at once foretold the threefold denial, which Peter passionately contradicted; Peter also protested at the feet-washing, and then impetuously demanded that Jesus wash him completely. Peter beckoned John to ask Jesus the identity of the betrayer; and although chosen to keep watch with James and John in the Garden of Gethsemane, Peter slept with them. At the moment of the arrest, however, it was Peter who struck out in defence of Jesus with his sword – only to be rebuked by Jesus.

When all the rest fled, Peter followed at a distance to the high priest's palace, where he was admitted to the court after the intervention of John with the portress. There he was accused of being one of Jesus's followers, denied three times that he knew Jesus – then remembered Jesus's prediction and bitterly repented. Luke adds that 'the Lord turned and looked at Peter'. If Mark's account of the trial before the Sanhedrin may be said to reveal the lack of witnesses of Jesus's admission to being the Christ, for which he was condemned as a blasphemer, then perhaps Peter's denial might well have prevented Peter himself being forced to give evidence of Jesus's Messiahship.

Various churches have been built on the possible sites of the high priest's palace to commemorate the trial and imprisonment of Jesus by Caiaphas, as well as Peter's denial and repentance. Some place the site on the top of the Western Hill, near the Armenian chapel, others prefer the remains covered by the Church of St Peter in Gallicantu, 'of the cock-crowing'. Here the story can be vividly reconstructed. Within the present church, over the high altar, is an illustration of the trial, which was conducted in the rock-hewn courtyard on the next level below the church. The prisoner is standing on a raised platform or dock, in the centre and with his back to the wall, chained by the wrists to escorts seated on either side of him. It is easy to picture this scene on the lower level, facing westwards into the hillside in which are cut staircases and galleries. On one of these Peter must have sat with the soldiers, warmed himself by the fire, and denied knowing his master.

On either side of the wall, behind the raised dock platform, the corners of the courtyard are cut square to a height of ten feet. In the very centre of the courtroom is the mouth of a bottle-necked prison, into which the condemned prisoner could be lowered after trial. Descending to a third level, there is a complete guardroom, all round the walls of which are still to be found the staples for the prisoners' chains (some consider this to have been a stable in Byzantine times). On one side there is a small window opening on to the bottle-necked condemned cell. Below this window, and left projecting from the floor when the guardroom was excavated from the living rock, is a block on which the guard stood to peer down into the gloom of the cell below him.

On the opposite side of the guardroom is the whipping-block. Here, tied up by the wrists with leather thongs through staples at the top, a belt round his waist secured to a staple at each side, the prisoner would be stretched up, taut and helpless. At his feet were two bowls carved in the rock, one for salt to disinfect his wounds, one for vinegar to revive him. Here, both Peter and John received the legal sentence of 'forty lashes less one', thirteen on each shoulder from the back, and thirteen on the chest from the front, were commanded not to preach Jesus as Christ, and then sent home. Yet they returned daily to the Temple to preach this very thing.

The Gospels do not mention Peter from the night of Jesus's trial to the morning of his resurrection, but the writer of the first Letter of Peter says that he was 'A witness of the sufferings of Christ' (1 Pet. 5:1). On Easter morning, Peter and John ran to the tomb, to find it empty. Both Luke and Paul report that Jesus appeared specially to Peter alone on the day of the resurrection. Certainly he shared with several others the appearance by the Lake of Galilee. Then John recognized Jesus; but Peter swam ashore to share the breakfast cooked on the fire of coals. There, Peter's love was thrice tested for his threefold denial: 'Simon, son of John, do you love me?' Peter then received his threefold commission to shepherd the flock of God. There, too, he received the prediction of his martyrdom. And there today the remains of the medieval chapel of 'Peter's Primacy' enclose a vast rock which projects out into the clear waters of the lake. The rock, known as the 'Table of the Lord', is still in its striking simplicity a silent witness to the resurrection tradition in Galilee, and to the commission of Peter as 'prince of the apostles'.

Peter takes command

After Jesus's ascension, at which he 'sent out' his apostles into the world, Peter at once assumed the leadership of the apostles. He suggested the choice of a replacement for Judas. He spoke for the apostles on the day of Pentecost, with great inspiration and effect. He was the first of the apostles to perform a miracle in the name of Jesus – healing the cripple at the Beautiful Gate of the Temple. He conducted the defence of John and himself before the Sanhedrin, and pronounced the condemnation of Ananias and Sapphira. He was soon renowned for his miracles done in the name of Jesus, and he and John were sent to Samaria where, through the laying-on of their hands, the Holy Spirit came to the baptized believers.

It was Peter who healed Aeneas, the paralytic at Lydda, and he raised to life Dorcas, the woman of many good works in Joppa. While in Joppa (now Jaffa), Peter received a vision convincing him, as he admitted, that 'God shows no partiality, but in every nation any one who fears him and does what is right is acceptable to him.' He then converted and baptized Cornelius, a Roman centurion, and his whole household at Caesarea. At the Council of Jerusalem, he upheld his decision to do this and was supported by Paul and Barnabas.

We know little of Peter's work outside Palestine. Paul mentions Peter's visit to Antioch (Gal. 2:11-21,) where he yielded to the demands of certain Jewish-Christians, in dissociating himself temporarily from the Gentiles. Peter seems to have visited Corinth (1 Cor. 1:12), and he may well have been engaged in evangelism in Rome itself before Paul's arrival. (Rom. 15:20-22) Certainly, Eusebius and Origen declare that he went to Rome and, as an old man, suffered martyrdom by crucifixion head downwards, during the reign of Nero, probably in AD 64.

The site of the present St Peter's Church in Rome, and of the first Constantinian basilica there, has been venerated by Christians from the earliest times as the site of the tomb of Peter. The first memorial over his grave was built in about 160. A vast five-aisled basilica was built by Constantine on the Vatican Hill above the traditional site of the grave. Two series of excavations instituted by Pope Paul XII, from 1940-51 and from 1953-7, have established what if anything has survived of the original grave. The apostle's body was certainly buried on the Vatican Hill, at a spot close to the gardens of Nero and their famous circus or sports stadium. The grave must have been a plain earth trench covered with large tiles. This whole area later came in time to be one of the largest burial-grounds in Rome and the apostle's grave became hemmed in by others, dating back to about the year 70 or 80. There are 2nd- or early 3rd-century Greek *graffiti*, cut in a dividing wall above the traditional site of the grave, which refer to Peter.

The First Letter

Of the two letters ascribed to Peter, the first is more likely to reflect the teaching and message of Peter himself than the second, which was written and attributed to him at least a hundred years after his death. The first is a message to the Churches in northern Asia Minor to help them meet the shock of sudden and violent persecution, to strengthen and reassure them in the faith, and to encourage them to remain firm in their allegiance to God. After the greeting there follows a long, perhaps baptismal discourse, unlike a simple letter in form or content, and without any personal or local references. This may have been a separate composition, with its own introduction and conclusion in the form of a sermon on the nature of the Christian life.

It assumes a basic knowledge of the Christian faith and it instructs the readers accordingly about baptism, regeneration, the nature of God, the sufferings of Jesus, and the Christian hope. The references to suffering and trials are of a general nature and do not indicate existing persecution. The mere profession of Christianity does not incur punishment, indeed those innocent of any wrongdoing can expect to be vindicated by the Roman magistrate. The Greek is excellent, the tone calm and tranquil.

The letter then begins to reflect an atmosphere of tension. The style is simple and direct, the language quick and nervous. Suffering is now a stark reality and their faith is put to the test; they are being persecuted for the very name of Christian by the authorities. Now is their judgment, their opportunity to share the sufferings of Christ in the brotherhood of his Church, that they may share his glory. The letter closes with greetings from the Church in Rome (here called Babylon), and from 'Mark my son'. The bearer was Silvanus.

There is a disagreement among scholars about the authorship of this letter. Some accept that it was written by Peter, explaining its style and language as the work of Silvanus, the secretary. In that case the persecution referred to must be Nero's of AD 64. But that persecution did not extend to the provinces of Asia Minor and Christianity did not reach Pontus by the Black Sea before 65. There was persecution of Christians under the Emperor Trajan (98-117) in Bythinia and Pontus, where the governor was Pliny the Younger. Pliny's own records of examinations under torture both of men and women have survived and accord with the description in 1 Peter. The letter is first described by Polycarp in 135, so must have been written between 64 and 135. It may perhaps be the composite work of Peter, Silvanus, and another writer, adapting it to the needs of a later persecution, using the name of Peter as a suitable martyr-apostle to encourage the suffering Christians of his time. The letter is important as not teaching the doctrine of a single author, but as a systematic presentation of the faith of the early Christian Church.

The Second Letter

This letter was undoubtedly written in the 2nd century under the name of Peter, in order to discredit views which the author thought unapostolic. The Greek style and the general tone is absolutely different from 1 Peter. Eusebius, writing in the 4th century, roundly declares that of all the writings in the name of Peter, 'only one epistle is genuine'. Certainly, this letter, 2 Peter, is dependent upon that of Jude. References to all Paul's letters also show that it was not written until after they had been collected into one corpus. The letter denounces false teachers with all the authority of an apostle. The inclusion within the New Testament of this letter is not based upon its authorship, but upon its intrinsic value recognized by the Church as the authentic voice of apostolic teaching. [Matt. 4:18; 10:2; 14:29; 16:6-23; 17:1; 26:37; Mark 3:16; 5:37; 8:32, 33; 9:2; 14:33; Luke 6:14; 8:51; 9:20-28; John 21:2-20; Acts 1:13, 15; 2:14, 38; 3:1-12, 4:13, 19; 5:3, 8, 9, 15, 29; 9:32-40; 10:5-48; 11:2-18; 12:3-18; 15:6-14; 1st and 2nd Letters of Peter]

PHANUEL (Gk. from the Heb. 'face of God') The father of the prophetess Anna and a member of the tribe of Asher. Anna was among those faithful Jews who, being in the Temple at Jerusalem at the time of the presentation of Jesus, 'gave thanks to God' and spoke of Jesus to all who were looking for the redemption of Jerusalem. [Luke 2:36]

PHARISEES (Gk. 'separated ones') At the time of Jesus, the Pharisees were the most powerful religious group among the Jews, and his constant opponents. Jesus continually denounced their external observance of the Law, their multitude of petty traditions, and particularly their self-righteousness.

The Pharisees were the successors of the 'Holy Ones' who had fought for religious freedom during the Greek occupation of Palestine from 332 BC. Like the 'Holy Ones' the Pharisees had 'separated' themselves by their pious efforts to maintain the Law. Though they were themselves mostly middle-class, they had become essentially the people's party, very different from the Sadducees, the party of the chief priests, who held aloof from the passionate enthusiasm of the Pharisees for righteousness. Unlike the Sadducees, they believed in angels and spirits as intermediaries between God and man, in resurrection after death, and in retribution in the world to come. Also unlike the Sadducees, the Pharisees held that the Tradition of the Elders was an authoritative interpretation of the Old Testament Law of Moses. They would not revolt against Gentile rule; if God was in charge of history, they held, it was not man's place to force his hand. Whereas the Zealot party burned to establish a national kingdom by force of arms, the Pharisees waited on God's intervention through the Messiah.

Though probably few in number – perhaps 6,000 at the time of Jesus – the Pharisees were much admired by the man in the street for their austerity, for their hatred of pagan rule and for their challenge to the rule of the chief priests. They fostered synagogue life and worship, calling people back to a study of the Law and its application to their own time. They consisted mainly of businessmen, shopkeepers, and teachers – but with some priests also.

Their 'fellowships' held regular meetings and prescribed rules for the admission of new members. These rules included the observance of seven 'hours of prayer', the Pharisaic interpretation of a tithe of one-tenth of all possessions to the Temple, fasting twice a week on the days when traditionally Moses ascended and came down from Mount Sinai, and performing scores of ritual washings and offerings, besides the complicated code of food laws and Sabbath regulations. All these were, of course, additions to the Mosaic commandments of the Law. The Pharisees regarded with scorn all those who did not come up to their own rigorous standards. Such people the Pharisees relegated to the depressed class of 'sinners', contact with whom rendered the Pharisee himself 'unclean'.

Opposition-group to Jesus

In the Gospel narratives the Pharisees are often linked with the Scribes, through whom they exerted their influence upon the minds of the people, for the Scribes presided in the local courts and taught in the local schools. It was inevitable that many Pharisees were bitterly opposed to Jesus, and constantly denounced by him. They rejected his claims to Messiahship. (John 9:16, 22) He condemned their ostentation, their hypocrisy, their doctrine of salvation by works, their impenitence and their lovelessness, which were so far from his own life and his teaching of the free forgiveness and love of God, culminating as it did in his death on the cross.

In the Gospels, the picture of the Pharisee is painted almost completely black and reflects the bitterness which later developed between the Christian Church and Rabbinic Judaism. This is particularly the case with Matthew's Gospel, where the denunciations of Scribes and Pharisees are especially virulent. But it is unlikely that these fierce and wholesale criticisms were directed by Jesus himself against the whole party, rather than against unworthy members of it. Indeed, some Pharisees played vital roles in the early Christian Church, including Nicodemus (John 3:1; 7:50, 51; 19:39), Gamaliel, who publicly defended the Apostles before the Sanhedrin (Acts 5:34-40), Joseph and Arimathea (Matt. 27:57; Mark 15:43; Luke 23:50; John 19:38), and certainly the Apostle Paul. (Phil. 3:5) Paul uses the title 'Pharisee' of himself, as a name of honour and respect: 'As to the law [I am] a Pharisee.'

The conflict between Jesus and the Pharisees occurred mainly in Galilee. During the passion of Jesus in Jerusalem, they remained in the background, the lead in the attack upon Jesus being taken by the Sadducees, although they combined with the Herodians to ask him a question about the payment of taxes to Rome. Luke records three occasions when Jesus was invited to meals in the houses of Pharisees. His conversation in the house of Simon the Pharisee (Luke 7:36) sums up the difference between his philosophy and that of those Pharisees who were scandalized at the company he kept.

On this occasion a woman with a bad reputation came in, and sitting behind Jesus anointed his feet, thereby according Jesus the treatment which Simon, his host, had neglected to offer his guest. When Simon criticized Jesus, thinking that surely he should have recognized the kind of woman she was and driven her away, Jesus replied with this parable: ' "A certain creditor had two debtors; one owed five hundred denarii, and the other fifty. When they could not pay, he forgave them both. Now which of them will love him more?" Simon answered, "The one, I suppose, to whom he forgave more." ' Then Jesus compared Simon's own lack of courtesy with the almost embarrassing attentions of the woman, explaining: 'Her sins, which are many, are forgiven, for she loved much; but he who is forgiven little, loves little.'

The letter of the Law

Perhaps the first point of basic disagreement between Jesus and certain of the Pharisees was in the interpretation of the Law of Moses, in the matter of Sabbath observance. When Jesus healed a man with a withered hand on the Sabbath (Mark 2:1-6), he challenged the Pharisees to say whether it was lawful to do good on such a day. He allowed his disciples to pluck and rub ears of corn, thus technically reaping and threshing on the Sabbath day (Mark 2:23-6). He justified his actions by declaring, 'The sabbath was made for man, not man for the sabbath; so the Son of man is lord even of the sabbath.' Jesus, thus quoting Deut. 5:12-15, indicated that the institution of the Sabbath was for man's benefit. He did not deny that his action was a breach of the Law, but justified it as meeting human need.

The Pharisees also criticized Jesus for allowing his disciples to eat without washing their hands, thus disobeying the Levitical hygienic regulations. Jesus declared, 'What comes out of a man is what defiles a man. For from within, out of the heart of man, come evil thoughts, fornication, theft, murder, adultery, coveting, wickedness, deceit, licentiousness, envy, slander, pride, foolishness. All these evil things come from within, and they defile a man.' (Mark 7:20-23) Jesus, as a loyal Jew, respected the Law of Moses and sought to fulfil it, but his idea of fulfilment was not that of many contemporary Scribes. He kept the Commandments; but he summarized their content in two positive principles:

'You shall love the Lord your God with all your heart, and with all your soul, and with all your might', (Deut. 6:5) and 'You shall love your neighbour as yourself.' (Lev. 19:18)

It is likely that the condemnation of the Pharisees by Jesus as reported in the Gospels has been over-emphasized, particularly in the Gospel of Matthew. It must be remembered that this Gospel was probably written at a time when the Judeo-Christians were divided into two parties. This division was based on and expressed in contradictory attitudes towards the observance by Gentiles of the Law of Moses. A 'circumcision party' held that all Gentile Christians must keep the Jewish Law and be circumcised. Many rejected this demand, considering the Law of Jesus sufficient for the Gentile Christians. The Gospel-writers appear to reflect this division of opinion in their presentation of the controversy between Jesus and the Pharisees. [Matt. 5:20; 9:14, 34; 15:1, 12; 16:1-12; 19:3; 23:2-29; Mark 2:16, 18, 24; 3:6; 8:11, 15; 12:13-17; Luke 5:30, 33; 6:2, 7; 7:36, 37, 39; 11:37-53; 12:1; 14:1-6; 16:14; John 1:24; 3:1; 7:32, 47, 48; 11:47, 57; Acts 15:5; 23:6-9; 26:5; Phil. 3:5]

PHILEMON (Gk. 'loving') This well-established member of the Christian Church at Colossae was the recipient of a personal letter from Paul the Apostle. It is the only surviving letter to Paul's vast personal correspondence, and the only letter in the New Testament addressed to an individual rather than to a community.

Philemon was evidently a wealthy man, the owner of slaves, able to entertain the local Christian congregation in his house. Paul's opening sentence to him refers to himself as 'a prisoner for Christ Jesus', and addresses Philemon as 'our beloved fellow worker'. The greeting embraces 'Apphia our sister', probably Philemon's wife, and 'Archippus our fellow soldier', probably Philemon's son. From Paul's reference to Archippus in his letter to the Church at Colossae (Col. 4:17), Archippus was a leader of their congregation. (*see* COLOSSIANS)

Writing in captivity, Paul had a particular reason and a favour to ask of his friend Philemon at Colossae. He also needed to write a general letter to the Colossian Church to counter certain false teaching, of which he had received reports from Epaphras, their first evangelist. Both letters were written at the same time and despatched from the same town to the same destination by the same messenger, Tychicus. In both letters Paul links with his own greeting the name of Timothy, his companion during his stay in Ephesus. In both letters he sends also greetings from Epaphras, Luke the physician, Demas, Aristarchus, and Mark the nephew of Barnabas. It is just possible that these letters were written during Paul's brief imprisonment in Ephesus, sometime during the years 54 and 57, but they are more likely to have been written during his long and leisurely period of house-arrest in Rome during the years of 61-3.

Advocate for a slave
During his captivity Paul was approached by an escaped slave called Onesimus. The Greek name means 'useful'. He had run away from his master Philemon in Colossae and had made his way to the teeming capital of Rome, a notorious hide-out for fugitive slaves. There, in destitution and danger, the hunted man had sought out the imprisoned Apostle Paul and had attached himself to him as his personal attendant. Paul came to know Onesimus's story, his unsatisfactory record as a slave to Philemon, whom he had robbed as

well as deserted – and to whom his very life was now forfeit on both accounts. Useless as Onesimus had been to Philemon, he became invaluable to Paul in his captivity. He had been taught by Paul and had apparently matured considerably in Christian character, for he was prepared to return – at the risk of his life – to the service of his deserted master, Philemon.

The sole purpose of Paul's 'covering letter' is to return Philemon's property with a plea not only for his forgiveness of Onesimus but for his new reception as a brother in Christ Jesus. Paul's letter is amazing in its tact, its tenderness, and its utter charm. It presumes to seek pardon for a slave for the most serious and the most easily identified offences against the common law: theft and flight. Speaking as a Christian apostle to one for whose conversion he is indirectly responsible, he does not begin to dictate, but delicately touches on their mutual obligations. The letter is a priceless memorial to the pastoral skill and affection of the apostle, in a way that his more theological treatises can never be.

Here, in the Greek style, is the opening thanksgiving and prayer addressed to Philemon: 'I thank my God always when I remember you in my prayers, because I hear of your love and of the faith which you have toward the Lord Jesus and all the saints, and I pray that the sharing of your faith may promote the knowledge of all the good that is ours in Christ. For I have derived much joy and comfort from your love, my brother, because the hearts of the saints have been refreshed through you.'

Then he gently begins his petition for Onesimus, as a father might for his own son. He even implies that he would have wished Philemon to return Onesimus to Rome in order to serve him in prison on behalf of Philemon. 'Accordingly, though I am bold enough in Christ to command you to do what is required, yet for love's sake I prefer to appeal to you – I, Paul, an ambassador and now a prisoner also for Christ Jesus – I appeal to you for my child, Onesimus, whose father I have become in my imprisonment. (Formerly he was useless to you, but now he is indeed useful to you and to me.) I am sending him back to you, sending my very heart. I would have been glad to keep him with me, in order that he might serve me on your behalf during my imprisonment for the gospel; but I preferred to do nothing without your consent in order that your goodness might not be by compulsion but of your own free will.'

Paul then proceeds to his daring request not only for Onesimus's forgiveness, but that he should be welcomed back as a brother, as Paul himself might expect to be received! Paul takes responsibility for whatever sum of money Onesimus owes to his master: taking the pen from his secretary (probably Timothy), Paul himself writes his bond in the required legal terms: 'I, Paul, write this with my own hand, I will repay it . . .' but adding, 'To say nothing of your owing me even your own self.'

Thus Paul closes his letter, in complete confidence of Philemon's willingness to do even more than he asks. Paul even asks on his own account that Philemon prepare his guest-chamber, as Paul expects shortly to be free to return to Asia. That Philemon preserved this letter and that it has been included in the New Testament surely shows that he granted Paul's request, though whether Onesimus returned to Rome, or Paul ever visited Colossae, we may never know for certain. According to tradition Philemon and his wife Apphia were martyred at Colossae and Onesimus became bishop of Ephesus.

This beautiful letter should surely convince all who accuse Paul of changing the simple message of Jesus into a complicated system of doctrine, that behind all his teaching lay the basic truth declared in the Sermon on the Mount.

This letter, too, is a milestone on the road to the emancipation of slaves; the principle that a slave be treated as a brother, that both Christian master and slave were the servants of Christ, and that all men are spiritually equals – this was ultimately and inevitably to destroy both the system and practice of slavery. [Letter to Philemon]

PHILETUS (Gk. 'worthy of love') A heretical teacher within the Christian community, probably at Ephesus or Troas, on the coast of Asia Minor, whom Paul found it necessary to excommunicate, as his teaching represented a real threat to the faith and loyalty of the local congregation.

In his last letter to Timothy, Paul is most insistent in his warnings against false teachers. Timothy needs to be a 'sound workman', 'handling the word rightly', avoiding 'what is ignoble', and exercising a strict supervision of his congregation. 'Remind them of this, and charge them before the Lord to avoid disputing about words, which does no good, but only ruins the hearers. Do your best to present yourself to God as one approved, a workman who has no need to be ashamed, rightly handling the word of truth. Avoid such godless chatter, for it will lead people into more and more ungodliness, and their talk will eat its way like gangrene. Among them are Hymenaeus and Philetus, who have swerved from the truth by holding that the resurrection is past already. They are upsetting the faith of some. But God's firm foundation stands.' (2 Tim. 2:14-19)

Exactly what the false teaching of Hymenaeus and Philetus was cannot be exactly or certainly determined. It is likely, however, to have been some early Gnosticism, like the Colossian heresy, robbing the resurrection of Jesus of its reality and substituting some allegorical explanation. Paul saw clearly that a purely mystical interpretation of the life and person of Jesus represented a real threat to the Christian faith in the true humanity of the Son of God, who came, lived, died, rose and returned to God, as 'the first fruits of the human race'. [2 Tim. 2:17]

PHILIP (Gk. 'lover of horses') **1. Philip the Apostle** Within the gospels of Mark, Matthew, and Luke, Philip's name occurs only in the list of apostles, linked with that of Nathanael Bar-Tolmai. In the Acts, his name is listed with Thomas among the apostles present at the election of Matthias in the Upper Room before Pentecost. The Fourth Gospel, however, describes a number of incidents involving Philip, from which some estimate of his character and personality may be deduced.

Philip was almost certainly a disciple of John the Baptist, because Jesus called him from among the crowds on the banks of the River Jordan where John was baptizing. The previous day, Jesus had met Andrew, who had introduced to Jesus his brother and Simon Peter. All three of them – Andrew, Peter, and Philip – came from the same town, Bethsaida, on the Lake of Galilee, and were fishermen. It was probably a day or two later that Philip brought his friend Nathanael to Jesus. Nathanael was a native of Cana, the rival and neighbouring town to Nazareth. Consequently, his sarcastic comment on Philip's enthusiastic acclamation of Jesus as Messiah had been, 'Can anything good come out of Nazareth?' Philip's reply was 'Come and see,' and the interview with Jesus evoked Nathanael's confession, 'Rabbi, you are the Son of God! You are the King of Israel!'

It seems from the story of the feeding of the five thousand that Philip was responsible for the provisioning of the party of disciples, or for their picnic rations. Certainly he was staggered at the idea of feeding such a crowd, when Jesus suggested buying bread for them. 'Two hundred denarii would not buy enough bread for each of them to get a little,' Philip answered, perhaps with more simplicity than accuracy! No doubt he was as horrified as the others when Jesus said, 'Make the people sit down,' and equally astonished at the outcome.

During Jesus's final visit to Jerusalem before the crucifixion, some Greeks had come up for the Passover. They approached Philip with the request, 'Sir, we wish to see Jesus.' Philip told Andrew and together they went to tell Jesus. Perhaps Philip again invited his enquirers to 'Come and see'.

Again, at the Last Supper, Philip's words to Jesus are recorded in the Fourth Gospel. Jesus had just reassured his disciples that wherever he is going they will follow, and has promised them 'I am the way, and the truth, and the life; no one comes to the Father, but by me. If you had known me, you would have known my Father also; henceforth you know him and have seen him.' Philip asks, 'Lord, show us the Father, and we shall be satisfied.' Jesus answers, 'Have I been with you so long, and yet you do not know me, Philip? He who has seen me has seen the Father . . . he who loves me will be

446

loved by my Father, and I will love him and manifest myself to him.'

It seems that Philip was a sincere person, very approachable and very practical, but not yet during Jesus's ministry so much a leader as a 'contact man', whose very simplicity called forth words of Jesus that are still deeply treasured: 'He who has seen me has seen the Father.'

Traditions contradict each other about Philip's later life. A 2nd-century Ephesian tradition says that he died at Hierapolis, where there is a beautiful Byzantine church, a hundred miles inland from Ephesus. A later tradition claims that Philip was crucified; thus in medieval art he is depicted either with five loaves or a cross. (Matt. 10:3; Mark 3:18; Luke 6:14; John 1:43-48; 6:5-7; 12:21, 22; 14:8-21; Acts 1:13]

2. Philip the Deacon and Evangelist This Philip is mentioned only in the Acts, first as the second of the seven deacons elected to administer charity in the daily distribution at Jerusalem, and secondly as a successful Christian evangelist in Samaria and Caesarea.

Deacon

He was a man 'of good repute, full of the Spirit and of wisdom', selected by the Hellenistic Greek-speaking Jews, and commissioned by the apostles with prayer and the laying-on of hands; he supervised the daily distribution of bread to the Hellenist widows and poor in Jerusalem.

The earliest members of the Christian Church in Jerusalem had been mostly pious Jews, who had continued to visit the Temple and to observe the Jewish Law. The original disciples of Jesus, perhaps from Galilee or from the neighbourhood of Jerusalem, were Aramaic-speaking. Now, as others, both Jews and foreigners, had come to settle in the city, sometimes residing near the Temple, the Christian Church had acquired new members from these newcomers. Christian evangelism had been particularly successful among the Hellenistic Jews, who spoke Greek instead of Aramaic. Consequently, there developed in Jerusalem two classes of Christian believers, the Hebrews and the Hellenists, both accepting the Messiahship of Jesus.

The welfare and relief of the needy have always been a characteristic of Judaism and the Law insists on providing for the fatherless and the widow, the slave and the stranger. The Christian community gladly accepted such obligations, as may be seen from the very considerable fund for poor-relief that Paul brought back to Jerusalem from his Mediterranean congregations. There developed, however, a sense of resentment among the Hellenists that their widows were being neglected in the daily distribution at Jerusalem. This threatened to cause some friction between these two groups, the Hebrews and the Hellenists.

The twelve apostles immediately took action, summoning the community as a whole body and ruling, 'It is not right that we should give up preaching the word of God to serve tables. Therefore, brethren, pick out from among you seven men of good repute, full of the Spirit and of wisdom, whom we may appoint to this duty. But we will devote ourselves to prayer and to the ministry of the word.' (Acts 6:2-4) The whole Christian community approved this course of action and they chose seven men to undertake the domestic and financial administration of the poor-relief. These seven deacons, as they later came to be called, the apostles

448

commissioned by prayer and the laying-on of their hands. Whatever the terms of their commission, certain of them are known to have been involved in teaching and evangelistic work, particularly Stephen and Philip.

The names of the seven – Stephen, Philip, Prochorus, Nicanor, Timon, Parmenas and Nicolaus – all indicate a Greek background, though most of them must have been of Jewish birth.

Evangelist

Following the martydom of Stephen and the persecution of Hellenistic Christians, Philip went to Samaria to preach to the people about the Messiah. 'And the multitudes with one accord gave heed to what was said by Philip, when they heard him and saw the signs which he did. For unclean spirits came out of many who were possessed, crying with a loud voice; and many who were paralysed or lame were healed. So there was much joy in that city.' (Acts 8:6-8)

Philip the Deacon became a successful evangelist, converting a magician called Simon. 'But when they believed Philip as he preached good news about the kingdom of God and the name of Jesus Christ, they were baptized, both men and women. Even Simon himself believed, and after being baptized he continued with Philip. And seeing signs and great miracles performed, he was amazed.' (Acts 8:12, 13) Philip's evangelistic efforts were confirmed by a visit from the Apostles Peter and John, as a result of which the Christians in Samaria were the first to receive the gift of the Holy Spirit by the 'laying on of hands with prayer'.

Philip is next described as intercepting the chariot of the chief treasurer of the queen of Ethiopia, on his way down from Jerusalem to Gaza. This court official was returning from a pilgrimage to the Holy City and was reading from the prophet Isaiah as he journeyed. Philip asked him if he knew about whom he was reading. The passage was from the Suffering Servant songs of the Second Isaiah: 'As a sheep led to the slaughter or a lamb before its shearer is dumb, so he opens not his mouth. In his humiliation justice was denied him. Who can describe his generation? For his life is taken up from the earth.' (Acts 8:32, 33) The man turned to Philip and asked, 'About whom, pray, does the prophet say this, about himself or about some one else?' Starting, therefore, with this text of scripture, Philip 'told him the good news of Jesus'. Further along the road, the Ethiopian was baptized by Philip at his own request. Later 'Philip was found at Azotus, and passing on he preached the gospel to all the towns till he came to Caesarea.' (Acts 8:40)

In about the year 58, it was at Caesarea that Paul and Luke were entertained by Philip and his four daughters, on Paul's final and fateful journey to Jerusalem. Certainly Philip and Paul had much in common, particularly their purpose in presenting the gospel of Jesus to the Gentiles. As with Philip the Apostle, traditions concerning the later life of this Philip are conflicting, but it is likely that he became a bishop in Lydia, the northern district of Asia Minor. [Acts 6:5; 8:5-40; 21:8]

3. Philip the Tetrarch *see* HEROD PHILIP

PHILIPPIANS The first European Christian community was founded in the year 50 by the Apostle Paul on his Second Journey, and was to receive from him a letter written some years later in prison at either Ephesus or Rome.

Luke and Philippi

Sailing from Troas to Neapolis via Samothrace, Paul and his companions arrived for the first time at Philippi. His companions were Silas, Timothy, and Luke, whose narrative at this point in Acts 16 suddenly changes from 'they' to 'we', implying that Luke the chronicler actually joined the party at Troas. When Paul sailed back from Philippi to Troas some five years later, returning to Jerusalem at the close of his Third Journey, Luke's narrative again resumes the first person plural, the 'we' section, which continues right back to Jerusalem. It is not therefore unlikely that Luke — though perhaps by birth a Syrian of Antioch — lived for some years at Troas or Philippi. At that time, too, there was at Philippi an excellent school of medicine, at which Luke the physician may have received his training. Certainly his detailed and vivid description of the events of Paul's first visit to Philippi is as graphic as any other passage in the Acts.

Luke's account reflects a touch of civic pride in what he calls 'Philippi, which is the leading city of the district of Macedonia, and a Roman colony'. The city, founded by Philip of Macedon, father of Alexander the Great, in the 4th century BC, had been built upon an ancient and strategic site near some gold-mines. It was near by that Octavius and Mark Antony defeated the forces of Brutus and Cassius in the year 42 BC, following the murder of Julius Caesar. Philippi had become a military centre of communication with the famous Via Egnatia, linking the Adriatic with the Aegean, passing through the centre of the city, whose inhabitants were very conscious of their Roman colonial status. Indeed, the population would have included many Latin-speaking Italian

451

veterans. Today, the ruins of Philippi and the military highway are still to be found eight miles northwest of the modern Kavalla, once the port of Neapolis.

Paul at Philippi

Paul found few Jews and no synagogue at Philippi. There was, however, a devout woman called Lydia, from the town of Thyatira in Asia Minor, who was in the purple-dye trade. When Paul and his companions were praying and preaching outside the gates of the city by the riverside, on the Sabbath, Lydia accepted Paul's witness and was converted. She and her household were baptized and insisted on the visitors going to stay in her house. It was to this Christian community in Philippi that Paul wrote later, when in prison, a letter full of happiness, gratitude, affection, and reassurance – reflecting little bitterness for the rough treatment he and Silas had received at Philippi, being arrested, beaten, and imprisoned without trial. (*see also* PAUL for the events during his Second Journey and visit to Philippi.)

An earlier letter?

Until this century, it was not doubted that this letter was, together with the other 'captivity epistles' – Colossians, Philemon, Ephesians, Timothy, and Titus – written from Rome, particularly in view of Paul's reference in this letter to both his imprisonment and his expected release. Lately, however, it has been pointed out that this letter has far more in common with Paul's earlier letters, reflecting the same problems in his Jewish relationship as are found in Galatians, and the same mood of danger and emergency to be found in 2 Corinthians.

A good argument for the writing of the letter from Ephesus is the amount of traffic implied between Philippi and the place of writing. Paul sends Timothy and expects him to return with news from Philippi. He plans to send Epaphroditus back to Philippi as soon as his recovery from illness is complete. If Paul were writing in Rome, it would be 850 miles and a month's journey one way to Philippi. Yet Paul expects Timothy to complete the return trip between the giving of the verdict and his possible execution. 'Even if I am to be poured as a libation upon the sacrificial offering of your faith, I am glad and rejoice with you all. Likewise you also should be glad and rejoice with me. I hope in the Lord Jesus to send Timothy to you soon, so that I may be cheered by news of you.' (Phil. 2:17-19) 'I hope therefore to send him just as soon as I see how it will go with me; and I trust in the Lord that shortly I myself shall come also.' (Phil. 2:23, 24) On the other hand, from Ephesus to Philippi is 250 miles and less than a week's journey. So we might perhaps conclude that the letter to Philippi was sent from Ephesus in the year 56 or 57, rather than from Rome some years later.

Anxiety at Philippi

Epaphroditus had brought a gift of money from Philippi to help Paul, and although Paul appears to have acknowledged it the Philippians had written again, perhaps displeased with what they considered a lack of appreciation. Paul's letter, which we have, in his reply to their second communication. Epaphroditus has been unwell and is anxious to return home, so Paul plans to send him as the bearer of the letter and explains why Epephroditus is returning. Paul knows the anxiety at Philippi for his own welfare and assures his friends there that he will send news soon by Timothy, if indeed he does not come himself.

453

The basic reason for writing, however, is to encourage the Philippians, themselves under persecution, to unity and steadfastness in their faith. Although Paul is himself in prison and apparently awaiting trial for his very life, yet his letter is full of happy confidence, affection, and reassurance. The words 'joy' and 'rejoice' occur no less than fourteen times within the four brief chapters of this letter, which must have given great comfort to its readers – besides some truly inspiring insights into Christian truth.

Unity in humility

What more beautiful expression of confidence could there be than Paul's opening greeting? 'I thank my God in all my remembrance of you, always in every prayer of mine for you all making my prayer with joy, thankful for your partnership in the gospel from the first day until now. And I am sure that he who began a good work in you will bring it to completion at the day of Jesus Christ.' (Phil. 1:3-6) What more sincere expression of his affection than this? 'For God is my witness, how I yearn for you all with the affection of Christ Jesus. And it is my prayer that your love may abound more and more, with knowledge and all discernment, so that you may approve what is excellent, and may be pure and blameless for the day of Christ.' (Phil. 1:8-10)

It seems that there are two parties within the Christian community of the city in which he is imprisoned. The one is inspired to speak out by his example and courage. The other is concerned to speak out in order to bring down even more trouble on Paul in his captivity. 'What then?' asks Paul. 'Only that in every way, whether in pretence or in truth, Christ is proclaimed;

and in that I rejoice.' (Phil. 1:18) Then his anxiety gets the better of his good spirits: 'I am hard pressed between the two,' he says. 'My desire is to depart and to be with Christ, for that is far better. But to remain in the flesh is more necessary on your account.' (Phil. 1:23-24)

Perhaps the most uplifting passage is his plea for unity in humility. 'Have this mind among yourselves, which you have in Christ Jesus, who, though he was in the form of God, did not count equality with God a thing to be grasped, but emptied himself, taking the form of a servant, being born in the likeness of men. And being found in human form he humbled himself and became obedient unto death, even death on a cross. Therefore God has highly exalted him and bestowed on him the name which is above every name, that at the name of Jesus every knee should bow, in heaven and on earth and under the earth, and every tongue confess that Jesus Christ is Lord, to the glory of God the Father.' (Phil. 2:5-11)

Then, incensed with those Judaizers who insisted on circumcision in addition to Christian baptism, Paul roundly declares, 'Look out for the dogs, look out for the evil-workers, look out for those who mutilate the flesh. For we are the true circumcision, who worship God in spirit, and glory in Christ Jesus, and put no confidence in the flesh. Though I myself have reason for confidence in the flesh also. If any other man thinks he has reason for confidence in the flesh, I have more: circumcised on the eighth day, of the people of Israel, of the tribe of Benjamin, a Hebrew born of Hebrews; as to the law a Pharisee, as to zeal a persecutor of the church, as to righteousness under the law blameless. But whatever gain I had, I counted as loss for the sake of

Christ. Indeed I count everything as loss because of the surpassing worth of knowing Christ Jesus my Lord. For his sake I have suffered the loss of all things, and count them as refuse, in order that I may gain Christ.' (Phil. 3:2-8)

It is a remarkably turbulent letter, as Paul's equilibrium is upset by some sudden provocation or anxiety added to the strain of his captivity. Yet he always seems to recover his tranquility. 'Therefore, my brethren, whom I love and long for, my joy and crown, stand firm thus in the Lord, my beloved. . . . Rejoice in the Lord always; again I will say, Rejoice. Let all men know your forbearance. The Lord is at hand. Have no anxiety about anything, but in everything by prayer and supplication with thanksgiving let your requests be made known to God. And the peace of God, which passes all understanding, will keep your hearts and your minds in Christ Jesus.' (Phil. 4:1, 4-7) [Phil. 1-4]

PHILOLOGUS (Gk. 'fond of learning) One of the Christians greeted by Paul at the close of his letter to the Church in Rome. Philologus is linked with the name of Julia, perhaps his wife, in a group or household of five, 'and all the saints who are with them'. Both names were common among Roman slaves. [Rom. 16:15]

PHLEGON (Gk. 'burning') The second of a list of five men, mentioned in a special greeting from Paul at the close of his letter to the Church in Rome. Perhaps Phlegon, his fellows, and 'the brethren who are with them' formed a household or small group within the larger Christian community. [Rom. 16:14]

PHOEBE (Gk. 'bright', 'radiant') 'Our sister Phoebe', as Paul called her, was the bearer of his letter to the Church in Rome, from her home town Corinth. She was in fact a deaconess or church-worker in the port of Cenchreae, on the east side of the Corinthian isthmus which faces the Aegean.

Paul asks for a special welcome to be given her 'in the Lord', and a 'welcome as befits the saints', and to help her with anything she needs. For Phoebe had been of great service both to Paul individually and to the Church as a whole.

The terms in which Paul speaks of Phoebe and her patronage indicate that she was of some wealth and social position within the community, as well as of some importance within the local congregation. [Rom. 16:1]

PHYGELUS A Christian disciple who, with Hermogenes and others in Asia, deserted Paul on his last arrest, perhaps at Troas and through the betrayal of Alexander the coppersmith. The last letter to Timothy conceals the drama of Paul's disastrous departure from Asia and arrival under arrest in Rome where, already convicted, he awaits execution. Many Asian Christians, under the threat of arrest for their association with Paul, simply did not manage to remain loyal. Among these, Paul mentioned by name those whose desertion represented the greatest disappointment, and particularly Phygelus and Hermogenes. [2 Tim. 1:15]

PILATE, PONTIUS Pontius Pilate was the fifth Roman procurator of Judea, Samaria, and Idumea, governing from the year 26 to 36, during which time he was officially responsible for the condemnation of Jesus on a charge of sedition, to be crucified in about the year 30. A good deal is known about Pilate, not just from the four Gospels, but from the contemporary Jewish secular historians Josephus and Philo, and also from the 4th-century Church historian Eusebius.

The name 'Pontius' was his family name and he came from a Roman family. The name 'Pilate' from the Latin *pilatus* means a 'pikeman', or one armed with the *pilum* or javelin. There are several legends about his origin, of which one is that he was the bastard son of Tyrus, king of Mainz, and was sent to Rome. There, so the story runs, he committed murder and was exiled to Pontus in Asia Minor, where he made good and was rewarded with the governorship of Judea. It is far more likely, however, that as the son of an eminent Roman family he underwent the usual diplomatic training, succeeding through other minor posts to the procuratorship of Judea – not a very coveted appointment in any case, and directly responsible to the emperor himself.

On his appointment in the year 26, some three years before the crucifixion of Jesus, he was about the same age as Jesus, in his early thirties. He was a proud, hot-tempered, obstinate and aristocratic young man, capable of childish behaviour when his will was crossed and as military-minded as his name suggests. His official residence was at the Roman port and colonial city of Caesarea on the Mediterranean coastline. At Jewish festivals and other potential emergencies, however, the procurator 'stood to' with his troops in Jerusalem – particularly at the time of Passover, when riots were frequent. Over all but Roman citizens the procurator's power was absolute. As one who had only recently reached the governorship, he was determined to make a success of it, and to keep the notoriously turbulent and nationalistic Jews in order.

His wife was Claudia Procula, granddaughter of the Emperor Augustus and illegitimate daughter of Claudia, third wife of the Emperor Tiberius. She was a princess royal, sophisticated, cultured, and sensitive. Perhaps it was through her that Pilate got this particular appointment, rather than for his diplomatic tact. The governors

458

of Judea did not usually get permission to take their wives, and although many women would have welcomed an excuse to stay in the comfort and society of Rome, Claudia was with him even in Jerusalem.

Events in Pilate's life before his appearance in the Gospels illustrate his character and capabilities. When he arrived in Judea, he discovered that there was no statue of the Roman emperor in Jerusalem. In fact it was the only city within the empire where people did not bow to the emperor's statue in the city square. Consequently, Pilate, concerned only to maintain the authority of Rome rather than to understand the outlook and problems of the Jews, decided to make an impression. When he entered Jerusalem for the first time, the Roman soldiers marched into the city with their images of the emperor on their standards. For the Roman with a dozen gods, this was one thing; for the Jew who believed in only one God, who did not allow graven images even of himself, this was an outrage. The Emperor Augustus had previously promised to grant Jerusalem immunity from such demands of the imperial cult. Having reached the Roman fortress, Pilate ordered the images to be put up on the walls facing down into the Temple, and returned himself to Caesarea. If the Jews attacked the fortress, he thought, they could be punished for revolt.

Outwitted by the high priest

Pilate, however, was a child in cunning compared with the high priest Caiaphas. The next day Jews streamed out of the city on their way down to Caesarea. They gathered others as they went and arrived 7,000 strong to surround Pilate's procuratorial residence. Pilate refused to listen to their deputation. For a whole week, the

7,000 picketed the palace, and every time Pilate emerged it was to find thousands of Jews at prayer for his own soul. At last his nerve was broken, and he gave orders for the Jews to gather in the *Agora* or market-place, where he would speak to them. Meanwhile his troops surrounded the square prepared to butcher the gathering crowd. The Jews, however, soon grasped the situation and, preferring to die than to suffer the images overlooking the Temple, they knelt down and waited, but the order was never given for the massacre and Pilate was humiliated.

A second incident showed a similar lack of sympathy on Pilate's part. He never met the demands of the Jews until their protests threatened to end in violence, likely to be reported back to Rome and thus endanger his own position. On this occasion, Pilate wanted to provide a fresh water-supply for Jerusalem by constructing in the grand manner an aqueduct to carry water six miles from some ancient reservoirs to the south of Jerusalem, beyond Bethlehem. The problem was not one of engineering so much as of the necessary funds. Pilate decided to raid the Temple treasury in order to finance the project. As each Jewish male paid three dollars or one guinea in Temple tax each year, there was a general uproar. Pilate sent his troops in plain clothes and armed with cudgels to suppress the riot, and himself gave the agreed signal for action. Thousands were trodden to death in the resulting panic and a very lurid account of the incident reached Rome. No doubt it was the high priest's intelligence and information service that procured for Pilate a very severe reprimand from Rome on this occasion.

Pilate's aqueduct is still to be seen following the contours of the hillsides, its stone vertebrae still showing signs of a lining with lead and lime mortar.

There is yet another incident, briefly mentioned by Luke (13:1), of Pilate's responsibility for the killing of some Galileans, when they were actually offering sacrifice in the Temple. In spite of such lapses into violence, Pilate must have been a strong and able administrator, for he remained ten years in office, while his four predecessors had governed only twenty years between them. Philo in fact describes Pilate as 'inflexible, merciless and obstinate' – not quite the impression given in the Gospels, where he appears as the pawn of Caiaphas. Both these aspects of his character can be reconciled, for the trial of Jesus took place in only the third year of his appointment, and his frustration and consequent lack of mercy appears to have progressively increased. He was not supported in his attitude by an imperial decree in the year 36, imposing a policy of greater tolerance and consideration towards Jews throughout the Roman Empire. As a result of this, he had to acquiesce to a demand from the Pharisees to remove the golden shields of portraits of the emperor and others, which had for years adorned the walls of Herod's citadel.

Soon after this further humiliation, Pilate made his final and fatal mistake. A crowd of Samaritans gathered for a religious ceremony on Mount Gerizim, their traditional place of sacrifice. Pilate interpreted their religious unrest as an act of revolt and brutally wiped out a neighbouring village in reprisal. The Samaritans complained to Vitellius, the Roman legate of Syria, and, as a result, Pilate was summoned to Antioch, examined, ordered to return to Rome, and finally exiled from Italy.

The term 'praetorium' is the name of the judicial seat of
the Roman governor or praetor at any given moment.
He established his praetorium simply by hanging his
shield at the gate and posting his tribune on guard,
whether in Jerusalem or Caesarea, at Herod's Palace or
at the Antonia Fortress.

A Hasmonean fort once stood to the west of the
Temple area to protect it from assault. Here Herod
built a vast fortress with the triple purpose not of pro-
tecting the Temple so much as suppressing riots and
preserving order within the Temple courtyards, and
securing the external defence of the city at its most vul-
nerable point. The fact that he called it after Mark Antony, the Roman conqueror of Syria and Palestine,
indicates his true purpose – that the Antonia should
successfully muzzle Jerusalem and her Jewish life. As
Josephus, the contemporary Jewish historian, said, 'The
city was dominated by the Temple and the Temple by
the Antonia.'

Less than a hundred years ago, the Dominican ar-
chaeologist Père Vincent described the fortress thus:
'This gigantic quadrilateral, cut almost entirely out of
the rocky hill, covered an area of 150 metres east to
west, by 80 metres north to south. It was protected by
powerful corner towers and enclosed installations as
complex and diverse as a palace and camp. The outstanding but characteristic feature of this complex was,
without doubt, the courtyard, about 2,500 metres
square, serving as a place of meeting between the city
and the Antonia. Extending over deep water-cisterns,
covered with a massive polished pavement, surrounded
by tall cloisters, this courtyard was really the heart of

the fortress whose activity it regulated. . . . Pilate had his tribunal set up within the courtyard, transformed for the occasion into the Praetorium, called indeed the "Pavement" *par excellence*. Where could one find more explicit evidence, more expressive and appropriate a setting for the place where Pilate pronounced the sentence which sent Jesus on his way to Calvary?'

Leaving the high priest's palace, prisoner and escort, followed by the crowd, must have passed on over the great viaduct across the Tyropoaen Valley. They must have left the city by the 'Fish Gate' and climbed the steep slope which ran alongside the ramparts of the north wall, to appear before the great double gate of the Antonia. The vast fortress, defended by a moat and scarp from the open country beyond, had its main gate outside the city wall, as though fearing less from without than within the city walls. And with good reason too, for though it dominated the Temple area, it was from here that trouble could be expected. Within the four corners of the great fortress, crammed with troops at such a time as Passover, Pilate had his own procurator's quarters in a little central tower facing down on to the Pavement.

To water thousands in a fortress often under siege must have demanded a phenomenal supply. This was yet another function of the Pavement, whose water runnels still lead down into the cavernous vaults below, where cistern-tops yet bear the marks of lock and chain, and whose counter-weights and pulleys are still to be seen.

On to this Pavement prisoner and escort proceeded, while the crowd, for fear of defilement before Passover, crammed by the thousand into the great double gateway. Pilate, seated in his curial chair at the head of his private stairway, must have gazed down upon the Pavement in disgust, having blotted his colonial copybook more than once and knowing himself to be outwitted by Caiaphas.

At the trial of Jesus

There are three rather different accounts of the trial of Jesus. Mark's version is closely followed by Matthew and is probably the earliest account, based on the memories of the Apostle Peter and published some thirty years after the event. This account reflects the undeniable fact that Jesus was convicted by the Roman authority, represented by Pilate. This fact was of some embarrassment to Christian propaganda throughout the Roman Empire. Morally the account holds the Jewish Sanhedrin and Caiaphas responsible, but the form of execution of the punishment was Roman and therefore the responsibility of Pilate.

After a second meeting of the Sanhedrin, early on the Friday morning, Jesus was bound and brought to Pilate. He was charged not with blasphemy, for which he had been sentenced by the Sanhedrin, but with the treason of claiming to be 'the King of the Jews'. 'And Pilate asked him, "Are you the King of the Jews?" And he answered him, "You have said so." And the chief priests accused him of many things. And Pilate again asked him, "Have you no answer to make? See how many charges they bring against you." But Jesus made no further answer, so that Pilate wondered.' (Mark 15:2-5)

To Pilate, Jesus's case appeared similar to that of Barabbas, another agitator with a more violent record; therefore he offered to release Jesus, who was seemingly a popular favourite. The crowd, swayed by the Sanhedrin, demanded the release of Barabbas and the crucifixion of Jesus. 'And Pilate said to them, "Why, what evil has he done?" but they shouted all the more, "Crucify him." So Pilate, wishing to satisfy the crowd, released for them Barabbas; and having scourged Jesus, he delivered him to be crucified.' (Mark 15:14, 15)

There is no further mention of Pilate in Mark's account, which throws little light on the feelings and motives of Pilate. He might have been expected to dismiss the case, without adequate evidence or cause for conviction. The prisoner silently refuses to refute the charge. Pilate, seemingly aware of the falseness of the accusation of treason, the 'envy' of the high priests and the insincerity of the people, yet delivered Jesus to be scourged and crucified. The writer is in fact more concerned with the purposeful progress of Jesus through his passion than with the characters of any of the personalities responsible.

Luke's version is noticeably different and he may have had access to an earlier and more accurate source than Mark. Writing, as he was, to the Roman aristocrat Theophilus, Luke tried to show that Rome – represented by Pilate – was responsible neither for the conviction nor the crucifixion of Jesus.

The threefold charge before Pilate is very specific: 'And they began to accuse him, saying, "We found this man perverting our nation, and forbidding us to give tribute to Caesar, and saying that he himself is Christ a king."' (Luke 23:2) However convinced of the innocence of the prisoner, Pilate could not disregard so detailed a charge of treason against the state. After some cross-examination of the prisoner, 'Pilate said to the chief priests and the multitudes, "I find no crime in this

465

man." But they were urgent, saying, "He stirs up the people, teaching throughout all Judea, from Galilee even to this place." ' (Luke 23:4, 5)

Hearing that Jesus was a Galilean, Pilate grasped his opportunity to pass the prisoner over to Herod Antipas, who happened to be in his castle at Jerusalem for the Passover festival. Herod, however, was more aware of the political and ecclesiastical issues involved in the case than was Pilate, and after making a fool of the prisoner, returned him to Pilate. Luke thus attributes the mocking of Jesus to the soldiers of Herod rather than those under Pilate's command.

Pilate, now faced with a second trial, attempted for the second time to acquit the prisoner. 'Pilate then called together the chief priests and the rulers and the people, and said to them, "You brought me this man as one who was perverting the people; and after examining him before you, behold, I did not find this man guilty of any of your charges against him; neither did Herod, for he sent him back to us. Behold, nothing deserving death has been done by him; I will therefore chastise him and release him." But they all cried out together, "Away with this man, and release to us Barabbas." ' (Luke 23:13-18)

When the crowd called for the release of Barabbas and the crucifixion of Jesus, 'He said to them, "Why, what evil has he done? I have found in him no crime deserving death; I will therefore chastise him and release him." . . . And their voices prevailed. So Pilate gave sentence that their demand should be granted.' (Luke 23:22-24) Luke makes no mention of a scourging and places the blame for Pilate's forced conviction of the prisoner, despite his threefold attempt at reprieve, firmly on Caiaphas and the Sanhedrin. Luke's portrait

466

of Pilate is that of a humane judge, unable to resist the pressure of the angry and riotous crowds.

John's version, though published at the end of the 1st century, after the death of Peter and almost all the others involved, is completely fresh and independent of the other accounts. How John got the record of the case before Pilate no one can tell; perhaps one of the officials told him, or even Pilate's wife, Procula; perhaps he himself risked ceremonial defilement before the Passover, entered the fortress, and heard the trial himself. Certainly John's account is beyond the art of fiction and carries the hallmark of truth, not least in its portrayal of the character of Pilate and particularly in his personal interrogation of the prisoner.

John's topography of the praetorium and the *Gabbatha,* or Pavement, is easily understood. Because Caiaphas and the Sanhedrin feared ritual defilement before the Passover, they refused to enter on to the Pavement, but waited in the great double gateway. It was as John says, 'early' – something before six o'clock – and Pilate was thus forced to go out and deal with them in the chill of the morning air. He would be uncomfortably reminded of religious scruples with which he felt scant sympathy. He demanded the written charge: 'What accusation do you bring against this man?' and was bluntly told: 'If this man were not an evildoer, we would not have handed him over.' In other words, the case had already been tried in their court and they were merely asking for the death-sentence to be confirmed. 'Pilate said to them, "Take him yourselves and judge him by your own law." The Jews said to him, "It is not lawful for us to put any man to death." ' (John 18:31)

No doubt, irritated by such a clumsy attempt to steam-roller him, Pilate insisted on hearing the full case.

Then he went inside and up into his private apartments in the central tower, followed by the prisoner now escorted by Romans. Pilate was unlikely perhaps to have been prepared to receive a prisoner quite so early in the morning, unless Caiaphas had warned him the night before of the nature and urgency of the case. Pilate would be expecting a charge of sedition and a prisoner capable of leading a dangerous revolt. He must have been surprised at the quiet figure before him, for he said 'Are you the King of the Jews?' ['Are you the Jewish Messiah?'] And the somewhat unconvincing rebel, Jesus, answered, 'Do you say this of your own accord, or did others say it to you about me?'

Then, with all the scorn and contempt of Rome for a subject race, 'Pilate answered, "Am I a Jew? Your own nation and the chief priests have handed you over to me; what have you done?"' (John 18:35) Vigorously, 'Jesus answered, "My kingship is not of this world; if my kingship were of this world, my servants would fight, that I might not be handed over to the Jews; but my kingship is not from the world."' (John 18:36) In other words: 'My kingdom does not belong to your kind of world.' Not surprisingly, Pilate could make nothing of that, except that somehow the prisoner was admitting to being a king and thus pleading 'guilty'. 'Pilate said to him, "So you are a king?" Jesus answered, "You say that I am a king. For this I was born, and for this I have come into the world, to bear witness to the truth. Every one who is of the truth hears my voice."' (John 18:37) However exasperated Pilate was by such a seemingly irrelevant and abstract answer, he must have grasped the utter harmlessness, if not the sincerity, of the prisoner.

Aware now that the case was being fradulently pre-

468

sented and that he was expected to act as a destructive tool of the Sanhedrin, he looked for a means of escape. He suggested the offer of the customary Passover amnesty; but he had forgotten Barabbas. 'He went out to the Jews again and told them, "I find no crime in him. But you have a custom that I should release one man for you at the Passover; will you have me release for you the King of the Jews?" They cried out again, "Not this man, but Barabbas!" Now Barabbas was a robber.' (John 18:39, 40)

Foiled in his purpose by the Barabbas fiasco, fearing the gathering crowd, Pilate had to think again. Here, Luke introduced the Herod episode as an abortive attempt by Pilate to escape from giving judgment. Perhaps it was the return of the prisoner in his mock regalia from Herod that suggested Pilate's next move. Pilate saw that he must do something to conciliate the Sanhedrin and invite the sympathy of the crowd. Therefore, in the hope of avoiding the death sentence, Pilate had the prisoner scourged. The scourge was a 'cat-o-nine-tails' loaded with crude pellets of lead and bone. The place of the scourging cannot now be known, but it probably took place in view of the people on the Pavement and at a column or post designed and used for the purpose.

After the scourging, John describes how the soldiers took him to their guardroom or quarters, before returning him to Pilate. It was in the guardroom that they had their opportunity to vent their detestation, as occupation forces, upon this representative of a subject race who had called himself a king. Just how they did so is well illustrated by carvings in the Pavement at the foot of the troops' stairways. Among a variety of knuckle-boards and hopscotch designs covering several flagstones, there are the following signs: the 'B' for Basilicus, meaning 'King', a rough and prickly crown, and finally a sabre. This is evidence of a game called 'King', described by Plautus as derived from the Saturnalia, in which a burlesque king is chosen, mockingly honoured and saluted, before being killed. So, in the crucifixion squad, each soldier would adopt as his stake one of the condemned prisoners. The winner in the game of bones would crown his own 'stake' with a crown of thorns in a mocking guardroom ceremony. The king, thus crowned, would receive his soldier's homage, his swagger-stick as a sceptre and his military cloak as a royal robe. All the guardroom would hail him *'Basilicus Judaiorum!'* This indeed gives meaning to the Gospel account of the mocking.

When the prisoner was returned to Pilate in a condition to draw pity from the crowd, Pilate presented him, with the words *'Ecce Homo!'* – 'Behold the Man!' – or more contemptuously perhaps, 'See, here the fellow is!' He had, however, underestimated the determination and cunning of Caiaphas, as he must have realized when the crowd still demanded the death penalty. In his frustration and annoyance, Pilate once again attempted to 'pass the buck': 'Take him yourselves and crucify him, for I find no crime in him.' This finally stung the Sanhedrin into stating their real case against the prisoner, for which they had themselves convicted him of blasphemy. 'The Jews answered him, "We have a law, and by that law he ought to die, because he has made himself the Son of God." When Pilate heard these words, he was the more afraid.' (John 19:7, 8)

Once again entering the praetorium, Pilate attempted to re-examine the prisoner, who had just been brutally scourged. His sudden fear may have been due to his growing apprehension that his prisoner was perhaps out of the ordinary. The sceptic had become perplexed and superstitious; he wished to test the prisoner's claim to divine origin: 'Where are you from?' But the prisoner remained silent. When Pilate reminded him of his procuratorial power of life and death, the prisoner calmly rejected both Pilate's authority and indeed Pilate's significance in the situation. 'Jesus answered him, "You would have no power over me unless it had been given you from above; therefore he who delivered me to you has the greater sin." ' (John 19:11) The real issue was between the prisoner and Caiaphas, in whose hands Pilate was merely a tool.

The truth of this was clearly shown within the next and final moments of this so-called trial. Pilate, more than ever convinced of the prisoner's innocence and harmlessness, once again went out to the crowd. But before he could even speak the Jews 'yelled' (the literal translation): ' "If you release this man, you are not Caesar's friend; every one who makes himself a king sets himself against Caesar." When Pilate heard these words, he brought Jesus out and sat down on the judgment seat at a place called The Pavement, and in Hebrew, *Gabbatha*. Now it was the day of Preparation of the Passover; it was about the sixth hour. He said to the Jews, "Here is your King!" They cried out, "Away with him, away with him, crucify him!" Pilate said to them, "Shall I crucify your King?" The chief priests answered, "We have no king but Caesar." ' (John 19:12-15)

Outmanoeuvred by a people whom he had not even begun to understand, his already precarious reputation in Rome dangerously threatened, deafened by the clamorous blood-lust of the crowd, Pilate's resistance collapsed. He signed the death warrant and handed the prisoner over for crucifixion. Perhaps he gained some revenge by his choice of words in the title nailed to the cross of Jesus in Hebrew, Latin and Greek: 'Jesus of Nazareth, the king of the Jews'.

'The chief priests of the Jews then said to Pilate, "Do not write, 'The King of the Jews', but, 'This man said, I am the King of the Jews.'" ' Pilate answered, "What I have written I have written." ' (John 19:21-22) Perhaps he felt some slight compensation in later granting the prisoner's corpse a decent burial.

Various traditions relate the execution of Pilate by Nero, his banishment to Vienne, his taking of his own life. The Abyssinian Church has made a saint of him. The Apostles' Creed has branded him throughout the universal Church by the words describing Jesus as 'crucified also for us under Pontius Pilate'. [Matt. 27; Mark 15; Luke 3:1; 13:1; 23:1-52; John 18, 19; Acts 3:13; 4:27; 13:28; 1 Tim. 6:13]

PORCIUS FESTUS (Gk. 'festal', 'joyful') *see* FESTUS

PRISCA (Gk. from the Lat. 'ancient') *see* AQUILA

PRISCILLA (Gk. from the Lat. 'ancient') *see* AQUILA

PROCHORUS (Gk. 'leader of the chorus') *see* NICO-LAUS

PUBLICANS (Lat. 'civil servants') *see* TAX-COLLECTORS

PUBLIUS The 'chief man', a Greek term for a high official on the island of Malta, who received and entertained Paul and the ship's company for three days, on the occasion of their shipwreck in the autumn of the year 60, during the voyage to Rome, where Paul was to appear before the imperial tribunal.

Near their place of landing on the rocky coastline, traditionally called St Paul's Bay, Publius owned an estate and offered them hospitality there. It so happened that the father of Publius was laid up with fever and dysentery, so Paul visited him and prayed over him, then, putting his hands on him, healed him. Other islanders consequently brought their sick to be cured and in return gave Paul presents. The following spring, after the entire company had wintered on the island, Julius, the centurion in charge of the escort, put his prisoners on another Alexandrian ship, bound for Puteoli on the Italian coast south of Rome. [Acts 28:7, 8]

PUDENS (Gk. 'modest') One of the four who sent their personal greetings at the close of Paul's final letter to Timothy in Ephesus, perhaps the last he ever wrote. From the grouping of the names, Pudens may well have been the husband of Claudia and father of Linus. Paul is writing from prison, presumably in Rome, after his conviction, and expecting execution. This family, not elsewhere mentioned in the New Testament, may have ministered to the final needs of Paul, along with the 'beloved physician', Luke, Paul's fellow-prisoner to the end. [2 Tim. 4:21]

PYRRHUS (Gk. 'fiery red') The father of Sopater of Beroea, near Thessalonica in Macedonia. Sopater was one of the representatives chosen to accompany Paul on his return to Jerusalem with the poor-relief collection from the various Christian Mediterranean communities. Fearing an ambush if he travelled via Corinth, Paul travelled overland through Macedonia, in the spring of a year around 58, as far as Troas on the coast of Asia Minor and so by sea to Caesarea and Jerusalem, with an escort of seven men, of whom the first, and perhaps the leader, was Sopater, son of Pyrrhus. [Acts 20:4]

Q

QUARTUS (Gk. from the Lat. 'fourth') A Christian in
Corinth who asked to send greetings to the Church in
Rome, at the close of Paul's letter to that congregation.
His name is the last among a long list of greetings and is
linked with those of Gaius and Erastus. An ancient tradition also lists him among the seventy early disciples,
whom Jesus sent out two by two, during his Galilean
ministry (Luke 10:1). [Rom. 16:23]

QUIRINIUS Governor of Syria, according to Luke, at
the time of the enrolment decreed by Caesar Augustus,
which compelled Joseph and Mary to register at his
family town Bethlehem, where Jesus was born.

Luke's efforts to record the exact date and circumstances of the birth of Jesus do not seem in complete
accord with the historical facts. It was not Roman custom to decree a census throughout the whole empire,
but for taxation purposes a particular province might be
enrolled, under the arrangements of the governor of
that province. The first Roman census of Palestine did
in fact take place in AD 6, on the occasion of Judea
being incorporated into the Roman province of Syria,
which was on the occasion of the dismissal of Archelaus
and his replacement by a Roman procurator. This Roman type of census and the subsequent degree of taxation appear to have been a new and bitter experience
for the Jews, for it aroused enormous resentment and a
revolt led by Judas of Gamala, cruelly suppressed by
the Roman authority. At that time, in AD 6, Quirinius
was indeed governor of Syria and possibly Luke may

have thought that the birth of Jesus coincided with that census.

On the other hand, Luke dates the early ministry of John the Baptist as the fifteenth year of the Emperor Tiberius, who only succeeded Augustus in AD 14. So Luke dates the beginning of both John and Jesus's ministries and calling of the disciples in the year 29. If Jesus was born in AD 6, he would have begun his ministry at about the age of 23, which seems too young. Matthew, however, states that Herod the Great was ruler at Jerusalem at the birth of Jesus and at the time of the slaughter of the innocents, perhaps up to two years later. As Herod the Great died in 4 BC, this could mean that Jesus was born between 6 and 4 BC. By Luke's reckoning, he would then have been about 33 years old at the start of his ministry.

It is, of course, possible that Herod conducted his own census in the last year or so of his reign, and that Luke muddled this with a Roman census in the time of Quirinius, AD 6-9. An Egyptian papyrus from AD 104 includes an ordinance for such a census. The presence of the woman was also required, in order to ascertain the number in each family. [Luke 2:2]

R

RHODA (Gk. 'rose') The servant-girl who acted as portress at the house of Mary the mother of John Mark in Jerusalem, and who recognized the voice of the Apostle Peter outside the door, but in her surprise and joy failed to let him in.

Herod Agrippa, in a personal persecution of the infant Christian Church, had already executed James the brother of John, and now had Peter arrested with the intention of presenting him to the Jews after Passover. Peter was imprisoned under a strong guard of sixteen soldiers; meanwhile the little Christian community prayed hard for his release. The very night before his trial, Peter was miraculously led out of his cell and through the prison gates by an angel, who left him in the street outside. Only then did Peter quite grasp what had happened and said to himself, 'Now I am sure that the Lord has sent his angel and rescued me from the hand of Herod and from all that the Jewish people were expecting.' (Acts 12:11)

Peter at once made his way to Mary's house, the headquarters of the Christians on Mount Zion and the first synagogue of the Christian congregation. While they were at prayer within, Peter knocked on the door and Rhoda came to answer. Recognizing his voice, in her joy she did not open the door, but ran in to say that Peter was at the gate. 'They said to her, "You are mad." But she insisted that it was so. They said, "It is his angel!" But Peter continued knocking; and when they opened, they saw him and were amazed. But motioning to them with his hand to be silent, he described to them how the Lord had brought him out of the prison.' (Acts 12:15-17) [Acts 12:13]

ROMANS The Romans were the rulers of Palestine throughout the New Testament period and for many centuries to come. Throughout the lives of Jesus and Paul, the Romans remain for the most part a power in the background, which emerges to dispense justice with a terrifying certainty. It was the Roman occupation forces who, as a matter of historical fact, crucified Jesus and, after long imprisonment, despatched Paul for trial to Rome. It was the Romans who exiled John in a penal colony on the rocky island of Patmos. And it was in Rome that the headquarters of the Christian Church was to be established by the end of the 2nd century.

The Roman Empire was a highly important factor in the successful spread of Christianity during the 1st century. The *Pax Romana* – the law and order on land and sea – lent security to the travels of the first apostles. As the Jewish synagogue provided a means of access to the minds of religious people, both Jews and Gentiles, so too the colloquial Greek (*lingua franca*) of the Roman world facilitated the transmission of the gospel. Christianity was by the Romans long regarded as a form of Judaism and enjoyed the privileges accorded to Judaism since the days of Julius Caesar. It was not until the persecution of Christians by the Emperor Nero, from AD 64, that there was any great conflict between Christianity and the Roman state.

Roman rule in Palestine

Since the capture of Jerusalem by Pompey in the year 63 BC, the whole of Syria had become a part of the Roman Empire. When Julius Caesar was besieged by the Egyptians at Alexandria, he escaped largely owing to the support of Jewish troops despatched by Antipater, the father of Herod the Great. As a reward, Antipater was given Roman citizenship and became procurator of all Jewish territory in Syria. His sons became governors, Phasael in Judea and Herod in Galilee. Despite the murder of Caesar in 44 BC, the rise and fall of Antony, and the shift of power to Octavian, under whose august rule began the golden age of the *Pax Romana,* the family of Antipater remained in power. Herod extended his authority from Galilee to become tetrarch of all the Jewish

477

territories and, when in Rome in 40 BC, was appointed king of Judea.

With the help of a Roman army, he made himself master of Jerusalem in 37 BC. In spite of domestic tragedies and private crimes, Herod proved himself a great builder, a clever politician, and an able ruler – though unpredictable and unpopular to the end of his days. (*see* HEROD 3.)

On Herod's death, at his own wish his kingdom was partitioned among three of his surviving sons: Judea, Samaria and Idumea to Archelaus as ethnarch; Galilee and Perea to Antipas as tetrarch; Gaulanitis and Trachonitis to Philip. None of these, however, had the diplomacy of his father. Archelaus is mentioned in the 'birth stories' of the First Gospel as reigning in Judea on the return of Mary and Joseph from Egypt. He ruled for ten years, before being charged in Rome with misgovernment and banished to Gaul. He was replaced by a Roman procurator, under Augustus a three-year appointment but under Tiberius considerably longer, and in the case of Pontius Pilate ten years. Pilate presided at the trial of Jesus and condemned him to crucifixion. He was recalled to Rome on a charge of oppression, convicted and banished in the year 36. The procurators were subordinate to the Roman legates of Syria, of whom one, Quirinius, is mentioned by Luke. The procurators resided in the military base and port of Caesarea, and were in command of 3,000 mercenaries, of which one cohort was permanently stationed in Jerusalem.

In spite of the appointment of the Herodian rulers, from the dismissal of Archelaus it was the Roman procurator who wielded the greatest power. Though he commanded mainly mercenary troops, he could call for the legions stationed in Syria. The Jews retained the right to administer their Jewish Law through their Scribal courts and their supreme Council, the Sanhedrin, but they could not execute the death sentence. The procurators had power to bring about the appointment and dismissal of the high priests. They could deploy their troops to support the collection of oppressive taxes. They became progressively more tactless and ruthless in dealing with the fanatical opposition of their subjects. The main cause of friction between the Jewish people and their Roman masters, however, was a difference in ideals. The new, pagan, materialistic state-worship was bound to conflict with the ancient Jewish faith. However much the Jews appreciated Roman law and order, they could not stomach the loss of liberty involved in maintaining the *Pax Romana*. Hence the rising tide of nationalism and resentment against the Roman authority as controlling the Holy City and indirectly the Temple itself. The Romans did not understand the puritanical fanaticism of the Jews, who in turn regarded the Romans as enemies both of their state and their religion.

For the most part, the Roman governors and procurators aimed at honest and impartial treatment of the provincials within their territories, but they were apt to be rigid, unimaginative and unsympathetic with peoples they did not understand. They found it particularly difficult to accept the point of view of the Jews, whose instincts and whose whole existence were bound up with their religion. The Romans were accustomed to despise the oriental cults of the eastern Mediterranean, and they found little difficulty in superimposing the additional cult of emperor-worship, as a token of loyalty to the ruling power. Faced with the racial pride, the national tradition, and religious fanaticism of the Jews, the Romans tried to meet the situation with concessions. They officially waived the demand for sacrifice to the emperor. For the most part they respected the sanctity of Jerusalem, though certain procurators were less conciliatory than others. Because the country was small and, politically, seemingly insignificant, the procurators appointed were 'little men' drawn from a lower social order. Felix, who imprisoned Paul without judgment for two years, was the brother of a freed slave. Not one procurator carried an ancient Roman name and it is not surprising that they were unequal to their task.

Claudius tried the brief experiment of appointing a native Jewish prince, Agrippa, who only survived to rule three years, and was replaced by a procurator. Even Tacitus, the Roman historian, admits that the methods of the procurators were too much for the patience of the Jews and, in AD 66, the revolt began. After some initial guerrilla successes, resistance was systematically worn down by the Roman general Vespasian before he was acclaimed emperor by his troops at Caesarea and returned to Rome. It was his son Titus who invested and besieged Jerusalem, burned the Temple, and destroyed the city in AD 70.

The gospel message and the whole life of Jesus are to be seen against a background of Roman military occupation and seething revolt. Only in the passion narratives is this political situation made explicitly clear, but there are various implications in earlier events. Jesus told his hearers in the Sermon on the Mount to be prepared to go a second mile with those who could compel them to go one mile. He was referring to the Roman soldier, who had the right to compel any native countryman to carry his military pack. Luke describes how Jesus was told about Galileans 'whose blood Pilate had mingled with their sacrifices' – thus implying the putting-down by the Romans of some petty revolt over the time of a Jewish festival. John describes the fear of the priests and Pharisees who said about Jesus, 'If we permit him to act thus the Romans will come and destroy both our Holy Place [the Temple] and our nation.' When Jesus entered Jerusalem on the first Palm Sunday, he foresaw and foretold the siege and destruction of the city. 'For the days shall come upon you, when your enemies will cast up a bank about you and surround you, and hem you in on every side, and dash you to the ground, you and your children within you, and they will not leave one stone upon another in you; because you did not know the time of your visitation.' (Luke 19:43-44)

The question of whether it was right to pay taxes to Caesar was a highly dangerous one. On Jesus's answer could depend either a complete loss of popularity for saying 'Yes' or a certain charge of treason for saying 'No.' In fact, he answered, 'Render to Caesar the things that are Caesar's and to God the things that are God's.'

The cold, callous cruelty of Roman justice is well illustrated by the narrative of the crucifixion, particularly as described by Mark. The scourging, the mocking in the guardroom, the method of crucifixion, all followed a common routine of execution calculated to induce fear and subjection. This impression is, however, in the Gospels relieved by the character of certain individuals – notably two centurions. One had built the synagogue in which Jesus taught at Capernaum, and displayed such faith in Jesus's ability to heal his son (or servant) that Jesus was astonished and declared, 'Not even in Israel have I found such faith.' The other centurion was in charge of the execution squad at the crucifixion and, seeing the courageous death of Jesus, declared, 'Truly this man was the son of God!' The words of the first centurion are still used by the priest at every Catholic Mass of the Latin Rite: 'Lord, I am not worthy that thou shouldest come under my roof, but speak the word only. . . .' The second centurion, to whom tradition has given the name Longinus and credited with conversion to Christianity, figures in the regular Western Catholic devotion called 'The Stations of the Cross'.

Romans and the early Church

The Third Gospel and the Acts, both the work of Luke, a highly educated and sensitive man, possibly a Gentile, were written to commend the Christian religion to the Greco-Roman public and authorities. These works are frankly tolerant of the Roman part in the crucifixion and of the Roman influence on the growth of the infant Church. They in turn set out to demand a tolerance for the Christian faith, in spite of the execution of its founder by a Roman procurator. Most of the letters of the New Testament were written by a Roman citizen, Paul, so here too we would expect to find a respect for Roman authority. If the writer of the first letter attributed to Peter was in fact Silas (otherwise called Silvanus), he too was a Roman citizen. As the writings of Paul were completed before the first outbreak of Christian persecution in Rome, under the Emperor Nero in AD 64, these documents indicate little Roman opposition to the early Christian Church. In Acts, the Roman centurion, Cornelius, converted by Peter at Joppa, and Julius, Paul's escort and protector on his way to Rome, play a vital part in the story. The Roman civil colonial authorities in Galatia, Philippi, Corinth, and Ephesus, however, appear to have been unpredictably uncaring or severe, and the Judean procurators uniformly ineffective, but there is no persecution.

Other New Testament writings, attributed to the period between AD 64 and the end of the 1st century, are marked by an insistence on the fact of persecution and the need for steadfast endurance. This is particularly to be seen in 1 Peter and Revelation. It was, nevertheless, in this period that the Christian Church at Rome grew in size and status, partly because being in the world's capital city, it was bound to become important, and partly because it was founded by the two great apostles, Peter and Paul. [John 11:48; Acts 16:12, 21, 37, 38; 22:25-27, 29; 23:27; 28:17]

Letter to the Romans

The first of Paul's letters, as they appear in the New Testament, is the longest and most influential, written at the height of the apostle's career. It conveys the richness of his personal experience of Jesus and the full maturity of his thinking. It is also his first work of Christian theology. Calmly and systematically, Paul sets forth the gospel which he has been preaching, often in situations of danger and difficulty which did not permit either calm or system. The general theme is the good news about Jesus and the reconciliation he has procured.

The letter was written in the winter months of 57-8 from Corinth, during Paul's Third Journey. It is unique in being addressed by Paul to a Christian community barely established and not yet visited by him. Consequently it is much less personal than his other letters, since he is not acquainted with those to whom he writes. It is rather more of a treatise than a letter – a treatise in which he works out at some length the line of thought more hastily expounded in his letter to the Galatians.

The letter to the Romans seems to have had a three-fold objective: to prepare his way for a visit to Rome; to enlist the help of Roman Christians for his mission in the West; and to provide a detailed exposition of the gospel. It is a document any Church would value; it was probably sent to other Christian communities besides that in Rome. Paul dictated his letters, but often added covering notes and greetings, sometimes in his own bold handwriting. The first fifteen of the letter's sixteen chapters are likely to constitute the original letter as sent to Rome, while the last three verses of Chapter 16 might well have been Paul's covering note accompanying the letter to Rome. It is also likely that a copy of the original letter would have been retained at Corinth.

Finally, the remarkable and lengthy series of individual greetings in the final chapter is hardly likely to have been included in his letter to Rome, a city which he had not yet visited. It is far more appropriate for a letter to the Christian community at Ephesus, where Paul had already spent three years and must have had countless friends. Many of the names of those greeted can in fact be linked with Ephesus. Moreover, the first postscript following the greetings is the sort of warning that would have been far more appropriate and natural in a letter to Ephesus than in one to Rome.

Paul warns against false and perverse teaching, contrary to what has already been taught. A similar warning was later addressed to the congregation at Colossae, and Paul personally warned the elders of Ephesus at their farwell meeting with him at Miletus (Acts 20:15-17). Therefore, it is possible that most of Chapter 16 was Paul's covering letter, enclosed with a copy of

484

his treatise to Rome, that was sent to Ephesus. Again, an early editor would have grafted the Ephesian greeting on to the end of the letter to Rome, closing the whole with the final doxology.

Message of salvation

Paul was brought up in observance of the Jewish Law. For him, God was essentially the God of righteousness. If God is absolute moral perfection, truth and goodness – then no form of evil can come near him without dissolving, like darkness in the sunlight. Paul tackles the problem of how man, who deliberately and constantly sins, can ever approach God and share life with him. The Law of Moses offers one solution. If men will fully obey the Law, they will be free from moral taint and they will be able to approach God. Paul, however, points out that unfortunately men have failed to obey either the Law revealed to Israel on Sinai, or the universal law of human conscience. Whether they have broken the whole Law or only a small part of it, all men are guilty and come short of God's perfection. The Mosaic Law, which should be a signpost to God, had become nothing but a warning notice.

The gospel message is that God himself has dealt with this problem by coming himself, in the person of Jesus, to this world. God, as Jesus, became 'Representative Man', and himself deliberately accepted the eventual consequences of evil by his own suffering and death on the cross. Anyone who entrusts his life to Jesus can now be accepted by God, through God's own personal act of atonement. Now, both salvation from the consequences of sin, and salvation that we may come into the presence of God in his holiness, has become a matter of

485

'believing' and not of 'achieving', gained by 'faith' rather than by 'works'.

Greeting and introduction

Paul's greeting includes his own credentials as 'a servant of Jesus Christ, called to be an apostle, set apart for the gospel of God'. He then gives a simple definition of the person and work of Jesus, as Messiah and Son of God: 'the gospel concerning his Son, who was descended from David according to the flesh and designated Son of God in power according to the Spirit of holiness by his resurrection from the dead, Jesus Christ our Lord, through whom we have received grace and apostleship to bring about the obedience of faith for the sake of his name among all the nations, including yourselves who are called to belong to Christ Jesus.' (Rom. 1:3-6)

Paul goes on to thank God for the Christian community in Rome, traditionally founded by Peter, but more probably founded by some of the 120 disciples addressed by Peter at Pentecost. Paul outlines his plan to come to Rome, despite delays, in order to bring them the Good News, for he says, 'I am not ashamed of the gospel: it is the power of God for salvation to every one who has faith, to the Jew first and also to the Greek' (Rom. 1:16), and he quotes the prophet Habakkuk: 'He who through faith is righteous shall live.'

Warning for Jews and Gentiles

Paul denounces the Gentiles for their reliance upon their own reasoning and the Jews for their reliance upon the Mosaic Law. Of the Gentiles he said, 'Claiming to be wise, they became fools, and exchanged the glory of the immortal God for images resembling mortal man or birds or animals or reptiles . . . though they know God's decree that those who do such things deserve to die, they not only do them but approve those who practise them.' (Rom. 1:22, 23, 32) Of the Jews Paul says, 'Therefore you have no excuse, O man, whoever you are, when you judge another; for in passing judgment upon him you condemn yourself, because you, the judge, are doing the very same thing. . . . Do you suppose, O man, that when you judge those who do such things and yet do them yourself, you will escape the judgment of God?' (Rom. 2:1, 3) Both must repent. 'There will be tribulation and distress for every human being who does evil, to the Jew first and also to the Greek, but glory and honour and peace for every one who does good, to the Jew first and also to the Greek. For God shows no partiality.' (Rom. 2:9-11) Paul then boldly asks: 'Then what advantage has the Jew?' Equally boldly Paul answers: 'Much in every way. To begin with, the Jews are entrusted with the oracles of God.' But it is not enough, for 'all men, both Jews and Greeks, are under the power of sin', and he goes on to answer from the Book of Psalms:

'None is righteous, no, not one;

no one understands, no one seeks for God.

All have turned aside, together they have gone wrong;

no one does good, not even one.' (Rom. 3:1, 2, 9-12)

The Mosaic Law does not justify but simply convicts of sin. It is only faith in Jesus that avails. Paul cites Abraham, the father of the faithful, as an example of a man justified by his faith. 'The promise to Abraham and his descendants, that they should inherit the world, did not come through the law but through the righteousness of faith. If it is the adherents of the law who are to be the heirs, faith is null and the promise is void.' (Rom. 4:13, 14) The promise depends on faith and is freely available to all Abraham's descendants, not only his descendants by Law, but also by faith. Abraham was indeed made 'the father of many nations'. His faith was a model of the Christian faith.

Freedom from sin

Salvation, therefore, comes by faith, as the response of man to the grace of God through Jesus and his cross, and by no human achievement of righteousness in obedience to a code of laws. But because the grace of God is all-sufficient, this does not entitle Christians to continue in their old evil habits without fear. Paul illustrates this from the practice of baptism, the initiation into the Christian life, showing that it necessarily involves death to the old sinful self and a rising to the new self. This does not make the Christian unable to sin, but it means that he no longer belongs to sin: he now belongs to Jesus, whose grace will inspire him to good conduct. That is why the Christian must keep himself holy, to present himself to God. 'So you must also consider yourselves dead to sin and alive to God in Christ Jesus.' (Rom. 6:11) Paul then launches into a direct psychological analysis of the experience of this salvation of sin. 'We know that the law is spiritual; but I am carnal, sold under sin. I do not understand my own actions. For I do not do what I want, but I do the very thing I hate. . . . Wretched man that I am! Who will deliver me from this body of death? Thanks be to God through Jesus Christ our Lord!' (Rom. 7:14, 15, 24, 25)

The universal Spirit

Paul goes on to compare those who live on a physical level with no expectation of further satisfaction when this is exhausted, and those who live by the Spirit of God. For Paul, this is the Spirit of Jesus that possesses his followers and makes them both the children and heirs of God. 'For all who are led by the Spirit of God are sons of God. . . . When we cry, "Abba! Father!" it is the Spirit himself bearing witness with our Spirit that we are children of God.' (Rom. 8:14-16)

At this point Paul – alternately the satirist, the philosopher, the rabbi, and the psychologist – now speaks with the vision of a poet, as he shows the function of the *universal* Spirit in the redemption of all created life. Paul explains that the story of the world is not yet complete, for Creation was purposefully made incomplete by the intention of God himself. The very gift of free-will and self-determination to man and the resultant risk of creating someone who may choose to crucify and reject you, is the only way to create a family of children, and not of robots. Indeed this very incompleteness of creation necessarily involves a process analagous to re-birth or re-creation. In this process, painful as it is, God himself is involved and is agonized – for the Spirit of God is within *all* and through all created life.

Paul himself was so filled and radiant with the Spirit, so truly alive, that he did not fear death. He had discovered a depth of life in the Spirit through his own experiences of betrayal and crucifixion. He had in a sense been down to hell, yet had survived, and in doing so had discovered the joy and purpose of living; so that he could truthfully exclaim, 'It is no longer I who live, but Christ who lives in me.' And again: 'Who shall separate us from the love of Christ? Shall tribulation, or distress, or persecution, or famine, or nakedness, or peril, or sword? . . . No, in all these things we are more than conquerors through him who loved us. For I am sure that neither death, nor life, nor angels, nor principalities, nor things present, nor things to come, nor powers, nor height, nor depth, nor anything else in all creation, will be able to separate us from the love of God in Christ Jesus our Lord.' (Rom. 8:35, 37-39)

The tragedy of Israel

The next three chapters of Paul's treatise are devoted to this subject and are a vindication of God's dealings with the Jews. Paul, as a student of the Hebrew Bible, begins by outlining the privileges, promises, and responsibilities of Israel within it. He is deeply, emotionally involved in the tragedy of Israel's rejection of the Messiahship of Jesus. 'My conscience bears me witness in the Holy Spirit, that I have great sorrow and unceasing anguish in my heart. For I could wish that I myself were accursed and cut off from Christ for the sake of my brethren, my kinsmen by race. They are Israelites, and to them belong the sonship, the glory, the covenants, the giving of the law, the worship, and the promises; to them belong the patriarchs, and of their race, according to the flesh, is the Christ. God who is over all be blessed for ever. Amen.' (Rom. 9:2-5)

Paul claims that God has kept his promise, that God is not unjust, but that he retains a freedom of choice in disposing of his blessings. He tries to show that the rejection of the Messiah by Israel has been foretold by the prophets and forseen by God — and that even this can be gathered up into God's purpose. Now, however, the order of events which Israel had been brought up to expect would be reversed. No longer would the Jews be saved first and the Gentiles saved later. The rejection of the Messiah by Israel would result in the salvation of the Gentiles.

'So I ask, have they stumbled so as to fall? By no means! But through their trespass salvation has come to the Gentiles, so as to make Israel jealous. Now if their trespass means riches for the world, and if their failure means riches for the Gentiles, how much more will their full inclusion mean! Now I am speaking to you Gentiles. Inasmuch then as I am an apostle to the Gentiles, I magnify my ministry in order to make my fellow Jews jealous, and thus save some of them.' (Rom. 11:11-14)

Paul, seeing that in fact the Church has been unsuccessful among the Jews, turns to the Gentiles. Writing to the very centre of the Roman Empire, he seeks to attract in the Church a nucleus of Gentiles from all parts of the world, in the hope that it will 'make my fellow Jews jealous'. For Paul, the Jews are still the chosen people – the olive-tree on to which the pagans have been grafted, and which awaits the regrafting of Israel. 'For if you have been cut from what is by nature a wild olive tree, and grafted, contrary to nature, into a cultivated olive tree, how much more will these natural branches be grafted back into their own olive tree.' (Rom. 11:24)

Charity and unity

Having disposed of some outstanding theological problems, Paul now declares that God brings those who are justified by their faith in Jesus into a new order of life in the Spirit. From this spiritual life, men derive the power to lead a good life and to display the righteousness of God in their Christian living. Similarly, by the indwelling of the Spirit, God's righteousness reshapes the conduct of men in society. Christians are therefore called to surrender their lives to God. 'I appeal to you therefore, brethren, by the mercies of God, to present

491

your bodies as a living sacrifice, holy and acceptable to God, which is your spiritual worship. Do not be conformed to this world but be transformed by the renewal of your mind, that you may prove what is the will of God, what is good and acceptable and perfect.' (Rom. 12:1, 2)

Christians must behave in humility and charity, acknowledging their various individual contributions to the Christian community, like the different faculties which contribute to the health of the human body. 'For as in one body we have many members, and all the members do not have the same function, so we, though many, are one body in Christ, and individually members one of another.' (Rom. 12:4, 5)

Paul's standard of Christian behaviour, like that of Jesus's Sermon on the Mount, is based on love and nonresistance. He demands that Christians submit themselves to the civil authority – and this at a time when nationalist feeling was building up to the crisis of the revolt in AD 66. Paul reminds his readers that the return of Jesus may be soon and that they are to be awake, ready, and waiting. They are to be tolerant of the behaviour of others, and gentle with the scruples of their brethren, not scoffing at their eating habits or their festival days. 'Why do you pass judgment on your brother? Or you, why do you despise your brother? For we shall all stand before the judgment seat of God. . . . So each of us shall give account of himself to God.' (Rom. 14:10, 12)

Paul exhorts Jewish and Gentile Christians to live in harmony and fellowship together. Their aim should be peace, the welfare and unity of the corporate life of the whole Church. 'May the God of hope fill you with all joy and peace in believing, so that by the power of the Holy Spirit you may abound in hope.' (Rom. 15:13)

Farewells and future plans

Paul outlines his plans to visit Rome *en route* for Spain, and asks for help and good wishes. First, however, he has to take the money contributed by the Christians in Greece to Jerusalem. It was appropriate, Paul said, that the Greeks – spiritual debtors to the Jewish-Christians – should contribute to their material needs. As soon as he has delivered this gift to Jerusalem, he will set out for Spain and visit them in Rome. 'I appeal to you, brethren, by our Lord Jesus Christ and by the love of the Spirit, to strive together with me in your prayers to God on my behalf, that I may be delivered from the unbelievers in Judea, and that my service for Jerusalem may be acceptable to the saints, so that by God's will I may come to you with joy and be refreshed in your company. The God of peace be with you all. Amen.' (Rom. 15:30-33)

As suggested above, the final chapter of the letter is probably Paul's covering letter when despatching a copy of his Roman letter to Ephesus. Certainly it is full of personal greetings, less likely perhaps to have been addressed to the Roman congregations which he had not yet visited. The primary purpose of the covering letter is the introduction of the deaconess Phoebe to the Ephesian congregation. He sends greetings to Aquila and Prisca, who in Ephesus had risked their own lives for Paul, together with an early Asian convert, Epaenetus, and a host of other friends. Paul's secretary, then Tertius, adds his own greeting.

Paul closes with a final doxology that may perhaps have been transferred from the end of the original letter to the Romans. 'Now to him who is able to strengthen you according to my gospel and the preaching of Jesus Christ, according to the revelation of the mystery which was kept secret for long ages but is now disclosed and through the prophetic writings is made known to all nations, according to the command of the eternal God, to bring about the obedience of Faith – to the only wise God be glory for evermore through Jesus Christ. Amen.' (Rom. 16:25-27) [John 11:48; Acts 16:21, 37, 38; 28:17; Rom. 1-16]

RUFUS (Gk. 'red') **1.** One of the sons of Simon of Cyrene, 'the father of Alexander and Rufus', who was compelled by the Roman execution squad to carry the cross-piece of the cross for Jesus on his way to Calvary. Only Mark mentions the sons by name, perhaps because they had become Christians and were known to his readers. Mark's Gospel is said to have been written in Rome during the year 64-5. Paul, in the final chapter of his letter to the Christians in Rome, includes a greeting to a Rufus, but there is no certain identification with the son of Simon of Cyrene. [Mark 15:21]

2. 'Rufus, eminent in the Lord, also his mother and mine.' Whether this greeting and others were in fact addressed to Rome or to Ephesus, there cannot be any certain identification of this family with that of Simon of Cyrene. The respect of Paul for the mother of Alexander and Rufus, coupled with Mark's mention of them by name, would seem, however, to strengthen the tradition that Simon of Cyrene and his family became Christians. [Rom. 16:13]

S

SADDUCEES (Gk. 'followers of Zadok' [Solomon's High Priest]) The Sadducees were a politico-religious party, holding the highest offices in church and state. They were prepared to compromise, for the sake of peace, with the Roman occupation forces, and consequently they frowned on the passive resistance of the Pharisees and on the aggressive nationalism of the Zealot freedom fighters. In return, they were allowed by the Romans to retain their power in the Temple and in the supreme Council, the Sanhedrin, and they guarded their position zealously. Indeed, the office of high priest was the appointment of Rome – much to the shame of the Jews – but Annas the Sadducee had so exerted his influence that six high priests in succession had been members of his own family, and Caiaphas, the seventh, was his own son-in-law. The importance of Caiaphas in the trial of Jesus gives some indication of the intrigue, the prestige, and the privileges of the Sadducees.

The high priest held the monopoly of the sale of animals for sacrifice, for which payment had to be made in Temple currency and on which they levied a rate of exchange. They also levied a tithe, or one-tenth of all their possessions, for the upkeep of the Temple, paid by every Jewish member of the population. The 'cleansing of the Temple' by Jesus represented a dangerous threat to both their authority and to their vested interests. This was the one occasion when Jesus accompanied his teaching with a violent demonstration to support his words: 'It is written, "My house shall be a house of prayer"; but you make it a den of robbers.' This undoubtedly took place within the eastern arcade of the Temple area, called Solomon's Porch, which was used at that time for limited public commerce.

Worldly self-interest

The worldly interests of the Sadducees led them in the same direction as the principles of their religion. Their very conservatism did not allow them to appreciate new doctrines such as resurrection. As wealthy aristocrats enjoying a privileged position in both church and state, they were indifferent to any hopes of a delivering Messiah. They were satisfied with their security under Roman patronage, and were very material in their pleasures. They did not believe in any after-life, except among the shades of Sheol, and so they set out to enjoy this life. For them there was no prospect of rewards or punishment in any future existence, nor was there time for troublesome traditions on earth. The Law was enough for them; there was no need to accept the new ideals of angels and spirits mediating between God and man. Scripture was the only authority for them, the 'hard-hearted rich', even if the 'pious poor' Pharisees preferred to saddle themselves with both scripture *and* tradition — even if, too, the masses of the people followed the Pharisees. They, the Sadducees, advocated a solid common-sense morality and political reality: for them any form of enthusiasm was unnecessary.

Jesus had few dealings with the Sadducees; they were not as influential in Galilee as they were in Jerusalem. John does not mention the Sadducees at all, but Matthew, Mark, and Luke all relate the question of the Sadducees to Jesus, on the day following his Palm Sunday triumphal entry into Jerusalem. Following the

Pharisees' question about the tribute money, and before the Scribes' question about the primary commandment, the Sadducees put their question about the resurrection. They probably hoped to ridicule both Jesus and the Pharisees by this story, for they did not believe in any resurrection.

'Teacher,' they asked, 'Moses wrote for us that if a man's brother dies, having a wife but no children, the man must take the wife and raise up children for his brother. Now there were seven brothers; the first took a wife, and died without children; and the second and the third took her, and likewise all seven left no children and died. Afterward the woman also died. In the resurrection, therefore, whose wife will the woman be? For the seven had her as wife.' Perhaps this was a stock question of the Sadducees; Jesus answered it in God's words to Moses himself: 'But that the dead are raised, even Moses showed, in the passage about the bush, where he calls the Lord the God of Abraham and the God of Isaac and the God of Jacob. Now he is not God of the dead, but of the living; for all live to him.' (Luke 20:28-38)

Agents of Jesus's death

Although the Sadducees are not often mentioned by name in the story of the passion, they are always included in references to the high priests. Caiaphas, as a matter of historical fact, was the architect of Jesus's crucifixion, and it is probable that it was the action of the Sadducees in the Sanhedrin that secured the conviction. It had been the Pharisees and high priests who had asked in the Council, when confronted by Jesus's progress in preaching, despite their efforts to trip him up, 'What are we to do? For this man performs many signs.

If we let him go on thus, every one will believe in him, and the Romans will come and destroy both our holy place and our nation.' It had been Caiaphas the Sadducee who replied, 'It is expedient for you that one man should die for the people.' (John 11:47-50)

That meant, of course, let him be handed over to the Roman authority, for in any case the Jews could not execute him. So in one act the Sadducees would destroy Jesus, put the blame on Rome, and pretend their own loyalty to Roman law and order. And from the day of that plot, 'they took counsel how to put him to death'. (John 11:53) *see also* ANNAS, CAIAPHAS, *and* SANHEDRIN [Matt. 3:7; 16:1, 6, 11, 12; 22:23, 34; Mark 12:18; Acts 4:1; 5:17; 23:6-8]

SALOME (Gk. from Heb. peaceful') **1. Salome, wife of Zebedee** Only Mark mentions this Salome by name as a watcher at the crucifixion of Jesus and as a visitor to his tomb on the Easter morning. Matthew mentions by name each of the other women, found in Mark, using the same order, 'Mary Magdalene, Mary the mother of James and Joses', but includes instead of the word 'Salome', the description: 'the mother of the sons of Zebedee'. More certain identification is not possible. Luke merely calls them 'the women'. All three Synoptic Gospels state that they had followed Jesus from Galilee and looked after him. All the women were early involved in the lakeside ministry of Jesus, Mary at Magdala, the other Mary and Salome both as mothers of his earliest disciples, Salome as the mother of James and John, who with Peter formed the inner circle of the twelve.

At some point during the Galilean ministry, these two brothers James and John came with a personal request to Jesus. Mark makes it clear that they presented their plea for themselves, but Matthew, perhaps to preserve the propriety and dignity of the apostles, puts the question into the mouth of the 'mother of the sons of Zebedee'. 'Then the mother of the sons of Zebedee came up to him, with her sons, and kneeling before him she asked him for something. And he said to her, "What do you want?" She said to him, "Command that these two sons of mine may sit, one at your right hand and one at your left, in your kingdom." But Jesus answered, "You do not know what you are asking. Are you able to drink the cup that I am to drink?" They said to him, "We are able." He said to them, "You will drink my cup, but to sit at my right hand and at my left is not mine to grant, but it is for those for whom it has been prepared by my Father." ' (Matt. 20:20-23) Indeed, it was Salome's first son James who drank of his master's cup, scarcely fifteen years later, when as a political victim of Herod Agrippa I, he was executed during an early persecution of the young Christian Church.

Salome, whose husband Zebedee must have been of some substance and status in the lakeside fishing trade, would have been a very useful member of the little group of women who provided for the needs of Jesus and his disciples, not only in Galilee, but also on their journeys to Jerusalem. [Mark 15:40, 41; 16:1 and, by implication, Matt. 20:20-23; 27:56]

2. Salome, daughter of Herodias This great-granddaughter of Herod the Great is chiefly remembered for the sordid scheme by which she danced for Herod Antipas and secured the execution of John the Baptist, at the instigation of her mother Herodias.

Salome's father was her great-uncle Herod Boethus, a private citizen in Rome and son of Herod the Great. Her mother was a granddaughter of Herod the Great, who contrived the assassination of both her father and grandmother. Salome's mother, Herodias, later married Herod Antipas, and the Gospels of Mark and Matthew mistakenly link her also with Philip the tetrarch, the brother of Antipas. Josephus, however, records the third marriage of Salome's mother Herodias with another Philip within the Herod family at Rome.

The account of the death of John the Baptist in Mark's Gospel reads like a popular legend of the prophet rebuking the king, along the lines of the Old Testament story of Elijah rebuking Ahab for appropriating Naboth's vineyard. John fearlessly condemned Antipas for taking Philip's wife, who was his own niece and consequently by law forbidden to be his wife. No doubt John also condemned Herodias for deserting her first husband to form an adulterous alliance with her uncle Antipas. Certainly, it was Herodias who bore a grudge against John, though Antipas is said to have respected and protected him.

'But an opportunity came when Herod on his birthday gave a banquet for his courtiers and officers and the leading men of Galilee. For when Herodias's daughter came in and danced, she pleased Herod and his guests; and the king said to the girl, "Ask me for whatever you wish, and I will grant it." And he vowed to her, "Whatever you ask me, I will give you, even half of my kingdom." And she went out, and said to her mother, "What shall I ask?" And she said, "The head of John the baptizer." And she came in immediately with haste to the king, and asked, saying, "I want you to give me at once the head of John the Baptist on a platter." And the king was exceedingly sorry; but because of his oath and his guests he did not want to break his word to her. And immediately the king sent a soldier of the guard and gave orders to bring his head.

He went and beheaded him in the prison, and brought his head on a platter, and gave it to the girl; and the girl gave it to her mother.' (Mark 6:21-28)

The execution took place, according to Josephus, in the fortress of Machareus beyond Jordan; his burial is supposed to have been at Samaria, where his tomb was honoured from the 4th century.

Richard Strauss's opera *Salome*, based on the play by Oscar Wilde, ends fancifully with the flogging to death of Salome at the close of Antipas's banquet. Salome at that time was less than sixteen years old and, according to the Jewish historian Josephus, later married Philip, the tetrarch of Iturea, Gaulanitis and Trachonitis. This Salome's name does not appear in the Gospels, except by implication as 'the daughter of Herodias'. *see* HEROD [Matt. 14:6; Mark 6:22]

SAMARITANS The capital of the northern kingdom of Israel, built by Omri, father of Ahab, stands on a hill 'bought from Shemer for two talents of silver' (hence the name Samaria), and is still to be seen a few miles north of the modern city of Nablus. The name Samaria came to be used for the district occupied by the ten northern tribes, bounded by Galilee, Jordan, and Judea.

During the lifetime of Jesus, Samaria was ruled until 4 BC by Herod the Great; he left it to Archelaus, who was deposed in AD 6 by the Romans, and they in turn appointed a series of procurators, answerable to the governor of the Roman province of Syria.

Tradition of independence

The history of Samaria is that of five distinct occupations: 1) Israelite, 2) Assyrian, 3) Persian, 4) Greek, 5) Roman. The Israelite city and royal capital of the northern kingdom was destroyed in 721 BC. The Assyrian colonial and administrative centre of Sargon for the next 400 years left little trace but for some crude walling on the acropolis. The Assyrian conquerors deported the leading inhabitants of the city, but imported settlers from Mesopotamia, who intermarried with the surviving population. These settlers practised their own religion, but were later instructed by an Israelite priest sent from Babylon. When, some two centuries later, the Jewish exiles were allowed to return and re-occupy Jerusalem, they found Judah under the administration of the governor of Samaria, appointed by the Persian Empire. They found their lack of political independence hard to bear, particularly as their religious scruples were offended by what they considered a debased form of Judaism, diluted with Assyrian customs, practised among the Samaritans. Nehemiah gained independence for Judah with its newly built Temple in Jerusalem.

The Samaritans built their own sanctuary on Mount Gerizim in about 400 BC, overlooking the ancient sanctuary at Shechem, Jacob's Well, and the traditional tomb of Joseph, from whom they claimed descent. By the 1st century, this sanctuary was in ruins. When the Jewish community accepted within their scriptures the Prophets and other writings of the Old Testament, the Samaritans did not do so, but confirmed their loyalty to the Five Books of Moses alone.

The woman of Samaria

Within the New Testament, this political and religious tension between Jew and Samaritan is well reflected in the Fourth Gospel account of the meeting of Jesus with the woman at Jacob's Well. On his way back from Jerusalem to Galilee by way of the highlands of Samaria, during his second day's travelling, Jesus rested at Jacob's Well and sent his disciples on to the next village to buy lunch. It was over his midday rest that he had that wonderful conversation with the much-married woman of Samaria, who teased him for his thirsty request for a drink: 'The Samaritan woman said to him, "How is it that you, a Jew, ask a drink of me, a woman of Samaria? For Jews have no dealings with Samaritans." ' (John 4:9) Jesus took his opportunity to teach her and answered, 'If you knew the gift of God, and who it is that it is saying to you, "Give me a drink," you would have asked him, and he would have given you living water.' (John 4:10)

She was by now plainly puzzled, but intrigued, and answered him, the Jewish rabbi, almost facetiously, Sir, you have nothing to draw with, and the well is deep; where do you get that living water? Are you greater than our father Jacob, who gave us the well and drank from it himself, and his sons, and his cattle?' (John 4:11-12) Today the well is still 105 feet deep and its identification is unquestioned. The biblical scholar Jerome describes the building of a church there in the 4th century, and the Bordeaux Pilgrim as early as 333 identified the well by its proximity to Joseph's Tomb. Since then the site has had an unbroken tradition.

Jesus said to her, 'Every one who drinks of this water will thirst again, but whoever drinks of the water that I shall give him will never thirst; the water that I shall give him will become in him a spring of water welling up to eternal life.' (John 4:13-14) Again puzzled and practical, for it is a good half-mile's carry back from the well to her village, with a full pitcher on her head, 'The woman said to him, "Sir, give me this water, that I may not thirst, nor come here to draw." ' (John 4:15)

Jesus then suggested that she call her husband, but

503

she, fearing exposure, denied she had a husband. Jesus, however, read her thoughts so clearly that she eagerly asked him, as a seer, to give his ruling on the vital question separating Jews and Samaritans. 'Sir, I perceive that you are a prophet. Our fathers worshipped on this mountain; and you say that in Jerusalem is the place where men ought to worship.' (John 4:19-20) Jesus gave his prophetic answer, 'Woman, believe me, the hour is coming when neither on this mountain nor in Jerusalem will you worship the Father. . . . God is spirit, and those who worship him must worship in spirit and truth.' (John 4:21, 24)

The woman still did not understand him and, expecting an obscure answer perhaps from such a prophet, she looked forward to the coming of the Christ who, when he came, would make it all plain. 'I know that Messiah is coming (he who is called Christ); when he comes, he will show us all things.' (John 4:25) Immediately Jesus completed his pastoral instruction with that stupendous affirmation: 'I who speak to you am he.' [John 4:7, 9]

The Good Samaritan

In answer to a certain lawyer's question, 'Who is my neighbour?' Jesus told the parable of the Good Samaritan, recorded in Luke's Gospel. The setting of the story would be well-known to his hearers. 'A man was going down from Jerusalem to Jericho, and he fell among robbers, who stripped him and beat him, and departed, leaving him half dead.' (Luke 10:30) The road drops down over the Mount of Olives, from 3,000 feet above sea-level to 1,300 feet below sea-level within a distance of 24 miles. It passes through a dry and arid wilderness of crags and boulders, which has always provided a wonderful hiding-place for brigands. At a point exactly halfway down, there is an old khan (or inn) overlooked today by the ruins of Roman and Crusader staging-posts. In the centre of its courtyard is a Roman well, which has for centuries been the local water-supply of the surrounding caravanserai. Many of Jesus's hearers would know that route all too well and may even have shared the experience of the man who 'fell among thieves'.

The story continues, depicting three travellers on the same road and their reactions to the naked and wounded man by the roadside. 'Now by chance a priest was going down that road; and when he saw him he passed by on the other side. So likewise a Levite, when he came to the place and saw him, passed by on the other side.' At this point, the hearers, who thought of their community in terms of Priests, Levites, and Israelites — as perhaps Christians today of bishops, clergy, and lay people — might have been confident that the hero would be an Israelite. Their shock and consternation when the hero turned out to be a hated Samaritan — one publicly cursed in the synagogues and whose evidence was unacceptable in a court of law — can be easily imagined.

'But a Samaritan, as he journeyed, came to where he was; and when he saw him, he had compassion, and went to him and bound up his wounds, pouring on oil and wine; then he set him on his own beast and brought him to an inn, and took care of him. And the next day he took out two denarii and gave them to the innkeeper, saying, "Take care of him; and whatever more you spend I will repay you when I come back."' (Luke 10:33-35) The parable did not exactly answer the question of the lawyer, 'Who is my neighbour?' but it illustrated graphically that neighbourhood was unlim-

ited, by race or religion. The only criterion for neighbourliness is need.

Hostility — and gratitude

Luke gives two further accounts of Samaritans.

Jesus and his disciples were on their way from Galilee to Jerusalem and sent messengers to make the necessary arrangements for accommodation along the
route. They came to a Samaritan village but were not
welcomed because they were Jews and were on the way
to Jerusalem. James and John, the hot-blooded 'sons of
thunder'; immediately asked Jesus: 'Lord, do you want
us to bid fire come down from heaven and consume
them?' Jesus turned and checked the brothers; they
went on to another village.

According to Josephus, 'it was a custom of Galileans
proceeding to the feasts at the holy city to journey
through Samaritan territory'. (*Antiquities*, xx, 6:1) On
one occasion Josephus records that in the Samaritan village of Gema 'A Galilean, one of a large company of
Jews journeying to the festival, was murdered.' (*Wars*,
II, 12:3) The Jews despised the Samaritans as 'the
foolish nation that dwells in Schechem' (Ecclesiasticus
1:25), and the Samaritans repaid them with scorn.

On another journey to Jerusalem on the same route,
Jesus healed ten lepers. Luke says that 'he was passing
along between Samaria and Galilee. And as he entered
a village, he was met by ten lepers' (Luke 17:11, 12).
The pilgrim route to Jerusalem would cross the border
into Samaria at Jenin where the road across the Plain of
Esdraelon cuts south through the foothills into the vale
of Dothan. Jenin, once called Ain Gannim, 'the gardens', is associated by a 15th-century tradition with the
village of the ten lepers. In the neighbouring hamlet of

Burkein, the Arabic-speaking Greek Orthodox congregation worship in a Church of the Ten Lepers, which they hold to be the site of the miracle. Gardens would indicate an appropriate and refreshing spot for the midday halt. It was also a crossroads at which pilgrims would gather from three different directions, those coming from the lakeside via Beth-shean, from Nazareth across the plain of Jezreel, and from the coast by the road among the Carmel range.

The lepers kept their distance and attracted Jesus's attention by shouting, ' "Jesus, Master, have mercy on us." When he saw them, he said to them, "Go and show yourselves to the priests." ' For Jewish lepers this would mean a visit to the Temple at Jerusalem, for they could only be pronounced clean after the necessary sacrificial rites. 'And as they went, they were cleansed,' says Luke, the physician. 'Then one of them, when he saw that he was healed, turned back, praising God with a loud voice; and he fell on his face at Jesus's feet, giving him thanks. Now he was a Samaritan.' (Luke 17:13-16) Jesus at once contrasted the gratitude of the Samaritan with the forgetfulness of the nine Jews. 'Were there not ten cleansed? Where are the nine? Was no one found to return and give praise to God except this foreigner? . . . Rise and go your way; your faith has made you well.' (Luke 17:17-19)

It is interesting to note that Pontius Pilate's recall to Rome in the year 36 was to answer charges of high-handed and savage repression of a Samaritan rising, on which charges he was found guilty and banished.

Samaria proved to be highly responsive to early Christian evangelism. In about the year 35, Philip, one of the seven deacons, was so successful as an evangelist that the Church in Jerusalem despatched the two Apostles Peter and John to consolidate this activity and officially establish the Christian community in Samaria.

Today, there are two Samaritan communities, numbering perhaps 200 souls in all. One is to be found in the area of the town of Nablus, on the slopes of Mount Gerizim, on which they continue to celebrate their Passover every spring. Within their synagogue, they treasure a very ancient Pentateuch. The other and smaller community is at Holon, near Tel Aviv. [Matt. 10:5; Luke 9:52; 10:33; 17:16; John 4:9, 39; 8:48]

SANHEDRIN (Gk. 'council') This supreme assembly of post-exilic Judaism was an aristocratic senate, composed of representatives of the priesthood and laity who from the 4th century BC, in the Persian and Greek occupations, came to the forefront of the Jewish people.

The Sanhedrin at Jerusalem was in origin and effect the first authority in the land, and the highest court of law to which the provincial courts turned for decisions in particularly difficult cases. The Sanhedrin's competence and reputation extended throughout world Jewry, though its greatest influence was in Judea. They held court at Jerusalem, within the Temple area, on the south of the priests' court in the 'Chamber of Hewn Stone'. The Temple police were at their disposal and probably effected the arrests of Jesus in Gethsemane and of the Apostle Paul within the Temple courts. The Sanhedrin also examined candidates for ordination to the priesthood, checking the purity of their priestly descent and their bodily fitness – as well as their other qualifications.

When Judea became a Roman province in AD 6, the Sanhedrin became the chief political agency, controlling the affairs of the eleven districts into which the Romans divided the land, and linking every town and village administratively to Jerusalem.

The presidency of the Sanhedrin, as a matter of privilege, belonged to the high priest. The Council consisted of 71 members, falling into the three main groups: the chief priests (sometimes called the 'rulers', Acts 4:5, 6), the elders (sometimes called the 'principal men of the people, Luke 19:47), and the scribes. These three groups or grades correspond with those who questioned the authority of Jesus for cleansing the Temple. (Mark 11:27)

The first group – the chief priests – included those who held the most important offices in the Temple: the anointed high priest and retired high priests, the Captain of the Temple, often the high priest's deputy, the leaders of the 24 weekly courses, the Temple overseers, and the Temple treasurers.

The hierarchy tended to fill all the chief positions from their own families as a matter of course. The ruling house of Annas held perhaps all the chief-priestly positions within its control, besides operating a flourishing trade in sacrificial victims within the court of the Gentiles, in the Temple. No less than eight members of this family held the supreme office of high priest: Annas himself, five sons, Caiaphas his son-in-law, and his grandson Matthias, from the year 65. Such a family virtually established the political as well as religious leadership of the nation.

Among the ruling priests, within the Sanhedrin and present at the trial of Peter and John in the early 30s, were Annas, the elderly and influential former high priest, his son-in-law Caiaphas, the ruling high priest, Jonathan, probably a captain of the Temple, a son of Annas, who succeeded Caiaphas, an unknown priest called Alexander, and others who held high-priestly office in Jerusalem. The family that ruled the Sanhedrin clearly held the leadership of the whole people.

The second group – the elders – were descended from those ancient ruling families who had held the leadership within the tribes and after the settlement in Canaan. The heads of these dominant families had directed the settlement and administration of the exiles in Babylon. After their return, the heads of such families had acted as representatives of the people, negotiating with the provincial governors, and directing the reconstruction of the Temple in the time of Ezra. The Sanhedrin grew out of the union of this secular nobility with the priestly aristocracy of those times.

Within the lifetime of Jesus one representative of this group was Joseph of Arimathea, a rich landowner, in whose tomb at Jerusalem the body of Jesus was buried. Josephus, the Jewish historian writing in the 1st century, describes the elders variously as 'notables', 'most eminent citizens', and 'leading men'. He describes the three groups within the Sanhedrin as the 'principal citizens, the chief priests, and the most notable Pharisees'. These elders were usually the heads of patrician families whose precedence was based on centuries-old privilege. They were usually men of great wealth; the Roman procurator was careful to choose such as his tax officials, for their office might involve them in considerable financial sacrifice. These were charged with assessing citizens for taxation and guaranteeing the correct payment from their own resources.

These first two groups within the Sanhedrin, the chief priests and the patricians, combined to hold the highest offices in church and state. In politics and religion, too, they combined from the 2nd century BC to form the politico-religious party called the 'Sadducees'. (*see* SAD-DUCEES) In the reign of the Hasmonean Queen Alexandra, beginning in 76 BC, the Pharisees gained a foothold in the Sanhedrin and gradually won the confidence and support of the people. In the century after Jesus, the political power of the high priests came to an abrupt end in the year 70, and the new class of Pharisaic Scribes overtook the more ancient class of priestly and lay nobility, founded on the privilege of birth.

The rise of this new upper class of Scribes, the third group within the Sanhedrin, was largely due to their knowledge of scripture and administrative capacity. Jewish communities usually chose Scribes rather than laymen for the office of judge or synagogue-ruler, simply because of their expertise in scriptural exegesis and tradition, as well as in civil and criminal jurisdiction. Thus many important appointments previously held by priests and laymen passed into the hands of the Scribes. Among such were Nicodemus (John 3:1; 7:50), Gamaliel (Acts 5:34), and, of course, the Apostle Paul (Acts 26:10, 11). (*see also* SCRIBES *and* PHARISEES)

The Sanhedrin is linked, in the pages of the New Testament, mainly with the trials of Jesus (*see also* CAIAPHAS *and* ANNAS), of Peter and John, of Stephen, and of the Apostle Paul. [Mark 14:53-56; 15:1; Acts 4:5, 23; 6:12, 15; 22:30; 23:1, 6-9]

SAPPHIRA (Aram. 'beautiful') The wife of the hypocrite who sold property, but appropriated some of the purchase-money, and only brought part of its value to give to the apostles for the Church. The Apostle Peter rebuked him sternly. This terrible indictment caused his immediate death. Three hours later, Sapphira arrived and, after similar cross-examination and for the same lie, was instantly punished by death. Whether legend or truth, this story reflects little mercy in Peter's dealings with this guilty couple. It seems that Luke, the narrator, may have regarded the sin of Ananias and Sapphira as a 'sin against the Holy Spirit'. [Acts 5:7-11]

SATAN (Heb., Gk. 'accuser' or 'adversary') In the early books of the Old Testament, the word is used in a general sense to denote an opponent or enemy. The first occasion it is used of a supernatural being is in the Book of Job, when the Satan – it is not yet a proper name – acts as the public prosecutor before God in heaven of his righteous servant Job. In the prophecies of Zechariah he plays the same part of accuser of the high priest Joshua. In the First Book of Chronicles Satan appears, a proper name for the first time, as the tempter of David.

According to one Jewish tradition, the Jews brought back the names of the angels from Babylon, but neither in Persian religion nor in Palestine was the belief in angels and demons a sudden growth. The many gods of the ancient oriental world were not completely eradicated by the growth of the belief in a single true God. Some of these old gods were down-graded into angels and agents of the one supreme God; others were degraded into demons and devils. Among these latter was a supernatural being – the Satan – whose function was to point out men's failings to God.

Jewish theology was somewhat influenced by Persian dualism, that is, the thought that there existed opposing kingdoms of good and evil, the one loyal to God, the other subject to the prince of devils, whether he was called Satan, Beelzebub, or by his Persian name Asmodeus. (Beelzebub was simply a degeneration of the Phoenician god Baal-Zebul, 'Lord of the Flies'.) The concept of Satan as public prosecutor may have developed from the function at the Persian court of an official called the 'King's eye', whose business it was to inform the king about his subjects.

In the text of the New Testament, the term Satan — transliterated from the Hebrew word — designates a personal devil. He is, however, known by various other names and descriptions, of which the most common in the Gospels is 'the devil', from the Greek word *diabolos,* meaning 'slanderer'. Elsewhere he is called 'Abaddon' or 'Apollyon' (Rev. 9:11), 'Deceiver of the whole world' (Rev. 12:9), 'Accuser' (Rev. 12:10), 'Adversary' (1 Pet. 5:8), 'Belial' (2 Cor. 6:15), 'The prince of the power of the air' (Eph. 2:2), 'the great dragon' and 'that ancient serpent' (Rev. 12:9). The Fourth Gospel includes many references to him by Jesus, as 'the evil one', 'the father of lies', 'a murderer from the beginning who has nothing to do with the truth, because there is no truth in him'. The writer of Jude describes him as the arch-enemy of the archangel Michael, cast out of heaven to roam the earth, as the 'prince of this world', a title thrice given him in the Fourth Gospel. This suggests the Jewish conception of the inherent evil of the present age and the good time expected in the age to come.

The first three Gospels describe the inward struggle of Jesus to face the implications and manner of his Messiahship in the form of three direct temptations by the devil in person.

The key to the understanding of the 'temptations' is to be found in the words of the divine voice at Jesus's baptism: 'Thou art my beloved Son; with thee I am well pleased.' (Mark 1:11) It was this fresh awareness of his sonship to God traumatically linked with that very clear reference to the Suffering Servant from Isaiah 52 (a reference repeated in all the Synoptic Gospels) that 'drove Jesus into the wilderness'. In that threatening environment, the evil one appeared, to offer him the means of escaping the cost of his Messiahship. The devil suggested various means of his gaining acceptance of God's kingdom among men but through the wrong means, the age-old means of coercing men's loyalty without first winning their hearts. These means included the bribery of the crowds by turning stones into bread, the spectacle and display of power in floating off the wing of the Temple down into the Kidron Valley, and finally the compromise of good with evil to secure the best of both worlds. All these Jesus rejected, using the words of scripture to confront and to confound the devil.

However literally we may interpret this experience, Jesus himself clearly recognized the existence and power of a kingdom of evil under the control of a supreme personality to whom he referred as 'Satan' or 'Be-elzebul'. The principal function of the Messiah was to destroy the works of Satan (Mark 1:24, 34; 3:11, 15). In the expulsion of devils or exorcism by his disciples during the mission of the seventy, Jesus saw the overthrow of Satan's power. (Luke 10:18) His disciples, too, interpreted Jesus's acts of exorcism as attacks on the power and influence on the devil.

After 'casting out a demon' from a dumb man, the scribes from Jerusalem accused Jesus of exorcising by the power of 'Be-elzebul, the prince of demons'. To them Jesus gave a very practical answer, 'But he, knowing their thoughts, said to them, "Every kingdom divided against itself is laid waste, and house falls upon house. And if Satan also is divided against himself, how will his kingdom stand? For you say that I cast out demons by Be-elzebul. And if I cast out demons by Be-elze-

514

bul, by whom do your sons cast them out? Therefore they shall be your judges. But if it is by the finger of God that I cast out demons, then the kingdom of God has come upon you." ' (Luke 11:17-20)

He then told a parable clearly illustrating that his arrival as Messiah was about to establish the kingdom of God in this world and would inexorably seize control, hitherto in the hands of the 'strong man', the 'prince of this world': 'When a strong man, fully armed, guards his own palace, his goods are in peace; but when one stronger than he assails him and overcomes him, he takes away his armour in which he trusted, and divides his spoil.' (Luke 11:21, 22)

The Apostle Paul shared the contemporary belief in the reality of the devil, whom he linked with the serpent in the garden of Eden, 'But I am afraid that as the serpent deceived Eve by his cunning, your thoughts will be led astray from a sincere and pure devotion to Christ'. (2 Cor. 11:3) 'For while your obedience is known to all ... I would have you wise as to what is good and guileless as to what is evil; then the God of peace will soon crush Satan under your feet.' (Rom. 16:19, 20)

The Book of Revelation contains a detailed account of the devil's persecution of the early Church, under the figure of the 'woman clothed with the sun, with the moon under her feet' whose new-born child is threatened by the dragon. The 'dream-picture' goes on to explain that the dragon, defeated in heaven, has been cast out into the earth. There, for a limited time, the war between good and evil will continue. 'Now war arose in heaven, Michael and his angels fighting against the dragon; and the dragon and his angels fought, but they were defeated and there was no longer any place for them in heaven. And the great dragon was thrown down, that ancient serpent, who is called the Devil and Satan, the deceiver of the whole world – he was thrown down to the earth, and his angels were thrown down with him. . . . Rejoice then, O heaven and you that dwell therein! But woe to you, O earth and sea, for the devil has come down to you in great wrath, because he knows that his time is short!' (Rev. 12:7-9, 12) [Matt. 12:26; Mark 8:33; Luke 10:18; 22:3; Acts 5:3; 26:18; Rom. 16:20; 1 Cor. 5:5; 2 Cor. 2:11; 12:7; 2 Thess. 2:9; 1 Tim. 1:20; Rev. 2:24; 20:7]

SAUL (of Tarsus) (Heb. 'asked of God') *see* PAUL

SCEVA The arch-priest or high priest, whose seven sons at Ephesus attempted exorcism in the name of 'Jesus whom Paul preaches', with disastrous results to themselves.

Luke, in Acts, describes Paul's long teaching activity in Ephesus, accompanied by an extraordinary sequence of healings and exorcisms of unclean spirits. Ephesus was a noted centre for magic and itinerant exorcists, both pagan and Jewish. Perhaps the 'sons of Sceva' were not literally brothers, but members of a guild of exorcists, led by a priest with the Latin name of Sceva. The patient upon whom they misused the name of Jesus, however, turned on them in insane fury and drove them away, stripped and wounded.

Luke goes on to describe the effect of this encounter: 'And this became known to all residents of Ephesus, both Jews and Greeks; and fear fell upon them all; and the name of the Lord Jesus was extolled. Many also of those who were now believers came, confessing and divulging their practices. And a number of those who practised magic arts brought their books together and burned them in the sight of all; and they counted the value of them and found it came to fifty thousand pieces of silver. So the word of the Lord grew and prevailed mightily.' (Acts 19:17-20) [Acts 19:14]

SCRIBES (Gk. from Heb. 'man of letters') The Scribes were the expert lawyers, who interpreted and extemporized the written Law by a mass of their own traditions. They were the acknowledged and respected teachers of the Law, both in the schools and in the courts.

Before the exile of the Jews to Babylon, the Scribes had been the public writers and secretaries. They had copied the Law and other manuscripts; in doing so they had become the leading authorities and interpreters of the Law. Ezra the Scribe, in the post-exilic period, had instructed the returned exiles in the study of the Law. So it was that the Scribes developed gradually into a professional class, devoted to the copying, exposition, and application of the Law. Then, during the Hellenistic period, when the Law and its observance were threatened by pagan and Greek influence, it was the Scribes, together with the Pharisees, who became the defenders and teachers of the Law to the common people, and even the magistrates.

By the time of Jesus, the Scribes had developed a complicated system of traditions to ensure the correct application of the Law. They had come to demand and to receive the deep respect of the people. The very title 'Rabbi', meaning 'My Teacher', by which some were known indicates the honour in which they were held. In the Gospels they are often linked with the Pharisees, whose convictions some Scribes shared as Pharisees. There were, however, Scribes within the Sanhedrin, the supreme Council, both Pharisaic and apparently Sadducean Scribes. These are mentioned among the members of the court which convicted Jesus of blasphemy in Jerusalem.

In Galilee, too, the Scribes were highly critical of Jesus's activities, particularly at Capernaum, where the synagogue congregation compared Jesus's authoritative preaching with the less inspired efforts of their Scribes. The Scribes objected strongly to Jesus's words of forgiveness to the paralytic, saying, 'Who can forgive sins but God alone?' Again, they complained at his eating with Matthew the publican and his colleagues. In the Gospel of Luke, Jesus replies to them with the parables of the lost and the found: the Lost Sheep, the Lost Coin, and the Prodigal Son – implying that he, Jesus, was sent to seek and to save those who were lost.

In Jerusalem, the Scribes were among the delegation that questioned Jesus's authority to drive the merchants out of the Temple. On at least two occasions an individual Scribe spoke to Jesus; when he was in the Temple, a Scribe asked which was the first commandment. Receiving and approving of Jesus's answer, he said: 'You are right, Teacher; you have truly said that he is one, and there is no other but he; and to love him with all the heart, and with all the understanding, and with all the strength, and to love one's neighbour as oneself, is much more than . . . sacrifice.' To which Jesus replied, 'You are not far from the kingdom of God.' Again, it was another Scribe who asked, 'Teacher, what shall I do to inherit eternal life?' then having partly answered his own question, the Scribe asked, 'And who is my neighbour?' It was in answer to this question that Jesus told him the story of the Good Samaritan and added, 'Go and do likewise.'

For the most part, however, the Gospels (and particularly that of Matthew) show Jesus in outspoken condemnation of the Scribes, together with the Pharisees. He saw that their mass of petty traditions often contra-

518

dicted the spirit of the Law, however much they preserved the letter of the Law. He felt that the Scribes, by their systematic codification, robbed the common people of any freedom of interpretation, according to their own conscience. The Scribes, he felt, 'set a fence around the law'. It is perhaps not surprising that many Scribes became his most bitter opponents and called forth from him a devastating denunciation – for their hypocrisy, their blindness, and their neglect of justice, mercy, and good faith. They sought to win for men the kingdom of Heaven by the meticulous observance of a written code. Jesus, in his Sermon on the Mount, set forward the two principles of self-sacrifice and service.

But the teaching of the Scribes had many virtues, as may be seen in the *Mishnah,* the earliest collection of Scribal teaching. It was a genuine attempt on the part of devoted scholars to interpret the Law so that men could be saved from unintentional transgression. There was much reference to other rabbis' opinions and little originality, but a vast amount of painstaking scholarship. The existence of the Law of Moses made the tradition of the Scribes necessary; for it was only by a traditional interpretation of the Law that it could be applied to the particular day and circumstances. For instance, if keeping the Sabbath involved not working, it was necessary for tradition to define what constituted work in that day and age. For Jesus, however, the Law was a matter of principles to be obeyed by a willing assent. *see also* PHARISEES [Matt. 5:20; 7:29; 16:21; 17:10; 20:18; 21:15; Mark 1:22; 2:6, 16; 8:31; 9:14; 10:33; 11:18; 12:28, 35, 38; 14:1; Luke 5:30; 6:7; 11:53; 20:1, 19; 22:2; 23:10; John 8:3; Acts 4:5; 6:12; 23:9]

SCYTHIAN (Gk. 'inhabitants of Scythia', but colloquially 'savages') The classical term for uncivilized foreigners, emanating from the name of the savage tribes in the steppe-lands beyond the Carpathians and the Caucasus, that is, to the north-east of the Roman Empire.

The Apostle Paul, writing to the Christian community at Colossae in Asia Minor, says that Christians have to put aside all the unworthy passions that belong to their baser nature. They are to have a new nature, formed after God's own likeness. Within this new Christian manhood there are to be no arbitrary divisions, as in the Roman world of Paul's day, where 'man is a wolf to his fellow man'. All men, says Paul, are made in the image of God. Divisions and antagonists have no meaning for the Christian. 'Here there cannot be Greek and Jew, circumcised and uncircumcised, barbarian, Scythian, slave, freeman, but Christ is all, and in all.' (Col. 3:11) The pairs of the words used are opposites, except for 'barbarian', the Greek term of vilification for any foreigner, and 'Scythian', the Roman equivalent. Both terms imply that these peoples neither spoke the language nor shared the culture of the Greeks and Romans, who consequently regarded them as totally uncivilized. [Col. 3:11]

SECUNDUS (Gk. from the Lat. 'second') One of two Thessalonian representatives chosen to accompany Paul on his return to Jerusalem with the poor-relief collected from the various Christian communities in the Mediterranean. Fearing an ambush if he travelled via Corinth, Paul travelled overland through Macedonia, in the spring of the year 58, as far as Troas on the coast of Asia Minor, and so by sea to Caesarea and Jerusalem, with an escort of seven men, of whom Secundus was one. [Acts 20:4]

SERGIUS PAULUS The Roman governor of the island

of Cyprus converted by Paul at Paphos on his First Journey.

When Paul, Barnabas, and Mark visited Cyprus in the year 46, on the first of Paul's Journeys, they fell in with a false prophet and sorcerer, who belonged to the suite of the Roman proconsul. It is quite in keeping with what is known of Roman colonial life that a learned Jew should have been attached to his household, that is, one who combined his philosophy with the exercise of magic or divination.

When Sergius Paulus invited Paul and Barnabas to present 'the word of God' to him, Elymas Bar-Jesus attempted to balk the teaching of the Christian gospel to his Roman master. Paul pronounced a curse upon him, as it were 'beating him at his own game', and inducing a temporary blindness, which both silenced the opposition and so impressed the governor that he accepted and believed the gospel proclaimed by Paul.

The name of Sergius Paulus occurs in the writings of Pliny the Elder about twenty years after this event; the name is also found in the works of the 3rd-century physician Galen. Two inscriptions have been found which include his name: the first contemporary with his lifetime and discovered in Cyprus, the second concerning the Christian family of a Sergius Paul in Asia Minor, at a rather later date. [Acts 13:7]

SILAS (Aram. from Heb. 'asked of God') A Roman citizen and companion of Paul on his Second Journey, AD 50-1, as far as to Corinth. Silas was still at Corinth when Paul wrote to the Christian community at Thessalonica, but then disappears entirely from the letters of Paul. He reappears as the emanuensis of Peter in Rome, perhaps thirteen years later. He is both the writer and bearer of Peter's letter to a group of Christian congregations in Asia Minor.

Silas first appears as one of two distinguished prophets, probably Jews of the Diaspora, commissioned as official delegates to convey the decision of the Council of Jerusalem to Antioch, in the year 49. The delegates were to deliver a written letter and to give orally this message, 'For it has seemed good to the Holy Spirit and to us to lay upon you no greater burden than these necessary things: that you abstain from what has been sacrificed to idols and from blood and from what is strangled and from unchastity. If you keep yourselves from these, you will do well. Farewell.' (Acts 15:28-29)

Silas and Judas gathered the community at Antioch and discharged their duty, with a wealth of advice and encouragement. They then returned, with greetings from Antioch, to Jerusalem. Silas, however, must have returned to Antioch by the spring of the year 50. Paul and Barnabas at Antioch had meanwhile planned to revisit together the young Churches in Cyprus and Galatia, but they disagreed on the question as to whether John Mark, Barnabas's nephew, should accompany them. Finally, they divided forces and Barnabas sailed with Mark for Cyprus, while Paul took Silas to encourage the Galatian Churches. The name Silas is the Aramaic form of Saul. He is called Silvanus in the correspondence with the Thessalonians, and was the bearer of Peter's first letter to the Church in Asia. Like Paul, Silas also was a Roman citizen.

Timothy was added to the team. Because Timothy was the son of a Greek married to a Jewess, Paul insisted on his circumcision, in order to remove obstacles to his working among Jews. Passing through Iconium and Antioch, impelled by some positive spiritual guidance, they did not turn south to the coast, but made their way through Phrygia and Troas, a port of the north-west coast of Asia Minor. Again, guided this time by the vision of a Macedonian calling for help, Paul sailed via Samothrace, over the Aegean, to Neapolis in Europe.

Taking to that great military highway, the Via Egnatia, which linked Rome and the east, Paul, Silas, and Timothy moved inland to Philippi, a Roman colony and city founded by the father of Alexander the Great. There being few Jews and no synagogue, Paul stayed with a devout Jewess called Lydia, a dealer in dyed cloth, whose household was the first in Europe to be converted and baptized. Paul was enabled to conduct house-meetings near the River Ganga.

Soon, however, an unpleasant incident put an end to their stay in Philippi. A certain soothsaying slave-girl with an evil spirit began following them, and Paul commanded the spirit to leave her. Her employers, who made considerable profit from her fortune-telling, had Paul and Silas arrested. Under pressure from the mob, the magistrates had Paul and Silas stripped, flogged, thrown into gaol, and put in the stocks. That night an earthquake released all the prisoners, and the gaoler was about to commit suicide when Paul called him and spoke to him about Jesus. He and his family were converted; they took their prisoners home to feed and care for them before returning them to the prison. When, the following morning, the magistrates sent the order for their release, Paul and Silas insisted on the magistrates themselves freeing them. Although Paul never forgot his degradation and suffering at Philippi, his letter to the Church there was full of affection and thanksgiving.

The party travelled seventy miles westwards along

the Via Egnatia to Thessalonica, the historical city and chief port of the Aegean. Paul preached on three consecutive Sabbaths in the synagogue, proving Jesus to be the Messiah, with some success among both Jews and Gentiles, men and women. With the help, however, of a market-place mob, the Jewish community stormed the house of one Jason, a Jew of the Diaspora, and accused him together with Paul and Silas of disloyalty to the Roman emperor, in declaring a rival king, Jesus. As a result, Paul and Silas left that night for Beroea, travelling west along the Via Egnatia.

When they arrived they went to the Jewish synagogue, where they were received with eagerness and much examining of the scriptures. Many believed and accepted the message of Paul and Silas; soon, however, Jews arrived from Thessalonica and, jealous of their success, incited the mob against them. Paul then set off to the coast, to make his way by sea to Athens, while Silas and Timothy remained some time at Beroea, with instructions to meet him at Corinth.

Some time later, they joined Paul at Corinth in an intense teaching mission, first within the synagogue and then in a Gentile household next to the synagogue. After eighteen months, following further friction with the Jews, Paul sailed from the port of Cenchreae, via Ephesus, and so to Antioch. Silas disappears from the story some time towards the end of the year 52. We know that he remained some considerable time with Paul at Corinth, because both the letters to the Christian community at Thessalonica are addressed, 'Paul, Silvanus, and Timothy, to the Church of the Thessalonians in God the Father and the Lord Jesus Christ: Grace to you and peace.'

How soon Silas began to work with Peter either in

Greece, Asia or Rome, we may never know. One theory is that, by the year 64, he was in Rome writing a letter for Peter – in far better Greek than was possible for Peter – to a group of Churches in northern Asia Minor. This letter (1 Peter) included a systematic presentation of the Christian faith within the early Church, together with a message of encouragement to Churches under the shock of a sudden and violent persecution. The whole is unlike a letter in form or content, but is a highly efficient composition. The Greek is excellent, the style deliberate and elaborate, the sentences balanced and polished, the tone calm and tranquil.

Although Luke's specific references to Silas are few and far between, he must have been a tremendously competent and useful member both of Paul's teaching team and also of the staff of the Apostle Peter in Rome. [Acts 15:22-40; 16:25, 29; 17:4, 10, 14, 15; 18:5; 2 Cor. 1:19; 1 Thess. 1:1; 2 Thess. 1:1; 1 Pet. 5:12]

SILVANUS *see* SILAS

SIMEON (Heb., Gk. 'hearing') **1. Simeon, the priest** The first-born son of every Jewish family had to be presented within the Temple at Jerusalem forty days after birth. In earlier, pagan times, the first son had often been sacrificed to the tribal god, as the first-fruit of the family. Now the Hebrew Law had adapted this primitive custom by demanding the offering of 5 shekels, in order to 'redeem' or buy back the child from God, to whom his life was owed.

The parents of Jesus took him up to Jerusalem to present him to the Lord, as demanded in the book of Exodus (13:2): 'Consecrate to me all the first-born; whatever is the first to open the womb among the people of Israel, both of man and of beast, is mine.' Mary and Joseph took with them the purification offering demanded in the Book of Leviticus (5:7) — 'two turtle-doves or two young pigeons'.

On this occasion, an upright and devout Jew called Simeon, who looked forward to the deliverance of Israel, met them in the Temple. He had been shown that he would not die without seeing 'the Lord's Christ'. Taking the child Jesus in his arms, he blessed God, saying: 'Lord, now lettest thou thy servant depart in peace, according to thy word; for mine eyes have seen thy salvation which thou hast prepared in the presence of all peoples, a light for revelation to the Gentiles, and for glory to thy people Israel.' (Luke 2:29-32)

Simeon's song has for over 1,500 years formed part of the evening offices of the Christian Church as the *Nunc Dimittis*.

As Simeon gave back the child Jesus into the arms of his mother and blessed the parents, he uttered the rather enigmatic prophecy: 'Behold, this child is set for the fall and rising of many in Israel, and for a sign that is spoken against (and a sword will pierce through your own soul also), that thoughts out of many hearts may be revealed.' (Luke 2:34-35)

This has generally been taken to refer to the anguish caused to Mary, mother of Jesus, at his crucifixion. So, too, the promise of universal salvation in Simeon's song, as recorded by Luke, 'a light for revelation to the Gentiles', may have been inspired by the Suffering Servant songs of the Second Isaiah. [Luke 2:25-35]

2. Simeon, called 'Niger' [R.S.V. Symeon] This man is listed among the prophets and teachers of the Christian Church in Antioch, who were 'guided by the Spirit' to select and despatch Paul and Barnabas on the First Journey to Cyprus and Galatia. These leaders at the headquarters of the Christian Church included Barnabas, himself a Cypriot-Jew, Simeon 'Niger', Lucius from Cyrene, Manaen, a one-time companion of Herod Antipas, and Paul the Apostle. [Acts 13:1]

3. Simeon, referring to Simon Peter [R.S.V. Symeon] *see* PETER

SIMON (Heb., Gk. 'hearing') There are no less than nine men of this name to be found within the New Testament.

1. Simon Peter
2. Simon, 'the Cananaean' or 'the Zealot'
3. Simon, brother of Jesus
4. Simon, the leper
5. Simon, the Pharisee
6. Simon, father of Judas Iscariot
7. Simon of Cyrene
8. Simon, the sorcerer
9. Simon, the tanner

1. Simon Peter *see* PETER

2. Simon, 'the Cananaean' or 'the Zealot' In the lists of the twelve apostles, Mark and Matthew call him 'the Cananaean', an Aramaic word meaning 'the zealous one' (not connected with Canaan, or with the village of Cana in Galilee). Luke uses the Greek word, 'the Zealot'. In each case, the implication may be that this Simon was a member of the Zealot party, the fanatical nationalist group whose guerrilla activities were designated to drive out the Roman occupation forces, but in fact provoked many bloody reprisals. The rise of the Zealots may be traced to the revolt of Judas of Gamala in AD 6; their story culminated in the disastrous revolt of AD 66, resulting in the fall and destruction of Jerusalem by the Romans in the year 70.

The Zealots found most of their support among the

hot-headed Galileans, whose tropical climate and temperament provided fertile soil for both political and religious dissent. Simon may well have come from the lakeside, like so many other early followers of Jesus. Luke, in both his Gospel and the Acts, links Simon with Judas among the apostles. Nothing further is known with certainty about these two, and an apocryphal work *The Passion of Simon and Jude* describes their preaching and martyrdom in Persia. They are still linked together on their combined feast-day in the Western Church on 28 October. [Matt. 10:4; Mark 3:18; Luke 6:15; Acts 1:13]

3. Simon, brother of Jesus This Simon is among the family of Jesus mentioned by the congregation at Nazareth, when they were impressed by Jesus's preaching. 'Is not this the carpenter, the son of Mary and brother of James and Joses and Judas and Simon, and are not his sisters here with us?' (Mark 6:3) John commented on the fact that in the last year of Jesus's life his own brothers did not believe in him. We do not know, however, whether Simon, like his brothers James, later became a member of the Christian Church. *see also* JOSEPH 2. [Matt. 13:55; Mark 6:3]

4. Simon, the leper The term 'leper' is used generally to apply to one with any skin disease, and Simon was a former sufferer who had been cured either by Jesus or by someone else. Mark and Matthew describe Simon the leper as living in Bethany, where he entertained Jesus at his house.

During the meal a woman came in with an alabaster jar of precious ointment, called nard. She broke the jar and poured the ointment on the head of Jesus. This may be interpreted as being a singular honour to the guest, or – more specifically – as symbolic of the anointing of the Messiah. Some of those present complained at what they considered a waste of good ointment, worth 300 silver denarii (a year's wages for a working man), that could have been given to the poor. Jesus, however, defended the woman with these words: 'Let her alone; why do you trouble her? She has done a beautiful thing to me. For you always have the poor with you, and whenever you will, you can do good to them; but you will not always have me. She has done what she could; she has anointed my body beforehand for burying. And truly, I say to you, wherever the gospel is preached in the whole world, what she has done will be told in memory of her.' (Mark 14:6-9)

This story in Mark and Matthew is sometimes linked and compared with a story in Luke's Gospel. (*see* SIMON 5.) The writer of the Fourth Gospel appears to use Mark's account of the anointing at Bethany as the basis of a similar story, and he seems to have incorporated some features from Luke's account, too. John puts the story in the context of Holy Week. The hosts are Mary, Martha, and Lazarus. Mary is the woman with the ointment. Judas Iscariot complains at the waste of money and Jesus's reply is nearly identical, 'Let her alone, let her keep it for the day of my burial. The poor you always have with you, but you do not always have me.' (John 12:7, 8) [Matt. 26:6; Mark 14:3]

5. Simon, the Pharisee He may have been identical with Simon 'the leper', whose story is recorded by Mark and Matthew, but the story of Simon the Pharisee as recorded by Luke has many distinct features and probably refers to another person and occasion.

The scene is set in Galilee, not Bethany. The woman is locally notorious – 'a woman of the city, who was a sinner' – and comes with the intention of making an act of penitence to Jesus. 'Standing behind him at his feet, weeping, she began to wet his feet with her tears, and wiped them with the hair of her head, and kissed his feet, and anointed them with the ointment.' (Luke 7:38)

Simon the Pharisee condescendingly looks on, assuming that a prophet like this rabbi Jesus will at least have the insight to see the sort of woman she is and therefore drive her away. When both the woman herself and Simon have waited long enough to have their true motives tested, Jesus, reading their minds, says to the Pharisee, ' "Simon, I have something to say to you." And he answered, "What is it, Teacher?" "A certain creditor had two debtors; one owed 500 denarii, and the other 50. When they could not pay, he forgave them both. Now which of them will love him more?" Simon answered, "The one, I suppose, to whom he forgave more." And he said to him, "You have judged rightly." ' (Luke 7:40-43) Then, turning to the woman whose uninhibited penitence and emotional abandon contrasted so clearly with the veiled criticism and discourteous condescension of the Pharisee, Jesus says, ' "Do you see this woman? I entered your house, you gave me no water for my feet, but she has wet my feet with her tears and wiped them with her hair. You gave me no kiss, but from the time I came in she has not ceased to kiss my feet. You did not anoint my head with oil, but she has anointed my feet with ointment. Therefore I tell you, her sins, which are many, are forgiven, for she loved much; but he who is forgiven little, loves little." And he said to her . . . 'Your faith has saved you; go in peace." ' (Luke 7:44-48)

Luke is now slow to notice and to compare the passion of penitence and the coldness of reason. With his deep sensitivity, Luke well knows that the basis of all forgiveness is love, and that the spring of love is often just this sense of forgiveness. [Luke 7:36-50]

6. Simon, father of Judas Iscariot Only the Fourth Gospel mentions the father of Judas. The family of the traitor-disciple hailed from the village of Kerioth, in southern Judea; hence the title *Ish-Kerioth,* meaning 'man of Kerioth'. [John 6:71; 13:2, 26]

7. Simon of Cyrene This Simon was the passer-by compelled to carry the cross of Jesus to the place of execution. Matthew and Luke describe him as of Cyrene, part of Libya in North Africa. Mark records that he was the father of Alexander and Rufus, rather as though these two sons had become Christians and were known to his readers, perhaps in Rome. Luke and Mark both say that Simon of Cyrene had 'come in from the country', as though he were on a Passover pilgrimage, either all the way from Cyrene or from the neighbouring countryside of Jerusalem. All three Synoptic Gospels state that he was pressed into the unpleasant job of carrying the cross-piece for the exhausted Jesus on his way to Calvary.

As the Roman routine of interrogation included a preliminary flogging and, once the prisoner was condemned, inevitably a scourging followed, it was not surprising that despite the encouragement of the lash many criminals collapsed on their way to execution. The drugged wine offered by the Guild of the Women of Jerusalem, at the Judgment Gate, served the double purpose of reviving and anaesthetizing the prisoners – yet this Jesus refused.

The writer of the Fourth Gospel specifically states that Jesus 'went out, bearing his own cross' to Golgotha, and makes no mention of Simon of Cyrene. Perhaps this was to contradict some rumour of the substitution of Simon for Jesus — not only in the carrying of the cross, but in the actual crucifixion. [Matt. 27:32; Mark 15:21; Luke 23:26]

8. Simon, the sorcerer After the stoning of Stephen and the persecution of Hellenized Christians in Jerusalem, Philip the Deacon carried out a mission to Samaria. His preaching and healing impressed the Samaritan community, among whom Simon Magus was a magician of considerable power and influence. Simon had for a long time worked his magic with such success that the people said, 'This man is that power of God which is called Great.' (Acts 8:10)

But Philip so impressed the Samaritans that they accepted his message of 'good news about the kingdom of God and the name of Jesus Christ'. They were baptized, including Simon the sorcerer, who 'continued with Philip. And seeing signs and great miracles performed, he was amazed' – hoping, perhaps, to learn more of this remarkable new power.

The apostles in Jerusalem followed up Philip's success by sending Peter and John to Samaria to teach and to confirm the Samaritans by the gift of the Holy Spirit, imposed by the laying-on of their hands. Simon was again highly impressed and tried to bribe the apostles with money, saying, 'Give me also this power, that any one on whom I lay my hands may receive the Holy Spirit.' Peter answered, ' "Your silver perish with you, because you thought you could obtain the gift of God with money! You have neither part nor lot in this matter, for your heart is not right before God. Repent therefore of this wickedness of yours, and pray to the Lord that, if possible, the intent of your heart may be forgiven you. For I see that you are in the gall of bitterness and in the bond of iniquity." And Simon answered,

"Pray for me to the Lord, that nothing of what you have said may come upon me." ' (Acts 8:19-24)

Peter's blistering rebuke seems to have taken effect in the resultant penitence of Simon. Post-apostolic traditions, however, credit this Simon with being the 'father of Christian heresy'. He is said by the historian Justin Martyr to have gone to Rome in the time of the Emperor Claudius (AD 41-54) and to have been the father of Gnosticism. [Acts 8:9-24]

9. Simon, the tanner After the conversion of Paul and his first visit to Jerusalem, Peter lived for some time in Joppa, lodging with a leather-tanner called Simon. It was to the house of this Simon that the Roman centurion Cornelius was sent to summon Peter to Caesarea.

It was on the roof of Simon's house at Joppa that Peter had his vision of the clean and unclean aninals, and his commission to accept the first Gentile members of the Christian Church. (*see also* CORNELIUS) The traditional site of the house of Simon the tanner was, until very recently, shown overlooking the harbour of ancient Joppa. [Acts 9:43; 10:6, 17, 32]

SOPATER A Christian from the town of Beroea, in northern Greece, the son of Pyrrhus. He is the first mentioned of the companions of Paul on his final journey from Corinth to Jerusalem. The companions were representatives of the cities whose Christian congregations had subscribed to the relief of the community in Jerusalem. [Acts 20:4]

SOSIPATER A Jewish-Christian in Rome, mentioned in the final greetings at the close of Paul's letter to the Christian community in Rome. Paul describes him as 'my compatriot', that is, a fellow-Jew.

Whether the final chapter of Paul's letter to Rome included messages to Christians at Ephesus or at Rome, the Sosipater who linked his greetings with those of Paul may well have been the same man as Sopater of Beroea. *see* SOPATER [Rom. 16:21]

SOSTHENES 1. The ruler of the synagogue at Corinth in the years 51 and 52, at the time of Paul's long stay there on his Second Journey, Sosthenes was also probably Paul's chief accuser before the new proconsul, Gallio, though whether he later became the Christian 'brother Sosthenes', Paul's emanuensis for his letter to the Christian Church, is a matter of guesswork.

The Apostle Paul had spent 18 months in Corinth, working with Aquila and Priscilla, both tentmaking and building up the young Christian Church in that very pagan city. No doubt, as elsewhere, the Jewish synagogue had provided both the pulpit and the congregation for Paul's preaching. Certainly it was the Jews, probably led by their synagogue ruler Sosthenes, who took Paul up before the tribunal, saying. 'This man is persuading men to worship God contrary to the Law.' Before Paul could even answer the charge, Gallio the proconsul, as the judge, dismissed the case with these words, 'If it were a matter of wrongdoing or vicious crime, I should have reason to bear with you, O Jews; but since it is a matter of questions about words and names and your own Law, see to it yourselves; I refuse to be a judge of these things.' (Acts 18:14, 15) And Gallio ordered the court to be cleared.

Gallio's decision was that the prosecution had no case, but the charge against Paul was a cunning one and quite different from that brought by the Jews at Thessalonica. There, they accused Paul and his followers of 'acting against the decrees of Caesar, saying that there is another king, Jesus,' at which the magistrates were somewhat disturbed, but must have realized that the accusation was absurd. Here at Corinth the Roman proconsul, Gallio, was asked to decide whether Paul's teaching was contrary to the Law and put him outside the pale of Judaism and, particularly, outside the toleration by the Roman law afforded to Jews. Gallio, however, had the philosophical temperament of his Stoic brother Seneca, and was far too good a lawyer to entertain such a charge. Furthermore, it was outside the competence of any Roman governor to decide whether a Jew had comitted an offence against the Jewish Law, and Gallio rightly refused to try the case. He simply acquitted Paul and cleared the court.

Immediately the Greeks, perhaps even those who had listened to Paul from the God-fearers' courtyard attached to the synagogue, seized Sosthenes, the ruler of the synagogue, and very possibly Paul's chief prosecutor. They beat Sosthenes in front of the tribunal, but Gallio 'paid no attention' or, as one text puts it, 'pretended not to see'. [Acts 18:17]

2. The Christian 'brother' who acted as Paul's emanuensis for his first letter to the Church at Corinth from Ephesus. 'Sosthenes' was an uncommon name and this man may well have been the ruler of the synagogue at Corinth. *see* SOSTHENES **1.**) Certainly this man was well-known in the Corinthian community only three years after the incident involving the first Sosthenes, and was probably trusted with the taking of a letter back to the Christian congregation at Corinth. [1 Cor. 1:1]

SPIRIT OF GOD The Holy Spirit is the life and activity of God at work in the world of nature and also in and through people. The Hebrew word for 'spirit' is the same as that for 'breath' or 'wind', and can even imply 'life', just as the English word 'spirit' forms the root of

535

others, such as 'inspire', 'expire', and 'respiration', meaning 'breath in life'.

The Old Testament is a record of God's transmission of his life and energy among his people. His universal spirit has first given life and then, as man has evolved and has become able to absorb it, a knowledge of God. This inspiration has taken place through the minds of those men in each age who have responded by their prayer and reason to God's progressive self-revelation. To such men as the Hebrew prophets and sages, God was gradually able through his Spirit to show his character, enabling the building-up of assessment within the minds of his people. They in turn looked forward to a more personal manifestation in the coming of his Chosen One, the Messiah.

Paul, acknowledging Jesus as the Messiah, wrote, 'God has shone in our minds to radiate the light of the knowledge of his glory on the face of Christ', and again, 'God was in Christ reconciling the world to himself.' The writer of the Fourth Gospel interpreted the coming of Jesus as the incarnation of the activity of God: 'And the Word became flesh and dwelt among us, full of grace and truth; we have beheld his glory, glory as of the only Son from the Father.'

At Pentecost, after Jesus had ceased to be seen among his followers, they underwent a spiritual experience which they identified as the coming of the Spirit, but with a new power, which they somehow associated with their master Jesus. They came to believe that his life and work continued, by the power of the Spirit within his Church.

Jesus and the Spirit

It was through the 'overshadowing' of the Spirit that Mary conceived the child Jesus. At his baptism the Spirit descended upon him in the form of a dove, the bird of peace, so many of which can still be seen flying down the River Jordan.

Immediately the Spirit drove him into the wilderness where he was tempted to escape from his Messianic calling, but from which he returned 'in the power of the Spirit' to begin his preaching in Galilee. In the synagogue at Nazareth he reads the Messianic prophecy of Isaiah 61: 'The Spirit of the Lord is upon me. . . .' He announces that he casts out devils by the Spirit of God and that the kingdom of God has arrived.

In the Fourth Gospel the teaching about the Spirit appears in characteristic form within the long discourse that follows the Last Supper. Here the writer uses the term *paraclete,* meaning literally an 'advocate', and referring to the task of helping Jesus's disciples after he has 'gone'. 'And I will pray the Father, and he will give you another Counsellor, to be with you for ever, even the Spirit of truth. . . .' (John 14:15-17) During his life on earth, Jesus had been their *paraclete,* revealing and teaching the truth. The world does not recognize the Spirit which replaces Jesus, and therefore does not receive the Spirit. The Spirit continues to do what Jesus did. The Spirit would remind and help his disciples and work through them.

Jesus tells the disciples that their grief at his departure is mistaken, for his going makes possible the sending of the Spirit. The Spirit will vindicate Jesus in the eyes of the world through his followers. The Spirit will guide the disciples to the truth and to a progressively fuller understanding of the truth in Jesus. As Jesus revealed God, the Father, so the Spirit will reveal Jesus. 'These things I have spoken to you, while I am still with you. But the Counsellor, the Holy Spirit, whom the Father will send in my name, he will teach you all things, and bring to your remembrance all that I have said to you.' (John 14:25, 26) Through the Spirit, the followers of Jesus will proclaim to the world the triumph of Jesus, the judgment of sinners, and the dethroning of evil. After the resurrection, Jesus breathes upon his disciples in the Upper Room, saying, 'Receive the Holy Spirit,' as if imparting to them his own personality. Indeed, for John, 'Life in the Spirit' begins at the resurrection rather than at Pentecost.

The Apostles and the Spirit

The story of Pentecost in the Acts probably reflects the feelings, rather than the facts, on this occasion. The apostles had met together in the Upper Room, when 'suddenly a sound came from heaven like the rush of a mighty wind, and it filled all the house where they were sitting. And there appeared to them tongues as of fire, distributed and resting on each one of them. And they were all filled with the Holy Spirit and began to speak in other tongues, as the Spirit gave them utterance.' (Acts 2:2-4)

Certainly this spiritual experience generated a tremendous feeling of enthusiasm, which fired their hearts and minds, so that their message was understood by the cosmopolitan crowds in Jerusalem for the feast of Weeks. As a result 3,000 were recorded as being baptized and added to the 120 disciples. Following Peter's cure of the cripple at the Beautiful Gate of the Temple, and the questioning and release of Peter by the Sanhedrin, the apostles met in prayer to thank God. As they prayed (after what was perhaps the first crisis following Pentecost) the house where they were assembled rocked; they were all filled anew with the Spirit of God and began to proclaim the word of God boldly.

Pentecost, originally a harvest festival, became for later Judaism a feast of the giving of the Law, the Torah. For the Christian Church, however, the Holy Spirit replaced the Torah as God's supreme gift to man. The writer of the First Gospel regarded the Sermon on the Mount as the new Torah. Luke, the author of both the Third Gospel and the Acts, talked of the 'Sermon on the Plains' – keeping the Mountain of Zion for the giving of the Spirit – as the new Torah. A Jewish-Christian in Jerusalem might well have seen the events of Pentecost as the proclamation of the Torah for the proselytes of the world. The miraculous activity of the Spirit vindicated the truth of the gospel message and the authority of the apostles to preach it.

Then, gradually, came a reduction of emphasis on the miraculous power of the Spirit. His personification as the prophetic, inspiring, and guiding power among them was steadily accepted by the leaders of the primitive Church, who could say with complete faith: 'It has seemed good to the Holy Spirit and to us' to do this or that, and they did so both with confidence and success. They were able by the laying-on of their hands to transmit the gift of the Spirit to others. While Peter was still speaking to the Roman centurion Cornelius and his family at Caesarea, the Holy Spirit came down on all his listeners. The Jewish believers were astonished to see that the Gentiles present shared this experience, even the speaking in strange languages. Peter at once ordered their baptism, the first Gentile baptism within the hitherto Judeo-Christian Church.

Paul's interpretation

The Spirit occupies a central place in Paul's theology. The key to its understanding lies in Paul's vision, at his conversion, of Jesus in his glory – 'I am Jesus'. From that moment Paul's own life was transfigured with a wonderful spiritual strength. As he said to the Church at Philippi, 'Our commonwealth is in heaven, and from it we await a Saviour, the Lord Jesus Christ, who will change our lowly body to be like his glorious body, by the power which enables him even to subject all things to himself.' (Phil. 3:20-21) No wonder Paul described Jesus as 'life-giving spirit', seeing the function of Jesus as being identical with that of the Spirit, though he tried to distinguish between the persons by such phrases as 'the Spirit of Him who raised Jesus from the dead', and 'God has given us the pledge of the Spirit'. The new life that Paul discovered through Jesus he could only speak of – as did the primitive Christian Church – as 'life in the Spirit', compared with the old life in the flesh.

To Paul, this 'life in the Spirit' meant the dwelling of Jesus within the Christian heart.

Our reconciliation with God is made possible only by the saving sacrifice of Jesus, together with our response. Our response is prompted and guided by the Spirit. We are justified – that is, judged to be righteous – by our faith in Jesus. We are made holy by the action of the Spirit within us. The primitive Church identified the Spirit as the inner impetus which pointed them to the perfect life of Jesus, and also gave them power to live that life 'in Christ Jesus'.

After Pentecost, there was a tendency in the Christian community to perceive the working of the Spirit only in the cruder expressions of speaking in tongues and relapsing into ecstasies of wild emotions. It was Paul who insisted that the real tokens of the Spirit were to be found in the steady, normal life of faith, and in the secret inward assurance of the children of God. 'Since the Spirit is our life, let us be directed by the Spirit.'

Paul is adamant that the power of the Spirit is fundamentally shown in love and charity: 'The love of God has been poured into our hearts by the Holy Spirit which has been given us.' It is this love, says Paul, that builds up the Body of Christ, his Church, and holds it together in unity, as a 'fellowship of the Holy Spirit'. This communion of the Christian community is expressed within the Eucharist of the Church. [Mark 1:8; Luke 4:18; 12:12; John 4:24; 16:13; 20:22; Acts 2:17; 11:15, 16; 2 Cor. 3:17; Gal. 5:16-18, 22, 25; Eph. 4:30; 1 Thess. 5:19; Heb. 9:14; 1 John 5:7; Rev. 1:10; 22:17; and elsewhere throughout the New Testament]

STACHYS (Gk. 'head of grain') One of the Christians warmly greeted by Paul, as 'my beloved', at the close of his letter to the Church at Rome. [Rom. 16:9]

STEPHANAS (Gk. 'crown' or 'wreath') Stephanas was a Corinthian Christian and householder, one of the first converts and founder-members of the Church at Corinth.

Writing from Ephesus in the year 55, during his Third Journey, to the Church in Corinth which he had founded some four years before, Paul closes his letter: 'I rejoice at the coming of Stephanas and Fortunatus and Achaicus, because they have made up for your absence; for they have refreshed my spirit as well as yours. Give recognition to such men.'

541

Apparently the household of Stephànas included slaves and employees, such as Fortunatus and Achaicus. This was the first household to have been converted by Paul – and the only household to have been baptized by Paul – in Corinth, on his Second Journey in the year 51. These three men had travelled to Ephesus on business, possibly carrying a letter to Paul from Corinth, and were probably present with Paul as he completed the dictation of his answering letter. [1 Cor. 1:16; 16:15, 17]

STEPHEN (Gk. 'crown' or 'wreath') Stephen was one of the seven Greek-speaking or Hellenist disciples of Jesus who were chosen to assist the apostles in the distribution of gifts to widows, after a dispute about this matter between the members of the first Christian Church in Jerusalem. These seven men are commonly called the seven deacons, although the word 'deacon' does not actually appear in the account of their appointment. The word is used because it was their duty to serve (Gk. *diakonein*) at the tables where gifts were distributed.

Stephen is described as a man full of faith, grace and spiritual power who, after his appointment to office in the church, 'did great wonders and signs among the people'. (Acts 6:8) There was a disputation between him and other Hellenists in Jerusalem, members of the synagogue called the Synagogue of the Freedmen, as well as Jews coming from Egypt and Asia Minor; these would of course be Hellenists and the debate would have been in Greek; no doubt it concerned Jesus. After this his opponents 'secretly instigated men who said, "We have heard him speak blasphemous words against Moses and God." ' At the trial of Stephen before the Council evidence was given by 'false witnesses' who said, 'This man never ceases to speak words against this

542

holy place and the law; for we have heard him say that this Jesus of Nazareth shall destroy this place, and will change the customs which Moses delivered to us' (Acts 6:13, 14). 'This place' undoubtedly signifies the Temple and the charge is like the charge brought against Jesus, that he said that he would destroy the Temple. (Mark 14:28; Matt. 26:61)

Stephen makes a long speech in his own defence. As reported in the Acts of the Apostles, he reviews the history of the people of God from the days of Abraham to those of King David and King Solomon. About the Temple he says, 'David . . . found favour in the sight of God and asked leave to find a habitation for the God of Jacob. But it was Solomon who built a house for him. Yet the Most High does not dwell in houses made with hands.' This is followed by a quotation from the Book of Isaiah, 'Heaven is my throne, and earth my footstool. What house will you build for me, says the Lord, or what is the place of my rest? . . .' (Acts 7:46-50, and compare Isa. 66:1, 2) It may be that this was taken to be an attack on the Temple, although the prophet quoted was most certainly a worshipper in the Temple. Stephen may be reacting to signs of opposition to what he is saying when he goes on, in an attack on the men standing around him, 'You stiff-necked people, uncircumcised in heart and ears, you always resist the Holy Spirit. As your fathers did, so do you.'

This leads on to a reference to Jesus, 'the Righteous One, whom you have now betrayed and murdered'. To this there was more opposition. 'They were enraged, and they ground their teeth against him.' Stephen, seeing a vision, declared, 'Behold, I see the heavens opened, and the Son of Man standing at the right hand of God.' (Acts 7:56) This is like the statement of Jesus to the chief priests, 'But from now on the Son of Man shall be seated at the right hand of the power of God.' (Luke 23:69, and compare Mark 14:62, Matt. 26:64) This is treated as blasphemy. 'They cried out with a loud voice and stopped their ears and rushed together upon him. Then they cast him out of the city and stoned him; and the witnesses laid down their garments at the feet of a young man named Saul. And as they were stoning Stephen, he prayed, "Lord Jesus, receive my spirit." And he knelt down and cried with a loud voice, "Lord, do not hold this sin against them." ' These last words are like some of the last words of Jesus, as reported in the Gospel of Luke, 'Father, forgive them. . . .' (Acts 7:59, 60; Luke 23:34)

The author of Acts no doubt wishes to suggest that the death of Stephen helped to prepare the conversion of Saul, who becomes the Apostle Paul. He describes its immediate result as a general flight from Jerusalem of the disciples of Jesus, except for the apostles who remained in the city. A widespread persecution of the Hellenist section of the Christian Church followed. The disciples scattered not only throughout Judea and Samaria (the whole Samaritan community 'received the word of God') but they carried the gospel message from Jerusalem across the entire Mediterranean world.

There are two different traditions about the place outside Jerusalem where Stephen was stoned. In the year 415, his body was identified. A priest named Lucian had a dream in which he thought that he saw Gamaliel and was told by him that Stephen was buried at Geth Gemal, some 22 miles south-west of Jerusalem. A body found in a tomb there was brought to Jerusalem and buried in the Zion Church on the Western Hill. In the year 460 the Empress Eudocia built a basilica and a monastery for the training of deacons outside the north gate of the city. These were dedicated to the memory of Stephen and his relics were brought to the basilica, to be buried under the altar. The buildings were destroyed in 614, rebuilt some years later, restored in the period of the crusades and finally demolished in the 12th century. Stephen being associated with them, the gate now known as the Damascus Gate, or the Shechem Gate, was called St Stephen's Gate and his death was commemorated near it. In 1881 the Dominicans acquired the site of the basilica built by the Empress Eudocia and they built the Church of St Stephen over the ancient remains which they found there. Beside it is the renowned *Ecole biblique et archéologique française*. It should, however, be remembered that when Stephen was stoned there was no city wall or city gate in the neighbourhood of the Damascus or Shechem Gate, which belongs to the 'Third Wall'.

Another tradition places the stoning of Stephen in the Kidron Valley; there is a Greek Orthodox Church on this traditional site at Gethsemane, where the road to Jericho crosses the valley. Stephen's name has been given, in modern times, to the east gate of the city, north of the Temple site. This gate, built by the Sultan Beibars and also called the Gate of the Lions, is named by the Eastern Christians and by the Muslim community the Gate of the Lady Mary, *Bab Sit Miriam,* on account of its proximity to the traditional sites of the birth and burial of Mary the mother of Jesus.

Stephen became one of the most popular of all the saints during the Middle Ages, especially in Western Christendom. His feast followed immediately after Christmas Day and in the canon of the Mass according to the Roman rite his name was commemorated. [Acts 6:5-8:2; 11:19; 22:20]

STOICS The Greco-Roman philosophers who, together with the Epicureans, questioned the teachings of Paul in Athens and brought him to speak publicly on the Areopagus, during his Second Journey in the years 50-2. Tradition, but without evidence, claims that the Stoic philosopher and statesman Seneca conducted a long correspondence with the Apostle Paul. Stoicism was essentially the philosophy of the 'Establishment' and upheld the official moral standards of the Roman Empire.

In origin, Stoicism was a school of philosophy founded at Athens by the Jew Zeno, 335-263 BC, and had many famous Roman and Greek exponents. The Stoics believed in law, the law of nature and the law of conscience. God was the immanent all-pervading energy by which the world was created and sustained. Nature is controlled and ordered by an indwelling and divine *logos* or reason. The essence of man is his mind and capacity to understand this reasonable order within the world. The good man is the wise man, who accepts his fate, detaches himself from the world outside himself and masters his own reactions to that world. Thus, in theory and often in practice, the Stoic achieved a self-centred freedom, happiness, and self-sufficiency, but without pity, pardon, or feeling. For the Stoic, God was an impersonal energy, and sin was an error in judgment that could be corrected.

It was not surprising, therefore, that Paul's teaching about God as the 'maker and Lord of heaven and earth', who now calls 'all men everywhere to repent', who has 'fixed a day on which he will judge the world in righteousness' by someone already appointed 'by raising him from the dead', was hardly likely to appeal to the Stoics. Such doctrines of a personal God demanding a personal obedience, or a personal judgment by a risen person, were foreign to the thinking of the Stoic philosophers. [Acts 17:18]

SUSANNA (Heb., Gk. 'lily') Mentioned by Luke as one of the band of women who provided for the needs of Jesus and his disciples, during their itinerant ministry in Galilee, from out of their own means. [Luke 8:3]

SYMEON *see* SIMEON **2.** *and* **3.**

SYNTYCHE (Gk. 'fortunate') One of the two women members of the Christian congregation at Philippi who had been disagreeing. Probably news of their quarrel was brought to Paul in prison by Epaphroditus. In the letter which Epaphroditus now took back to Philippi, Paul wrote this appeal, 'I entreat Euodia and I entreat Syntyche to agree in the Lord. And I ask you also, true yokefellow, help these women, for they have laboured side by side with me in the gospel together with Clement and the rest of my fellow workers, whose names are in the book of life.' (Phil. 4:2, 3) The 'true yokefellow' referred to might well be an elder in their congregation, or may be read as the proper name 'Syzygus'. [Phil. 4:2]

SYRIANS All the people living north of Palestine, as far as the Euphrates, were named in biblical Hebrew '*Aram*', translated loosely as 'Syrians' or 'Arameans'. In nomadic groups they emerged from Mesopotamia, moving westwards in the 12th century BC. In the time of David, Solomon, and the Kings, there were several small kingdoms or city-states often at war with Israel. The language of these peoples is to be found in sections of the Books of Ezra and Daniel; later various Aramaic dialects were used in different parts of greater Syria, in Mesopotamia and Persia. Syria was the meeting-place of different cultures and religions, of Judaism, Hellenism, Gnosticism, and those of Persia and the East.

In the year 312 BC, a Syrian empire was founded by Seleucus, a general of Alexander the Great, and greatly extended by Antiochus the Great a century later. In a decisive battle of the Panium in 198 BC, near the sources of the Jordan, Antiochus defeated the army of Ptolemy V of Egypt and ended the Ptolemaic occupation of Palestine. He was finally defeated by the Romans in 190 BC at the battle of Magnesia, and Palestine and Jerusalem came under Syrian domination. His successor Antiochus Epiphanes provoked the Maccabean revolt by appointing a Hellenist-Jewish high priest and introducing the Hellenistic state religion. The Syrian armies finally withdrew in 145 BC, and yielded to Judah's demand for independence.

From 64 BC Syria became a Roman province, whose governor ruled from the ancient Seleucid capital at Antioch, on the Orontes. After Rome and Alexandria, Antioch was the third city of the Roman Empire, with a population of half a million, and of great political, econimic, and cultural importance, with the fine Mediterranean seaport of Seleucia some sixteen miles away. The Roman procurators of Judea and Samaria were directly responsible to the governors of Syria, and it was the Roman governor of Syria, Vitellius, who finally dismissed Pontius Pilate and sent him to Rome on the charge of cruelty. It was from bases in Syria that Vespasian launched his troops into Galilee in the year 67 and directed the siege of Jerusalem.

Within the New Testament narrative, Luke mentions Jesus's brief reference to 'Naaman the Syrian' to illustrate how the Jews had consistently rejected their prophets and were likely to reject him as Messiah. 'A prophet is not without honour except in his own country.' But when Jesus referred to the Gentile widow of Zarephath in Sidon, and Naaman the Syrian general, as examples of a more ready faith in the prophets Elijah and Elisha, the people of Nazareth were sufficiently enraged to attempt to stone him.

The greatest significance of Syria and Syrians within the story of the Christian Church is, without doubt, the fact that Saul the Persecutor was converted into Paul the Apostle on the road to Damascus, and that Antioch became the headquarters and centre of Christian activity among the Gentiles throughout Asia. It is possible that Luke the Evangelist hailed from Antioch and many scholars would say that the Gospel of Matthew was written in Syria. [Luke 4:27]

SYRO-PHOENICIAN The Phoenicians were a seafaring people, inhabiting the coastal strip north of the port of Acre and west of the Lebanon range. They were the people who in about 1500 BC had begun to develop a cuneiform alphabet of 30 letters, and they made extensive use of writing. They were primarily a nation of traders with a wide field of activity within the Mediterranean area, founding the city of Carthage in Tunisia, sailing as far as Spain and even to the south-west of Britain. The Phoenician cities of Byblos, Tyre, and Sidon transacted commerce with merchants from Egypt, Mesopotamia, Asia Minor, Cyprus, and Crete. Solomon recruited Phoenicians to man his navy, and used Phoenician labour in the construction of his Temple. Ahab married the Tyrian princess Jezebel.

From the 4th century BC, following the famous adventures of the Carthaginian general Hannibal and the Punic colonists, the *Syro*-Phoenicians were so-called to distinguish them from the Africans.

In the 1st century, the Phoenician coast was part of the Roman province of Syria. Jesus visited the district of Tyre and Sidon on the one occasion that we know he, the Jewish rabbi, crossed the border into foreign territory. Although he was in search of peace and quiet, after his busy ministry among the crowds at the lakeside of Galilee, he was accosted by a Syro-Phoenician woman appealing to him to heal her daughter. Both Mark and Matthew recount the story, though apparently they draw from different sources and their accounts are complementary.

Mark indicates that she was Greek by religion, Matthew that she was a Canaanite. She probably spoke in the common Greek of the Mediterranean world. Her little daughter was 'possessed by an unclean spirit' (the common term for describing epilepsy). She must have known the reputation of this Jewish rabbi, for she entreated him, crying repeatedly, 'Have mercy on me, O Lord, Son of David.' Jesus, however, did not answer her. She continued to pester Jesus until his embarrassed disciples begged him to 'send her away, for she is crying after us.' Jesus answered, 'I was sent only to the lost sheep of the house of Israel.'

At this point, the woman knelt in front of him, saying, 'Lord, help me.' Jesus then answered her, 'It is not fair to take the children's bread and throw it to the dogs,' meaning 'It is not right to spend the message for your own people on Gentiles.' Jesus's choice of words shows that he had his tongue in his cheek. He spoke with affection and humour. The sense of the words is rather: 'It is not fair to throw the kid's bread to puppies.'

The woman caught the tone of his banter and answered him in the same vein. The sense of her answer is: 'Yes, Lord, but the pups can lick up the crumbs under the master's table.' She thus accepted his decision, yet trusted him and believed that she would be comforted by someone who spoke and thought on her own level. Then Jesus responded to her need: 'O woman, great is your faith! Be it done for you as you desire,' and her daughter was instantly cured. Or, as Mark puts it, ' "For this saying you may go your way; the demon has left your daughter." And she went home, and found the child lying in bed, and the demon gone.' (Mark 7:-29, 30) [Matt. 15:21-28; Mark 7:26]

T

TABITHA (Aram. *Tabeitha;* Gk. *Dorcas,* meaning in Greece, 'roe'; in Syria and Africa, 'gazelle') A woman whose life had been 'full of good works and acts of charity' fell ill and died at Lydda, where her body was laid out in an upper room. The Christian disciples at Lydda, hearing that Peter was in the nearby coastal town of Joppa, sent two men to fetch him without delay. When Peter arrived in the upper room, all the local widows were wailing and displaying the clothes that Tabitha had made. He put them all outside, then knelt and prayed; finally, turning to the body, he said, 'Tabitha, rise.' Luke, the recorder of this incident, adds, 'She opened her eyes, and when she saw Peter sat up. And he gave her his hand and lifted her up. . . . And it became known throughout all Joppa, and many believed in the Lord.' (Acts 9:40-42)

This story has remarkable similarities to the raising of Jairus's daughter, as recorded in Mark 5:38-42 and

Matt. 9:25, particularly the weeping and the putting out of the women from the death chamber, and the Aramaic words spoken by Peter. Jesus had said to Jairus's daughter, *'Talitha cumi'* ('daughter, arise') and Peter *'Tabitha cumi'*. Luke adds that her name could be translated 'Dorcas' or 'Gazelle'. [Acts 9:36, 40]

TAX-COLLECTORS (from the Lat. 'civil servants') These are the 'publicans' mentioned in the Synoptic Gospels, so called from the Latin *publicani,* referring to people employed in collecting the state, or public, revenue. The collection of taxes within the provinces of the Roman Empire was auctioned in Rome to financial companies. The highest bid was accepted, and the companies sold their rights to collect in different areas of the province to smaller speculators. The result was often an exorbitant rate of taxation, for exceeding the original bid to the imperial colonial administration.

Consequently the publicans were highly unpopular members of society, particularly as they could call upon the support of the Roman colonial governor and his military forces. Those Jews who were willing to earn a living by extorting high rates from their fellow compatriots, in order to pay their Roman masters, were doubly despised and disliked. Moreover, as their business transactions brought them into close and constant touch with Gentiles and they were deemed to be dishonest anyway, publicans were regarded as sinners and outside the Law.

The chief source of taxation tended to be the frontier customs, which were usually collected in the towns astride the main roads leading to the frontiers. Thus Capernaum and Jericho were both towns in which Jesus was likely to meet publicans, besides in Jerusalem and the provincial towns.

The Jordan River formed the natural frontier between the territory of Herod Antipas in Galilee and that of Herod Philip in Gaulanitis. Capernaum, the nearest lakeside town west of the frontier, was the natural frontier customs-post astride the main road to Damascus. Jericho was the town nearest the river and on the main trade route to Gerasa, Philadelphia, and the southern towns of the Decapolis. It was here that Jesus met the tax-superintendent Zacchaeus. Indeed, it has been recently suggested that the present name of the site of Capernaum, 'Tel-Hum', may be a corruption of the Greek word for 'custom house', *telonium*.

Certainly there must have been a busy harbour with boats from neighbouring ports loading and off-loading the dried fish and local wares of Galilee, the silks and spices of Damascus, the fruit and produce of the plain of Gennesaret. It was here perhaps by the quayside or the roadside that the shadow of Jesus fell across the customs ledger of Matthew, the publican. In the words of Matthew's Gospel: 'He said to him, "Follow me." And he rose and followed him.' (*see* MATTHEW)

Luke alone tells the delightful story of the chief tax-collector, Zacchaeus, who was very rich because the Jericho taxes constituted a fruitful source of income and he had contracted for the right of collecting the revenues of that district. When Jesus came to Jericho, probably among the crowds of pilgrims on the way up to Jerusalem for the Passover festival, Zacchaeus wanted to meet him. He was, however, a little man, and he therefore went on ahead and climbed into a tree overlooking the road along which Jesus was likely to come. As Jesus came level with him, he looked up, and called to him, 'Zacchaeus, make haste and come down; for I must stay at your house today.' (Luke 19:5) Zacchaeus made haste to come down and received Jesus joyfully.

When the crowds saw what had happened, they were resentful and murmured, ' "He has gone in to be the guest of a man who is a sinner." And Zacchaeus stood and said to the Lord, "Behold, Lord, the half of my goods I give to the poor; and if I have defrauded any one of anything, I restore it fourfold." And Jesus said to him, "Today salvation has come to this house, since he also is a son of Abraham. For the Son of man came to seek and to save the lost." ' (Luke 19:7-10)

Luke brings out very clearly Jesus's application of the word 'lost' to the publicans, as though their livelihood made them inevitably 'sinners'. Luke described how the 'tax-collectors and sinners' were attracted to Jesus and came near to listen to him. But the Pharisees and Scribes grumbled to the disciples, 'Why does your teacher eat with tax-collectors and sinners?' In answer, Jesus told them parables, all with the same theme of 'lost and found'. 'What man of you, having a hundred sheep, if he has lost one of them, does not leave the ninety-nine in the wilderness, and go after the one which is lost, until he finds it? And when he has found it, he lays it on his shoulders, rejoicing. And when he comes home, he calls together his friends and his neighbours, saying to them, "Rejoice with me, for I have found my sheep which was lost." ' (Luke 15:4-6)

'Or what woman, having ten silver coins, if she loses one coin, does not light a lamp and sweep the house and seek diligently until she finds it? And when she has found it, she calls together her friends and neighbours, saying, "Rejoice with me, for I have found the coin which I had lost." Just so, I tell you, there is joy before the angels of God over one sinner who repents.' (Luke 15:8-10)

The third parable is that of the prodigal son and his elder brother. The prodigal demanded his share of his father's property, went and wasted it in a far country, but 'came to himself' and returned in penitence to his father. The father, in forgiveness, fêted him, saying, 'bring quickly the best robe, and put it on him; and put a ring on his hand, and shoes on his feet; and bring the fatted calf and kill it, and let us eat and make merry; for this my son was dead, and is alive again; he was lost, and is found.' (Luke 15:22-24)

The elder son, however (and here Jesus undoubtedly was referring to the resentful Scribes and Pharisees), complained that the father had forgiven the prodigal (indicating the publicans who were repentant and attentive to Jesus). The elder son jealously answered him: 'Lo, these many years I have served you, and I never disobeyed your command; yet you never gave me a kid, that I might make merry with my friends. But when this son of yours came, who had devoured your living with harlots, you killed for him the fatted calf!' (Luke 15:29, 30)

The father sums up the lesson of all three parables, that the Scribes and Pharisees should rejoice at and not resent the new-found penitence of the publicans. 'It was fitting to make merry and be glad, for this your brother was dead, and is alive; he was lost, and is found.' (Luke 15:32)

There is no doubt that Luke correctly interpreted Jesus's sense of vocation, in dealing with the publicans and sinners, 'to seek and to save the lost'.

The well-known parable of the Pharisee and the publican, also to be found in Luke's Gospel (18:9-14) tends to caricature both men. The Pharisee is depicted parading his virtues, while the publican is shown in penitence imploring God's mercy. 'The tax-collector, standing far off, would not even lift up his eyes to heaven, but beat his breast, saying "God be merciful to me a sinner".' Jesus's hearers might well have been amused at this portrait and surprised to hear that 'this man went down to his house justified, rather than the other'. [Matt. 5:46; 21:31; Mark 2:14-17; Luke 3:12; 7:27, 29, 30, 34; 15:1; 18:9-14; 19:1-10]

TERTIUS (Gk. from the Lat. 'third') The man who actually wrote the letter to the Christian Church in Rome, at Paul's dictation, added his own personal greeting at what he must have thought the end of Paul's greetings. Paul, however, added a further three names. It was Paul's custom, at the end of his letters, to take the pen from the hand of his emanuensis and add a final message in his own bold handwriting. (cf. Gal. 6:11; Col. 4:18; 2 Thess. 3:17) [Rom. 16:22]

TERTULLUS The Roman prosecuting attorney, employed by the Sanhedrin to present their case against the Apostle Paul before the procurator Felix at Caesarea in the year 60.

It was not unusual for Roman advocates, used to Roman court procedure, to be hired by the people resident in Roman provinces. Tertullus made a very competent speech for the prosecution, opening with a compliment to Felix to win his goodwill. 'Since through you we enjoy much peace, and since by your provision, most excellent Felix, reforms are introduced on behalf of this nation, in every way and everywhere we accept this with all gratitude. But, to detain you no further, I beg you in your kindness to hear us briefly.' (Acts 24:2, 4) He then declared Paul to be a perfect pest as (1) an agitator, (2) a ringleader of the Nazarenes, and (3) as a desecrator of the Temple. Finally he invited Felix to examine Paul himself to ascertain the truth of these charges. The speech, whether as spoken by Tertullus, or condensed by Luke, is a masterpiece of brevity. Paul's defence of himself, however, was more than a match for the prosecution, for Paul was equally well-trained in the famous law school of Troas. [Acts 24:1, 2]

THADDAEUS (Gk. from the Heb. 'large-hearted', 'courageous') One of the twelve apostles of Jesus, whose name is to be found only in the Gospels of Mark and Matthew. Elsewhere (in Luke, John, and Acts) the equivalent name is Judas.

The Fourth Gospel refers to one of the twelve as 'Judas (not Iscariot)', when at the Last Supper he asks Jesus: 'Lord, how is it that you will manifest yourself to us and not to the world?' It is, therefore, reasonable to identify Thaddaeus and Judas as the same person, with James as their father. (The name Lebbaeus is included as an alternative to Thaddaeus only in some minor manuscripts at Matt. 10:3, and also in the Western Text only at Mark 3:18, but Lebbaeus is not to be found in the Revised Standard Version.) The actual wording in Luke's list is 'Judas, son of James', implying either that James was his father or his brother. If this Judas was the writer of the Letter of Jude, the last in the New Testament, then he does in fact refer to himself as 'Jude, a servant of Jesus Christ and brother of James'. [Matt. 10:3; Mark 3:18]

THEOPHILUS (Gk. 'lover of God') The unknown addressee of both the Gospel of Luke and the Acts of the Apostles. The title given him in the Gospel, 'Most excellent', elsewhere (Acts 23:26) used to 'His Excellency the governor Felix', procurator of Judea, indicates a specific person of some social prominence. The title would well have fitted a Roman official of equestrian rank.

This man had heard by repute about Jesus and his followers, and probably had requested further information. He received two scrolls, one about the birth, life, ministry, death and resurrection of Jesus, the other a selection of events connected with the society formed by the followers of this Jesus, particularly Peter and Paul.

The writer of these two volumes, Luke, tried to give an accurate account of the life of Jesus and the growth of the early Church that would appeal to Romans. He, himself possibly a Gentile, presents to his probably Roman reader the universal importance of the Gospel of Jesus. He does not lay the blame for the execution of Jesus primarily upon the Romans, but upon the Jews; nor does he present Jesus as a criminal condemned for crimes against the state and the authority of Rome. Rather, Luke presents Jesus as a Jew with a message of world-wide interest and significance, yet misunderstood and convicted by his own people, despite the efforts of the Roman authorities in power.

The theory that the Acts were originally written as a brief for the defence of Paul before the imperial tribunal presents some chronological difficulties, as the Gospel is not likely to have been completed before Paul's execution. Nevertheless, this double work must have been of considerable value to the progress of the Christian Church in Rome, of which it is only reasonable to suppose that Theophilus became an influential and well-instructed Christian. [Luke 1:3; Acts 1:1]

THESSALONIANS (Gk. 'inhabitants of Salonika') Thessalonica, the modern Salonika, was, in Paul's time, the capital of Macedonia. The Thessalonians were evangelized by Paul, Silas, and Timothy on the Second

Journey, and the events are described in Acts 17: 'Now when they had passed through Amphipolis and Apollonia, they came to Thessalonica, where there was a synagogue of the Jews. And Paul went in, as was his custom, and for three weeks he argued with them from the scriptures, explaining and proving that it was necessary for the Christ to suffer and to rise from the dead, and saying, "This Jesus, whom I proclaim to you, is the Christ." And some of them were persuaded, and joined Paul and Silas; as did a great many of the devout Greeks and not a few of the leading women.' It was not long, however, before the Jews accused Paul and his companions of breaking 'the decrees of Caesar, saying that there is another king, Jesus'. It is likely that Paul's stay lasted much longer than three weeks – more likely three months, during which time he was supported by gifts of money from Christians at Philippi (Phil. 4:16), and these must have taken some time in collection and delivery. When Paul moved on to Beroea and word of his success reached Thessalonica, his opponents followed him and hunted him out of town again, so he went on to Athens and to Corinth.

It seems that Paul was anxious about the young Thessalonian Christian community, mostly Gentiles and persecuted by members of the synagogue. Paul's own character had been impugned and he had been accused of deception, immorality, and fraud, so he sent Timothy back from Beroea to keep them 'firm and strong in the faith' and prevent them from being unsettled. Timothy returned to Paul in Corinth with good reports of the Thessalonians, their faith is Jesus, and their love for Paul. Paul then wrote his first letter (1 Thess.) in AD 51, to send his gratitude and affection for their perseverance. He also answered two questions: one about

559

those who die before the Second Coming of Jesus, and the other about the time of his coming. 'But we would not have you ignorant, brethren, concerning those who are asleep, that you may not grieve as others do who have no hope. For since we believe that Jesus died and rose again, even so, through Jesus, God will bring with him those who have fallen asleep. For this we declare to you by the word of the Lord, that we who are alive, who are left until the coming of the Lord, shall not precede those who have fallen asleep. For the Lord himself will descend from heaven with a cry of command, with the archangel's call, and with the sound of the trumpet of God. And the dead in Christ will rise first; then we who are alive, who are left, shall be caught up together with them in the clouds to meet the Lord in the air; and so we shall always be with the Lord. Therefore comfort one another with these words.' (1 Thess. 4:13-18)

As for the hour of Christ's coming, Paul wrote: 'But you are not in darkness, brethren, for that day to surprise you like a thief. For you are all sons of light and sons of the day; we are not of the night or of darkness . . . but, since we belong to the day, let us be sober, and put on the breastplate of faith and love, and for a helmet the hope of salvation. For God has not destined us for wrath, but to obtain salvation through our Lord Jesus Christ, who died for us that whether we wake or sleep we might live with him. . . . May the God of peace himself sanctify you wholly; and may your spirit and soul and body be kept sound and blameless at the coming of our Lord Jesus Christ.' (1 Thess. 5:4, 5, 8-10, 23)

The newly-founded congregation continued to make progress in real unity and love, still in the face of considerable opposition and persecution from the synagogue. Paul, therefore, wrote again to encourage them to persevere. 'So then, brethren, stand firm and hold to the traditions which you were taught by us, either by word of mouth or by letter. Now may our Lord Jesus Christ himself, and God our Father, who loved us and gave us eternal comfort and good hope through grace, comfort your hearts and establish them in every good work and word.' (2 Thess. 2:15-17)

Paul also tells them not to get excited too soon or to be alarmed by any rumour that they have missed the second coming of Jesus. They are to follow the example of Paul and his companions, in working day and night for the Lord. 'For we hear that some of you are living in idleness, mere busybodies, not doing any work. Now such persons we command and exhort in the Lord Jesus Christ to do their work in quietness and to earn their own living. . . . If any one refuses to obey what we say in this letter, note that man, and have nothing to do with him, that he may be ashamed. Do not look on him as an enemy, but warn him as a brother.' (2 Thess. 3:11, 12, 14, 15)

The patience, affection, and pastoral skill of Paul are shown very clearly in the Thessalonian correspondence, together with a vivid impression of his personality. He ends his second letter with a prayer and farewell wishes: 'Now may the Lord of peace himself give you peace at all times in all ways. The Lord be with you all. I, Paul, write this greeting with my own hand. This is the mark in every letter of mine; it is the way I write. The grace of our Lord Jesus Christ be with you all.' (2 Thess. 3:16-18)

The Thessalonian Church was renowned for its orthodoxy and steadfastness in the years that followed. Its early martyrs included the three sisters SS Agape,

Chionia, and Irene, with St Demetrius, later patron of the city; and the first bishop of Thessalonica was probably Gaius. [Acts 17:1-9, 11, 13; 20:4; 27:2; 1st and 2nd Letters to the Thessalonians]

THEUDAS (Gk. 'gift of God') A Jewish fanatic who with his 400 followers revolted against Roman authority in Palestine during the early years of the 1st century; they were ruthlessly wiped out.

The great Pharisee and rabbi Gamaliel quoted the stories of both Theudas and Judas the Galilean as unsuccessful leaders of pseudo-Messianic movements, in a speech to the Sanhedrin at the trial of the Apostles Peter and John. Gamaliel's advice was to leave the apostles alone and to trust God either to further or to destroy the movement, rather than themselves to take any drastic action against the Christian leaders at that time.

Judea was in those years seething with revolts and pretenders, and it is historically impossible to know the names of all the leaders involved. Josephus mentions a Theudas, who led a very much larger body than 400 in an uprising in AD 44, but Gamaliel's speech was made some years before that. Gamaliel's second and presumably later example, Judas of Galilee, led his revolt in the year 6, so the Theudas to whom he referred was probably active before that date. That is, of course, unless the whole reference to Theudas is an inaccurate and later interpretation of the writer or some editor. Luke, the writer of Acts, was not able to check his dates as can a modern historian. [Acts 5:36]

THOMAS (Gk. from Aram. 'twin') The loyal and practical, down-to-earth, 'seeing-is-believing' disciple of Jesus, whose doubts of the resurrection dissolved in the presence of his risen master.

The name of Thomas is included in the lists of apostles in each of the Synoptic Gospels and in the roll of those who, in the Upper Room after the ascension of Jesus, elected a replacement for Judas and received the Spirit at Pentecost. Nothing further is mentioned about him in the New Testament outside the Fourth Gospel, where he is called 'the Twin'. John, however, mentions four different occasions when the presence of Thomas was significant to the gospel story.

The first occasion was when Jesus had been hounded out of Jerusalem to seek safety in some quiet village, possibly Ephraim among the hills several miles to the north of the city and overlooking the wilderness of Judea. Suddenly the news of the illness of Lazarus of Bethany arrived; Jesus at once decided to go back to him at Bethany, within two miles of Jerusalem. Thomas was frightened, but loyal. He knew well the danger involved, but volunteered to accompany him in very blunt if realistic terms: 'Let us also go, that we may die with him.' (John 11:16)

The second incident took place at the Last Supper, in the Upper Room on the Western Hill, on Maundy Thursday night. Jesus had been preparing his disciples for his coming departure: 'And when I go and prepare a place for you, I will come again and will take you to myself, that where I am you may be also. And you know the way where I am going.' (John 14:3, 4) Thomas at once interrupted him, 'Lord, we do not know where you are going; how can we know the way?' (John 14:5) It was not as though the others knew any more than Thomas, but he was not the sort to let his master get away with something that he, Thomas, did not understand. No doubt Christians should be thankful for Thomas's question, which evoked such an answer. 'Jesus said to him, "I am the way, and the truth, and the

563

life; no one comes to the Father, but by me. If you had known me, you would have known my Father also; henceforth you know him and have seen him." '

The third occasion was in the same room, but after the resurrection of Jesus. On the Easter night, Thomas had not been with the others when Jesus first came to them. When the others had told him, Thomas had not been able to believe them. Perhaps he felt they had succumbed to wishful thinking or had seen a ghost. His reply to them was quite typical of the man, absolutely practical: 'Unless I see in his hands the print of the nails, and place my finger in the mark of the nails, and place my hand in his side, I will not believe.' (John 20:25)

A week later, the disciples were again all together in the Upper Room and this time Thomas was with them. Though the doors were barred for fear of the Jews, again Jesus was there. Thomas's doubts and demands provided both Jesus and the evangelists with just the opportunity that was needed, to bring home the reality of the resurrection to the disciples both then and now. Jesus called Thomas over to touch the scars of crucifixion: 'Put your finger here, and see my hands; and put out your hand, and place it in my side; do not be faithless, but believing.' (John 20:27)

In that moment Thomas must have seen both the body on the cross, hanging by hands and feet, the side opened by the soldier's spear, and his living friend and master. As these two figures fused together, so Thomas leapt the gap between loyalty to a friend and adoring faith in God himself. His ponderous pessimism and lonely doubts disappeared, and he identified his friend as both 'My Lord and my God!'

The final reference to Thomas is among the seven

disciples who went fishing on the Lake of Galilee, when at dawn they met Jesus on the shore, and landed a miraculous draught of fish. Thomas is mentioned only second to Simon Peter in this final post-resurrection story of Jesus.

Later traditions claim that Thomas found his way to Persia and south India, where he was reputedly the founder of the ancient Mar Thoma Church, in Travancore and Cochin, now called Kerala. He is credited with an apocryphal gospel, that in fact dates from the 2nd century. [Matt. 10:3; Mark 3:18; Luke 6:15; John 11:16; 14:5; 20:24-28; 21:2; Acts 1:13]

TIBERIUS The Roman emperor whose years of rule (AD 14-37) include the ministry and crucifixion of Jesus. In fact, Luke dates the beginning of Jesus's public life as 'in the fifteenth year of the reign of Tiberius Caesar'.

Born in 42 BC, son of the Empress Livia, wife of Augustus, by her first husband Tiberius Claudius Nero, this Tiberius Julius Caesar Augustus served with military honours in Europe and the East. As Augustus his step-father had no heir, Tiberius was his successor. Augustus, however, disliked and distrusted him, and Tiberius was a lonely and unpopular figure, despite his able administration and determination to continue the foreign and domestic policy of his august predecessor.

It was in honour of the Emperor Tiberius that Herod Antipas built Tiberias, during the lifetime of Jesus, near the hot springs already famous throughout the Roman world. A great castle built to accommodate his court dominated the town from the hillside.

The local Jewish population avoided the artificial pagan township and despised Herod's oriental court. To them also, the town was unclean because it was built on the site of a cemetery. In the 2nd century, the rabbis officially declared the purity of the site and, thereafter, Tiberias became the seat of the Sanhedrin. [Luke 3:1]

TIMAEUS (Gk. from Heb. 'to be unclean') Father of the blind beggar Bartimaeus at Jericho, whose sight was restored by Jesus. Bartimaeus was the first person publicly to proclaim the Messiahship of Jesus. *see* BARTIMAEUS [Mark 10:46]

TIMON *see* NICOLAUS

TIMOTHY (Gk. 'honouring God') The closest companion and messenger of Paul the Apostle, Timothy was called by Paul his 'dear and faithful child in the Lord', his 'brother', or his 'fellow-worker'. Timothy appears to have been entirely at Paul's disposal from Paul's visit to Lystra on the Second Journey until the time of Paul's death in Rome, a period of perhaps 17 years.

Timid nature, weak health

A much younger man than Paul (who knew his grandmother Lois), Timothy was by nature reserved and timid. 'When Timothy comes, see that you put him at ease among you, for he is doing the work of the Lord, as I am. So let no one despise him. Speed him on his way in peace, that he may return to me; for I am expecting him with the brethren.' (1 Cor. 16:10, 11) Paul nevertheless commissioned Timothy to strengthen the recalcitrant Corinthians in their faith and in their loyalty to Paul; and he writes in the same vein to the persecuted Thessalonian congregation, 'We sent Timothy, our brother and God's servant in the gospel of Christ, to establish you in your faith and to exhort you, that no one be moved by these afflictions. You yourselves know that this is to be our lot.' (1 Thess. 3:2, 3)

For all his shyness, Timothy could be trusted above many others for his pastoral concern and his gentle tact in dealing with awkward situations. When in prison, Paul wrote to the Christian community at Philippi, 'I hope in the Lord Jesus to send Timothy to you soon, so that I may be cheered by news of you. I have no one like him, who will be genuinely anxious for your welfare. They all look after their own interests, not those of Jesus Christ. But Timothy's worth you know, how as a son with a father he has served with me in the gospel.' (Phil. 2:19-22) Although Timothy may have been subject to 'frequent ailments' (1 Tim. 5:23), he seems to have been constantly ready to undertake dangerous journeys on difficult errands for Paul. His deliberate action leading to his martyrdom (some thirty years after Paul's) shows a similar courage, if not quite the same aggressive initiative as that of the apostle.

Timothy was a native of Lystra in Lycaonia, a town visited twice by Paul and Barnabas on their First Journey. On the first occasion Paul had been stoned and left for dead, so Timothy was under no illusions as to the cost and danger of discipleship. A few years later, when Paul returned to Lystra, this time with Silas, Timothy was already a respected member of the Christian congregation, as was his grandmother Lois and his mother Eunice, both Jewesses. His father, however, was a Gentile, and Timothy consequently was uncircumcised. Perhaps to placate the Jewish community, or – more likely – because circumcision was still imposed by the Jewish Law, Paul decided that Timothy should undergo the operation rather than be hindered in his ministry. Certainly his Jewish mother would have seen to his education in the Old Testament scriptures.

Paul and Silas took Timothy along with them on their

journey over to Macedonia. Somehow Timothy escaped the very rough treatment suffered by Paul and Silas at Philippi, and he does not seem to have been involved in the episode which incensed the Jews at Thessalonica. When Paul went on to Athens, Silas and Timothy stayed for some time at Beroea and Thessalonica before joining Paul at Corinth. We do not know at what point in Timothy's career he was ordained by the laying-on of hands by Paul and others. We do not know whether he accompanied Paul back to Antioch between the Second and Third Journeys. But we do know that Timothy and another disciple named Erastus were Paul's 'helpers' during his long teaching ministry at Ephesus, which may well have been interrupted by some crisis involving danger. Timothy acted as Paul's messenger to carry the Corinthian correspondence from Ephesus, and his name is linked with Paul's in letters to Thessalonica, Colossae, and Philippi.

At the end of Paul's Third Journey, Timothy was among the large group of disciples who met Paul at Troas and shared a Eucharist the night before Paul sailed for Jerusalem. But we do not know whether Timothy accompanied Paul or shared any of his imprisonment at Caesarea. It seems that Luke acted as Paul's secretary and companion until his arrival in Rome; from then onwards there is little evidence of Paul's movements, let alone those of his companions. If Paul's letter to Philippi or to Colossae, whether to the congregation or to Philemon, were written in Rome, then certainly Timothy was with Paul in Rome.

Whether the letters to Timothy were written by Paul or not, it is certain that Paul sent Timothy as his representative to Ephesus, to teach for some considerable time. We know that Paul sent for Timothy to bring his scrolls and cloak before winter set in – but not whether Timothy arrived before Paul's execution. The final chapter of the letter to Hebrew Christians may just possibly have been an appendix added by Paul himself. Its last message is that Timothy has been set free from some imprisonment and that Paul hopes he will arrive in time to be with him.

Eusebius, the 4th-century historian and bishop of Caesarea, records that Timothy became the first bishop of Ephesus. An apocryphal Acts of Timothy, dating from the same period, describes his martyrdom on 22 January in the year 97, when protesting at the licentious festivities in honour of Diana of the Ephesians. His relics are believed to have been translated to Constantinople in the year 356. [Acts 16:1; 17:14, 15; 18:5; 19:22; 20:4; Rom. 16:21; 1 Cor. 4:17; 16:10; 2 Cor. 1:1, 19; Col. 1:1, 1 Thess. 1:1; 3:2, 6; 2 Thess. 1:1; 1st and 2nd Letters to Timothy; Philem. 1; Heb. 13:23]

Timothy, Letters to

The two brief letters to Timothy and the one to Titus concern Church organization and discipline rather than doctrine. They reflect the situation in the Christian Church at the close of the 1st century.

Together with the letter to Titus, the letters to Timothy have, since the 18th century, been called the 'pastoral epistles', being primarily addressed to pastors. All three are in full agreement in their religious and ethical teaching; they deal virtually with the same problems in the same words. They were clearly written in a period not covered by the narrative in the Acts of the Apostles; they cannot be 'fitted in' to Paul's life as related in the Acts. They show little of Paul's power of thought and expression, nor of his depth and originality.

If Paul is to be considered as their author, we must suppose that Paul was released from his first imprisonment in Rome, as Agrippa anticipated. The second letter to Timothy does indicate some continuation of ministry in Asia before his final arrest, trial, and execution.

Briefly, the arguments against their Pauline authorship are these. The first letter purports to be sent from Macedonia to Ephesus, but the only time (Acts 19:22) Paul went from Ephesus to Macedonia, he sent Timothy on ahead of him. The letter to Titus in Crete, calling him to meet Paul in Nicopolis, on the west coast of Achaia, presupposes a long period of teaching activity in Crete. But there is no mention in the Acts of Paul conducting such a mission, nor would there have been time for him to make more than a cursory visit to Crete from Corinth. The last letter to Timothy presupposes another imprisonment in Rome, and purports to be written on the eve of Paul's martyrdom. This letter, typical of Paul in style and language. The letter's final chapter would seem to include a genuine fragment of some Pauline letter, with so vivid a description of his situation and feelings as he awaits execution that it may well be the last message he ever sent.

'For I am already on the point of being sacrificed; the time of my departure has come. I have fought the good fight, I have finished the race, I have kept the faith. Henceforth there is laid up for me the crown of righteousness, which the Lord, the righteous judge, will award me on that Day, and not only to me but also to all who have loved his appearing. Do your best to come to me soon. For Demas, in love with this present world, has deserted me and gone to Thessalonica; Crescens has gone to Galatia, Titus to Dalmatia. Luke alone is with me. Get Mark and bring him with you; for he is very useful in serving me. Tychicus I have sent to Ephesus. When you come, bring the cloak that I left with Carpus at Troas, also the books, and above all the parchments. Alexander the coppersmith did me great harm; the Lord will requite him for his deeds. Beware of him yourself, for he strongly opposed our message. At my first defence no one took my part; all deserted me. May it not be charged against them! But the Lord stood by me and gave me strength to proclaim the word fully, that all the Gentiles might hear it. So I was rescued from the lion's mouth. The Lord will rescue me from every evil and save me for his heavenly kingdom. To him be the glory for ever and ever. Amen.' (2 Tim. 4:6-18)

From the evidence, therefore, we may conclude that the 'pastoral epistles' are the work of an admirer of Paul who, employing Paul's theology and vocabulary, used both his name and brief notes of his correspondence in a desire to impress his readers with the need to hold fast to Paul's teachings of faith and practice.

The Church of the period in which the author is writing is not as it was in Paul's day. It no longer consists of scattered and struggling little communities, held together by the occasional visits of apostolic leaders. The conditions described in these 'pastoral epistles' indicate a more firmly-established and organized Church, officered by bishops, deacons, and elders. These letters give a useful picture of the Church at the close of its apostolic age, when as an institution it is taking shape, when its practices are becoming a system, and its beliefs are being formulated into a creed.

The letters do not constitute a systematic 'Manual of Church Order', but they are much concerned with the duties of Church leaders. 'Now a bishop must be above reproach, the husband of one wife, temperate, sensible, dignified, hospitable, an apt teacher, no drunkard, not violent but gentle, not quarrelsome, and no lover of money. He must manage his own household well, keeping his children submissive and respectful in every way.' (1 Tim. 3:2-4) 'Deacons likewise must be serious, not double-tongued, not addicted to much wine, not greedy for gain; they must hold the mystery of the faith with a clear conscience. And let them also be tested first; then if they prove themselves blameless let them serve as deacons.' (1 Tim. 3:8-10) 'Do not rebuke an older man but exhort him as you would a father; treat younger men like brothers, older women like mothers, younger women like sisters, in all purity. Honour widows who are real widows.' (1 Tim. 5:1-3)

The writer is also concerned to preserve the faith, as 'deposited' by the Apostle Paul, as a bastion against all false teaching. 'But as for you, continue in what you have learned and have firmly believed, knowing from whom you learned it and how from childhood you have been acquainted with the sacred writings which are able to instruct you for salvation through faith in Christ Jesus. All scripture is inspired by God and profitable for teaching, for reproof, for correction, and for training in righteousness, that the man of God may be complete, equipped for every good work.' (2 Tim. 3:14-17)

Perhaps the greatest contrast between this writer and Paul himself is that, unlike Paul (whose ethics are based on the guidance of the Holy Spirit), the writer appears primarily guided by the need for prudence and good order within the Church. And indeed his wise, practical councils have helped to mould both the organization and the ethical teaching of the historical Church through the centuries.

His outlook is exactly shared by Clement of Rome, in the letter to the Corinthian Church written in the year 96. He is quoted by Ignatius, bishop of Antioch at the close of the 1st century. Thus it is probable that the pastoral letters belong to the end of the 1st century. [1st and 2nd Letters to Timothy]

TITIUS *see* JUSTUS **2.**

TITUS (Gk. Titos, a praenomen only, the surname being lost) A Greek Christian for nearly twenty years associated with the Apostle Paul, for whom he acted successfully in Corinth. Titus became a leader of the Church in Corinth, in Dalmatia, on the Adriatic, and finally Crete. He was also the addressee of one of the pastoral letters attributed to Paul.

No mention of Titus is made by Luke in the Acts of the Apostles, but Paul frequently refers to him in the Corinthian correspondence, once in his last letter to Timothy. Titus is first introduced in the Letter to the Galatians as on the delegation from Antioch accompanying Paul and Barnabas to Jerusalem round about the year 49. Opinions differ as to whether this visit is that recorded in Acts 11, or that in Acts 15, for the Council.

The Council was called to deliberate the necessity of circumcision for all Christians and the observance of the Law of Moses by Gentile Christians, for salvation. Many Christians in Jerusalem resented the acceptance of Gentile Christians, particularly within the headquarters of the Church, at Antioch in Syria. The accounts of the Council vary. Luke says that the Apostle Peter, speaking out of his personal experience (*see* CORNELIUS), supported the Antiochene delegation and secured a generous judgment from James and the elders of the

Church. Paul implies that he himself had forced the issue by taking the Gentile Christian Titus, who was not circumcised, to be a test case. 'Then, after fourteen years, I went up again to Jerusalem with Barnabas, taking Titus along with me. I went up by revelation; and I laid before them (but privately before those who were of repute) the gospel which I preach among the Gentiles, lest somehow I should be running or had run in vain. But even Titus, who was with me, was not compelled to be circumcised, though he was a Greek.' (Gal. 2:1-3)

Some years later during his Third Journey and while he was at Ephesus, Paul had bad news of the Church at Corinth. He heard that a party spirit prevailed in the community and that a particularly grave case of immorality had arisen within the Church. Paul dealt with these questions in a letter now known to us as 1 Corinthians, which he sent by sea, while Timothy took the land route to deal with the situation in person. Neither the letter nor Timothy's visit achieved the desired effect, and Paul himself sailed for Corinth. Even he was not able to secure a reform within the Corinthian Christian community and, after being grossly insulted, he sailed back to Ephesus. From there, he wrote a 'severe letter', his third, possibly to be found in 2 Cor. 10-13, which was carried by Titus, an older and more experienced man than Timothy. This letter demanded a proper respect of the Christian Church in Corinth. In this letter, Paul wrote, 'Did I take advantage of you through any of those whom I sent to you? I urged Titus to go. . . .' (2 Cor. 17, 18)

Paul was so anxious about the outcome of his appeal to the Corinthian Church to mend its ways that he had barely closed his ministry at Ephesus before setting out via Troas, to intercept Titus on his return from Corinth through Macedonia. Somewhere *en route* he met Titus, who at last brought him the good news that the Corinthian Church was ready to conform, and that they had already by a majority censured the person who had insulted Paul. Paul immediately wrote his fourth letter, to be found in 2 Cor. 1-9, omitting the content of his preliminary letter. In this last letter, he forgave his antagonist, closed the controversy, and arranged for a collection for the poor Christians at Jerusalem.

In this letter, Paul warmly expressed his relief and gratitude at the report of Titus. 'When I came to Troas to preach the gospel of Christ, a door was opened for me in the Lord; but my mind could not rest because I did not find my brother Titus there. So I took leave of them and went on to Macedonia.' (2 Cor. 2:12, 13) 'But God, who comforts the downcast, comforted us by the coming of Titus, and not only by his coming but also by the comfort with which he was comforted in you, as he told us of your longing, your mourning, your zeal for me, so that I rejoiced still more. For even if I made you sorry with my letter, I do not regret it (though I did regret it), for I see that that letter grieved you, though only for a while. As it is, I rejoice, not because you were grieved, but because you were grieved into repenting. . . . I do not mean that others should be eased and you burdened, but that as a matter of equality your abundance at the present time should supply their want, so that their abundance may supply your want, that there may be equality. As it is written, "He who gathered much had nothing over, and he who gathered little had no lack." ' (2 Cor. 7:6-9; 8:13-15)

Paul clearly valued the pastoral skill and tact of his veteran comrade, Titus, without whose efforts the story of the Christian community in Corinth might have been very different. It was to Titus therefore that Paul committed the care of that congregation, and the task of completing the collection for poor-relief, giving him this final letter to deliver to Corinth. 'Accordingly we have urged Titus that as he had already made a beginning, he should also complete among you this gracious work. . . . Thanks be to God who puts the same earnest care for you into the heart of Titus. For he not only accepted our appeal, but being himself very earnest he is going to you of his own accord. . . . As for Titus, he is my partner and fellow worker in your service; and as for our brethren, they are messengers of the churches, the glory of Christ.' (2 Cor. 8:6, 16, 17, 23)

The last reference to Titus is to be found in Paul's final letter to Timothy. Paul, re-arrested, condemned, and awaiting execution, is depressed by the scattering of his followers, even though for the most part they are concerned with the continuation of his work throughout the Mediterranean Churches. Titus, at Paul's request, had gone to Dalmatia on the east coast of the Adriatic, probably to Nicopolis.

The pastoral letter addressed to Titus and attributed to Paul, if written by the apostle, must belong to the period between Paul's two imprisonments in Rome. In this letter, Titus is represented as left in charge of the organization of the Christian Church on the island of Crete where, according to the historian Eusebius, he became the first bishop. His traditional burial-place is at Gortyna, the ancient capital of Crete, though his head is venerated as a relic in St Mark's, Venice. *see also* CRETANS

(For discussion on the date, authorship, origin and contents of the pastoral letters, *see* TIMOTHY) [2 Cor.

2:13; 7:6, 13, 14; 8:6-23; 12:18; Gal. 2:1, 3; 2 Tim. 4:10; Titus 1:4]

TROPHIMUS (Gk. 'nourishing') A Gentile Christian from Ephesus, one of Paul's escorts on his final visit to Jerusalem, where he was indirectly the cause of Paul's arrest. Trophimus began to accompany Paul on his final journey to Rome, but fell ill and stayed at Miletus, on the south-west coast of Asia Minor.

As one of the two Asian representatives, Trophimus the Ephesian was chosen to accompany Paul on his return to Jerusalem with the poor-relief collection from the various Christian communities on the Mediterranean. Fearing an ambush if he travelled via Corinth, Paul went overland through Macedonia, in the spring of the year 58, as far as Troas on the coast of Asia Minor, and so by sea to Caesarea and Jerusalem, with an escort of seven men. They met the others at Troas, returned by sea to Caesarea, and went up to Jerusalem.

There, at the suggestion of James, the leader of the Christian Church in Jerusalem, Paul was advised to undergo a week's ritual purification in the Temple and to pay the expenses of four companions who with him were under a vow, to reassure the Jews of his adherence to the Law of Moses. When the week was nearly up, some Jews from Asia who had seen him in the Temple, but had also met him in the city with Trophimus the Ephesian, jumped to the hasty conclusion that Paul had taken Trophimus into the Temple. They dragged Paul out of the Temple and intended to lynch him, but he was rescued by the Antonia guard, who took him into protective custody. From this moment, Paul was never free until after his release by the imperial tribunal at Rome. Thus, indirectly, Trophimus was responsible for

Paul's arrest, imprisonment, and appeal to Caesar at Rome.

We next hear of Trophimus several years later, after Paul's acquittal and return to Asia, his re-arrest possibly at Troas, and his return in chains to Rome. Writing his final letter to Timothy, Paul comments that, on their way back to Rome – perhaps via Ephesus – Trophimus became ill at Miletus and had to be left there.

According to tradition, Trophimus was martyred during Nero's persecution at Rome, after the year 64. [Acts 20:4; 21:29; 2 Tim. 4:20]

TRYPHAENA (Gk. 'dainty') One of two Christian women greeted by Paul at the close of his letter to the congregation in Rome as 'workers in the Lord'. The similarity of their names (both from a common root in the Greek word for 'luxurious living') gives rise to the supposition that Tryphaena and Tryphosa were sisters, if not twins. Both names are found in Latin inscriptions of the period, for members of the imperial household. Tryphaena was sometimes used of Jewish women, and was the name of the queen from Pontus, in Asia Minor, who befriended the early Christian virgin Thecla, in the apocryphal *Acts of Paul and Thecla*. [Rom. 16:12]

TRYPHOSA *see* TRYPHAENA

TYCHICUS (Gk. 'fortuitous') An Ephesian convert and one of the two Asian representatives chosen to accompany Paul on his return to Jerusalem with the poor-relief collection from the various Christian communities on the Mediterranean. Fearing an ambush if he travelled via Corinth, Paul went overland through Macedonia in the spring of the year 58 as far as Troas on the coast of Asia Minor, with an escort of seven men. They met the others at Troas, returned by sea to Caesarea, and went up to Jerusalem. Three men – Aristarchus,

Timothy, and Tychicus — were later Paul's fellow-prisoners in Rome.

Tychicus is not mentioned as having accompanied Paul on his voyage to Rome. He was, however, commissioned by Paul to deliver the letter to the Christian Church in Colossae, together with Onesimus, the escaped slave of his master Philemon, to whom Paul restored him. (*see* PHILEMON) Tychicus, besides taking the general letter to the Church at Colossae and the personal letter to Philemon, was also the bearer of several copies of a circular letter to various churches in Asia, of which the epsistle to Ephesians was one. (*see* EPHESIANS)

It would seem that Tychicus was the man who was capable of dealing with doctrinal questions arising from Paul's various letters to the Church in Asia. Paul commends him warmly to the Christian congregations at Colossae, Ephesus, and wherever else the circular letter was to be delivered in Asia. 'Tychicus will tell you all about my affairs; he is a beloved brother and faithful minister and fellow servant in the Lord. I have sent him to you for this very purpose, that you may know how we are and that he may encourage your hearts, and with him Onesimus, the faithful and beloved brother, who is one of yourselves. They will tell you of everything that has taken place here.' (Col. 4:7-9)

In both these letters, Paul wrote to correct some strange and heretical teachings that were gaining ground within the Asian Churches, particularly perhaps within the Lycus Valley and the area of Ephesus. News of these strange doctrines was reported to Paul in prison by Epaphras, one of the evangelists trained by Paul at Ephesus on his Third Journey. He reported that certain teachers at Colossae, trying to combine within Christianity what they considered to be best in both Judaism and Hellenism, emphasized on the one hand such demands of the Jewish Law as the keeping of festivals and of the Sabbath and the hygiene laws. On the other hand, they devalued the material and physical, regarding the human body with contempt, not thinking that the physical birth and death of the Man Jesus was able to secure the reconciliation of the world with God. They questioned the uniqueness of Jesus Christ in God's scheme of salvation, which they felt they could only be achieved by supernatural means.

Tychicus was entrusted with Paul's remarkable replies. The Letter to the Colossians was undoubtedly the first draft of Paul's attempt to combat this theosophy, and to restate the all-sufficiency of Jesus the Messiah within God's scheme of salvation. The circular letter, our Letter to the Ephesians, was possibly a carefully and purposefully revised form of the first letter into a magnificent exposition of the 'mystery' of God's purpose in history, and of the new life within the Christian Church. Tychicus was the bearer of the 'very crown of all Paul's epistles'.

These letters were probably despatched from Rome in the year 61 or 62. Following Paul's release, return to Asia Minor, re-arrest and return in chains to Rome, he again mentions Tychicus in his letters to Titus and Timothy. To the former he suggests sending either Tychicus or Artemas as an assistant. To the latter, in the final report of the disposition and whereabouts of his companions. Paul tells Timothy that he has sent back Tychicus to Ephesus. Tychicus is one of the quiet but key figures in the history of the Asian communities, who have been described as the 'seed-plot of the Christian Church'. [Acts 20:4; Eph. 6:21; Col. 4:7; 2 Tim. 4:12; Titus 3:12]

TYRANNUS (Gk. 'tyrant') The teacher at Ephesus in whose lecture-room, or school, Paul taught over a period of two years, in the siesta hours of noon to four.

For three months, Paul had taught fearlessly in the synagogue, arguing the Christian message and persuading people of the Messiahship of Jesus. The opposition, however, hardened and Paul decided to withdraw from the synagogue – as he had done at Corinth also – into some alternative accommodation. It must have required an enormous effort of endurance to continue, throughout the middle of the day in the heat, teaching for two whole years. As a result, however, all the interested Jews and Greeks of Asia benefited from a period of continuous teaching. This accounts for the sound foundation of the Seven Churches in Asia, which later became known as the 'seed-plot' of Christianity in the time of John the Divine.

No doubt Tyrannus had heard Paul in the synagogue and offered his own accommodation to the apostle. He was possibly himself a proselyte to the Jewish faith or an attendant in the Gentile courtyard of the synagogue. [Acts 19:9]

U–Z

URBANUS One of the Christians greeted by Paul as 'our fellow-worker in Christ', at the close of his letter to the Church in Rome. Urbanus was a common slave name, often found within the emperor's own household. [Rom. 16:9]

WISE MEN *see* MAGI

ZACCHAEUS (Gk. from Heb. 'pure') Luke alone tells the delightful story of the chief tax-collector, Zacchaeus, who was very rich because the Jericho taxes constituted a fruitful source of income and he had contracted for the right of collecting the revenues of that district. When Jesus came to Jericho, probably among the crowds of pilgrims on the way up to Jerusalem for the Passover festival, Zacchaeus wanted to meet him. He was, however, a little man, and he therefore went on ahead and climbed into a tree overlooking the road along which Jesus was likely to come. As Jesus came level with him, he looked up, and called to him, 'Zacchaeus, make haste and come down; for I must stay at your house today.' (Luke 19:5) Zacchaeus made haste to come down and received Jesus joyfully.

When the crowds saw what had happened, they were resentful and murmured, ' "He has gone in to be the guest of a man who is a sinner." And Zacchaeus stood and said to the Lord, "Behold, Lord, the half of my goods I give to the poor; and if I have defrauded any one of anything, I restore it fourfold." And Jesus said to him, "Today salvation has come to this house, since he also is a son of Abraham. For the Son of man came to seek and to save the lost." ' (Luke 19:7-10)

Luke brings out very clearly Jesus's application of the word 'lost' to the publicans, as though their livelihood made them inevitably 'sinners'. Luke described how the 'tax-collectors and sinners' were attracted to Jesus and came near to listen to him, but the Pharisees and Scribes grumbled to the disciples, 'Why does your teacher eat with tax-collectors and sinners?' (Matt. 9:11) In defence of Zacchaeus, Jesus called him 'a son of Abraham', a good Jew, despite his profession.

In Jericho of the New Testament period, houses with

ossuaries have been found, belonging to rich men. Jericho was then as now a popular winter resort, near to which Herod had a magnificent water-garden at the mouth of the Kelt Gorge. [Luke 19:1-10]

ZACHARIAS (Gk. from Heb. 'whom Yahweh remembered') *see* ZECHARIAH

ZEALOTS (Gk. 'zealous one') The name given to those Jews who, from Maccabean times in the 1st and 2nd centuries BC to the fall of the fortress of Masada in the spring of AD 73, were impelled by a fanatical nationalism. Considering themselves the agents of God to deliver their nation from the foreign oppressors, under a banner of 'No rule but the Law – No King but God', they became increasingly violent in their resistance both to the Roman occupation forces and to their own people who sympathized with Hellenism.

Following the example of the Maccabean resistance to the efforts of the Seleucid king, Antiochus Epiphanes, to force Greek customs and religion upon the Jews, Judas the Galilean of Gamala led a considerable revolt in protest at the introduction of a Roman census on the incorporation of Judea in AD 6. (*see* JUDAS **4.**) Theudas led another uprising in about the year 42. (*see* THEUDAS) Both these were quoted by the Pharisee Gamaliel as unsuccessful if patriotic attempts at a national deliverance impelled by religious motives.

The Gospels (Luke 6:15) give only one specific reference to the name Zealot (*see* SIMON **2.**) but include many incidents involving the probable activities of the Zealot party. Among these is the report of certain Galileans 'whose blood Pilate had mingled with their sacrifices'. Galilee, its climate and people, was fertile soil for discontent and revolt. (*see* GALILEANS) There is a similar comment on some eighteen men who were killed when a tower in Siloam fell on them, perhaps while they were undermining some Roman fortification. Jesus said of the Galileans: 'Do you think that these Galileans were worse sinners than all of the other Galileans, because they suffered thus? I tell you, No; but unless you repent you will all likewise perish.' (Luke 13:2, 3) And of the other victims he said, 'Of those eighteen upon whom the tower in Siloam fell and killed them, do you think that they were worse offenders than all the others who dwelt in Jerusalem? I tell you, No; but unless you repent you will all likewise perish.' (Luke 13:4, 5)

Perhaps Barabbas, who was released by Pilate instead of Jesus, was a Zealot leader, a mistaken claimant for the Messiahship who left his followers to suffer, while accepting his own release. The remark of one of the bandits crucified with Jesus implies a possible comparison between Barabbas and Jesus on his cross: 'Are you not the Christ? Save *yourself and us!*' Perhaps Judas Iscariot also was a Zealot, whose impatient aspirations for his master as Messiah led him in desperation to betray him in order to force Jesus's hand. For neither theory is there material evidence (*see* BARABBAS *and* JUDAS 1.), but it would have been surprising if the Zealots had not at least considered exploiting Jesus for their cause. John clearly says that the people wanted to make Jesus king in Galilee, and that his movements were restricted by the threat of such demonstrations.

The Jews who conspired to assassinate Paul at Jerusalem were perhaps Zealots, acting in defence of the Law. 'When it was day, the Jews made a plot and bound themselves by an oath neither to eat nor drink till they had killed Paul. There were more than forty who made this conspiracy. And they went to the chief priests and elders, and said, "We have strictly bound ourselves by an oath to taste no food till we have killed Paul." ' (Acts 23:12-14)

In the years that followed, partly as a result of the Hellenistic policies of the Emperor Nero, partly from the corrupt and harsh administration of the Roman procurators, the persistent trouble-making of the Zealots reached a climax. Open hostility broke out in the year 66, when Gessius Florus, the governor, demanded funds from the Temple treasury. The Jews refused and suspended the daily sacrifice for the emperor: from then onwards the Zealots led the people in open revolt, resulting in the cruel suppression of Galilee and the disastrous siege of Jerusalem. There, with the Zealots divided into two opposing factions, the aristocrats on the west hill, the commoners on the east of the city under John of Gischala, with the Romans under Titus along the Mount of Olives, the Antonia Fortress was taken, the Temple burnt and the city sacked. Of the remaining Zealot fortresses, Herodium (near Bethlehem) and Machaerus (beyond Jordan) rapidly fell, but Masada survived until the spring of 73. The ruins of Masada and the suicidal story of this last stronghold bear witness to all that was best and all that was worst in the character of the Zealots. [Luke 6:15]

ZEBEDEE (Gk. from Heb. 'my gift') The father of James and John, who together with Peter made up the inner circle of Jesus's disciples, and husband of Salome, Zebedee was a fisherman of some substance, employing a hired crew and at least one sizeable boat for deep-water fishing. He allowed and enabled his wife Salome to give financial help to Jesus and his disciples. He may himself have been a disciple with his two sons, first of John the Baptist and then of Jesus.

A particularly interesting possibility is that the firm

of 'Zebedee and Sons, of Galilee' was contracted to supply fish to the high priest's palace in Jerusalem. This would account for the welcome of John Bar-Zebedee by the portress at the high priest's courtyard. 'Simon Peter followed Jesus, and so did another disciple. As this disciple was known to the high priest, he entered the court of the high priest along with Jesus, while Peter stood outside at the door.' (John 18:15-16) There exists a traditional site, in the upper city of Jerusalem, of the 'fish-shop of Zebedee', on which the Crusaders built a little cruciform church, now occupied by an Arab coffee-house.

Luke (5:3) describes Jesus borrowing Simon Peter's boat, from which to speak to the crowds on shore, and goes on to tell the story of the miraculous draught of fishes that Peter found in the deep water. They had let down their nets, but these were bursting with the quantity of the shoal they had thus enclosed. They had to signal to their partners to come and help them bring the catch on board. Having filled both boats, they began to sink with the sheer weight of fish. No wonder Simon Peter, the expert deep-water fisherman, was astonished, and Luke adds, 'so were also James and John, sons of Zebedee, who were partners with Simon'. It was after such an experience that the two sets of brothers, Simon and Andrew, James and John, must have decided to leave their homes to follow Jesus. As Mark puts it, 'And going on a little farther, he saw James the son of Zebedee and John his brother, who were in their boat mending the nets. And immediately he called them; and they left their father Zebedee in the boat with the hired servants, and followed him.' (Mark 1:19, 20)

If Simon and Andrew came from Bethsaida at the north-west of the lake, it is probable that Zebedee's home was on that part of the coastline, though their best fishing-grounds were along the north-west shore. Here the silt from the exit of the River Jordan, flowing down from the slopes of Hermon, still attracts the fish and provides their food. It is a mistake to think of the fisher-disciples of Jesus as all poor, simple, rustic peasants; Zebedee and his family were of great skill and considerable business acumen and substance. *see* SALOME **1.** *and* BOANERGES [Matt. 4:21; 10:2; 20:20; 26:37; 27:56; Mark 1:20; 3:17; 10:35; Luke 5:10; John 21:2]

ZECHARIAH *or* **ZACHARIAH** (Gk. from Heb. 'whom Yahweh remembered') Only Luke names the parents of John the Baptist and tells the story of John's birth. Zechariah, his father, belonged to the Abijah section of the priesthood. He and his wife Elizabeth, also a descendant of Aaron, were devout and scrupulous in their observance of the Law, but they were childless and both of them were getting on in years.

The twenty-four families of the 'sons of Aaron' were responsible in rotation for service in the Temple at Jerusalem. Within each family, two individuals were chosen by lot each day to tend the brazier on the altar of incense in front ot the Most Holy Place, one in the morning and one in the evening. On the occasion that Zechariah was chosen for the great privilege of entering the sanctuary to burn incense there, the congregation remaining outside at prayer, Zechariah received a vision.

He saw an angel standing on the altar of incense and he was overcome with fright. He heard the angel speaking to him. 'Do not be afraid, Zechariah, for your prayer is heard, and your wife Elizabeth will bear you a son, and you shall call his name John. And you will have joy and gladness, and many will rejoice at his birth; for he will be great before the Lord, and he shall drink no wine nor strong drink, and he will be filled with the Holy Spirit, even from his mother's womb. And he will turn many of the sons of Israel to the Lord their God, and he will go before him in the spirit and power of Elijah, to turn the hearts of the fathers to the children, and the disobedient to the wisdom of the just, to make ready for the Lord a people prepared.' (Luke 1:13-17) To this Zechariah replied, ' "How shall I know this? For I am an old man, and my wife is advanced in years." And the angel answered him, "I am Gabriel, who stand in the presence of God; and I was sent to speak to you, and to bring you this good news. And behold, you will be silent and unable to speak until the day that these things come to pass, because you did not believe my words, which will be fulfilled in their time." ' (Luke 1:18-20) When at last Zechariah went out of the sanctuary to greet the people, he was unable to speak and could only make signs to them. They perceived that he had received a vision within the sanctuary.

In due time, he returned home, and his wife Elizabeth conceived. Six months later, Mary, the future mother of Jesus and cousin of Zechariah's wife Elizabeth, visited and stayed with them for some three months. It was not, however, until after the birth of his child, his circumcision and naming, that Zechariah received back his power of speech. At the ceremony of circumcision on the eighth day, their family and friends were going to name the child 'Zechariah' after his father. Elizabeth, however, insisted on his being called 'John', despite their protests that no one else in the family had that name. Finally they appealed to Zechariah, the father, who wrote on a tablet: 'His name is John', as the angel Gabriel had instructed him. At that instant, his power of speech returned. Luke records him as praising God in a prophetic poem, which has since become part of the liturgy of the Christian Church. It is full of Old Testament phrases and reflects the Messianic hopes of pious Jews of that time. It looks forward to the coming deliverance of the Lord Most High, whose forerunner and prophet the little child, John, was to become.

'Blessed be the Lord God of Israel, for he has visited and redeemed his people, and has raised up a horn of salvation for us in the house of his servant David,

as he spoke by the mouth of his holy prophets from of old,

that we should be saved from our enemies,

and from the hand of all who hate us;

to perform the mercy promised to our fathers,

and to remember his holy covenant,

the oath which he swore to our father Abraham, to grant us

that we, being delivered from the hand of our enemies, might serve him without fear,

in holiness and righteousness before him all the days of our life.

And you, child, will be called the prophet of the Most High;

for you will go before the Lord to prepare his ways,

to give knowledge of salvation to his people

in the forgiveness of their sins,

through the tender mercy of our God,

when the day shall dawn upon us from on high

to give light to those who sit in darkness and in the
shadow of death,
to guide our feet into the way of peace.'

(Luke 1:68-79)

According to a later tradition, Zechariah was murdered in the Temple at the command of Herod. *see* ELIZ-
ABETH [Luke 1:5-79; Matt. 23:35; Luke 11:51]

ZENAS A lawyer whose services, together with those of
the biblical scholar Apollos, Paul requested in his letter
to Titus. Paul, writing probably from Macedonia to Titus in Crete at the end of the year 64, following his
release from prison in Rome, asks Titus to meet him at
Nicopolis on the Dalmatian coast of the Adriatic. We
do not know why Paul needed the services of the lawyer
Zenas at Nicopolis. [Titus 3:13]

ZEUS (Gk. *Zeus*, Lat. *Jupiter*) The chief and father-
figure of the gods of Olympus, known to the Greeks as
'Zeus' and to the Romans as 'Jupiter', whose messenger
or spokesman was known as 'Hermes' to the Greeks
and 'Mercury' to the Romans.

During the First Journey of Paul in the years 46-8,
he and Barnabas had arrived at Lystra, a city of Lycaonia in Pisidia, in the Roman province of Galatia,
now central Asia Minor. Here there was no synagogue,
so Paul preached in the open air. There was a man outside the Temple, a cripple from birth, who had never
walked. He was probably placed at the entrance to the
local temple of Zeus to attract sympathy and alms from
the worshippers. 'He listened to Paul speaking; and
Paul, looking intently at him and seeing that he had
faith to be made well, said in a loud voice, "Stand upright on your feet." And he sprang up and walked.'
(Acts 14:9, 10)

When the crowd saw what had happened, they were

convinced that these visitors were more than mere mortals, and shouted out in their own Lycaonian dialect, 'The gods have come down to us in the likeness of men!' They called Barnabas 'Zeus', perhaps for his tall and dignified appearance, and they called Paul 'Hermes', 'because he was the chief speaker'. The priest of the temple of Zeus, who emerged from his temple 'in front of the city, brought oxen and garlands to the gates and wanted to offer sacrifice with the people'. Seeing the visitors outside his temple and the cripple healed, the priest assumed that Zeus with Hermes had visited his own shrine and had worked this miracle of healing.

At this point, Paul and Barnabas, who had not understood what was happening nor the shouting in the local dialect, suddenly grasped the situation, tore their clothes in the traditional manner of displaying grief and cried out to the people, 'Men, why are you doing this? We also are men, of like nature with you, and bring you good news, that you should turn from these vain things to a living God who made the heaven and the earth and the sea and all that is in them. In past generations he allowed all the nations to walk in their own ways; yet he did not leave himself without witness, for he did good and gave you from heaven rains and fruitful seasons, satisfying your hearts with food and gladness.' (Acts 14:11-18)

The Roman writer, Ovid, tells the beautiful story of an aged couple, Baucis and Philemon, who lived in the neighbouring district of Phrygia and were similarly visited by Zeus and Hermes. The gods granted their wish that they should tend the temple of Zeus together and that neither should outlive the other. On their death, at the entrance to the temple two trees appeared, whose leaves whispered together in the wind. [Acts 14:12] those who die before the Second Coming of Jesus; and the other about the time of his coming. "But we would not have you ignorant, brethren, concerning those who